YITZ GREENBERG
AND
MODERN ORTHODOXY
THE ROAD NOT TAKEN

The studies in this volume emerged from the First Annual Oxford Summer Institute on Modern and Contemporary Judaism at the Oxford Centre for Hebrew and Jewish Studies, University of Oxford.

Funds for this volume made available through the generosity of

Jack and Giti Bendheim

The Maimonides Fund

The Susan and Jack Lapin Fund for Jewish Continuity (AJC)

YITZ GREENBERG AND MODERN ORTHODOXY

THE ROAD NOT TAKEN

ADAM FERZIGER,
MIRI FREUD-KANDEL,
AND STEVEN BAYME
Editors

Boston
2019

© Academic Studies Press, 2019
All rights reserved.
ISBN 978-1-618116147 (paperback)
ISBN 978-1-618117502 (ebook)

Book design by PHi Business Solutions.

Cover design by Ivan Grave.
On the cover: Photo of Dr. Greenberg, *Masmid* 1966, p. 4.
Courtesy of the Yeshiva University Archives.

Published by the Borderlines Foundation for Academic Studies
with Academic Studies Press.
1577 Beacon street,
Brookline, MA 02446, USA
www.borderlinesfoundation.org
press@academicstudiespress.com
www.academicstudiespress.com

Library of Congress Cataloging in Publication Data:
The biographical record for this title is available from the Library of Congress.
Identifiers: LCCN 2019942083 (print).

The following text is excerpted from the dedication of *Masmid* 1966, the Yeshiva College (Yeshiva University) Yearbook:

Dr. Greenberg's significance lies in that he is the personification of the aim of Yeshiva University. Never reluctant to draw parallels and show differences between the heritage of classical Judaism and modern Western culture, Dr. Greenberg's ultimate goal for himself, his students, and the institution is "synthesis" in its highest form.

The dedication of *Masmid* to Dr. Greenberg is only a small token of our deep esteem for him. Perhaps the only true recognition that can be given to such a a man is our self-dedication towards reaching our goal of Torah U'Madah.

Contents

Editors' Foreword   1
    Adam S. Ferziger, Miri Freud-Kandel, and Steven Bayme
Modern Orthodoxy and the Road Not Taken:
A Retrospective View   7
    Irving (Yitz) Greenberg

PART ONE
Law and Theology   55

1. History and Halakhah   55
    Steven T. Katz
2. Rabbi Yitz Greenberg's Covenantal Theory of Bioethics   67
    Alan Jotkowitz
3. Irving Greenberg's Theology of Hybrid Judaism   81
    Darren Kleinberg
4. On the Meaning and Significance of Revelation for
Orthodox Judaism   96
    James Kugel
5. Divine Hiddenness and Human Input: The Potential
Contribution of a Postmodern View of Revelation to
Yitz Greenberg's Holocaust Theology   107
    Tamar Ross
6. Modern Orthodoxy and Religious Truth   129
    Marc B. Shapiro
7. On Revelation, Heresy, and Mesorah—from Louis Jacobs
to the TheTorah.com   146
    Miri Freud-Kandel

PART TWO
Past and Present — 172

   8 What Is "Modern" in Modern Orthodoxy? — 172
       Alan Brill

   9 Can Modern Orthodoxy Survive? — 193
       Jack Wertheimer

  10 Where Have All the Rabbis Gone? The Changing Character of the Orthodox Rabbinate and its Causes — 211
       Samuel C. Heilman

  11 Modern Orthodox Responses to the Liberalization of Sexual Mores — 224
       Sylvia Barack Fishman

  12 "The Road Not Taken" and "The One Less Traveled": The Greenberg–Lichtenstein Exchange and Contemporary Orthodoxy — 254
       Adam S. Ferziger

Editors and Contributors — 289
Index — 293

Editors' Foreword

ADAM S. FERZIGER, MIRI FREUD-KANDEL, AND
STEVEN BAYME

In late June 2014, sixteen scholars from around the globe gathered at the Oxford Centre for Hebrew and Jewish Studies in the bucolic Yarnton Manor in the Oxfordshire countryside, for the first (now annual) Oxford Summer Institute on Modern and Contemporary Judaism. The goal of this inaugural event was to facilitate in-depth engagement with the contributions of Rabbi Dr. Irving "Yitz" Greenberg, concentrating particularly on the historical ramifications of his theological and public stances. Consideration was given to his lifelong and complex encounter with the Modern Orthodox stream of American Judaism and the extent to which his teachings functioned as "the road not taken." Toward these aims, each of the participants prepared a first draft of a research study that was distributed in advance. These papers then served as the springboards for the seminar sessions.

This auspicious gathering was most certainly characterized by deep appreciation for Greenberg's original outlook, which is predicated on his profound dedication to God, Torah, the Jewish people, and humanity. But this was by no means gratuitous homage or naive esteem. On the contrary, those in attendance understood that the most genuine form of admiration for a thinker and leader of his stature—especially one who continues to produce path-breaking writings and speak out publicly—is to examine rigorously and critically his ideas and legacy.

Others might have found it overwhelming, if not discouraging, to experience the depth and array of piercing analysis to which Greenberg's positions and works were subjected. The appreciative manner in which Yitz—and his wife Blu—listened to their counterparts, and in parallel the gentle assertiveness with which he challenged points that were raised, was decisive in facilitating healthy and candid discourse.

This volume brings together updated versions of many of the papers that were first presented at the Oxford Summer Institute. In the interim, each was revised in response to the dynamic deliberations that took place and new materials that have subsequently appeared, as well as the critical comments of anonymous readers who evaluated them for their academic quality. We are confident that the creative process that was nurtured has resulted in a substantive contribution to research on the religious, historical, and social trajectories of contemporary Judaism, and, similarly will engender fresh thinking on crucial theological and ideological postures that will ultimately enrich Jewish life.

***

Greenberg, as detailed in his own contribution to this volume, grew up in an Orthodox Jewish home in the Borough Park section of Brooklyn. He was educated in Orthodox Jewish schools that provided both religious and secular studies and encouraged integration into American life, and subsequently in a more traditionalist-oriented advanced yeshiva, where he gained rabbinical ordination. In 1959, while completing his Harvard University PhD in American history, he was appointed a full-time faculty member at Yeshiva College (Yeshiva University), the banner institution of the burgeoning "Modern Orthodox" camp within American Jewry. A few years later, he accepted the position of rabbi of the Riverdale Jewish Center, a synagogue in an area of New York that had only recently attracted Orthodox Jews. Over the course of the 1960s his reputation soared as a dynamic academic, communal rabbi, public activist, and creative educator intent on advancing an expansive approach to Orthodox Jewish engagement with contemporary intellectual and cultural trends. Subsequently, his progressive alienation from the increasingly more conservative directions of the Modern Orthodox sector was given concrete expression, when he simultaneously resigned from Yeshiva University and the Riverdale Jewish Center rabbinate in 1972. Henceforth, his public career focused on spreading Jewish knowledge and enhancing identification of the broader American Jewish population with their heritage. Here, too, his efforts met with considerable excitement and wide support. Some referred to him as "the rabbi of American Jewry." He also emerged as a groundbreaking post-Holocaust theologian. While Greenberg remained a committed Orthodox Jew, outside his local community his formal public role within mainstream late twentieth and early twenty-first century Orthodox life was relatively limited.

Greenberg's interests span a broad range of concerns. He introduced one of the earliest university courses on the Holocaust and served as executive director of the United States Holocaust Commission, which in turn recommended the establishment of the United States Holocaust Memorial Museum in the nation's capital. He was the founding dean of Salanter Akiba Riverdale Academy, commonly known as SAR Academy, in Riverdale, New York, the progressive Modern Orthodox day school predicated on the "open classroom" approach. He has written widely on the challenges posed by Jewish power as well as those of new medical technologies, and joined his wife Blu as one of the original champions of Orthodox feminism. He has also long been a major voice advocating enhanced dialogue with Christian leaders, while his covenantal theology—which emerged as a theological response to the Holocaust—elevates humanity to that of a partner in God's creation, which means that humanity must take responsibility for both universal and particularistic betterment.

Notwithstanding the unparalleled degree of enthusiasm Greenberg elicited in the 1960s at Yeshiva University, at Yavneh (the Orthodox collegiate association), and at his own Modern Orthodox congregation, his enormous personal impact upon communal leaders who diligently pursued his lectures and writings, and the inspiration that many have drawn from his ideas, as far as the trajectory of Modern Orthodox Judaism was concerned, his was "the road not taken." The Oxford Summer Institute was dedicated to examining this circumstance in order to provide fresh insight both into the place of Greenberg in the social and intellectual history of late twentieth and early twenty-first century Judaism, and the specific evolution of its Modern Orthodox subtrend.

The scholars gathered at Oxford explored this issue and related questions through a series of papers focused on Greenberg's intellectual interests and activities. The contributions themselves fell under two discrete rubrics: analysis of subjects central to his interests and theology, and the historical unfolding and contemporary manifestation of Modern Orthodoxy.

The volume opens with a personal statement by Greenberg on his journey within American Orthodoxy from childhood onward. The ensuing section is entitled "Law and Theology." Steven Katz analyzes the core components of Greenberg's covenantal theology, which, in his view, presents fundamental challenges to the believing Modern Orthodox Jew. Alan Jotkowitz explores Greenberg's views on questions of medical ethics and demonstrates how covenantal ethics may help professionals navigate the different and often conflicting directions suggested by technology, research, and the human needs of health care. Darren Kleinberg roots Greenberg's religious pluralism within his theology of covenant and Holocaust, which enables Greenberg to engage positively diverse religious systems, both Jewish and non-Jewish. In his contribution, James Kugel explicates that which he considers to be the core understandings of revelation that are identifiable within foundational

Jewish thought. Building upon the work of Rabbi Abraham Isaac Kook on the *Akedah* story (biblical binding of Isaac), Tamar Ross puts forward a view of revelation that is more fluid and dynamic than the concept of submission embraced by other Orthodox thinkers such as Rabbi Dr. Joseph B. Soloveitchik. Ross suggests that her approach offers a potential avenue for strengthening the philosophical foundations of some of Greenberg's central perceptions. Marc Shapiro explores Greenberg's wholehearted embrace of the concept of revelation extending to other faiths, particularly Christianity, and compares Greenberg's interfaith work with contemporary Jewish and non-Jewish thinkers and theologians. Shapiro suggests that the notion of multiple covenants, shared in various degrees by Greenberg, Eugene Korn, Shlomo Riskin, and Jonathan Sacks, poses problems for traditional claims of revelation as containing absolute truth. Miri Freud-Kandel, also concentrating on approaches to revelation, analyzes the implications of modern biblical scholarship for contemporary Orthodox views of *Torah min hashamayim*. She traces the evolution of this question from the Louis Jacobs controversy in Britain in the 1960s to the growth of *TheTorah.com* in the twenty-first century.

The third section, "Past and Present," begins with Alan Brill's exploration of the taxonomy of the nomenclature "Modern Orthodoxy," and its evolution into a religious movement, comparing it with currents in contemporary Christianity. Jack Wertheimer reflects on the sustaining power of Modern Orthodoxy and raises concerns about its future survival, especially given defections to its left and the specter of Haredization on its right. Samuel Heilman considers changes in the Orthodox rabbinate, noting that had Greenberg's model been followed by more successors in the pulpit rabbinate, they may well have posed a formidable alternative to the predominant Orthodox drift rightward. Sylvia Barack-Fishman contextualizes Greenberg's views on sexuality within the overall courtship and dating patterns of contemporary Orthodox Jews. Finally, Adam Ferziger's essay closes the volume by reconsidering, in light of later developments, the debate between Greenberg and Rabbi Dr. Aharon Lichtenstein that arose in the spring of 1966. Ferziger posits that by evaluating ideas articulated subsequently by Lichtenstein as well as his students, it emerges that numerous approaches first deemed radical when broached by Greenberg, in time gained traction within Lichtenstein's milieu. To be sure, he does not ignore the significant distinctions between the two figures that existed in the 1960s, nor those that grew even stronger in later years. Ferziger's essay, as such, serves both as a retrospective on changing currents within Orthodoxy and a statement to the fact that Greenberg's views, although clearly representing "the road not taken," continue to have resonance within the Orthodox spectrum.

Beyond the individual essays, the volume covers many of Greenberg's multifold interests and contributions to Jewish intellectual life. The initial gathering was held some eight months after the release of the 2013 Pew Survey of American Jewry. Its findings suggested that the Modern Orthodox make up one-third of the Orthodox population but just three percent of American Jews. While indicating demographic weaknesses within Modern Orthodoxy, notable signs of creativity were considered during the course of the Oxford Summer Institute. The development of new rabbinical seminaries, including those ordaining women rabbis, the phenomena of Partnership Minyanim, and new approaches to biblical scholarship, among others, clearly challenge some of Orthodoxy's long-held boundaries, yet they also indicate vibrant efforts to address some of the issues that Greenberg first raised. Indeed, the more recent 2017 Nishma study of Modern Orthodoxy identified a constituency thirsting for fresh thinking on critical issues. In this light, the current volume offers readers the opportunity to examine in-depth the trenchant and candid efforts of one of the most thoughtful and earnest voices to emerge from within American Orthodoxy to address the theological and moral concerns that characterize our times.

***

Many individuals coalesced to make this volume possible. We thank all of the participants at the inaugural Oxford Summer Institute on Modern and Contemporary Judaism, including Arye Edrei, Zev Farber, Michael Fishbane, Melissa Raphael, and Margie Tolstoy, who each prepared learned and thought-provoking presentations and contributed profoundly to cultivating the seminar's energy and novel discourse. That event, and the entire framework that has developed since, could not have come to fruition without the support and guidance of Professor Martin Goodman, former president of the Oxford Centre for Hebrew and Jewish Studies, University of Oxford, and its outstanding staff. We thank Professor Judith Olszowy-Schlanger, who began serving as president in the fall of 2018, for her encouragement during the final stages. We are grateful to the authors whose essays are contained in this volume, who all took the time to research and write their original papers and then later revised them, for their dedication and patience. We also commend the anonymous reviewers, who took their mandate quite seriously by offering both sharp criticisms and, when they thought it fruitful, helpful directions for improvement to each of the contributors.

Funding for the initial Oxford Summer Institute was provided by: The Targum Shlishi Foundation (Aryeh and Raquel Rubin—who spearheaded the efforts to support this project),[1] The Rothschild Foundation (Hanadiv) Europe, Harvey Beker, Harold Grinspoon, Michael G. Jesselson, Matthew and Gladys Maryles, Peter and Naomi Neustadter, and Zahava and Moshael Straus. Publication of this volume was made possible by Jack and Giti Bendheim, The Maimonides Fund, and the Susan and Jack Lapin Fund for Jewish Continuity at the American Jewish Committee. The editors thank each of the donors for their generosity.

Our most profound appreciation, of course, is to Yitz Greenberg, who has dedicated his life to engaging core ideals and experiences of Jews and Judaism with profound scholarship, deep-seated morality, and religious commitment—and a passionate desire to advance the world toward a better place.

Adam S. Ferziger (Ramat-Gan), Miri Freud-Kandel (Oxford), and Steven Bayme (New York)
Adar 5779/March 2019

---

1 The Targum Shlishi Foundation sponsors the website Rabbiirvinggreenberg.com, which includes a comprehensive bibliography and accessible copies of most of Greenberg's writings, as well as other relevant documents and records. This website has served as an invaluable resource for many of the authors of this volume.

Modern Orthodoxy and the Road Not Taken: A Retrospective View

IRVING (YITZ) GREENBERG

The Oxford conference of 2014 set off a wave of self-reflection, with particular reference to my relationship to and role in Modern Orthodoxy. While the text below includes much of my presentation then, it covers a broader set of issues and offers my analyses of the different roads that the leadership of the community and I took—and why.[1]

The essential insight of the conference was that since the 1960s, Modern Orthodoxy has not taken the road that I advocated. However, neither did it continue on the road it was on. I was the product of an earlier iteration of Modern Orthodoxy, and the policies I advocated in the 1960s could have been projected as the next natural steps for the movement. In the course of taking a different

---

1 In 2014, I expressed appreciation for the conference's engagement with my thinking, noting that there had been little thoughtful critique of my work over the previous four decades. This was to my detriment, because all thinkers need intelligent criticism to correct errors or check excesses. In the absence of such criticism, one does not learn an essential element of all good thinking (i.e., knowledge of the limits of these views). A notable example of a rare but very helpful critique was Steven Katz's essay "Voluntary Covenant: Irving Greenberg on Faith after the Holocaust," in *Historicism, the Holocaust, and Zionism: Critical Studies in Modern Jewish Thought and History*, ed. Steven T. Katz (New York: New York University Press, 1992), 225–50, which was by far the most intelligent summary and searching critique of my theological responses to the Shoah.

  I also want to thank Steven Bayme and Judith Weil for a close reading and critique of this article, which clarified many points and saved me from various errors in judgment or insight.

road, Modern Orthodoxy changed much of its cultural direction and religious style, and I argue that it took its eye off the distinctive mission and contribution of Modern Orthodoxy to pursue a copy of Haredi Orthodoxy. In other words, in choosing a different road, it lost its way.

GROWING UP IN MODERN ORTHODOXY

My parents were immigrants. My father was a *musmach* of Rav Hayim Brysker and a classic mitnagged, fully observant, a *talmid chacham*, who communicated the ultimacy of learning Torah. He also insisted that the Torah had a strong sense of justice and that God's primary demand was not ritual, but proper conduct between people (*bayn adam la'chavero*). His greatest dream was that his children should become American, at home in the country and loyal to its best values. He strongly conveyed the message that Christians in America were different from those in Poland. As they treated us well, so should we respect them and treat them with full ethical integrity. He understood that one of the prices of Americanization was that some people would become less observant or be influenced in their behaviors by American norms. He did not see such people as betrayers of the tradition or as evil.

Temple Beth El was the haute Modern Orthodox shul in Boro Park. My father was the rabbi of the *beit midrash*, teaching Talmud in Yiddish, while upstairs the rabbi spoke in English. The shul featured world-famous *chazzanim*, such as Moshe Koussevitsky. It had a choir and even installed an organ (but it was never, ever played). There was one Conservative congregation in the neighborhood, Temple Emanuel, which was completely traditional in all its services, but allowed mixed seating. The leadership of both synagogues treated each other with respect. Sometimes on holidays, after praying in his own shul, my father would stop off with me to hear the other Koussevitsky brother, David, at Temple Emanuel, because he wanted me to hear the beautiful *chazzanut*.

America had a certain normative weight in mid-twentieth century Modern Orthodox religious life. It was taken for granted that there were some people who worked or went in to their business on Shabbat, because that was the price of integrating in America. It was not seen as permitted activity, but those people were not looked down on or denied *aliyot* or synagogue honors. Temple Emanuel was seen not as the lair of some heretical, rebellious group, but as reflecting the price that some people paid out of respect for American customs.

At that time American Modern Orthodoxy was Zionist to the core. I was nurtured by the religious Zionist youth movement, then called HaShomer

Hadati (renamed Bnei Akiva after 1948). Profound Religious Zionist experiences inspired my teenage years, including demonstrating for and fundraising in support of the nascent state of Israel. All our Zionist activities were coeducational. We sang together and danced in concentric, if separate, circles. From the Hebrew Institute of Boro Park elementary school, I went on to attend Yeshiva University High School. I already had the idea that Modern Orthodoxy meant positive interaction with American culture. I read widely in American and world literature, and I even had some glimmers of the idea of a synthesis between the two cultures.

In college this positive attitude took the form of the decision to become a college professor teaching history. This was a highly respected profession, representing success in America. For some of my peers, becoming an American rabbi (Conservative/English-speaking/well-paid) was an equivalent form of successful Americanization. Young Modern Orthodox men did not think much of becoming a *rosh yeshiva*. Most of my teachers in advanced Jewish studies were European-born and -cultured.

There was one digression from my steady journey on the path of Modern Orthodoxy. I was planning to go to Yeshiva College, when I encountered Beit Yosef Novaredok, a yeshiva of the extreme right wing of the Mussar movement. All the teachers and the students were refugees—survivors of Siberia or of the concentration camps—who had settled in Boro Park. The *rosh yeshiva* told my father that they were thinking of taking in a few American boys, and, since my father respected him as a real *talmid chacham*, my father suggested that I take a look at the school, even though he was agnostic about Mussar. I stumbled into an intense meeting of learning *mussar b'hispaylus*, a highly emotional session of chanting and acting out Mussar moral maxims, and was so moved that I decided to attend this yeshiva.

This decision had a tremendous impact on my life in three ways. First, Beit Yosef was a hotbed of premodern yiddishkeit, and the religious dimension was not "filtered" by the modern. There was a sense of *hashgachah*, that God was close and directing everything in life. It was a profound religious encounter which showed me the limits of Modern Orthodoxy—or, rather, that it needed to be deepened (i.e., less domesticated spiritually).

This insight planted seeds that did not bear fruit until decades later. I sensed that Modern Orthodoxy had gone too far in accommodating the conventional, modern, rational reading of religion. It needed to restore an intense religious experience dimension to its life. This could be carried out in the form of a synthesis with the religious experiential component of the premodern culture or by going deeper into modernity to a level that recognized and enabled an ongoing access to religious experience.

Secondly, Beit Yosef continued the tremendous emphasis on the centrality of ethics, the importance of character-building, the need for ongoing self-analysis and self-criticism. This reshaped my life. It taught me that Judaism was about human beings and about making a person into a mensch. The school focused on character and on personal development. The goal was to break the ego, by concentrating on self-criticism and self-analysis and simultaneously working to improve personal characteristics (overcoming anger, honors-seeking, impatience) and intensify respect for the other. This was the beginning of my thinking of Judaism as a way of shaping people into *tzelem Elokim*, the image of God.

The third profound effect of Beit Yosef was a by-product of my rebbe's decision to switch the special class for the American boys to the afternoon hours, which allowed me to go to Brooklyn College in the morning. There I encountered all the intellectual issues that I might have avoided had I gone to Yeshiva College or to Brooklyn College at night. I was introduced to the challenges of history/critical studies and of philosophy of religion, as well as to the conflicts between science and religion. Each of these challenges was a shock. Neither my father nor the *rosh yeshiva* had answers for the burning questions raised by my college courses. This really forced me to become Modern Orthodox. I could not retreat to the fundamentalist position, because I had already been exposed to the contradictions and to the debunking cultures/studies of modern civilization. I did not want to turn secular. This drove me toward Modern Orthodoxy, in the form of a synthesis and reconciliation between the two cultures.

Thanks to its dynamism, my yeshiva made another contribution to my religious life. It showed me that I could live dialectically. I could feel the religion was absolutely true, God was very much present, and the mitzvot were commanded. Nevertheless, in the mornings, I could learn about science, evolution, and the understanding of the Torah as not literal. This caused turmoil and religious searching and rethinking. But thanks to Beit Yosef and its profoundly persuasive religious culture, the Torah remained very serious and retained its ultimate claims.

For the rest of my professional career, the greatest impact of Beit Yosef was in its emphasis on *zikui harabim*, "the highest calling," which was to share and teach Torah to everyone else. In Poland when one finished studying and received ordination from the school, the expectation was that the graduate would go out and start another yeshiva. At Novaredok they emphasized that you had to be a Jewish educator and spread Torah to the Jewish people. I dreamed of creating an educational enrichment outreach to the whole Jewish community. That urge never left me, and it came to dominate my career. Also, there is no question that the Beit Yosef experience seared into my soul that religion and Jewish identity were of ultimate significance. They remained central instead of shriveling or disappearing as they did in the lives of many other ambitious sons of immigrant Jews who entered American society and climbed the ladder to success.

The paradox was that another part of myself wanted to be Irving Greenberg, an echt academic. I wanted to fulfill my father's dream of becoming all-American. That is why I determined to go to Harvard, fortified by my conviction that the philanthropists who would support my educational mission to the Jews lived in Boston.

For the next decade, I lived with these two polar navigational stars. Guided by the religious vision I received from the yeshiva, I felt called to Young Israel of Brookline synagogue, where it was revealed to me that the Feuerstein family, an Orthodox philanthropic family just rising to national prominence, would back me in initiating a major religious outreach to the Jewish world. In the end, however, although I connected well with the family, they did not underwrite my vision of *zikui harabim*. They were moving to strengthen Torah U'Mesorah, the organizational seedbed of the burgeoning day school–movement. In the process, they handed that organization over to the spiritual guidance of the *roshei yeshiva* of the traditional yeshivot.[2] At that time, I did not grasp the significance of the move.

RABBI SOLOVEITCHIK'S INFLUENCE

In Boston, Rabbi Joseph B. Soloveitchik, a giant among Modern Orthodox thinkers, had already set up the Maimonides Day School as coeducational, even in Jewish/sacred studies. He internalized the American norm as calling for women to have an education as good as the men, and introduced the study of Talmud for women—although this directly went against a Talmudic ruling that was the standard in Orthodox schools worldwide.[3]

When I encountered him in person in Boston, after I moved there for my graduate studies, I had a great and unequivocal experience. We met in his weekly *shiurim* (Torah lectures), given for the Boston Chevra Shas, and later I

---

2 Rabbi Soloveitchik kept the Maimonides School away from that influence.
3 Maimonides Day School was founded in 1937. See the discussion in Seth Farber, *An American Orthodox Dreamer: Rabbi Joseph B. Soloveitchik and Boston's Maimonides School* (Hanover, NH: University Press of New England, 2004).

participated in *shiurim* at his home, in summer sessions, and other opportunities. He inspired me to be a Modern Orthodox Jew for life.

I had already received *smicha* and considered myself a serious, learned Jew. Yet he reframed my understanding and taught me much richer patterns of meaning for everything that I knew: "The *halachah* became more than the sum of its thousands of observances and details. It was the system by which to live humanly, a way to seize life whole, a confrontation with the dilemmas and anxieties of existence."[4]

Rabbi Soloveitchik modeled a true openness to modern culture and how one could learn from it and use its categories to find the deeper meaning in every aspect of Torah. It seemed obvious to me that his thinking had been immensely upgraded and his ways of interpretation broadened and deepened by his exposure to new paradigms of philosophy and science in PhD studies at the University of Berlin. Perhaps drawing from his struggles when he encountered secular studies, he showed his students how to ask questions boldly and thus get better answers from the sources. No one had ever articulated for me, as he did, the poetry, spirituality, and profoundly intellectual dimensions of the tradition. He encouraged me to pursue my secular studies and to find religious insight and explanatory paradigms for my spiritual explorations. I loved the man.

Years later, I came to understand his weaknesses. He had a strong apologetics streak. He would weave an idealized frame around a tradition that was so persuasive that it would blind him (and others) to actual problems or human suffering in the real situation. Most of all, he did not fully grapple with the reality that rethinking the tradition in the new setting would require revisions in moral assumptions, halakhic regulations, and understanding of classic concepts such as revelation, authority, and miracles. He did some of the necessary rethinking—as in improving women's education, by stressing the universal against the tribal in Orthodox ethics; and *halakha*, by redefining miracles,[5] etc. However, he often did this not by openly saying that there was a problem,

---

4 Irving Greenberg, *The Jewish Way* (New York: Summit, 1988) 7–8.
5 See, for example, his treatment of miracles in Joseph B. Soloveitchik, *The Emergence of Ethical Man*, ed. Michael S. Berger (Jersey City, NJ: KTAV, 2005), 187–91. He wrote: "The word 'miracle' in Hebrew does not possess the connotation of the supernatural. It has never been placed on a transcendental level. 'Miracle' (*pele, nes*) describes only an outstanding event which causes amazement. … Whether God planned that history adjust itself to natural catastrophe, or vice versa … is irrelevant" (187–8). The timing of the Exodus miracles makes them a miracle. Thus, Soloveitchik fits miracles into an unchanging natural order without openly repudiating the supernaturalistic conception or acknowledging how strong the fundamentalist conception is in the Bible and traditions.

but by asserting his view as if it were the traditional or Torah view. He did this without acknowledging that the tribal or premodern view was widely present in the sources and maybe even dominant among his peers. Furthermore, he did not come to grips with such issues as historical development. This left the door open for some students, fundamentalist and legalistic in their thinking, to take over his legacy and develop it so as to become congruent with yeshivish/Haredi Orthodoxy.

This is not meant to diminish Rabbi Soloveitchik's contribution to my development. His ideas continued to shape my thinking and stimulate new insights in later years. Decades after, his idea that the Torah must work in every civilization took me to the next step on the path of synthesis. I concluded that the new modern civilization was so dynamic—and had brought with it such political/economic/social advances—that it would win out historically and become pretty much universal. Already most of the Jews of the world had willingly joined this cultural system. The Holocaust wiped out the largest part of those that had not. The expulsion of the Arab Jews from Muslim lands after the birth of Israel transferred that large fraction of premodern Jewry into the setting of modernity. Therefore, Judaism must be able to live and flourish in modernity's physical/cultural environment. Jewish identity and religion had to evolve and successfully adapt to this new context. Following Soloveitchik's line of reasoning, I concluded that belief in the eternity of Torah mandated that we must develop the religious understanding and cultural resources needed to enable Torah to function effectively and evoke loyalty in the new environment. Finding a shelter and/or staying out of modern civilization was wrong and probably futile.

No less important: modernity and some of its assumptions would have to be modified or reshaped to enable this successful integration without assimilation. It seemed to me that these needed changes were implicit in the unfolding of postmodernism. I concluded that the Orthodox, who correctly believed that the whole tradition should be brought with us in the new culture, would need to upgrade various moral positions in our heritage, lest it be experienced as ethically inferior. Successful adaptation would also require wider or more sophisticated understandings of classical concepts such as revelation (*Torah min hashamayim*), authority, covenant, etc. We would also be required to adjust the balance in the tradition between heteronomy and autonomy, between universal and particular, discipline and restriction, experiential and expression, individual and community—even as we would need to correct the host culture and rebalance various standard ideas and values of modernity. My belief in the divinity of Torah gave me the confidence that this could be done and that Judaism could compete successfully in this civilization.

The groundwork for such an approach was laid down by Rabbi Soloveitchik, who portrayed the Haredi worldview as fundamentally flawed, in that it refused to engage with modernity or the political realities that necessitated Zionism. The underlying Haredi assumption that the Torah could not maintain itself in a modern dynamic culture or function within the urban, methodologically sophisticated, university-educated milieu, he said, denied the eternality of Torah.[6] Thus, despite its resemblance to ultra-Orthodoxy, Modern Orthodoxy at that time was affirming a very different conception of religion: that ours is a Torah of life which must be lived in its time, in every era. Therefore it must engage and be credible in the new, modern culture of humanity.[7] To me this implied that Modern Orthodoxy was committed to get even more involved in contemporary culture and needed to develop the capacity to show that the Torah could function credibly and sanctify life in it.

The next logical historical step could have been an affirmation that Modern Orthodoxy was defined by a commitment to enter fully into the new culture, while maintaining the whole Torah. The legitimate outcome of that aspiration would be a deeper mutual fructification.

THE HOLOCAUST TRANSFORMS MY THINKING: PLURALISM FOLLOWS

As I see it today, the problem with Modern Orthodoxy of the '50s and '60s was that it had a shallow understanding of (or would not deal with) the hardest issues raised by modernity. If one understood modern culture in depth, the problems that most of my teachers and the Modern Orthodox books I read, dealt with and offered answers to, were not credible. In truth, I did not feel that I had answers for the contradictions and challenges that I met in college. At the same time, the religious experience in the yeshiva was so gripping, and I was so in love with my family and my religious life, that I was not going to give up religion just because of these deep questions. I concluded that I would have to fashion a religious understanding that would be persuasive (and magnetic and livable) in the presence of an unfiltered modernity.

---

6 See Joseph B. Soloveitchik, *Hamesh Drashot* [in Hebrew], trans. David Telsner (Jerusalem: Machon Tal Orot, 1974), 97–100, 111–13.
7 Ibid.

Graduate studies in American Intellectual History at Harvard from 1953 to 1959 enriched my knowledge base and deepened my love for America. However, they had relatively little impact on the competing intellectual/cultural claims of religion and modern culture on my understanding. Marrying Blu Genauer in 1957 became a major intellectual/spiritual factor in the further development of my thinking and work, which unfolded as we grew in mutual interaction over the years.

I completed my PhD in the summer of 1959, but I still had not resolved the two impulses in me. When I was offered an academic position at Yeshiva University, it was a kind of fence straddle. Yeshiva University engaged in Jewish education, so I would have some entrée into the Jewish *chinuch* world, and the dean told me he wanted to improve the intellectual quality of the college, so I could be a high-level academic. I sensed that this could lead to an advance level of synthesis between religion and modernity. Soon after I arrived, a group of the new faculty, headed by Aharon Lichtenstein, Charles Liebman, and myself, started meeting regularly to discuss issues of Modern Orthodoxy and to consider how to improve Orthodox/Yeshiva education. That aspiration—for interaction and synthesis between the two parts of the school—was the key to my accepting the offer from Yeshiva University.

The next major turning point in my intellectual/theological life came in 1961, when I received a Fulbright scholarship to teach at Tel Aviv University. As religious Jews, we chose to live in Jerusalem. The week we moved there, a friend called to say that he could obtain really hard-to-get tickets to attend the Eichmann trial in its last week. I replied, "No, don't bother. I can read about it in the newspaper." Yet within a couple of weeks, I became totally caught up in the Shoah, spending most of my time at Yad Vashem Holocaust Memorial Authority in Jerusalem.

Twice a week I would drive to Tel Aviv to teach American intellectual history at the university. The rest of the time I was immersed in the Holocaust. It was an overwhelming and devastating experience for which I was wholly unprepared. Heretofore I had been a happy, religiously fulfilled Orthodox Jew. But there was no way I could reconcile what I was reading at Yad Vashem with my traditional outlook and what I thought was God's role in the world. Nor could I resolve the contradiction between the depth of horror that I relived all day and the return home, seeing Jerusalem bursting with life and meeting Blu and our son Moshe daily, growing, kicking, laughing. There was an irreconcilable contrast between drowning in death all day and being flooded with life at night. On the one hand, the Jewish people were alive; God was alive; and the covenant was being fulfilled before my eyes as Jerusalem was rebuilt. On the other hand, the Shoah had occurred, and death seemed to have been victorious, with divine intervention nowhere in sight. The struggle to resolve these two realities became pivotal. To this day, the tension between Israel and the Holocaust, between life and death, between God present and God totally absent, is something I wrestle with and feel constantly.[8]

The yearlong experience in 1961 changed my life trajectory in another way. I no longer wanted to be an academic; I wanted to work primarily for the Jewish religion and to heal and bind up the wounds of the Jewish people. When I came back to Yeshiva University and wanted to teach Jewish studies, Dr. Samuel Belkin, president of Yeshiva University, said, "With your Harvard PhD, why would you want to teach Jewish history?" As a classic Modern Orthodox Jew of those days, he had internalized the higher status of that which was American.

With encouragement from my students, I decided to introduce a course on the Holocaust. The course was approved by the faculty, but for two years in a row the dean vetoed it. He feared that it would destroy the credibility of the rigorous and highly successful premedical program. He finally signed on the course when I changed its name to "Totalitarianism and Ideology in the Twentieth Century." But the administration's inadequate understanding of the need to come to a new relationship with the secular/general culture continued to dog my steps, and I had to fight for every Jewish-themed course that I wanted to teach.

That struggle partly explains how I ended up becoming rabbi at the Riverdale Jewish Center in 1965. I had never wanted to be a pulpit rabbi, but I was looking for an outlet to serve the Jewish people full-time, and the shul offered me the opportunity to focus completely on Jewish matters. Initially, I did not leave Yeshiva University, but the shul came to be the center of my life and gave me the chance to build a community, create a school, and explore theologically my burning questions about tradition, modernity, and the Holocaust.

As I struggled with the theological conundrum of the Holocaust, I came to see that Modern Orthodoxy was not the sole legitimate Jewish position—nor was it a fully adequate one. Neither before, during, or after the catastrophe, did Orthodoxy (or any of the other movements) have the answers. In fact, the rest of Jewry—especially American, secular, Federation-oriented Jews—were

---

8 See Irving Greenberg, "Cloud of Smoke, Pillar of Fire: Judaism, Christianity and Modernity After the Holocaust," in *Auschwitz: Beginning of a New Era? Reflections on the Holocaust*, ed. Eva Fleischner (New York: KTAV, 1977), 7–55.

ahead of the Orthodox in focusing on the Holocaust and the centrality of Israel. I looked at the other religious and secular Jewish movements with new respect—not least for their heroism (and that of all Jews) in reaffirming their Jewishness in the face of such a monstrous past and future danger. The conclusion was that Modern Orthodoxy, all by itself, was not adequate to meeting the challenge of the Shoah.

The study of the Holocaust also drove me to Jewish–Christian dialogue. I was convinced that Christians had set the Jews up for the Nazi onslaught through the teaching of contempt over the millennia. Blu and I openly stated that our goal was to stop Christianity's teaching of hatred. Yet we soon discovered that the Christians that we engaged with were ahead of us in wanting to clean up Christianity. They wanted it to stop being associated with spreading hatred. They were ahead of us on other issues too, such as *tikkun olam*. Seeing their religious and moral lives, I began to recognize that Christianity had positive and redemptive elements. We saw the power in the religious ways and the moral force and inspiration in Christian ethical teachings. This moved me away from the unthinking, patronizing feeling that Christianity was only a good religion in that it incorporated so many positive Jewish teachings.[9] The process of dialogue was an instructive and moving experience. This led me to think that the same procedure should be tried among Jews. Thus was born the core element of CLAL—a center for intra-Jewish dialogue and pluralism. Literally meaning "everyone" in Hebrew, CLAL was also an acronym for the National Jewish Center for Learning and Leadership.

Another post-Shoah experience that led to pluralism came through a friendship with Rabbi David Hartman. In 1965 Hartman convened a group of rabbis to study together, and he invited me to join with him in planning an institute. We called it the Canadian Center for Advanced Jewish Studies. In addition to Orthodox rabbis, we extended invitations to Eugene Borowitz and Emil Fackenheim, and other Conservative and Reform rabbis.

As we met for a week of intensive learning and conversation, I quickly concluded that the concepts underlying their movements were validated by the fact that they could produce such learned and faithful people. Out of an exchange with Jakob Petuchowski, I came to see that Jewish law was unfair to women with respect to the laws governing the issuance of a *get* (Jewish divorce document). Until that moment, I had complacently assumed that the halakha was entirely

---

9 See Irving Greenberg, *For the Sake of Heaven and Earth: The New Encounter between Judaism and Christianity* (Philadelphia: Jewish Publication Society, 2004), 3–48.

adequate and Reform Jews made changes lightly because they knew little or nothing about it. The encounter with Petuchowski and the other Reform rabbis crystallized my nascent pluralism. I concluded that not only were Reform Jews performing a service by reaching Jews that Orthodoxy could not, but also there were corrections needed in Modern Orthodoxy.

I was no less inspired by making a deep personal connection with Emil Fackenheim, whose critique of modern thought lit my path toward a synthesis (between equals) of modernity and tradition. He joined in my conviction that the Holocaust was a turning point in Jewish and general history—and this buoyed me when many colleagues and peers rejected any attempt to give theological weight to the catastrophe.

I was so inspired by this pluralist group that I considered it to be my spiritually sustaining community. This gave me the inner fortitude to defy the growing attempt to enclose Modern Orthodoxy and marginalize all who challenged the emerging centrist consensus. At that time, I had no institutional framework to act out my pluralism, but this Canadian experience provided a prototype for my conception of CLAL in the 1970s. I emerged from these summer institutes convinced that dialogue with liberal Jews and learning from them would help me become a better Orthodox Jew.

But the Yeshiva University community was moving in the reverse direction, becoming convinced that cutting off from the liberal Jews and reducing the influence of modern values would serve Orthodoxy better.

THE 1960S AND THEIR IMPACT

A year after I went to Yeshiva University, the 1960s arrived in America. In the 1950s the dominant tone had been monocultural. When I came to Harvard, for the first two years I did not wear my *kipa*. Without being told, I understood that this was a religious symbol outside of the regnant culture. Only in the third year did I decide to come out of the closet and wear the *kipa*. Most of my Modern Orthodox peers continued not to wear head coverings in public, non-Jewish spaces.

Then came the cultural revolution of the 1960s. There was a new mix of utopianism and pragmatism and a dream that America could quickly transform itself and also create a culture for an individualist, self-fulfilling, just society. The United States would be multicultural and open to all. Those groups hitherto suffering discrimination—blacks, women, gays—would become fully integrated and empowered, and would flourish. Many people mentally added Jews to the list. I was optimistic that this would be good for the Jews—for if "black was beautiful," then Jews could express themselves distinctively and outwardly as well.

As humanism, optimism, and multiculturalism came to the fore in America, the university was the environment where these rising values swept the field. The number of students attending university grew rapidly, while the number of Jews going to college exploded. Clearly, the college experience would become a decisive force not only in American life generally, but especially in the Jewish community.[10] I became the adult advisor/spiritual leader for Yavneh, a student-initiated Orthodox college group whose founders sought to sustain Orthodox life and observance on campus. Yavneh's programs encouraged students to embrace the understandings (which often challenged the simple traditional education they had received) and reach a higher-level synthesis of the tradition with American culture. This work was an ideal outlet for my spiritual and educational calling.[11] It led me to reflect more generally about the challenge to American Jewry's capacity to live fully and maintain its distinctiveness in the rapidly opening society.[12] I also saw new opportunities for Jewish education. If ethnic studies were introduced to uphold multiculturalism, then Jewish studies could also be introduced. They could overcome some of the weaknesses of the shallow or nonexistent Jewish education given to many Jewish children.

By the middle of the decade, the definition of my calling to do *zikui harabim* widened. I wanted to help the Jewish people adapt to living distinctively while participating fully in an open society. Most American Jews were focused on becoming American, and the programs of the community institutions stressed nonsectarianism and universal liberal values. What would happen when Jews were totally accepted? Would there be enough Jewish content left in their lives to function as Jews? Once being Jewish (and the Jewish message) lost the protective tariff of antisemitism, would American Jews buy the total American package, including assimilation? The initial impact of the college experience was, in most cases, to diminish or erode Jewish identity. This was an early

---

10 See Irving Greenberg, "Jewish Survival and the College Campus," *Judaism: A Quarterly Journal of Jewish Life and Thought* 17, no. 3 (1968): 259–81.
11 See Benny Kraut, *The Greening of American Orthodox Judaism: Yavneh in the 1960s* (Cincinnati: Hebrew Union College Press, 2011).
12 Irving Greenberg, "Adventure in Freedom—Or Escape from Freedom? Jewish Identity in America," *American Jewish Historical Quarterly* 55, no. 1 (September 1965): 5–21.

warning that most Jews' identity was shallowly nurtured and highly dependent on the now rapidly disappearing cultural shelter and ethnic exclusion.[13]

Now that through the State of Israel the Jews were responding by taking power in history, this called for revision in thinking on many fronts. Gradually, the Holocaust and Israel were becoming more prominent in American Jewish consciousness. There was an urgent need to recover the primacy of Jewish identity, especially if the community was to have the intestinal fortitude needed to stand up for Israel in times of difficulty. Jews who grasped the nature and lessons of the Holocaust would be empowered to reshape the host culture, even as they joined the new society. I believed that to stay religiously Orthodox in an open society meant that one had to critique, and not merely passively adapt, to the society.

In 1963, inspired by Jacob Birnbaum, Blu and I became active in the Student Struggle for Soviet Jewry. The movement was particularly appealing to Modern Orthodox Jews. SSSJ had a strong *clal yisrael* (Jewish solidarity) orientation and was driven by the determination not to allow a repeat of the abandonment of European Jewry in the Holocaust. No less important was the participants' absorption of the American message of activism. This included imitating the role model of college students in challenging the establishment and taking the lead to protest and transform American politics. The mainstream Jewish organizations hesitated, because they were not yet comfortable with actively asserting distinctive Jewish interests and causes in the American public domain. Similarly, the Haredi religious leadership—including the European *roshei yeshiva* at Yeshiva University—held back, because they internalized the traditional Jewish outsider fear of confronting or offending political authorities.

The '60s activism and spirit of communalism was also expressed in my work at Riverdale Jewish Center. The goal was to nurture a synagogue that was a community, not just a house of prayer. We started SAR Academy to create a day school that would give a higher-level integration of Jewish and Western culture.

I became involved with the student group that took over the General Assembly of the Jewish Federations and demanded a more Jewish agenda for the community, with priority funding for Jewish education and culture. Conservative Rabbi Steven Shaw, a pioneer religious activist, introduced me to the world of federations. The takeover evoked tremendous resonance in the American Jewish community. This convinced me of the power and value of working in a pluralistic manner to foster a more Jewish agenda. In 1974 Steve

---

13 See the extended treatment of these issues in the articles cited in "Adventure in Freedom."

joined Elie Wiesel and me to found CLAL (then called the National Jewish Conference Center).

Throughout, I kept in touch with Jewish studies, which were growing rapidly in the university world. In 1970 a group of scholars came together to create the Association for Jewish Studies to encourage the growth, set standards, and nurture the expanding cohort of Jewish scholars who taught in this field. I saw academic Jewish studies as an important part of the Jewish future: since the overwhelming majority of Jewish students were going to attend university, Jewish learning and identity would have to make it there. Jewish studies professors overwhelmingly insisted that the academic standards in Jewish studies must be upheld and kept at a higher level than ethnic studies that suffered from undue politicization. I believed that university-level Jewish studies would constitute an affirmation of pluralism and of Judaism's presence at the highest levels of culture and civilization, which would inspire Jewish students and nurture their Jewish identity. My task and that of all Jewish educators was to communicate a culture and identity that were so vital that they would not want to give them up.

I remained deeply engaged with general societal developments. Jewish and American seem to be a recipe for synergy and achievement. The highlight was the Soviet Jewry movement, which injected itself into America's Cold War with Communism and gave an American patriotic stamp to a deeply Jewish cause. Many Modern Orthodox Jews reached out to the general community (Jewish and American) through these activities. To me, the message was that when Orthodoxy/Judaism joined in the general society, it grew stronger. It achieved its goals and positively influenced many others.

I also was further drawn into Jewish–Christian dialogue, which offered the promise of the best of the '60s—freedom, justice, pluralism, mutual respect—in the interreligious area. Blu and I joined with a group of friends to form *ha-Tzaad ha-Rishon* (the First Step), a project to integrate black Hebrews into the mainstream American Jewish community. I also became involved with the anti–Vietnam War movement, mainly through leading a group of Yeshiva University students to participate in the national Moratorium Shabbat in Washington, DC. In this process, I was invited to give a paper on behalf of the Orthodox community/Rabbinical Council of America during a symposium on the war sponsored by the Synagogue Council of America. This later led to testimony before the Senate Foreign Affairs committee. At a time when most Orthodox Jews and rabbis were staunch defenders of the government policy, I offered a nuanced critique of how and why the well-intentioned war had gone wrong and should be terminated.[14] It is noteworthy that the Rabbinical Council of America itself was still open enough to the liberal winds of the '60s that it would allow me and my slightly avant-garde views to represent Orthodoxy officially. I identified with the spirit of the '60s and was convinced that Modern Orthodoxy, indeed, all of Jewry, should march boldly into the brave new world being born.

Later, I reacted against the excesses—the mindless, extreme radicalism of some elements —and came under the influence of Norman Podhoretz and *Commentary* magazine, and was persuaded that many of the neoconservative criticisms and social policy alternatives were correct. Nevertheless, I remained convinced that many of the social advances and political liberalizations were also positive. They needed to be checked and limited, not repealed.

RECOIL FROM THE '60S AND THE RISE OF ULTRA-ORTHODOXY

Many people in the Modern Orthodox rabbinate and at Yeshiva University were far from satisfied, let alone fulfilled, by the social/cultural trends in the 1960s. The social changes were frequently accompanied by open expressions of disrespect for tradition. Many were threatened by the intellectual challenges and scholarly critiques of Orthodox ideas and beliefs. As they saw it, the college experience was undermining the religious positions of Jewish traditional students. They feared that Orthodox students would be lost to heresy, while the Jewish social identity of all students could well be swept away in the maelstrom of acceptance and activism.

At Yavneh we had an internal argument. The student leaders wanted to invite speakers from non-Orthodox circles, including Conservative rabbis and scholars, and I felt that the students needed to learn how to handle a variety of non-Orthodox and even anti-religious views. Allowing exposure to a wider set of scholars and thinking was also consistent with the pluralistic culture of the university—to which I believed that Modern Orthodoxy had to adapt in the long term. Norman Lamm (future president of Yeshiva University) and Aharon Lichtenstein (son-in-law of Rabbi Soloveitchik and future Religious Zionist yeshiva head) opposed this wider opening, because they feared that it might

---

14 For an extended treatment of my thinking and of the issues involved from a Modern Orthodox point of view, see Joshua M. Feigelson, "Into the Public Sphere: *Halakha* as an Ethic of Power," in "Relationship, Power, and Holy Secularity: Rabbi Yitz Greenberg and American Jewish Life, 1966–1983" (PhD diss., Northwestern University, 2015), 75–104.

undermine the students' orthodoxy. I lost the argument, and the restrictive policy was adopted. I did not recognize the underlying signal—that Modern Orthodox educators were calling a halt to the openness and seeking to return to the use of shelter and exclusion in order to keep people on the reservation. Nor did I grasp the significance of the pushback and psychological withdrawal gathering strength inside Modern Orthodoxy.

The biggest factor in the turn away from the road on which I had embarked was the strengthening of Haredi Orthodoxy and its increasing influence on Modern Orthodoxy. I drew the lesson of the Shoah to mean that Modern Orthodoxy should reach out to affirm and work with its partners in the covenant of fate (*brit goral*) (i.e., liberal religious and secular movements). The Jews in those groups felt deeply Jewish, and embraced Jewish history and suffering and responsibility to each other (and Israel) and took action on all these fronts.[15] The ultra-Orthodox shared the covenant of destiny with the Modern Orthodox—belief in a divinely given Torah, the binding nature of halakha, etc.—but they were weak on the issues of common fate, and in their extreme wing, the Satmar Hasidim, they spurned Israel as the work of the devil.[16] The modern community's leadership turned toward the Haredim and their policies in the hope of warding off assimilation, and over the next few decades the ultra-Orthodox pulled the Modern Orthodox into their orbit and persuaded them that the Haredim were their only legitimate partners. As the Modern Orthodox became convinced that the two groups were one and the same community, the Haredi halakhic authorities became the dominant force in both communities.

In convincing the Modern Orthodox that the two communities and policies should be united against other Jews who deviated on religious ideology and observance, the Haredim undid the historic impact of Zionism, which had led to the greatest Jewish triumph of the past two millennia by saving the Jewish future. Since 1948, religious Zionists had failed to go forward with a renewal

---

15 See Rabbi Soloveitchik's formulation of the two dimensions of *brit goral* and *yiud* (covenant of fate and destiny) in his essay, "Kol Dodi Dofek," in Joseph B. Soloveitchik, *Fate and Destiny: From the Holocaust to the State of Israel*, trans. Lawrence S. Kaplan (Hoboken, NJ: KTAV, 1992), where he clearly delineates the covenant of fate as the most basic foundation of the covenant of the Jewish people. Through this category, he legitimated the nonreligious Zionist Jews and their institutions as valid partners in the covenant of Israel, though he did not apply this articulation to the non-Orthodox denominations in America.
16 See Joel Teitelbaum, *Al HaGeulah v'al HaTemurah* (Brooklyn, NY: Jerusalem Publishing, 1967).

of halakha in light of living in a sovereign Jewish state, and control of *psak* and halakha steadily passed to the Haredim. American Modern Orthodoxy made the same error. While they intensified their own Zionism, they ignored the ongoing anti-Zionism of some ultra-Orthodox, as well as the fact that living by ultra-Orthodox halakha would make it impossible for Israel to function. They ignored the lessons of the Holocaust and allowed shared beliefs and religious practices to override the more fundamental bonds of common fate and historical challenge, which should have led them to close ranks with *clal yisrael* (the majority of whom are non-Orthodox) and to try to work together to create a viable Jewish identity and culture inside modernity.

In a historical irony, the Haredim, who pronounced the Holocaust to be God's punishment for Jewry's modernization and Zionism, channeled the impact of the Shoah to strengthen themselves. Internally, they used the catastrophe to justify rejecting modernity entirely. Externally, they drew on the broader Jewish community's reaction of nostalgia for the lost world of tradition, and guilt for not having done more to save European Jewry, to elicit strong financial and social support to rebuild Haredi life. As the ultra-Orthodox grew in numbers and rebuilt their institutional infrastructure, their influence on the Modern Orthodox expanded steadily—until it became dominant.

THE LICHTENSTEIN–GREENBERG EXCHANGE IN *THE COMMENTATOR*

The Lichtenstein–Greenberg exchange that appeared in Yeshiva University's student publication the *Commentator* in 1966 was a signal of the internal shift underway in Modern Orthodoxy.[17] Thanks to my encounter with the Shoah and Israel, I located my religious positions primarily in relation to the small circle of pluralistic rabbis to which I had connected, and I no longer had an accurate political reading of the intellectual/policy parameters of the nascent centrist Modern Orthodox.

In my interviews for the initial article, I wanted to put new thinking before my community and get them to take the next step forward by credibly meeting the intellectual/moral criteria of the post-Shoah, positive '60s culture. This included respect for (and cooperation with) the non-Orthodox, new thinking on historical and biblical studies, more openness to equality

---

17 "Dr. Greenberg Discusses Orthodoxy, YU, Viet Nam, & Sex," *Commentator*, April 28, 1966.

norms and to more natural male-female connections. I also felt that there should be greater willingness to critique internal community issues, instead of dutifully assuming that the authorities are always right.

I sought to reduce the conflict by use of Marrano language—to hint and offer layers of double meaning—so the traditionalists could read these views more traditionally, while the progressives could see the implications and go further with them. I felt keenly that the students were torn between the conservative/traditionalist values they were being taught by the *roshei yeshiva*, and exposure to their social reality, which was influenced by the general American atmosphere. While I rejected the emerging culture of promiscuity and abrogation of restraint, I believed that there was a need for a more egalitarian and socially connected ethic governing gender relationships, and that the growing emphasis on prohibiting *yichud* (a male and female meeting in private) and the later *shomer negiah* (aggressive prohibition on any touching) ethos went too far. They reflected ultra-Orthodox norms of discomfort/distaste for sexuality and an insistence on women's intrinsic sexual provocativeness and built the religious/ethical social ethic on heightened social separation, just when the general society was moving toward greater mixing and social interaction. Personally, I believed that in a more interconnected culture, relationships between men and women would be healthier, more respectful, and more humanly fulfilling. However, I put this exploratory thinking forward in vague language so that those who understood would understand (*ha-mayvin yavin*). I was similarly vague in speaking about liberal religious Jews, trying to sound positive rather than explicitly pluralist.

When the article appeared, there was an explosion. The younger traditionalist faculty and advanced students leaped on my words to spell out the most radical possible meanings to maximize the community's recoil. They sought to turn the moment into an opportunity to crush what they considered deviant views and to enshrine the growing traditionalism. They tried to get Rabbi Joseph B. Soloveitchik, the most authoritative rabbinical figure and Modern Orthodox theologian, to denounce my statements, but he declined to do so. His son-in-law and protégé, Aharon Lichtenstein, stepped up. He had the Harvard credentials, as well as the learning, and he wrote a sharp critique.[18] This led to a rejoinder from me and another from him, in which he skewered my equivocations. I am not proud of the way I handled this. However, I did not

---

18 "Rav Lichtenstein Writes Letter to Dr. Greenberg," *Commentator*, Thursday, June 2, 1966.

want to lose the community, nor had I developed the inner clarity and toughness needed to get the community to face up to these issues. I still believe that I needed to put fresh views forward, because Modern Orthodoxy was getting a full blast of the society's novel ideas, while the religious leadership was putting its head in the sand. I understood the community's recoil, because I myself had struggled and felt uncomfortable or even pained to make some of the proposed changes. However, I saw such a rethinking as part of a necessary reconceptualization of Judaism, especially the need to remove unethical or degrading attitudes toward Others.

A close reading of Lichtenstein's responses shows that he conceded the correctness of my main points, even as he sharply critiqued the excessively frank and too candid aspect of my writing. On the substance, he was arguing with a viewpoint that erred in parts but offered a legitimate alternative, if contested, view. He often said he believed that the students were not ready or strong enough intellectually or in their belief to deal with these issues positively. Instead of recruiting the leadership to figure out a way to upgrade the students' education and ability to cope, he wrote in a way that seemed to rule out explorations of such topics. And his critique of my language and style was so sharp that most of the public—and his conservative colleagues—read the rejoinder as a repudiation, rather than a nuanced disagreement. His article was exceedingly valuable and heavily utilized by the most conservative elements at Yeshiva University to argue that my views were beyond the pale. Although Lichtenstein personally later on dealt with me as a legitimate *bar plugta* (partner in an intellectual disagreement), he did not publicly contradict the misuse of his critique. Nor did he express objection to the growing use of the method of suppression of views deemed dangerous.

In his response to the initial interview, Lichtenstein dismissed my argument that the Modern Orthodox must allow maximum freedom of exploration and generate a culture within which people could feel safe even if they made errors in articulating new ideas to deal with the challenge to tradition. He concluded that the need for such a culture of exploration was overruled by the danger of heavy losses of Torah loyalties. We had previously argued about this problem at Yavneh, the Orthodox college student organization we both supported. He was upset by the thought that even a single student might be lost to Orthodoxy due to these exposures. I argued that only by being exposed to the full blast of the general culture could the system mature enough to maintain itself. I used the analogy of a mutated disease for which the population's immune system was not strong enough: Since we could not permanently shelter our students from cultural/spiritual/social challenges, we had to expose them and help them develop a new immunity—trusting and believing that our Torah and our students were up to the challenges. He countered by asking how many patients would get deathly sick as the immune system evolved. I replied that any short-term gain from sheltering the students would be offset by widespread losses among those that could not or would not seek shelter. The only hope was to develop a new strain of student/Jewish identity that could live safely and thrive in the new culture.

I also argued that he was underestimating the students, that most would have the resilience to absorb shocks and/or come back after. He accused me of being cavalier about the high risks. I replied that the filter/shelter approach would not work, as the emerging culture was too magnetic. Even if we could save a minority who would accept our direction and not listen to the general culture or to heretical ideas, we would be abandoning the bulk of the Jewish people, which was completely unsheltered. I was anxious about the potential losses, but I felt that the path of filter/shelter would delay or distract from the development that was crucial.

Lichtenstein's *Commentator* article and the way it was used confirmed that he and the emerging centrist leadership would not support the exploration of these dangerous issues. In the '70's and '80s, this rightward shift took on the form of systematically excluding people like Hartman and me from the conversation. My views became off limits, and Yeshiva University students and centrist laymen heard only those from the right and never from the left. Modern Orthodox leadership went along with this exclusion, sometimes at the behest of the right and sometimes in anticipatory compliance with the right's growing dominance of community policy. Modern Orthodox institutional leadership folded and/or drifted, as American Modern Orthodoxy moved steadily toward the Haredi position in most areas of rabbinical adjudication, education, and community policy.

THE *HAREDIZATION* OF MODERN ORTHODOXY

The ultra-Orthodox were determinedly opposed to any connection with the non-Orthodox community. In the 1970s, the *roshei yeshiva* of the great yeshivot put out a prohibition on Orthodox participation in the Synagogue Council of America, in which all three denominations sat together as equals, and in local boards of rabbis. They did not invite Rabbi Soloveitchik to sign. In his lifetime, they rarely missed the chance to treat him as a deviant, for his embrace of Zionism and modernity. For his part, Soloveitchik never did sign, but he did not fight back or legitimate intra-faith activity either. He temporized, arguing that vis-a-vis the federal government and American society, multidenominational representation of Jewry was needed and inescapable. However, as to internal spiritual matters, the non-Orthodox were not to be recognized as legitimate. Although his ambiguous instruction enabled the RCA and Union of Orthodox Jewish Congregations to continue cooperating with liberal groups, they were continuously criticized from the right and increasingly on the defensive. Thus, they steadily reduced the extent of cooperation. As Soloveitchik aged and grew sick, the younger Yeshiva University rebbes aggressively affirmed the exclusion agenda.

This trend also held true in Jewish–Christian dialogue. In 1965 Soloveitchik gave policy guidance for interfaith relations: Dialogue was permitted on issues of social welfare and the common good; conversations on theology and matters of substantive religious/spiritual import were ruled out. As I saw it, he was attempting to triangulate the modern values that called for dialogue—especially as Christians were actively revising negative teachings on Jewry and Judaism for the good—with the traditionalist rejection of Christianity and opposition to any dialogue. His guidance was turned into a ruling and applied to ever more restricted Orthodox participation in religious dialogue. Orthodox individuals made important contributions to the Jewish–Christian dialogue (including David Hartman, Michael Wyschogrod, and me, among others), but this work was boycotted by the Modern Orthodox establishment.[19]

The outcome of all this was that, starting in the 1960s, American Modern Orthodoxy engaged in a steady retreat from its more modern positions, its leadership deferring to and adopting the ultra-Orthodox stances in most areas of Jewish law, education, and community policy. Examples include kashrut (*glatt kosher* standards of Hungarian Hasidim became the only legitimate ones), gender separation (synagogues without separate seating and *mechizahs* were excluded from membership in the Orthodox Union, and elementary schools were required by Torah U'Mesorah to separate boys and girls), women's modesty (wives were expected to cover their hair in accordance with Haredi standards), and outreach (the National Conference of Synagogue Youth was primarily staffed by graduates of traditional yeshivas).

Yeshiva University's spiritual leadership was taken over by rabbinic faculty who were yeshivish/Haredi in their religious orientation, their halakhic rulings,

---

19 Wyschogrod gave courses at Yeshiva University but never taught about his interfaith work or his important theological interaction with (Barthian) Christianity.

and their educational methods. They did not repudiate secular studies openly, but they tried to reduce the demands of secular studies on their students' time. They opposed any cooperation with non-Orthodox groups in Zionism or in any other areas. In their teachings, modern America became not something to emulate or learn from, but the source of never-ending temptation and heresy. They prohibited feminism or greater tolerance for gays and lesbians in the Orthodox community and defined them as cardinal sins (*yehareg v'al ya'avor*). Egalitarian practices such as women's tefillah groups or partnership minyanim were labelled *darkei ha'emori* (ways of the pagans) and *hukkot hagoyim* (imitating the laws of the Gentiles). Perhaps their most profound philosophical and moral reversal was expressed in the reassertion of the particularist, anti-goy (Gentile) elements in the tradition—to the point of communicating that only Jews were fully in the category of *tzelem elokim* (created in God's image).[20] They were completely legalistic in their religious thinking and pretty much dismissed any role for values such as justice or for human emotions in the halakhic equation. Thus, in the name of continuing Soloveitchik's tradition of learning, they reversed his religious/theological paradigm. In the process, they turned Yeshiva University, the flagship institution of Modern Orthodoxy, into a training ground for Haredi-lite clergy and laymen. To be sure, YU continued to retain students who were dedicated to the ideals of *Torah U'madda*. Moreover, as noted below, YU also enhanced its academic Jewish studies offerings, including study of Bible and rabbinics, which in turn broadened the education of students, in some cases preparing them for leadership positions within twenty-first-century Modern Orthodoxy. Yet the overriding outlook reflected the attitudes and the legal approach of the Haredi community. In sum, the legal decisions and policies adopted in the second half of the twentieth century met the needs of the Haredi community, but made it more difficult for Modern Orthodox Jews to be credible by American standards or to keep less observant Jews inside Modern Orthodox institutions.

Another result of these trends was that Modern Orthodoxy became less able to serve and strengthen the broader Jewish community. The exception was where individuals moved to reach out and serve in the Federation world, in the community day schools, and even in the Hebrew schools of the liberal movements. Over these decades, some of the most important civil servants

---

20 When Chief Rabbi Isaac Unterman gave a lecture endorsing the saving of life (*pikuach nefesh*) of Gentiles on Shabbat, because of *darkei shalom*, Rabbi Soloveitchik privately told a group of faculty that this saving was obligatory because Gentiles are unequivocally *tzelem elokim*.

and spiritual leaders of American Jewry were Modern Orthodox Jews. I would cite Elie Wiesel, Abe Foxman, Malcolm Hoenlein, and Barry Shrage as the top people in their respective fields, with tremendous influence in the broader Jewish community. Steven Bayme ran the American Jewish Committee's Jewish Communal Affairs Department and steered AJC's Jewish policies into far more focused Jewish policies and educational efforts than its Americanizing leadership had done in the past. Marvin Hier, who was more centrist, created a hugely successful Jewish defense organization, the Simon Wiesenthal Center, by transcending religious and denominational lines, even as he honored Orthodox observance in its programs. These individuals were the exceptions who proved the rule. Had Orthodoxy moved to the left and toward *clal yisrael*, it would have been welcomed with open arms and been offered many professional outlets. Then it would have given strength and stability to the rest of the community.

WORKING FOR *CLAL YISRAEL* AS A MODERN ORTHODOX JEW; LOSING GROUND IN MODERN ORTHODOXY

Throughout this period, I shifted my professional activity toward *clal yisrael*. Not surprisingly, this intensified the evolution of my theology toward embracing and justifying the behaviors of the whole Jewish people, which considerably pushed my understanding of Orthodoxy and its principles toward the left, religiously and culturally.

In the '60s and '70s—and due in no small measure to student activism—Jewish studies spread rapidly in the university world. Despite some academics' resistance, student pressure forced more and more schools to offer courses on the Holocaust. This became the most widely taught course in Jewish studies on campus. It was clear to me that Jewish studies programs would give the community a chance to reach a rapidly surging number of its young who were going to college. Despite a conscious push by some Jewish studies academics against allowing any affirmative, nonacademic role for these studies, the courses did have positive impacts on the Jewish identity of Jewish students and offered many Jewish students the opportunity to experience high-level Jewish education—unlike the minimal, shallow Hebrew/Sunday school experience of many young American Jews.

The symbolism of Judaism's presence in the central halls of Western culture, in itself, affected many Jewish students to view their identity more favorably. I became convinced early on that to maintain believability and attractive power in the university culture, Judaism would have to become more individualized, more internalized, more activist-oriented, more nuanced, and more responsive to the growing openness and pluralism of the general society. And this would be good for Judaism and enable Jews to maintain their identity in the emerging, wide-open culture.

I was equally convinced that Modern Orthodoxy should move in the same direction. If it did, it could flourish and influence more people than ever before. A disproportionate number of Modern Orthodox Jews became Jewish studies faculty. On the other hand, the growing yeshivish and centrist elements recoiled from Jewish studies and tried to convince their students to avoid exposure to these academic approaches.[21]

In 1970, a group of academics came together to form the Association for Jewish Studies in order to facilitate its rapid growth, nurture younger scholars and provide outlets for scholarship, as well as to protect the high academic standards of the discipline. I joined the founders' group and argued for an open acknowledgment of the potential for Jewish studies playing a properly delimited role in nurturing Jewish culture and identity on campus. Most of the scholars were focused on attaining academic respectability and were not particularly willing to acknowledge the identity dimension of these courses.[22] Nevertheless, over the next four decades, Jewish studies grew apace. Tens of thousands of Jewish students, as well as non-Jewish, took these courses. Universities eagerly sought Jewish funding, and the community responded. The effect was one of the most positive Jewish educational upgrades in American Jewish history. Happily, academic standards were protected and upheld during this process.

By 1972, I came to the conclusion that despite my great satisfaction and fulfillment in building a synagogue, day school, and community, I was failing to deliver the message of the Holocaust and Israel as turning points to the broader Jewish community. When I was offered the position of creating a Jewish studies department at City College of the City University of New York, I took it. I

---

21 Yeshiva University, paradoxically, upgraded its academic Jewish studies faculty and scholarship even as the yeshiva's atmosphere and teachings turned against such methods. The result was a growing bifurcation in which the more *frum* (religiously intense) students and those more devoted to Talmud and halakha studies were less open (or turned antagonistic) to academic Jewish studies. The school was a long way from the 1960s Soloveitchikian- or Samuel Belkin–inspired visions of synthesis.
22 See especially Irving Greenberg, "Scholarship and Continuity: Dilemma and Dialectic," and Gerson D. Cohen, "An Embarrassment of Riches: Reflections on the Conditions of American Jewish Scholarship in 1969," in *The Teaching of Judaica in American Universities: The Proceedings of a Colloquium*, ed. Leon Jick (New York: KTAV Publishing House, 1970), 115–29, 135–50.

believed that, as an academic, at least I could more easily write and publish on the significance of the Holocaust and its lessons for Jews in the world. I also hoped that the post might give me a launching pad for a pluralist center for thought and education that could reach out with a dual message: American Jews must grow in Jewish knowledge and identity in order to participate in American society without assimilating. Jewish religion, ethics, culture, and relations with other groups must be rethought in the context of the Holocaust and Israel.

As chair of the new department, I convinced the administration to appoint Elie Wiesel as a Distinguished Professor of Jewish Studies at City College—even though he was a writer and did not have an advanced academic degree. This was his first full-time, adequately paid professional position that enabled him to spread his wings. Elie continuously wrote and lectured widely, articulating the weight of the Shoah and the need to confront it and draw conclusions. He modeled the dignity and moral force of the survivors and called for human solidarity and joint action to prevent any repetition of genocide or persecution.

After numerous conversations, Elie decided to serve as cofounder of CLAL with me. In 1973, with the aid of a legacy left to City College, which the administration designated for Jewish studies, we brought in the third cofounder, Rabbi Steven Shaw. He served as our guide as CLAL, initially called the National Jewish Conference Center, reached out. We targeted the federations with an agenda to make them more Jewish by casting Jewish learning, across all denominational lines, as a fundamental resource for leaders' personal identity. Typically, this experience also led the leaders to establish more Jewish priorities in Federation decisions in communal policy, religious activity, and educational funding.

When we started the organization, I believed that there was a race on between the possibility of renaissance and rebirth in a supportive, pluralist American society, against a growing assimilation and disintegration. The negative outcome would win if an ill-educated, religiously infantile Jewry entered totally into the most open and accepting culture of all time. I sometimes put it that CLAL's goal was to push up the angle of ascent of the wave of renewal, so that when the ascending curve met the downward curve of assimilation, there would be enough engaged Jews to successfully complete the adaptation of Jewry/Judaism into modern civilization. Sadly, the Pew survey of 2013 suggested that the two curves will interact in a much lower level of communal engagement and educational fortification than we had dreamed.

CLAL's other main theme was that Jewish communities must come to grips with the Holocaust and the State of Israel as transforming Jewish religion and self-understanding. One implication was that all Jews were in this task together. CLAL was built on the principle of pluralism.[23] The staff was recruited from plural denominations. The courses were pluralist and academic level. Plural religious services were offered at CLAL retreats and institutes. Special programs were created to bring rabbis and rabbinical students together across denominational lines, to learn from each other and to dialogue on religious policies and issues.

This open affirmation of pluralism clashed with Modern Orthodoxy's move to the right. While a disproportionate number of CLAL's professional staff and lay leadership were Modern Orthodox (due to my roots, contacts, and past activity in the community), the organization itself was increasingly marginalized by the Orthodox. Norman Lamm, by then president of Yeshiva University, whose leading donors included nonobservant Jews, participated in the first two CLAL conferences on the theme of preserving "one Jewish people," but he stopped coming after that, as he explained, due to the backlash from the right. The number of rabbinical students from Yeshiva University who came to our seminars also declined as the school stopped openly sponsoring such activities.

As the growing polarization in Jewry inflamed Jewish life, I felt that the pluralism work was even more urgent. The fraying of ties with Orthodox Jews helped tilt the balance inside the Reform movement, which adopted an official declaration recognizing patrilineal descent as sufficient for identification as a Jew, as traditional Reform rabbinic leadership wrote off their concern to stay in relationship with the Orthodox (whom they perceived as now totally delegitimating them). Similarly, as Modern Orthodoxy became a satellite of ultra-Orthodox policies, the Synagogue Council of America broke down, and the Orthodox withdrew.

I felt that giving up the principle of pluralism would be a gross betrayal of the lessons of the Holocaust and Israel, even though I saw that it was undermining my residual standing in Modern Orthodoxy. My stand was popular in the rest of the community. CLAL attracted lots of support thanks to holding up the banner of pluralism, including support from the shrinking number of progressive Modern Orthodox.

---

23 I felt it was time to apply Soloveitchik's categories of *brit goral* and *yiud* to the liberal denominations for maximum effectiveness in the fight against assimilation. See Irving Greenberg, "Toward a Principled Pluralism," in "Will There Be One Jewish People By the Year 2000?," *Perspectives*, June 1985 (New York: National Jewish Center for Learning and Leadership [CLAL]).

Nevertheless, most Orthodox rabbis were convinced that pluralism was subversive of Orthodoxy because it weakened the Orthodox monopoly of being the (only) "authentic" Jews. More and more colleagues grew distant because they were upset by CLAL programs. Critiques and delegitimating broadsides proliferated in the Orthodox community. The Agudath Israel publication, *The Jewish Observer*, published a scathing attack on Norman Lamm for consorting with a heretic (me) and on Modern Orthodoxy for tolerating me and my beyond heresy, unspeakable writings on Christianity. After one such attack, a national Jewish leader called me, "Cheer up," he said. "They may be questioning if you are Orthodox inside the community. But you are the most popular Orthodox rabbi in the country—if you ask non-Orthodox Jews."

The climax of the backlash came when I was brought up before the Rabbinical Council of America's Honor Committee on charges of what might be called conduct unbecoming an Orthodox rabbi. The committee consisted of past presidents of the RCA, and its mandate was upholding/enforcing religious standards of Orthodox rabbis. Its powers included recommending sanctions, up to expulsion from the council. I was offended at this "criminalization" of my views and considered rejecting the summons and resigning. However, I saw myself to be an Orthodox rabbi and wanted my views to be recognized as legitimate inside the community. Hence, I decided to go through the process.

The main charge was that I, an Orthodox rabbi, was violating Torah law by running religious services (Conservative, Reform, etc.) whose practices such as mixed seating, and the like, violated halakha. There was a secondary charge of teaching heresy, which I gathered was because I wrote about Christianity. For some people, applying pluralism to Christianity was even more shocking, but they shied away from openly punishing such views. They were worried that if the news leaked publicly, this would evoke a backlash from Christians, so the charge of heresy was mostly soft-pedaled throughout the process.

The main charge was technically false. We had made a decision at CLAL that only a rabbi ordained in a particular denomination would lead services of that kind. CLAL felt this requirement was necessary to send a message that we did not consider all rabbis and services as interchangeable. We were pluralists, not relativists. However, at a deeper level the charge was true. As head of CLAL, I hired those diverse rabbis and aided them. Also, I enthusiastically taught Torah at those services, as I did in synagogues, from Orthodox to Reconstructionist, around the country. I explained to the committee that this was the meaning of being a pluralist. I did not run non-Orthodox services, but I did enable and make them available to others.

The committee members responded that this constituted a denial of the existence of all norms and standards. How could I, as an Orthodox rabbi, enable and participate in religious services that violated halakha? My response was that, although I personally prayed in an Orthodox minyan because I agreed that liberal services violated certain religious laws, nevertheless, I was convinced that God heard and accepted the prayers of liberal Jews, and, having been there, I could testify that the divine presence was palpably there in such synagogues and gatherings. Moreover, liberal religious services were reaching Jews whom neither I nor Orthodoxy could reach. They were uplifting them religiously and confirming their Jewish identity, and were therefore a valid and constructive part of *clal yisrael*. It was in our interest to strengthen and improve their religious performances, if we could.

The committee asked me to stop giving the liberal services legitimacy by teaching Torah there. I rejected that demand unequivocally; I would teach Torah in any place or to any person willing to learn with me. They asked me what my practice was when I taught Torah in non-Orthodox services. I explained that I personally davened beforehand, but showed respect for the congregation, standing up and sitting down as appropriate; I informed my hosts that I wanted them not to offer me honors such as *aliyot*, but if there was a slipup I did not refuse, because that would constitute degrading the service or embarrassing the people.

The committee again charged that I was undermining norms and distinctions. I was frustrated that a number of the past presidents simply could not grasp the idea of pluralism, and I was troubled by the fact that a number of them could, but would not defend me or try to stop the rush to judgment and condemnation.

By then, Lamm was under heavy pressure to stop the process, and he persuaded one of the past presidents of the RCA to negotiate a stand-down. As a concession, I offered never to take any honors in non-Orthodox synagogues, to make it clear that I honored distinctions and that I was Orthodox. Thus the matter ended with no action or public report. Although my antagonists did not achieve their maximum goals, I think they won a victory in that they confirmed my marginalization inside the movement.

Sadly, the Modern Orthodox institutional leadership never saw that they had an even larger stake than I did in keeping the widest possible spectrum inside Modern Orthodoxy, that no matter how far down the road of Haredization they went, Yeshiva University and centrists would always be seen as inauthentic, class-B Haredim. Nor did they stand up for the right of others in the community to advocate pluralism or even a big-tent Orthodoxy. They just gave in to the right.

The Modern Orthodox leadership paid a heavy price for their capitulation. When Norman Lamm called to tell me that he would no longer participate in CLAL programs, I pointed out that he was yielding to the Haredi trend, instead of defending the Modern Orthodox alternative approach. In the process, he was acquiescing in the delegitimization of me, of pluralism, and of CLAL's (and all other *clal yisrael*) program activity. I told him that by doing this, he was cutting off the branch on which he was sitting: it would leave him as the most left, most modern spiritual voice in Modern Orthodoxy. But he needed the left as an integral part of Modern Orthodoxy, so that he could lead from the center. By abandoning the left, he was marginalizing himself.

Lamm did, in fact, become marginalized at Yeshiva University, particularly inside the rabbinical seminary. While many students still looked up to him, the growing majority of intense learners internalized a Haredized version of Modern Orthodoxy. They identified with and guided themselves by the rulings, policies and values of the yeshivish/Haredi world. I saw that all this was happening but could not do much. Modern Orthodox leadership did not want to help itself. Most leaders hesitated to articulate that the "moderns" needed distinctive policies and halakhic procedures.

Nor could CLAL do much to arrest the process of growing divisiveness and radicalization within the denominations. CLAL played an important role in moving the Federation world toward a more Jewish agenda and toward greater emphasis on living and learning Jewishly for the lay leadership. Teaching and shaping the communal agenda toward Jewish education and culture consumed almost all my time. This program side of the organization kept growing and succeeding. The interdenominational and pluralism work, the dialogues, the conferences on one Jewish people, the joint rabbinic learning also grew—but their impact was overwhelmed by the polarization and growing interdenominational antagonism. Separation and sectarianism surged as each side felt that its more radical policies were justified by the increasingly partisan programs of the other side.

In one area, however, CLAL's focus, theme, and program work on the centrality of the Shoah and of Israel in Jewish life broke through beyond my wildest dreams. Stuart Eizenstat, chief domestic affairs adviser to President Jimmy Carter, had been deeply involved in CLAL. He was profoundly affected by its teachings, both on the need for intensive Jewish education for his children and the importance of the Holocaust. When the president was seeking an outreach gesture to American Jewry, Eizenstat proposed that he make it a national Holocaust memorial. Elie Wiesel was appointed chairman of the President's Commission on the Holocaust, and I was named to serve as executive director.

Wiesel, brilliantly and charismatically, led the commission to grasp the enormity of the event and its important implications for all of humanity, and it recommended a museum to tell the narrative and to influence the American educational system. This was an almost unimaginable breakthrough. It meant that the Holocaust Memorial Center would be created on behalf of all Americans. It was placed on the National Mall, the sacred ground of the American people, with the sponsorship and imprimatur of the government of the United States. The US Holocaust Memorial Museum has become the third most popularly visited museum on the Mall. The overall program included a commitment by the United States government to hold a National Day of Commemoration of the Holocaust on or about Yom HaShoah.

In my judgement, the US Holocaust Museum and its program validated one of the finest promises of the 1960s. America would become a pluralist culture in which Jews could be themselves fully. They could even help shape and upgrade American life through their values.

Before and after 1979, the ZACHOR Holocaust Resource Center worked with local Jewish communities to create similar communal Holocaust memorial centers. This stemmed from our conviction that only an institution focused on the event and offering an immersive encounter followed by education could do justice, and educate the Jewish/general public, to the centrality of this event in Jewish and general history. By the 1980s, I had concluded that my contribution to *zikui harabim*—educating the public—should focus on creating two historic institutions for Jewry, new institutions that could express and channel educationally the new historical era unfolding in Jewish history. One was the Holocaust Memorial Center. I believed that a local Holocaust memorial center would become a permanent institution in every major Jewish community. This would enable Jews to confront the event, to draw its implications, and to channel them into Jewish education and culture.

Nevertheless, in 1980, I determined to return to CLAL to work full-time and not stay on as director of the US Holocaust Museum. As central as raising Holocaust consciousness was, I believed that the even more fundamental task was to assure the future of Jewry in an open society by upgrading Jewish identity and saturating the community with Jewish culture. I wanted to give my life's priority to enriching Jewish life internally. CLAL offered classes, and especially retreats, to enrich Jewish identity. Through CLAL, I wanted to focus on the creation of retreat centers to offer immersive Jewish learning and living experiences for Jewish communal leaders and, eventually, to all lay people. I remain convinced that offering a total environment, immersive group experience of Jewish living at many points in life (including day schools, camp and youth movements, Israel trips, and extended studies in the Land of Israel for college students, as well as adult retreats) will implant and nurture a Jewish identity vital enough to enable full participation in American society without assimilation or losing the primacy of Jewishness.

I consider my giving this priority to Jewish communal/educational work to be the outcome of my own identity as a Modern Orthodox Jew. Although I had become an unabashed pluralist by the 1970s, all my projects and programs were deeply rooted in the Modern Orthodox commitment to learning Torah as the key to living a successful Jewish life. I often thought of myself as a representative of Modern Orthodoxy, serving the entire Jewish people. CLAL—and I— pushed the Federations to serve kosher food and to respect Jewish holidays in all their programs. This was important for the Modern Orthodox participants and would be viewed as a sign of respect for Jewish unity and Jewish heritage. Most of the Jewish community recognized my rootedness in Modern Orthodoxy and gave the denomination credit for my activities.

When Birthright Israel was started, the founding philanthropists saw it as an outreach program to connect to the unaffiliated. A number of leaders proposed to exclude Modern Orthodox young people on the grounds that they did not need such a program, whereas their inclusion would put the total costs beyond the fundraising capabilities. I and our son J. J., z"l, executive director of Jewish Life Network, staffed the planning group. We insisted that the principle of *clal yisrael*/Jewish unity demanded their inclusion. Though we had to put ourselves and our professional roles on the line, we won the argument, and in actual practice, Orthodox participation has been strong and Orthodox providers have attained the largest market share of the trips.

CLAL was not successful in creating a retreat center or convincing American Jewish communities to construct their own. However, CLAL and I personally continued to offer individual and communal retreats with great impact. I remain convinced that a universal program of retreats, offered free to younger adults and/or young marrieds and/or new parents and/or all adults, is the single most powerful option to confirm Jewish identity and reverse the process of assimilation in America. Unfortunately, the community has not been able to put this option together.

There were other initiatives that failed to take off, such as universal Jewish prekindergarten and service learning. We created MAKOR, a Jewish outreach institution which presented as a secular, nondenominational music performance space and restaurant, to attract young Jews in their 20s and 30s, and offered classes in Hebrew and Jewish culture, as well as art programs and Jewish holiday experiences. For a time MAKOR was an important venue for young adult nightlife in New York, but it closed after its leadership moved to the 92nd St. Y. As a result, outreach has remained an outlier in the general Jewish community, primarily the province either of non-Orthodox or of premodern, mostly ultra-Orthodox missionary groups.

In the 1980s, I visited England on behalf of CLAL. The trip included giving talks at Orthodox venues and at Liberal and Reform conferences as well. When Chief Rabbi Immanuel Jakobovits learned of this schedule, he told me that if I did not cancel my talks at the liberal groups, all the Orthodox invitations would be withdrawn. It was the policy of the Orthodox United Synagogue not to recognize or legitimate non-Orthodox groups. I pleaded with him that British Jewry was facing the opening up of British society and that all the religious groupings would be needed to cope with the challenge. I argued that the exclusion policy was inconsistent and bordering on hypocrisy. After all, he participated in interfaith conversations with Christians, which the United Synagogue actively supported in order to establish its civic, democratic bona fides with the general society, yet he refused to speak or dialogue with the liberal Jewish denominations. I also pointed out that this policy of accommodation to the growing ultra-Orthodox community was weakening the Modern Orthodox. Intra-religious dialogue would strengthen the Modern Orthodox lay people and equip them to handle better the modern ideas coming at them from the general society. In the absence of internal deepening and dialogue, the Modern Orthodox would be cannibalized from the right and from the left. Some would move toward the ultra-Orthodox—seeking shelter or believing that they were more authentic—while most would drift into liberal and/or assimilating communities.

Rabbi Jakobovits acknowledged that my scenario was a likely one, but insisted that the policies would continue. He predicted that the ultra-Orthodox would become dominant, and he was not going to fight them. I pointed out that modern civilization would not go away and that Judaism would have to work out some adjustments to function effectively in the dominant civilization. Modeling this capacity to participate and maintain distinctiveness could be the special purpose and contribution of Modern Orthodoxy to Diaspora Jewry. He acknowledged this argument also, then said that when the Haredim were the only Jews left, the others having assimilated, they would deal with the issues and make the necessary adjustments. To which my response was: let us make the adjustments now while we still have most of the Jews with us. He was unmoved. The Orthodox invitations were mostly withdrawn—except that from Rabbi Jeffrey Cohen, a liberal and independent Orthodox rabbi of one of the largest United Synagogue congregations.

Within the United Kingdom, the Haredi takeover of the policies of Orthodox institutions continued. The halakhic, educational policy-setting mostly passed from the chief rabbi to the London Beth Din, dominated by Haredi Torah scholars. An accommodating conversion policy would have reduced intermarriage and the disintegrating impact of intermarriage on Jewish affiliation and identity. Instead, the Beth Din developed one of the most restrictive conversion processes in Diaspora Jewry. This served well the Haredi community who were counting on social distance and exclusion to keep intermarriage out of their ranks. It served badly the majority of British Jews, whose children were rapidly integrating in the general society.

The dominance of the ultra-Orthodox London Beth Din continued and even intensified under Jakobovits's successor, Rabbi Jonathan Sacks. He brilliantly reached out in dialogue with the general culture and society and made a great spiritual/moral/political contribution to Britain. However, internally, he deferred to the London Beth Din and the ultra-Orthodox. Jews' College, the fountainhead of British Modern Orthodoxy, continued to decline and finally closed its ordination program. In response to pressure from colleagues in the British rabbinate, Sacks removed one of his most important theological insights from the second edition of his important book, *The Dignity of Difference*: his unequivocal pluralist statement that God spoke to Jews through Judaism, to Christians through Christianity, and to Muslims through Islam.[24]

I never could make up my mind as to what motivated the Modern Orthodox leadership in America, Great Britain, and elsewhere to allow the ultra-Orthodox to take over and to set policy. Were they politically intimidated? Did they feel that the yeshivish/Haredi movement was more authentic, or its leadership more learned, than they were? Or, did they become convinced that this Haredi development was an irreversible historical tide? When he completed his term as chief rabbi, Jonathan Sacks made a stinging critique of the ultra-Orthodox policies and tendencies. This made clear that he never

---

24 Jonathan Sacks, *The Dignity of Difference: How to Avoid the Clash of Civilizations* (London: Continuum, 2002).

abandoned the Modern Orthodox view, but that did not retroactively change the Haredi dominance of Orthodox communal policies.

Also in the 1980s, I noticed that four Modern Orthodox spiritual leaders in Israel that I greatly admired had built remarkable educational platforms. Yet all four stalwarts were being attacked: Adin Steinsaltz's bona fides as an Orthodox authority was impugned on the grounds that his Talmud edition departed from the traditional pagination and used modern, historical material in the commentary. Aharon Lichtenstein was denounced for a willingness to forfeit sacred land and for supporting a traditional peace movement. Shlomo Riskin was challenged for a step he took to advance women's learning. David Hartman was condemned for his religious pluralism.

I went to Israel and visited all four with a proposal: We five should take a stand and put out a joint statement. We did not agree with each other on all religious matters or doctrines. However, we were all trying to advance the place of Torah and its teachings and values in Jewish life from a Modern Orthodox standpoint. The issues were formidable, and the obstacles were great. Therefore, we needed a culture that sought truth and would strive for understandings that could inspire modern people. We could call on our fellow Modern Orthodox Jews to come together and repudiate delegitimating attacks designed to suppress religious development. Our arguments should be *l'shem shamayim* (for the sake of heaven), assuming that the opposing group was operating out of goodwill, a desire to arrive at Torah's truth and to live by its guidelines.

I went to see Hartman first; he was willing, but he warned me that Lichtenstein considered him beyond the pale. Then I spoke to Steinsaltz and Riskin, and they came up with similar answers: despite attacks, each considered himself well-ensconced within Orthodoxy and felt that any such joint activity would only weaken his position.

When I met with Aharon, he heard me out and gave the following response (paraphrased): "As far as I am concerned, Hartman has crossed the line and is out. I don't know where you are. Some people tell me that you have crossed the line. But since I'm not in America and have not followed you closely, I will simply suspend judgment. Steinsaltz and Riskin stand on their own two feet … I am a Rosh Yeshiva. My priority is teaching Torah and educating as many students as I can. The Yeshiva world is my world. I am not about to do anything that damages my priority to help out you or Hartman for the sake of a nebulous, more open culture that could as likely harm as help the students' *emunah* and *yirat shamayim*." I told him that I understood his realism and the prudence of his answer. However, I felt that Modern Orthodoxy was being strangled slowly.

Opening up its culture would be lifesaving for it, and would serve the Jewish people better. He demurred.

So my proposal for a joint statement went nowhere. The shunning of the left continued apace. Lichtenstein was a great *rosh yeshiva* for another thirty years; his voice for a mature, moderate, ethical Judaism inspired many, and his role model uplifted the national-religious community. But his voice was relatively drowned out by the unchecked, often louder, more politically extreme and spiritually sectarian voices. The uncontested assertions from the right extended their sway in the Centrist Orthodox community. Legalism and ritual punctiliousness grew, and ethical focus shrank. Discomfort with modernity and negative attitudes toward Gentiles and other outsiders strengthened. Modern Orthodoxy continued to decline.

TOWARD A POSTMODERN JEWISH CULTURE AND A POSTMODERN ORTHODOXY

By the 1990s, I became convinced that the Jewish community had to move beyond its commitment to modernity and its internalization of modern values and assumptions, toward a new synthesis of Judaism and postmodernity. Modern Orthodoxy also had to reformulate itself as "Postmodern" Orthodoxy.

A word about postmodernity. Some readers will classify this phenomenon with the denial of the existence of objective facts and truth. Some equate it with the insistence that all truth claims are specious fronts for subjective, agenda-driven narratives. Such a culture frequently comes with an atmosphere of anything goes and claims that all identities are purely social constructs, protean, easily adopted and lightly shed. I consider this version to be an overextended, distortedly crystallized version of the true insights of postmodernity.

All truths are inescapably articulated and understood in a social and historical context. The wrong conclusion to be drawn from this is a worldview of relativism or nihilism. The right response is to acknowledge the subjectivity, seek to offset and filter it with a hermeneutic of skepticism and with cross-cultural comparisons and insights. What is right about postmodern culture, and what needs to be incorporated into our religious beliefs and systems? The best approach is to recover as many voices from the past and present as possible, so as to allow for a 360-degree view of the truth and/or the issue.

Postmodernity emerged as humanity has lived through and recognized the fallacies and failures of modernity. This includes the methodological insight that many of the binaries held up by modern culture were not objective, as claimed, but constructed. Therefore, the forced choices between science and religion, or facts and values, are not correct; nor are reason and science objective and authoritative, while faith is emotional and inferior. This means that it is all right to believe, side by side with science. In this culture, religious experience is both possible and authentic. When we acknowledge that divinity and belief are not fully accessible to language and objects, this insight enables us to grasp metaphors, poetry, and narrative models of faith.

Many truths of modernity and the very strengths that led to the upgrading of life and increased human dignity turned destructive or even catastrophic when extended beyond their limits or allowed to go out of control. The correct response is not to reject such phenomena as universalism, industrialization, commerce, technology, bureaucracy, but to employ them with limits, corrective mechanisms, and countervailing forces and norms.

Thus, postmodernity enables us to take the best insights and moral improvements of our culture into our traditions. The equality of women, the legitimacy of various forms of sexuality, affirmation of embodiment and the dignity of the body—which were fought by Orthodoxy as the spoor of modernity—can now be embraced and embedded in traditional culture and worldview. Similarly, postmodernity enables us to embrace every aspect of the heritage fully and incorporate it into a vital religious life. The transcendence of Divinity and the eternality of Torah—hitherto impugned by modern categories of understanding—can now be recovered.

Sociologically, the monolithic authority of modernity carried a tacit message to Jews: give up being different, in return for full admission to the club. Postmodernity's message is: you are here by right. Being Jewish and different is kosher. In this mode, pluralism becomes not the abandonment of absolutes and a way-station to relativism and moral indifference. It becomes a way of intensively affirming our religion, along with an acknowledgment that other religions may contribute to the world or even enrich our religious lives.

Finally, a healthy postmodernity embraces the human assumption of power. Whole new vistas of *tikkun olam* have opened up. At the same time, limits, covenantal standards and partnership with God and humans are essential to prevent this process of development from turning into unrestrained growth—that is, cancer, be it biological, political, or moral.

As I saw it, by the 1990s, Judaism had to evolve into a postmodern formulation. Already in 1979 I had written that, since the "idol worship of modernity has been broken in the Holocaust ..., correcting the excessive modernization of Modern Orthodox, Conservative, Reform and secular Jews is a major task ... we should be looking for a post-modern position ... This would include major growth and synthesis between Torah values and post-modern values and insights ... a major renewal of Modern Orthodoxy."[25]

I felt that the binary, either/or positions taken by Orthodox, Conservative and Reform in the first stage of modernity were all partially right and partially wrong. Many of these denominational conflicts stemmed from modern cultural assumptions and standards. On issues such as accepting or rejecting modern values (democracy and equality, or universal morality), meeting modern intellectual criteria as established by historical and critical methods, or the authority of reason and of tradition, the accumulation of evidence had become overwhelming. For people living in the culture, the issues had been settled decisively. Therefore, the real challenge was not whether, but how, to respond. I concluded that the valid responses were spaced along a spectrum. Consequently, pluralist responses were legitimate and necessary, especially if the whole Jewish people was to make it into the new culture.

By then, my primary teaching opportunities were at CLAL and at the Wexner Heritage Program. Both settings were pluralist in their working principles, with a widely diversified student cohort. While I never stopped being Modern Orthodox in my religious practice and institutional affiliations, I had become a pluralist. I affirmed the legitimacy of all the denominations and considered that denominational loyalties should be secondary to *clal yisrael* needs.

I believed the task of Jewish educators was to fight the values-free, nihilistic reading of postmodernity. The mission of Modern Orthodoxy was to join others in articulating the Jewish tradition and culture in a credible way in this emerging civilization. The postmodern Orthodox could make a special contribution in the process, because they were deeply grounded in and had access to the resources of the whole tradition. Yet they were close enough and integrated enough to learn how to make it fully credible in the new culture. It was urgent that they take leadership. If the level of Jewish culture and identity was not upgraded and intensified—the need to do this was the great insight and strength of Orthodoxy—then there was a high risk of broad-scale assimilation.

The Haredi effort to evade this culture was futile. The postmodern culture, at least in America, was even more open to Jews—so 95 percent of the Jewish community went into it enthusiastically. As I saw it, ultra-Orthodoxy's success in creating some shelter and building itself as the counterculture was impressive, but

---

25 Irving Greenberg, "Orthodox Judaism and the Holocaust," *Gesher* 71 (1979): 55–82.

was useful, essentially, only for itself. In choosing and carrying out these policies, it wrote off the bulk of the Jewish community. Furthermore, I estimated that this shelter solution would not last more than a generation or two. Therefore, I concluded that Modern Orthodoxy had a mission to go fully into the postmodern culture alongside the bulk of Jewry and show the way to a successful integration.

This community could provide important leadership, role models, and social heft to Jewry. To do this, Modern Orthodoxy would have to incorporate the positive moral and intellectual advances of modernity into its Torah heritage. Clearly, this would place a great strain on its capacity to grow and to reformulate the vital center of its tradition. I was convinced that on balance, democracy, pluralism, humanism, feminism, individualism, self-expression, this-worldliness, affirmation of the body and pleasure, cultural creativity, and variety of expression were moral and spiritual advances that the tradition should incorporate (while also critiquing and modifying them). Furthermore, both science and historical/critical studies had deepened our understanding of reality. The tradition needed to acknowledge these achievements and properly and persuasively reformulate the classic doctrines of revelation (that is, the understanding of commandment and of *Torah min hashamayim*), the continuity and eternity of tradition, and the covenant, in a manner credible to people with a new understanding through the postmodern lens.[26] By the light of the classic tradition, Jewry would critique, reshape, and put dialectical limits on postmodern culture—to the betterment of both. All the other strains of Jewish identity and strands of Jewish culture/religion would have to undergo a parallel process of upgrade, correction, and integration.

By the '90s, the right wing/centrists had frozen me out, so that neither my voice nor sympathetic views were heard in places like Yeshiva University, the Orthodox Union, or the Rabbinical Council of America. When I received an invitation from a small student group at Yeshiva to speak to them, posted signs announcing the lecture were torn down and replaced by signs stating that the

---

26 In recent years, two important postmodern Orthodox statements have emerged. One is the posthumous publications of the works of Rav Shagar (Shimon Gershon Rosenberg); see especially his comments on postmodernism in *Luhot v'Shivrei Luhot* (Tablets and Broken Tablets) (Tel Aviv: Yediot-Sifrei Hemed, 2013), 428–40. The other important address to the issues of historicity, narrative, and revelation is Yehuda Gellman, *This Was from God: A Contemporary Theology of Torah and History* (Boston: Academic Studies Press, 2016). TheTorah.com is a website which connects Orthodox/observant Jews with contemporary biblical historical-critical scholarship to enable Jews who accept the divinity of Torah to learn from (and possibly integrate) critical scholarship.

lecture had been canceled. (I went anyway, and there were fewer than ten students present. They reported that the action was taken at the instigation of the *roshei yeshiva*, but when I reported the incident, Lamm said, "I had no idea.")

In the 1990s, I worked with Michael Steinhardt to create a model of entrepreneurial philanthropy, designed to innovate educational formats and enable the community to meet the culture/identity challenge. Through the Jewish Life Network/Steinhardt Foundation, we sought to build out the communal educational/experiential infrastructure needed to nurture Jewish identity in the open society. JLN/SF was a leader, especially in the creation of immersive experiences (Birthright Israel), day schools (through the Partnership for Excellence in Jewish Education), and camps (through the Grinspoon Foundation).

Michael Steinhardt was persuaded that it was in the interest of the broader Jewish community (and of his goals) to revive Modern Orthodoxy. He put up matching money, and I was able to recruit a group of Modern Orthodox philanthropists to fund a new outlet for a progressive, communal-oriented Orthodoxy, which we called EDAH. EDAH's programming leaned over backward not to appear too progressive. It repeatedly stressed that it was only advocating pluralism within Orthodoxy. Its slogan "the courage to be modern and Orthodox" captured the fear of delegitimization by the right and a desire for their approval. Steinhardt was disillusioned by EDAH's inability to mount a serious challenge to the rightward drift, and dropped out.

EDAH was ahead of its time. There were no self-affirming, proudly Modern Orthodox institutions to stand in solidarity with it. Nor did it have a self-aware, battle-seasoned lay leadership that wanted to reclaim the direction of the community. EDAH offered its administrative leadership to an outstanding and iconic Modern Orthodox rabbi, Rabbi Saul Berman, who managed to sustain it for a decade of modest programming and cautious policy moves before it closed.

Nevertheless, the left of Modern Orthodoxy began to stir. Thanks to such stalwarts as Blu Greenberg, Rabbi Avi Weiss, and a host of lay leaders, the Jewish Orthodox Feminist Alliance (JOFA), Yeshivat Chovevei Torah (YCT), and Yeshivat Maharat began the work of rebuilding a genuine, open Modern Orthodoxy. The International Rabbinical Fellowship (IRF) was founded by Rabbis Avi Weiss and Marc Angel to serve as a rabbinic organization for more progressive Orthodox rabbis—especially as the RCA continued to move to the right. (The RCA refused to recognize the ordination of those who graduated YCT and would not admit them to membership because the views taught at the school were openly progressive Orthodox.) The IRF membership is now over two hundred rabbis.

As these groups strengthened, I discovered that my views were no longer as decidedly different from the Orthodox camp's spectrum than in the past. I have supported and helped these new groups, including teaching under their auspices but have not been active in their consolidation. Honestly, I had not expected these developments in my lifetime. I often think of the Talmudic dictum *zachu–melachtam naaseyt al yedei acheyrim* (If people are lucky/worthy, their work is done for them by others).[27]

These organizations are only finding their way. Furthermore, they are continuously fending off delegitimating attacks from the Haredi community and the centrist institutions, such as Yeshiva University and the RCA. This pressure holds them down to some extent. That said, they are mostly not where I am. For example, they are not yet pluralist. They have not yet arrived at the understanding of the need to mature beyond Modern Orthodoxy into a postmodern Orthodoxy. Nevertheless, they are highly significant. They shed new light on the terminology that I represent, the road not taken for Modern Orthodoxy.

I believe that history will record that in the past half century, Modern Orthodoxy (especially its leadership) lost its way and turned onto the path of halakhic reaction, communal separation, and seeking cultural shelter. Instead of growing and moving forward into postmodernity, it retreated and turned toward the ghetto/shelter of premodernity. This rightward turn made it miss two historic missions that it could have fulfilled. One was to lead the world Jewish community to successfully master the forces of assimilation and alienation from their religious heritage by offering an integrated, intellectually, and morally credible Jewish way of life in the heart of (post)modern civilization. The other was to recalibrate the relationship of Judaism and Christianity, ending the Christian denigration of Jewish religion and enabling both faiths to partner in teaching and modeling the covenant of redemption for the world.

THE DECLINE AND REBIRTH OF (POST)MODERN ORTHODOXY

The flight from history and responsibility has been close to catastrophic for Modern Orthodoxy, which now amounts to only 3 percent of American Jewry.[28] It has lost many of the young people who were educated by the Haredi/

---

27 BT Berakhot 35b.
28 "A Portrait of Jewish Americans, Findings from a Pew Research Center Survey of U.S. Jews, 2013," http://www.pewresearch.org/wp-content/uploads/sites/7/2013/10/jewish-american-full-report-for-web.pdf.

yeshivish rebbes staffing its institutions, either because the campus atmosphere and academic studies of the best universities undermined their belief systems and observance patterns, or because they moved even further to the right and became ultra-Orthodox.

The decline of Modern Orthodoxy has been no less harmful to the general Jewish community, as their ability to synthesize modernity and tradition and show all Jews how to live Jewishly in the world has been damaged. As Modern Orthodoxy weakened and its leadership deferred to the right, the Haredim took control of the religious public agenda. They installed Haredi-friendly policies that were inimical to the best interests of other groups. These policies included delegitimation of non-Orthodox groups, rather than cooperative strengthening of the community's educational infrastructure and/or joint outreach to the unaffiliated.

In Israel, the Modern Orthodox failed to check strident Haredi attacks on liberal Judaism or the use of their role in government coalitions to exclude non-Haredim from public spaces (such as the Kotel/Western Wall). These policies alienated many American Jews from the Jewish state and hurt Israel's image as a democracy. Yet the Centrist Orthodox were persuaded to stand in solidarity with the Haredim in both countries—even though the ultra-Orthodox frequently demeaned Modern and even some Centrist Orthodox rabbis or denied the legitimacy of Modern Orthodox practices and rabbinic conversions.

An impossibly demanding, exclusionary conversion policy was enforced by the Israeli chief rabbinate and was generally followed by the Centrist Orthodox in America. As the American Jewish community was participating intensely in the general society, Jews met and fell in love with non-Jews, while many Gentiles became interested in Judaism and open to conversion, especially to marry a Jew. Instead of helping them stay Jewish by easing entry of prospective converts into the general Jewish community, Orthodox requirements were considerably tightened. The legitimacy of all liberal conversions, no matter how rigorously or seriously done, were denied, even though statistics showed that such converts and their spouses became considerably more affiliated and participatory in Jewish life than those who intermarried but did not convert. The outcome was that the surge in intermarriage was bleeding people out of Jewry—whereas a more *clal yisrael*–oriented, welcoming conversion policy could have turned interfaith relationships into a recruitment tool for the Jewish people.

In Israel, 300,000 Russian *olim* were ready to become full citizens and join the Jewish religion to be one with the Jewish majority. They served in the IDF (Israel Defense Force), putting their lives on the line to protect the Jewish state, but they were presented with the demand that they become ultra-observant in order to be converted. The ultra-Orthodox rabbinic staff's treatment of the would-be converts during the process, and their all-out assaults and denial of legitimacy to those who went through a more lenient Orthodox process, also alienated the community, so Israeli Russian public opinion turned against conversion.

The ultra-Orthodox educational system made students less qualified to contribute to the contemporary polity, economy, and scientific/technological culture. Although the Modern Orthodox did get highly educated and contributed much, as they became more influenced by ultra-Orthodox values, this reduced or cramped their participation. At a time when Israel and Jewry took on political sovereignty and the creation of a military infrastructure to defend it, the Haredim taught that everything depended on being right with God—as a substitute for an army which they did not join. They diminished the moral dimension of the religion in favor of pleasing God with religious behaviorism. This reduced the Orthodox contribution to solving the moral dilemmas of exercising power.

Haredi influence stimulated the growth of the *hardal* grouping inside Religious Zionism. These ultra-religious nationalists translated the worldview that all depended on God into messianist policies. Their visions would not be bound by political/military realities, by Israeli government authority, or by international public opinion.

The reduction of modern influences and increasing withdrawal from contact with people of other viewpoints led to considerable growth of anti-Arab prejudice and hostility to Christian minorities among Orthodox Jews. The religious community and its voters repeatedly became an obstacle to exploring peace possibilities, or they supported restrictions on civil rights and democratic practices.

In 2017 the Union of Orthodox Jewish Congregations of America (OU) ruled that "a woman should not be appointed to serve in a clergy position."[29] This prohibition was a response to the spread of Orthodox women's ordination and service as clergy in communities both in the United States and Israel. This was stimulated by the steady advance of women to leadership in politics, education, business, and professions, as well as the overwhelming triumph in American and Israeli society of the principle that women are fully equal to men and should be treated that way. The prohibition of women serving as clergy was

---

29 See www.rabbis.org/pdfs/Responses-of-OU-Rabbinic-Panel.pdf.

justified on three specific halakhic grounds and on a global "halakhic ethos." Each of the rationales fits the Haredi community perfectly but is dissonant with the actual way of life of Modern Orthodox Jews.

The Haredi Agudath Israel of America and its rabbinic leadership had already proclaimed these developments to be beyond Orthodoxy, but they continued, so the traditionalists within the Orthodox Union sought to reverse this direction within Modern Orthodoxy. However, the ruling is out of step with the Modern Orthodox reality and its prevalent values. Most Modern Orthodox Jews perceive women's equality as morally superior to women's inequality. The 2017 ruling makes it harder to function as a Modern Orthodox Jew. Many Modern Orthodox young people are in college/university settings where exclusion of women from leadership roles is deadly to their ethical standing and religious credibility among their peers. Like the other rulings above, this policy forces Modern Orthodox Jews to move to the right or lose out.

What makes this policy destructive to Modern Orthodoxy is that it was handed down by seven rabbis, six of them from Yeshiva University, the flagship center of Modern Orthodoxy. Under that cover, it presents as a halakhic ruling to be legitimately imposed on Modern Orthodox synagogues and laypeople. It gives no halakhic weight to the existence of Modern Orthodox authorities, who rule that women can be ordained and can serve as rabbis.

This ruling continues the domination of Haredi values on Modern Orthodox life. These values have been so damaging to the modern community and have strengthened the Haredim at the expense of the Modern Orthodox, steadily driving out more Americanized, less traditional Jews. In 1960, based on my personal observations and the results of demographic studies in some local communities, I estimated that the Orthodox were around 20 percent of the adult national Jewish community. Perhaps half of Modern Orthodox synagogue membership was comprised of semi-observant or nonobservant Jews who identified as Orthodox. Their numbers and the institutions they supported gave heft to the Modern Orthodox community. Three decades later, these Jews or their children were gone, and the term "non-observant Orthodox" was viewed as an oxymoron inside the community. In the 1990 National Jewish Population Survey, Orthodoxy was down to 7.7 percent of American Jewry. Almost all that decline was in Modern Orthodoxy.

The same outcome holds true in Jewish education. Separate gender education honored Haredi norms, but served as a signal to non-Orthodox parents that Jewish day school was un-American. The single biggest obstacle to day-school enrollment was the widespread feeling among non-Orthodox American

Jews that they wanted maximum social integration in American life for their children. Gender segregation and other Haredi practices (such as restricting women's singing) put the day schools into an "alien" box. Once labeled this way, the schools found it hard to get out of being categorized as on the fringe. Outside the large metropolitan centers, the typical Jewish day school was started and driven by Modern Orthodox families, but needed non-Orthodox registration to survive financially. As the schools adopted a more Haredi atmosphere, they lost registration, struggled financially, and became less relevant to the rest of the Jewish families. In some communities, parents started Solomon Schechter (Conservative) schools or more sectarian schools. Both developments weakened the Modern Orthodox or the community day schools.

The 2013 Pew survey of American Jewry shows the cumulative impact of these policies, which drove off the less traditional, more Americanized Jews. In the half century from 1960 on, Modern Orthodoxy lost more than 50 percent of its membership. This decline, which was recognized as stemming from the move to the right, was rationalized by Modern Orthodox leadership as the creation of a more solid, observant core constituency. This was true to a point. However, the larger part of Modern Orthodoxy (led by Yeshiva University) distanced itself from American culture. Most called themselves centrist, not "modern." This group, de facto, had become Haredi-lite. Since many in its community were still exposed to American jobs, culture, and standards, especially when its sons and daughters went to regular colleges and universities, the community continued to bleed children from its committed families.

THE ROAD TO BE TAKEN

There are people who despair of Modern Orthodoxy's future. If you believe that the Jewish people can live without the Torah (and 85 percent of Jewry reject ultra-Orthodox religion), then Modern Orthodoxy may well disappear. If you believe that the Torah can live without the Jewish people—and this is the implication of an Orthodoxy that insists on the premodern way of life, which 95 percent of Jewry will not accept—then Modern Orthodoxy may well disappear. However, if you believe that both cannot live without each other, then Modern Orthodoxy will have to be reborn. The community/movement must reinvent itself to survive and to nurture Jews in this new postmodern culture.

This long-awaited rebirth is happening before our eyes now. It is now plausible that Modern Orthodoxy will turn onto the same road that *clal yisrael* is on: a way to postmodernity that is illuminated by the orienting events of the

Holocaust and the State of Israel, which signal a turn to taking political and military power in a responsible and morally restrained way. On this road, Jews will participate fully in scientific, medical, technological, and cultural breakthroughs, while upholding the moral restraints and spiritual guidelines of the tradition—alongside and in tandem with all people. Strengthened by Modern Orthodox teaching and models, all Jews will act out of Jewish values and see challenges through a Jewish lens, but they will acknowledge the dignity, validity, and contribution of other religions and national cultures.

In preparation for that development—which may well occur after my lifetime—I have worked for the past thirty years to create a Jewish narrative that could be persuasive in an open society in the full presence of other religions and cultures. Part of its credibility is that it affirms the other religions and respects them rather than dismissing them. This thinking started in the '60s with the notion of the centrality of *tzelem elokim*, the dignity of all persons created in the image of God. Next came pluralism. Once one encounters the power and contribution of other religions and religious trends, how can one go on affirming the absolute claims of one's own tradition? Pluralism holds the continuing authority (and even absolute demands) of one's own tradition, while acknowledging that there are other, sometimes even contradictory, teachings that are also valid. I continue to believe that pluralism is the only acceptable alternative to relativism. The fundamentalist upholding of absolutism requires creating a shelter or forcibly reducing the presence of other religions and cultures. Such a policy is morally flawed and spiritually warped—as can be seen in those countries where fundamentalism rules supreme. The policy is also likely doomed to failure as technology, more and more, interconnects people and their traditions.

I have gone through three waves of interpretation of pluralism. In the first wave, I derived pluralism from the tradition's building blocks of *tzelem elokim* and covenant. This included coming to understand Christianity—and trying to formulate a Jewish relationship to it—as an independent, dignified religion which has a genuine covenantal relationship with God (the same God as the Jewish people's).

In the second wave—reworking the understanding of the covenant in the light of the Shoah—I articulated the concept of a voluntary covenant. In the Holocaust, the covenant was broken and then reaccepted by the Jewish people, voluntarily, out of love of God, love of the Torah, and love of the vision of *tikkun olam*—even by those who did not believe in God. This formulation was used to delegitimate me and my thinking, particularly in Haredi and centrist circles. This is another example of the constant tension between trying to navigate by the light of the new orienting events while seeking to uphold and participate in Modern Orthodoxy. I was pained by my loss of credibility in the community. Still, I believed that I must faithfully interpret the religious revelation of our time. I never lost hope that Modern Orthodoxy would grow religiously, then it would acknowledge and integrate these new events and come to understand where it should stand religiously.

This struggle led to the next round of thinking—articulated in a narrative theology that has not yet been published. This interpretation is focused on a repeated divine *tzimtzum*. The initial divine self-limitation constitutes the entry into the covenant in the biblical stage. The next stage was a summons to Jewry to take on a more active role in the covenant. That Jewish response to God's call is expressed in the world and culture of rabbinic Judaism. I believe that since the beginning of modernity, we have been living through a third divine *tzimtzum*. This constitutes a call to the Jewish people and to all humanity to take power and assume full responsibility for the realization of the covenant. This third-stage human response is meant to be out of love, free will, and full, autonomous identification with the goal of *tikkun olam*. Therefore, the interpretive paradigm is not one of God breaking the covenant and Jewry voluntarily reaccepting it. The better understanding is that the covenant was always meant to be an educational process. God intended (as it were) that the human partners develop, then grow up, and become empowered enough to take full responsibility. Having given over the mandate to the human partners, the Divine did not shirk responsibility during the Holocaust; God was present and infinitely shared the pain and torment of the Jews. However, humanity did not exercise its responsibility.

Part of the failure to act in the Shoah stemmed from the inherited absolutist denigration of Judaism and hatred of Jewry. Another factor was modern humanity's loss of the sense of being covenanted (i.e., a partner in Creation and history). This failure of understanding has led to increasing human arrogance and self-deification, which is being expressed in exploitation of Creation and other human beings. These tendencies have become a threat to all life, as exemplified in climate change and species destruction. The failure to preserve the sense of partnership was aided and abetted by religious groups who have insisted that, out of respect for God, humanity should not take on powers that were once beyond it, nor should humans assume roles that were seen in the past as in the realm of the Divine. But an important part of the Jewish mission is to teach the ongoing power and relevance of the partnership. Jewry can be a role model on how to follow the (totally hidden but totally present) God into the new era of human empowerment, without becoming idolatrous. Thus, Jewry can become again a "light unto the nations" even as it persists and pursues its own covenantal goals.

As for Modern Orthodoxy, it cannot be the whole answer for every Jew; nor can it save Jewry or the tradition all by itself. Still, I hope that it will relocate itself in the center of Jewish life—and lead the charge into postmodernity. Being in the center means that one mediates, as Moses and the great prophets and rabbis did, between God and the people, between tradition and the need for change, between the entire heritage and postmodernity. When it lost its way, Centrist Orthodoxy located itself in the faux center—halfway between the Orthodox left and Satmar. But that actually placed them on the extreme right margin of *clal yisrael*, with 95 percent of the Jews living to their left, operating by different cultural assumptions and struggling with alternative moral paradigms and existential challenges. Modern Orthodoxy must relocate itself solidly inside postmodernity, sharing the fate, the challenges, and the experiences of all of Israel. Then it will be able to deepen the tradition, incorporate new methods, insights, and values, while connecting all people to the deepest levels of the entire heritage. This is the road that I believe will still be taken.

Part One

Law and Theology

CHAPTER 1

History and Halakhah

STEVEN T. KATZ

1. INTRODUCTORY COMMENTS

I am delighted and honored to participate in this volume dealing with the thought of Rabbi Irving "Yitz" Greenberg. Rabbi Greenberg and I have been friends for decades, and I have been a dialogue partner and friendly critic of certain aspects of his theological views during this time. Though I have found central features of his theological reflections problematic, I have seen his work continually grow and mature in depth and now believe that he should be recognized as a theologian of the first rank.

In reading Greenberg's work, one cannot but be impressed with his broad erudition and command of the history of Jewish thought. He moves seamlessly from the biblical, through the rabbinic and medieval eras, and then on to the modern period and the Shoah and its implications. Moreover, his exegetical sensitivity and insight into particular texts and issues is exceptional. In his explanations and discussions, well-known biblical and rabbinic passages often acquire a new clarity and deep meaning, while his critiques of specific theological positions (e.g., of Reform Judaism and the Haredi version of Orthodox Judaism), are often remarkably insightful.

It is also a testimonial to Rabbi Greenberg's seriousness and the authenticity of his search for truth that he is willing to reconsider dubious ideas present in his own earlier studies, for example, the idea of a "voluntary covenant" and "moment faith."

2. EXEGESIS OF THE MAIN CLAIM

Though Greenberg's views have continued to evolve, his basic theoretical model remains what I would call "Greenbergian Hegelianism." By this I mean that, like Hegel, Greenberg is a devoted student of the significance of history, in his case Jewish history, or, the history of the Jewish people, and is committed to arguing for the significance of this historical experience vis-à-vis theological truth and reflection. One could therefore fairly say that his work is an investigation of the theological meaning of the movement of Jews through time. It begins with the patriarchs and the historical narratives of the Torah, focused on the Exodus from Egypt and the revelation of the Law at Sinai, continues with probing reflections on the destruction of the First and Second Temples and the Jewish people's responses thereto, moves forward through the medieval period with informed commentary on Moses Maimonides and the medieval halakhists and kabbalists, and then takes us into the modern period beginning with the expulsion from Spain in 1492 from Portugal in 1496, and the emergence of the Jewish community of Safed in the sixteenth century. He then intelligently reviews the era of revolutionary modernity beginning with the French Revolution and explores the significance of the previously unthinkable possibility of Jews becoming citizens of the nation states in which they lived. Finally, this long historical narrative climaxes in the two monumental and revolutionary events of the twentieth century: the Shoah and the recreation of a Jewish commonwealth in the Land of Israel.[1]

For Greenberg, like Hegel, this historical narrative moves essentially in one progressive direction—albeit with acknowledged detours and backsliding, the Holocaust being the most notable. And, for Greenberg, central to his explanation of this upward direction is the traditional theological notion of *brit* = covenant. On his reading of the movement of history, the covenant contributes to the perfection of the world. It provides a paradigm of what life should be like, and how one might go about achieving this ideal state of social and communal existence that has as its goal the fundamental transformation of human existence. For this reason, Judaism is best described as a "hope" that has as its central ambition the fundamental transformation of human existence. Most importantly, this covenant is defined by Greenberg as a partnership "between God and man" entered into by both partners without coercion, i.e., made by both man and God as a "free choice."

---

1 See, for example, Irving Greeberg, "Judaism and History: Historical Events and Religious Change," *Ancient Roots and Modern Meaning: A Contemporary Reader in Jewish Identity*, ed. Jerry V. Diller (New York: Bloch Publishing, 1978), 139–62.

However, despite the foundational, phenomenological structure of the covenant, the pattern of God's relationship to Israel, as manifest in historical reality, changes in fundamental ways over time. In the biblical era God is present, visible, and directly intervenes in a powerful way into history, as in the dramatic revelation of the divine will in the Exodus from Egypt and the conquest of the Land of Israel under Joshua. Also, after the conquest of the Land of Israel and the establishment of the Davidic monarchy, the presence of God was felt in the First Temple with immediacy and an overwhelming sense of awe. The mystery of the Holy of Holies and the meaning that the sacrificial cult carried conveyed a profound sense of the presence of the divine within the community of the people of Israel. In contrast, after the destruction of the First Temple in 586 BCE, and Israel's return from the Babylonian exile in 538 BCE, and then the construction of the Second Temple (which traditionally is dated to have begun in 516 BCE) the situation had changed. The Second Temple did not carry the same transcendental weight and the sense of the Almighty's immediate reality was less intense. Greenberg also notes that in the Second Temple period, during which time the story of Esther occurs, the book of Esther does not mention God. God has become less apparent, less visible, and now appears in Jewish history less directly, more obliquely, than had been the case earlier.

After the destruction of the Second Temple in 70 CE, the Divine becomes even more remote and appears less concerned to manifest His overt power in the flow of history. Now the sages and the people of Israel assume a more active role in responding to the destruction of the Second Temple and in taking fundamental steps to assure the continued vitality and meaningfulness of their religious tradition. This is evident most especially in the foundational role played by the rabbis of the Talmudic era, who led the Jewish people without new and direct divine revelation. Hence, there is a profound difference in style and content between rabbinic and prophetic leadership.

But history did not end in 70 CE nor in the post-70 CE exile. Rather, as Greenberg argues, the *zimzum*, the "contraction," of God's public and obvious role in Jewish (and world) history, continued to increase during the Middle Ages and climaxed in our time with the Holocaust. Nevertheless, in spite of His hiddenness, there always remains what Greenberg describes as a sustaining presence of God in history. In effect, the metaphysical paradox working itself out within the unfolding of history is that, as God becomes more hidden, God comes closer to men and women. Thus, even though rabbinic Judaism does not depend for its continuity on direct revelatory moments it creates a way of life in which the Jewish people still sense the divine reality.

The essential insight that Greenberg would here emphasize is that God becomes more "hidden" in history not because He is actually absent or because humans are becoming more alienated from the transcendent but rather because men and women have responded to their historical experience by becoming more mature and aware of their own capacities for altering the world. Thus, they can relate to God with independence and integrity rather than as passive, mute, frightened creatures. In actuality, in a dialectical movement shared together by God and Israel, the transcendental withdrawal of God is inextricably linked with what Greenberg sees as the growing level of human responsibility, of men and women taking responsibility for themselves and their world. This growing maturity and taking of responsibility is moreover to be recognized not as the disconfirmation of the covenant but rather as its fulfillment.

This drama, revealed in the "evolution" of history, leads to Greenberg's well-known and seductive schema that in the Bible and biblical era, "God was the senior partner," in the rabbinic era "an equal partner," and in the modern era "a junior partner." As Greenberg has written in an as yet unpublished manuscript:

> Out of respect for humans, God calibrates the elements of force and limits coercion in the encounter. God wants humans to grow into full capacity, i.e., to want the good for its own sake and to seek it without pressure or punishment. God wants humans to join in the task of tikkun olam out of love for God (and God's vision) and love of fellow human (and wanting the best for them). The degree of Divine visibility and intervention is greater at the beginning to get humans' attention and to motivate them to take on covenant and responsibility. As they develop more, the Divine role is "reduced" – really, reconfigured – to operate as role modeling: it is to be experienced as persuasion and education and less as command or authority.

What is particularly important about this evolutionary metaphysical deconstruction of the history of Israel (and the nations) is that it carries with it a demand for normative reevaluations and ethical reconsiderations. It is not just the evolution of history that is significant. Human and societal evolution is as well. Thus, for example, in his exegesis of the biblical rules governing the institution of slavery, and in his review of the status of women and the rules of marriage in the Mishnah, Greenberg explains that these rules were interpreted and reinterpreted by the *Tannaim* (sages of the Mishnah) and later scholars in ways that were increasingly sensitive to the existential and ethical implications carried by these issues. In this way they showed that they understood the need for more equal and ethical readings of these societal norms. This obligation to continually re-study and reinterpret the Torah's regulations continues into our own time. As history unfolds and the Jews mature they are called on—are obligated—to look ever more deeply into the moral core of their religious-halakhic traditions. And most essentially, after the Shoah we live in a situation where, as Greenberg wrote in an early essay, "The Holocaust challenges the claims of all the standards that compete for modern man's loyalties."[2]

What Greenberg takes away from this theological explanation of Jewish history is that men and women are now challenged to do better morally (i.e., to be more responsible for ourselves, others, the people of Israel, and humanity in general). Therefore, Greenberg's historical/metaphysical decipherment concludes by making profound moral demands. His "progressive" historical narrative, in which God finally, in our time, becomes the "junior partner," entails that not only is *God* not visibly active in historical events but also that men and women are also wholly, or nearly wholly, responsible for what occurs in history. They are most definitely responsible for all social and ethical norms. Accordingly, all inherited teachings and orthodoxies require reexamination in accordance with our modern, elevated social and ethical sensibilities.

These telling observations and entailments about our relation to inherited normative demands and values are, self-evidently, exceedingly consequential, especially for those who would retain some form of orthodoxy, in our case, Orthodox Judaism. They force us to address directly the foundational Jewish subjects of the Torah and Halakhah. We will return to these cardinal issues in our critical reflections below.

3. CRITICAL REFLECTIONS

There is something fundamentally persuasive about Greenberg's historical model. It is hard to deny that history, including Jewish history, both as an empirical matter as well as a phenomenological philosophical datum, appears to have moved over time to higher and higher levels of ethical sensitivity, increased humanitarian concern, more developed concepts of human equality, and more

---

2 Irving Greenberg, "Cloud of Smoke, Pillar of Fire: Judaism, Christianity and Modernity after the Holocaust," *Auschwitz: Beginning of a New Era? Reflections on the Holocaust*, ed. Eva Fleischner (New York: Ktav, 1977), 213.

capacious notions of human and societal freedom. And as Greenberg so persuasively recounts and deconstructs this history, this is exactly what God wanted. God is the ultimate guarantor of this process of liberation and its main booster. Moreover, and for our present discussion a matter of considerable significance, Greenberg perceives this positive "advance" as being not only desirable but also relatively "frictionless" over against Orthodox Jewish belief.

But are matters quite so simple? Is this covenantal progress as deciphered by Greenberg so conceptually (and existentially) benign? Is the concept of *brit* = covenant so flexible and nonjudgmental, so malleable and approving? Is all of this remarkable change and "advance" to be experienced solely, or even mainly as, in Greenberg's words, "persuasion and election" and less as communal command or authority?

To help clarify these interrelated theological questions, and others that flow naturally, even necessarily, from them, I would raise five critical issues for reflection.

Issue 1

In an age of "autonomy" in which Jews are the "senior partner" in their covenantal relationship with God, and fidelity to the covenant is defined as "the transformation of history" and "a hope," is the Halakhah still binding? Two linked queries are here relevant:

> (a) *Does the Halakhah possess authority, even, in keeping with Jewish tradition, absolute authority?* I begin with this question because I hold the view that there is only one important question in religious matters, both conceptual and existential, and that question is: Who or what has authority? Once this inquiry is resolved everything else moves smoothly forward. If the Halakhah still has authority, then many things follow. If it does not, then many other very different things follow. In the present instance, in light of Greenberg's theological claims, it thus needs to be asked: For Jews to live a "covenantal life," must they live according to traditional, authoritative, halakhic rules, or are these rules "negotiable," possessing no binding authority?
>
> (b) In the modern era, a second, related question needs also to be confronted, namely: *Even if one posits the continued salience of Halakhah, must the Halakhah of today be essentially monolithic?* That is, must the Halakhah be governed, as in the past, by a specific set of men who

possess the requisite rabbinical knowledge and whose rulings are all made within the traditional halakhic circle (i.e., in a fundamentally monolithic form), or can—even must—the Halakhah, after modernity, Auschwitz, and the recreation of the State of Israel, be pluralistic?

The crucial existential-theological dilemma raised by these questions is that if the answer to our first question is "No, Halakhah is not *the* religious Jewish authority," then we are no longer thinking and living religiously within an Orthodox circumstance. Alternatively, if the Halakhah *is* the authority, then we are not in a realm in which God is a "junior partner." Certainly, the Halakhah is decided by human beings, but in such a way that the halakhic authorities claim direct divine sanction and authority. I recognize that this very complex issue (i.e., the nature of the halakhic process and how it operates) needs much more analysis than can be offered here. However, readers need to ponder this both in this context and more generally. Moreover, by definition, it is not inconsequential that the Halakhah is meant to severely circumscribe human autonomy.

Second, if we *are* living in an age where human agency and the *zimzum* of God are paramount, can we declare, with authority, that Reform, Reconstructionist, and Conservative religious formulations—whether described by their adherents as Halakhah or not—are to be rejected? But if these nonorthodox forms of Jewish practice and Halakhah *are* acceptable (i.e., are legitimated as the religious equal of Orthodox interpretation and practice), then the Orthodox position has no superior claim to truth, nor are its rulemaking procedures more authoritative than those of other groups. Indeed, in this scenario, Judaism has become a smorgasbord of spiritual options.

At this juncture I would also note that Greenberg, if I understand his view correctly, wants to reply to this cluster of methodological concerns that modern pluralism in religious matters (i.e., Halakhah), is *not* a radical break with the logic and tradition of covenant but is, rather, its natural outgrowth and "transformation." This makes good sense given that he wants, despite all talk of evolution, change, diversity, and pluralism, to maintain an "Orthodox" position. But here the very complex term "transformation" needs close examination. For when is "X becomes Y" considered to be an act, a process, of transformation, and when is it something different, even radically different? Put another way, when is the concept, the process, of transformation conceptually and actionably legitimate, and when is it a term that in fact serves to represent discontinuous change?

Issue 2

Greenberg, with great sophistication, turns to the interpretation of history, to history itself, to substantiate and verify his covenantal vision of the evolution of the Jewish spirit through time. It is this subtle and well-informed reading that is the foundation for his normative judgments, both halakhic and non-halakhic. It needs, however, to be appreciated that while he talks of empirical events as the test of his view, and claims that history confirms his understanding of the meaning of history, the deconstruction and interpretation of Israel's history for both halakhic and non-halakhic purposes is not a simple matter of reading the historical record "as it is." Rather, it is a very complex situation based on assumptions and structural conceptions. Accordingly, the meaning of Jewish history is the outcome of diverse interpretive rules and intricate hermeneutical techniques. Vis-à-vis Halakhah, this means that drawing halakhic conclusions from historical experience is not a simple nor a direct procedure. So, for example, on the basis of the Holocaust experience, Greenberg draws the strong halakhic conclusion that the Halakhah needs to change, to become more just and equitable in certain ways, in response to what the Holocaust was, especially the ethnic and gender principles on which it was predicated.

But the Lubavitcher Rebbe, the Munkatcher Rebbe, and the Haredi world read this history very differently. For them, the empirical historical event of the Holocaust was proof certain that the Jews were being punished for violating the "Halakhah," and the correct response to the death camps is, therefore, meticulous traditional halakhic observance, not the "transformation" of the Halakhah. Again, Greenberg's revered teacher, Rav Joseph Soloveitchik, while not endorsing the traditional view of *mipnei hataeinu* (because of our sins), as the "explanation" of the Holocaust, also demanded the maintenance and perpetuation of the halakhic tradition with little change. He certainly would not endorse changes in the Halakhah because of the Shoah.[3]

Furthermore, to take a very different example, Richard Rubenstein "read" the empirical event of the murder of six million Jews as "proving" *let din ve-let dayan* (there is neither justice nor Judge). That is, the Shoah is proof that the Halakhah, though of sociological and communal significance à la Mordechai Kaplan, has no ontological standing. I would also recall in passing that the German Protestant, Pastor Dean Gruber, who was Richard Rubenstein's theological discussion

---

3 See *Wrestling with God: Jewish Theological Responses during and after the Holocaust*, eds. Steven T. Katz, Shlomo Biderman, and Gershon Greenberg (Oxford and New York: Oxford University Press, 2007).

partner, thought that it was theologically correct to understand the murder of a million Jewish children by the forces of the Hitler state as a contemporary verification of the historical-theological claim that Jews were to be eternally punished for the first-century crime of deicide. Alternatively, the Roman Catholic Church has, since Vatican II, rejected this time-honored Christian belief. Getting at the "meaning" of history is no simple thing.[4]

Issue 3

In a related, though different, way relative to the deconstruction and conceptualization of historical experience, I would ask another question that bears centrally on the theological-covenantal interpretation of modern Jewish history: *Where is God relative to the creation and maintenance of the State of Israel?* Does it make sense to claim that the state is *reshit zemihat geulateynu* (the beginning of the dawn of our redemption), as it is described in the standard prayer for the State of Israel, in any traditional sense? In relation to this seminal topic, one can talk about God as a "junior partner" and the obvious role of human activity in the creation and maintenance of the State of Israel. But if one chooses to do so, what do such assertions really mean? Why not just talk of human enterprise and activity in this historical happening? Given the revised conception of God as "hidden" and "contracted" (*zimzum*), what does the invocation of God add to the description and explanation of events? For God to be understood to have played some truly meaningful role in this dramatic adventure, we need more than a claim that God's *zimzum* is a sign of His presence. On what criteria, empirical and otherwise, do we decide to include God in the necessary description of the relevant details that make up this narrative? And on what criteria do we decide to simply leave God out of the description as it appears to provide no added agency or influence? Can it be that to talk about *zimzum* here is only to speak of one's own faith rather than to make claims that are theologically or historically significant?

Issue 4

Returning directly to thinking about the status and value of the Halakhah in our time relative to Greenberg's schema, it is apposite, in light of the changes that have occurred in the modern era, to ask whether the Reform Jews might not be right. Did they not do what Greenberg asks that we all do (i.e., measure the

---

[4] For more on this issue see the essays in Steven T. Katz, *Post-Holocaust Dialogues: Critical Studies in Modern Jewish Thought* (New York: New York University Press, 1983).

Halakhah by a meta-halakhic ethical norm, in their case Kantian morality, and adjust Jewish practice accordingly)?[5]

Here one must acknowledge that Greenberg appears to have the weight of moral sensitivity—and it is a significant weight—on his side. Modern ethical norms do, on occasion, require halakhic changes given the record of the past. However, at this juncture we encounter a truly vexing issue. Who is the ultimate arbiter of the moral domain? (And, fundamentally related, who is the arbiter of the religious domain?) I note that the original conference at which an earlier version of this essay was presented was held in the United Kingdom, then a member of the European Union, and that the European Union has, in various ways, objected to circumcision as barbaric and incompatible with modern European ethical values. The same type of "moral" objection to Jewish Orthodox practice has also arisen in many European countries relative to *kashrut*. In addition, the topic of "who is a Jew" became a subject of public debate in England not long ago relative to admission to Jewish day schools. So we are confronted by a very real, very immediate moral challenge: should Jews abandon *brit milah* and *kashrut*, and revise the classical, normative definitions of "who is a Jew" because these practices were not thought to be ethical by European civilization in 2016 (or since)?

In this context, the very complicated matter of the relationship of Halakhah, morality, and sociology becomes relevant, even inescapable. For when is change truly warranted and when is it merely a capitulation to sociological pressures? I remind readers that changing the Halakhah is, at least in theory, altogether different from changing human social conventions or political constitutions. The transcendental claims made for the Torah as divine revelation, and for the Torah as the source of the Halakhah, raise difficult issues about how one interprets the Torah, how one draws laws from it, how one goes about making alterations in the law (Halakhah), and what limits exist vis-à-vis making such changes. The Torah *she-be'al peh* (the Oral Tradition) does acknowledge, however carefully, sociological phenomena but it does not recognize sociological forces as ultimate.

Issue 5

Every theological proposition and every theological position has logical and metaphysical implications and involves specific theological "costs"—which is

---

5 See Irving Greenberg, "Covenantal Pluralism." *Journal of Ecumenical Studies* 34, 3 (summer 1997): 425–436.

to recognize in this context that the key issue raised directly and profoundly by Greenberg's evolutionary theology is not only what it offers that is insightful, original, and persuasive, but also what it denies, makes difficult, and brings into doubt. That is to say, Greenberg is free, especially in our post-Holocaust age, to redefine "God" (and other foundational concepts) as he wishes. But, having redefined God (and other basic theological concepts) he must attend to the myriad conceptual and metaphysical consequences of having done so. Accordingly, one must inquire: what happens to the traditional "God of Judaism" in his revisionist theological schema?

Specifically, what conceptual and ontological corollaries flow from conceiving of God as a "junior partner"? And are these implications that I assume will be significant acceptable in particular to Orthodox Jews, or is their cost (i.e., what they entail), too high? Consider, for instance, what the costs are if God is now a "junior partner" relative to such cardinal notions as reward and punishment, God as the underwriter and enforcer of morality, the character of Torah law, the meaning of revelation, the idea of mitzvot, the understanding of redemption, and other eschatological notions. Is God as a "junior partner" capable of being the guarantor of moral rules? Is He capable of insuring the ultimate messianic fulfillment that Greenberg repeatedly discusses? The deep structure of Jewish messianism is meant to guarantee that in the end good triumphs and evil is defeated, and that there is a moral balance in creation. Can a God who is a "junior partner" be responsible for, and guarantee, this outcome? And can a "junior partner" be the source of authority sufficient for the demands of the regimen of mitzvot?

Again, when the Divine is defined as, and perceived as, a "junior partner," is sin still a viable, meaningful idea, or is it now only a metaphor of a sort? Does God "save" both personally and communally? What becomes of Yom Kippur when God is a "junior partner?" Does the whole cycle of the *aseret yemei teshuvah* (the Ten Days of Repentance), culminating in fasting and self-debasement on Yom Kippur, make any sense if men and women are now the "senior partner"? What sense does it make to pray for forgiveness, redemption, and life from a "junior partner"? Why think that the traditional practices of *teshuvah*, *tefillah*, and *tzedakah* (repentance, prayer, and charity) that are central to the rituals of Yom Kippur, will have any power to "avert the *gezerah*" (the evil decree), or even why we should think them necessary when interrelating with a "junior partner"?

More generally, we all know that the term mitzvah, commandment, derives its meaning, its power, from the belief that the mitzvot are grounded in the will of a Divine Commander. Can God as a "junior partner" still be a *mezaveh*, a commander? Or do both the concepts of "commander" and "commandment" become, in our age, simply metaphors that remind us of a past that is no more?

In addressing the meaning of concepts like mitzvot and revelation, it is moreover apposite to remind ourselves that while Greenberg's comments on the changing context in which people "hear God's revelation" are certainly correct and raise a fundamental point, one has at the same time to be aware that there is always a competing dialectic vis-à-vis God's revelation. Which is to say, we do not want to claim that we hear God's voice, that God speaks to us, only in conformity with *our* "context" and norms because this would be to relativize and reduce God's voice to our hearing. One should always think of God's revelation as potentially or actually challenging our context and as possibly speaking to us in an unfamiliar voice that calls into question the assumptions and values of our own time.

4. CONCLUSION

Rabbi Greenberg has many elemental and consequential things to teach us. His work is, despite my critical questions, profound and repercussive. But it is not yet complete.

CHAPTER 2

Rabbi Yitz Greenberg's Covenantal Theory of Bioethics

ALAN JOTKOWITZ

Covenant plays a central role in the theology of Rabbi Yitz Greenberg (RYG) and other contemporary theologians. The purpose of this paper is to discuss how RYG's covenantal ethics relates to practical questions in medical ethics and compare his theology to other religious bioethicists.

It is appropriate in a paper first delivered in Oxford, to start with the words of the former British chief rabbi and founder of the academic discipline of Jewish medical ethics (JME), Lord Immanuel Jakobovits, who writes in explaining his approach to moral questions in medicine:

> Now in Judaism we know of no intrinsic rights. Indeed, there is no word for rights in the very language of the Hebrew Bible and of the classic sources of Jewish law. In the moral vocabulary of the Jewish discipline of life we speak of human duties, not of human rights, of obligations not entitlement. The Decalogue is a list of Ten Commandments not a bill of Human Rights. In the charity legislation of the Bible, for instance, it is the rich man who is commanded to support the poor, not the poor man who has the right to demand support from the rich. In Jewish law a doctor is obligated to come to the rescue of his stricken fellow-man and to perform any operation he considers essential for the life of the patient, even if the patient refuses his consent or

prefers to die. Once again, the emphasis is on the physician's responsibility to heal, to offer service, more than on the patient's right to be treated.[1]

The eminent legal scholar Robert Cover makes a similar point:

> Every legal culture has its fundamental words. ... The word "rights" is a highly evocative one for those of us who have grown up in the post-enlightenment secular society of the West. ... Judaism is, itself, a legal culture of great antiquity. ... When I am asked to reflect upon Judaism and human rights, therefore, the first thought that comes to mind is that the categories are wrong. I do not mean, of course, that basic ideas of human dignity and worth are not powerfully expressed in the Jewish legal and literary traditions. Rather, I mean that because it is a legal tradition, Judaism has its own categories for expressing through law the worth and dignity of each human being. ... The principal word in Jewish law, which occupies a place equivalent in evocative force to the American legal system's "rights," is the word "mitzvah" which literally means commandment but has a general meaning closer to "incumbent obligation." ... All law was given at Sinai, and therefore all law is related back to the ultimate heteronomous event.[2]

Rabbi Jakobovits's theology of duty certainly had an impact on his practical ethical decision-making. For example, he writes:

> In Jewish law the consent of a patient is not required for any operation medically deemed necessary for his health. Indeed, even if he wished to avoid the operation and submit to danger as a means to penitence through suffering, he should be forced to undergo the treatment against his will if necessary.[3]

And regarding truth telling, "The rabbis insisted on maintaining the patient's hopefulness not merely by withholding information of his imminent death, but by positive means to encourage his confidence in recovery."[4]

---

1 Immanuel Jakobovits, *The Timely and the Timeless: Jews, Judaism and Society in a Storm-Tossed Decade* (London: Vallentine Mitchell, 1977), 128.
2 Robert Cover, "Obligation—A Jewish Jurisprudence of the Social Order," *Journal of Law and Religion* 5 (1987): 65–74.
3 Immanuel Jakobovits, *Journal of a Rabbi* (New York: Living Books, 1966), 158.
4 Immanuel Jakobovits, *Jewish Medical Ethics: A Comparative and Historical Study of the Jewish Religious Attitude to Medicine and Its Practice* (New York: Bloch, 1975), 120.

These positions regarding consent and honesty are difficult for many moderns to accept; nonetheless, in Rabbi Jakobovits's conception of medical ethics duty takes precedence over autonomy. Rabbi Jakobovits was responding to the trend to make human rights the dominant theme in modern bioethics. This was first expressed by the Protestant theologian Joseph Fletcher at the Lowell Lectures given at Harvard University in 1949:

> We shall attempt, as reasonably as may be, to plead the ethical case for our human rights to use contraceptives, to seek insemination anonymously from a donor, to be sterilized, and to receive a merciful death from a medically competent euthanasiast. We believe we can show, at the very least, that any absolute prohibition of these boons of medicine is morally unjustified, subversive of human dignity, and most serious of all spiritually oppressive.[5]

Fletcher maintained "that the ethical judgments I have reached are within the range and provision of Christian theology, but that would be all that could be claimed for them. The bias of my ethical standpoint, apart from its frame of reference in Christian faith, is probably best pinpointed as personalist."[6]

Fletcher's theology was groundbreaking in that it argued for honesty in the doctor-patient relationship and provided an ethical response to the Roman Catholic Church's opposition of contraception and artificial reproduction. Fletcher's defense of euthanasia based on human rights also anticipated the "right to die" movement. But in recent years we have seen abuses of this "right." For example, in Belgium euthanasia was recently extended to children of all ages and the legality of involuntary euthanasia is being debated. The Netherlands under the Groningen Protocol also approves of euthanizing severely disabled infants, and infanticide or "after-birth abortion" is now seriously being debated in the medical ethics literature.

Complete honesty in the doctor-patient relationship is also being questioned. One of the basic tenets of modern bioethics, partly based on the work of Fletcher, is that the patient is the sole and best decision maker about their healthcare preferences. The bioethicist John Lantos maintains that in some instances the patient or his or her family is unable to make the most appropriate and best decision, particularly when dealing with end-of-life issues. In fact, he is one of the few bioethicists who believes that a "slow code" is appropriate

---

5 Joseph Fletcher, *Morals and Medicine* (Boston: Beacon Press 1960), 25.
6 Ibid., preface.

in certain circumstances. He calls this approach the ambiguous approach and argues

> The patients or families for whom the ambiguous approach might be beneficial are those who recognize that death is inevitable, who would not necessarily find death unwelcome in the circumstances, but who cannot—for whatever reason—allow themselves to feel that they were complicit in authorizing the death. In such situations, the patient or family member needs some wiggle room, some ambiguity, with regard to their own role in a decision to withhold or withdraw some form of life support.[7]

RYG's covenantal ethics of medicine offers a third approach.

> Judaism teaches that there is a covenant between God and humanity, and not just with the Jewish people. The human role in this covenant is to perfect the world … to perfect the world means that the human is called upon not to accept the world as it is, but to improve it and complete it.[8]

He calls this a covenant of power. The example he brings is the ritual of circumcision (which currently is under attack worldwide from human rights activists). "The removal of the foreskin is a symbol that one does not simply accept the biological given. Rather the human task is to perfect the body, complete it, and remove whatever imperfections it has."[9] Not surprisingly he learned this idea from his great teacher, Rabbi Joseph B. Soloveitchik, who famously developed a theology of human dignity and postulated a religious obligation for man to improve the world that God created. Failure to do so is a religious and ethical failure. RYG adds a redemptive element to this covenant of power.

> Hence the ultimate achievement of being in the divine image would be pure life and the absolute triumph of life. Isaiah in his description of the Messianic period uses that language specifically "death will be swallowed

---

7 John D. Lantos and William L. Meadow, "Should the 'Slow Code' Be Resuscitated?" *The American Journal of Bioethics* 11, no. 11 (2011): 8–12.
8 Irving Greenberg, *Toward a Covenantal Ethic of Medicine* in *Jewish Values in Bioethics*, ed. L. Meier (New York: Human Sciences Press, 1986), 128. RYG's covenantal ethic of medicine flows naturally from his general theology of covenant. See, for example, "Covenantal Pluralism," *Journal of Ecumenical Studies* 34, no. 3 (1997): 425–36.
9 Ibid., 129.

up in eternity" ... according to classic Judaism this is the ultimate goal of humanity and all humans are called to participate in this process.[10]

This redemptive aspect also has practical applications crucial to RYG's covenantal ethics—societal issues such as public health and universal access to care and expanding healthcare to include the economic, political, and social environment. Not surprisingly, this is consistent with the World Health Organization (WHO) definition of health as a state of complete physical and social well-being and not merely the absence of disease or infirmity. Somewhat surprisingly for someone so personally and theologically affected by the Holocaust, RYG maintains that this charge for man to conquer the world has no limits "The covenantal response is that the limits are non-existent. I submit that the fear of genetic engineering, the fear of medical control, is in part derived from the inherited ethic of powerlessness, whereby there is deemed something sacrilegious in our ability to gain control over life."[11]

RYG adds another element to this covenant of power, partnership, which is also modeled on the covenant between man and God. "The key is the concept of partnership and not just power for its own sake. The Bible which commands humans to shape the world and conquer it turns around and demands respect for that world. The classic limit is Shabbat."[12] In the covenantal model of medical ethics, the limits are when the physician pretends to be God and when the doctor infringes on the human dignity of the patient. Man acting like God is a form of idolatry and forgetting human dignity is an affront to the partnership aspect of the ethical covenant.

In limiting this covenant of power, the Holocaust certainly has impacted on RYG's thought.

> In Germany in the 1930s, medical doctors experimented on the mentally retarded to develop the very process of gassing which became the preferred method of mass killing during the Holocaust. This is precisely the challenge of the dialectic. On the one hand, unlimited power is a religious calling. On the other hand, one must have no illusions: such power is available for evil and destruction.[13]

---

10 Ibid.
11 Ibid., 137.
12 Ibid., 134.
13 Ibid., 138–9.

In arguing for the dignity of the human body even after death, RYG recalls the Nazi practice of turning the ashes of cremated Jewish bodies into soap and fertilizer. He continues, "In the Holocaust, Hitler was God, or Mengele was God, or Eichmann was God; they had total control over life and death. In this form, power turned out to be demonic and cancerous rather than life-giving."[14]

The use of covenant is a powerful tool in developing a modern bioethic but difficulties arise when theologians argue over the nature of the covenant. For example, the Protestant theologian Paul Ramsey, also basing his arguments on covenant, maintains that human ethical relations should be modeled on the relationship of God to man and therefore there exists an unbreakable bond of covenantal loyalty between men (delivered as one of the Beecher lectures at Yale in 1969, twenty years after Fletcher's lectures and partly as a response to them).[15] This is interpreted to mean that man must always act with love and charity toward his fellow man. In most instances this means using all one's power to cure his or her illness, but in the case of the suffering terminal patient it means easing the dying process. The emphasis for Ramsey is on relieving the suffering of the patient and on maintaining a human presence until his or her last breath. Active euthanasia is considered a violation of this covenant. Ramsey was also opposed to many forms of artificial reproduction because he viewed it as intruding upon the power of God and as a violation of the holy covenant of marriage ordained by God.[16] In Ramsey's deontological approach, the covenant is expressed in rules and ethical principles that govern moral behavior. The covenant of Ramsey is almost the exact opposite of RYG's covenant of power.

Not surprisingly, the use of covenantal theory has not caught on among traditional decisors. As mentioned, it is open to a myriad of interpretations and *poskim* are very hesitant about using non-Talmudic sources in reaching halakhic conclusions. However, echoes of it can be found in the works of some authorities. For example, Rabbi Waldenberg was opposed to cosmetic surgery because "one should know and believe that there is no creator like God and he created each person in a unique way and one should not add or detract from this creation."[17] In performing plastic surgery, the physician oversteps his boundaries and competes with God for power. For similar reasons Rabbi Waldenberg was also opposed to all forms of artificial reproduction. He writes:

---

14 Ibid., 141.
15 Paul Ramsey, *The Patient as Person* (New Haven, CT: Yale University Press, 1970).
16 Paul Ramsey, *On Moral Medicine: Theological Perspectives in Medical Ethics*, eds. Stephen E. Lammers and Allen Verhey (Grand Rapids, MI: Eerdmans, 1987).
17 Responsa Tzitz Eliezer 11:41.

> The future of the process of artificial reproduction is to create a "laboratory child" which means that the pregnancy and birth will all occur outside the body of the woman in the laboratory. And there is also a plan to create a human clone ... and this will cause destruction and loss of the human spirit and will rule in all problems of conception and it will turn into a science without any humanity. Many scientists have already expressed their deep fears about this future ... that will create a new being without free choice and without familial relationships and this will also create fear and confusion among many regular people. And therefore what have we accomplished with the creation of these new beings that do not fulfill the obligation to procreate found in the holy Torah and only cause complicated problems that are bound to set the human race back a thousand degrees.[18]

Rabbi Moshe Feinstein, the other great decisor of questions relating to medical halakhah, did not have these theological concerns regarding cosmetic surgery or artificial reproduction, which he permitted using classical halakhic arguments.

If the great halakhic decisors did not use covenantal approaches to help decide questions in modern medical ethics, is RYG's covenant of power and partnership relevant to future scholarship in Jewish medical ethics? I believe it is. Recently I was asked to participate in a forum on the future of Jewish medical ethics. The following are among the issues I raised. An authentic Jewish ethical response is heavily dependent on Talmudic sources and precedent. However, many modern ethical questions simply have no precedent in the Jewish sources, as Louis Newman has pointed out in his landmark article "On Woodchoppers and Respirators: The Problem of Interpretation in Contemporary Jewish Ethics."[19] For example, in trying to determine halakhic motherhood in a case of surrogacy, some authorities cite the discussion dealing with the laws of *orlah*: Fruit from the first three years of the life of a tree is forbidden to eat. A branch from a tree that is five years old and not obligated in *orlah* and grafted onto a two-year-old tree, legally makes the grafted branch part of the two-year-old tree and one is forbidden to eat its fruit.[20] It follows, some argue, that if one

---
18 Responsa Tzitz Eliezer, part 15:45.
19 Louis E. Newman. "Woodchoppers and Respirators: The Problem of Interpretation in Contemporary Jewish Ethics," *Modern Judaism* 10, no. 2 (1990): 17–42.
20 Shulkhan Aruch, Yoreh Deah 294:16.

implants a zygote into the womb of a woman, it becomes part of her; the gestational mother should therefore be recognized as the child's legal mother. Other scholars brings proofs from the Talmudic discussions of olive trees swept away by a river, whether a fetus can acquire property, whether one is allowed to eat meat cooked in the milk of a female animal unable to conceive, and how one is allowed to have sexual relations with his pregnant wife and not be in violation of the prohibition of incest.

Bioethicist Ronit Irshai takes issue with this rabbinic approach to the resolution of the maternity issue:

> How could it be that in a dilemma so complicated from a moral perspective like surrogacy that who the mother is has been reduced simply to a technical halakhic question? How can it be that all the halakhic efforts and wisdom has been dedicated to just looking for the appropriate analogy which will prove whether the birth mother or the genetic donor is the deciding factor, with all the other moral issues at stake? How can it be that hardly any of the decisors feels uncomfortable with the proposed analogies, some of which are taken from the plant world and have no relevance to real life, to the feelings of a mother, or to human relationships?[21]

When there are no specific halakhic parallels, many *poskim* use aggadic sources, particularly in the field of JME. In answering the question of whether a dying patient should be treated aggressively, Rabbi Feinstein looks to the story of Rebbe's (Judah the Nasi/Prince) death in determining the halakhah:

> On the day that Rebbe was dying the Rabbis instituted a fast and begged for mercy and proclaimed that anyone who said that Rebbe is dying should be stabbed with a knife. The housemaid of Rebbe climbed to the roof and said the heavens are requesting Rebbe and the earth is requesting Rebbe, may it be your will that the earth should overcome the heavens. When she saw how many times Rebbe had to go to the bathroom and remove his tefillin and the suffering involved, she said may it be your will that the heavens will overcome the earth. When she saw that the students continued to pray she took an urn and threw it to the ground the students

---

21 Ronit Ir-Shai, "Fertility and Jewish Law: Feminist Perspectives on Gender, Culture, Religion, and Law" (PhD diss., Bar-Ilan University, 2006).

stopped praying (because of the sound of the urn breaking) and Rebbe's soul departed.[22]

Other questions are more difficult to find relevant halakhic sources for. For example, as the possibility of cloning could not have been anticipated by Talmudic sages, there is clearly no normative tradition that could help answer the question. Therefore, modern decisors have had to rely on Talmudic narratives for guidance. In a Talmudic legend known as the golem story, the ancient sage Rava stated:

> If they wish, righteous people could create a world. Rava created a man [by using the book called Sefer Yetzirah that teaches how to combine the letters of the Divine Name] and he sent it to Rabi Zeira. Rabi Zeira spoke with it and it did not respond. Rabi Zeira then stated, "You are created by my colleague return to your dust," (i.e., die).[23]

This strange story has been used by some as a source for a Jewish perspective on cloning. But the difficulties with using this source might be even more problematic than the previous narratives quoted. It is not clear from the legend if Rava was right in creating the man; Rabi Zeira for one felt that the creature should die. There is also much theoretical discussion on the legal status of the creature. There are those who claim that because it could not speak, Rabi Zeira did not consider it a person and therefore felt it should be killed. Others claim that because the creature was not the product of a mother's womb, Rabi Zeira did not consider it a person. In response to these difficulties, Rabbi J. D. Bleich has written:

> There may be—and there probably are—questions to which conventional halakhic methodology provides no solutions. When that occurs, there is only one solution: confession of ignorance. That, too, is a halakhic answer ... The one thing we must not do is engage in "desperate attempts to preserve a semblance of halakhic reasoning"—including the drawing of inappropriate analogies, construction of conceptual models, and derivation of halakhic norms from philosophical or aggadic notions.[24]

---

22 Babylonian Talmud [B. T.] Ketubot 104a.
23 B. T. Sanhedrin 65b.
24 J. David Bleich, "Maternal Identity Revisited," in *Jewish Law and the New Reproductive Technologies*, ed. Emanuel Feldman and Joel B, Wolowelsky (Hoboken, NJ: Ktav Publishing House, Inc.), 113–14.

Rabbi Emmanuel Rackman has even gone as far as to suggest in relation to triage specifically and other medical ethics dilemmas in general that the halakhah offers no guidance.

> When one must choose between two persons, who will live and who will die, the decision must be that of the person who will act upon it and not that of the state or any of its duly authorized agents. ... [T]he rich legal literature of Judaism provides him with no imperatives. No court will authorize his action in advance and no functionary of the state will or should be his surrogate to decide for him. The only sanction he may suffer will come from his conscience and public opinion. His problem is exclusively ethical and not legal in character. ... It seems to me that human beings who are confronted with the problem of making a choice must evaluate all the circumstances and make their own decision.[25]

Rabbi Rackman furthers his position by claiming "No Jew who was directly or indirectly involved in an abortion was punished. The decision pro or con was always a moral decision. There were no sanctions. Similarly with regard to mercy killings ... Thus while euthanasia is prohibited it is virtually nothing more than a sin punishable only by God."[26]

However, Rabbi Rackman's broad assertion that the halakhah is neutral regarding moral decisions relating to questions of life and death is difficult to defend. The halakhah is unequivocal in stating that non-Jews are deserving of capital punishment for performing an abortion and it is absolutely forbidden for a Jew or non-Jew to kill a terminally ill patient. The fact that in both cases one might be not be actually punished either due to the fact that Jewish courts have no jurisdiction over non-Jews or a technical exemption that the court does not carry out a death sentence if one kills a terminally ill patient, does not in the least mean that the decision is left to the individual. Halakhah does not shy away from rendering legal decisions even to the most difficult moral questions. The fact that there has and always will be a difference of opinion does not give the individual the freedom to decide. Halakhah does not offer "guidance" in these situations but binding directives.

---

25 Emanuel Rackman, "Priorities in the Right to Life," in *Tradition and Transition: Essays Presented to Chief Rabbi Sir Rabbi Immanuel Jakobovits to Celebrate Twenty Years in Office*, ed. Jonathan Sacks (London: Jews College Publication, 1986), 235–44.
26 Ibid.

RYG's covenantal model of medical ethics can help us find a way out of this quagmire. Based on theological arguments, it embraces technological and scientific advances while maintaining respect for human dignity. This model would embrace all modes of artificial reproduction but might limit physician-assisted suicide because of the possibility of a physician abusing his or her power and due to the ever-present specter of the Holocaust. But problems persist with the practical application of this covenant of power. Where should the line be drawn in this conflict between power and idolatry? For example, is reproductive cloning a religious charge, or is it the physician playing "God"? Other modern bioethical dilemmas need to be judged according to this covenant. For example, is it ethical to take semen from a young accident victim, or is it moral to conceive a child through IVF to be a kidney donor for a dying sibling?

Another question related to Jewish medical ethics is: What is the relevance of the field to general medical ethics? In other words, why should a non-Jew care about what the Jewish tradition says about a particular area? Daniel Callahan has argued that for the benefit of an extensive exposure "to the accumulated wisdom and knowledge that are the fruit of long established religious traditions. I do not have to be Jewish to find it profitable and illuminating to see how the great rabbinical teachers have tried to understand moral problems over the centuries."[27] From a different perspective, David Novak has long claimed that halakhah and particularly the seven universal commandments, from which most of JME is derived, are rooted in natural law and therefore have universal applicability.[28]

RYG's covenant based on the biblical covenant between God and humanity is explicitly not limited to Jewish bioethics and is touted as a model for all. This contention is much easier for believers in the monotheistic religions that share a common theological heritage with Judaism to accept. But this covenant of power might be more difficult for followers of Eastern religions or cultures to accept, as RYG himself notes. Regarding vegetarianism, which is widely practiced in India, he writes, "The Jewish tradition permits meat to be eaten by Jews, precisely because it realized that if one protects animal life, above all else, one is going to end up in a situation where sacred cows walk the street undisturbed and well fed, while humans starve to death every day."[29]

---

27 Daniel Callahan, "Religion and the Secularization of Bioethics," Hastings Center Report, Special Supplement: *Theology, Religious Traditions and Bioethics* 20, no. 4 (1990): 2–4.
28 David Novak, *The Sanctity of Human Life* (Washington, DC: Georgetown University Press 2007).
29 Irving Greenberg, *Toward a Covenantal Ethic of Medicine in Jewish Values in Bioethics*, ed. Levi Meier (New York: Human Sciences Press, 1986).

In modern secular medical ethics, there is a consensus that the ultimate decision maker should be the patient or their surrogate. Autonomy is one of the four basic principles of modern bioethics; however, from a Jewish perspective the rabbi has traditionally been the final arbiter of bioethical dilemmas that overlap with halakhic issues. In a covenantal ethic of medicine, the question arises of who the ultimate authority is—and whether this authority is able to translate ethical principles into practical guidance. Does a person decide for himself or herself the appropriate covenantal approach to a moral dilemma, or does there exist a mechanism for how to reach a consensus on a proper ethical response to a pressing dilemma?

JME has traditionally been focused on the relatively straightforward clinical questions such as how aggressively to treat a patient at the end of life or in which cases an abortion is permitted. However, there should be much more to a Jewish approach to these questions; the answers should also reflect the traditional concern with character development and supererogatory behavior. For example, beyond the question of whether an elderly demented patient should be fed, which relates to the question of quality of life versus sanctity of life, the commandment to respect your parents and the obligation to feed them should enter into the discourse.[30] The requirements of Bikur Cholim (visiting the sick) and confession before death and how they are done appropriately should be a factor in the Jewish discussion of the doctor-patient relationship and professionalism.[31] However, this perspective has been missing in many modern presentations of JME, which tend to focus more on the dry legal issues and less on how these dilemmas relate to the development of an altruistic and empathetic personality. These latter concerns have been a staple of those concerned with virtue ethics, and RYG's model of power and partnership also needs to relate to them. Notwithstanding these concerns, RYG's covenantal ethic of medicine can help physicians, researchers, and patients navigate the increasingly complex world of the interaction between medical research, technological advancements, and caring for the sick.

---

30 Alan B. Jotkowitz, A. Mark Clarfield, and Shimon Glick, "The Care of Patients with Dementia. A Modern Jewish Ethical Perspective," *Journal of the American Geriatrics Society* 53 (2005): 881–84.

31 Alan B. Jotkowitz and A. Mark Clarfield, "The Physician as Comforter," *European Journal of Internal Medicine* 16 (2005): 95–96. Alan Jotkowitz and Shimon Glick, "Confession at the End of Life: A Jewish Perspective," *Journal of Palliative Care* 21 (2005): 57–58.

POSTSCRIPT

As I wrote these words a controversy erupted in Israel on the ethical question of the force feeding of imprisoned hunger strikers. In August 2015, the Israeli parliament passed a law permitting the forced feeding of hunger strikers, and in response the Israel Medical Association filed a brief to the High Court of Justice challenging the law on the basis that it is illegal and unethical.[32] A group of highly respected Israeli ethicists, physicians, and philosophers then released a position paper justifying the use of force-feeding in certain circumstances in order to save the prisoner's life. The issue has also arisen regarding the force-feeding of hunger strikers at Guantanamo Bay by American military personnel, and there too opponents have labeled the procedure medical complicity in torture.[33]

Opponents of force-feeding base their opposition on two ethical principles, patient autonomy and a refusal to perform potentially harmful, painful, and invasive procedures without the patient's consent. According to most bioethicists, the World Medical Association, and other leading medical organizations, it is unethical to force treatment upon a competent patient.[34] Proponents of the procedure invoke the ethical principle of sanctity of life and concern for the public interest if the prisoners were to die. In addition, they claim that many hunger strikers do not really want to die and feeding them might be in their best interests.

The ethical conflict between autonomy and sanctity of life is of course not new, but what is striking about the public debate is the inability of both sides to see the ethical validity of the other approach and to understand the complexities of each individual case of political hunger strikers. As Michael Gross has pointed out, it makes a world of difference who the strikers are and if their demands are realistic and not a threat to the public safety. In many cases of political hunger strikers, creative solutions were found to their demands and an accommodation was reached ending the strike nonviolently.[35]

---

32 Ethan Miller, "Force Feeding Law Legally and Ethically Flawed, Medical Official Says," *The Times of Israel*, August 12, 2015, http://www.timesofisrael.com/force-feeding-law-legally-and-ethically-flawed-medical-official-says/.
33 Sarah M. Dougherty, Jennifer Leaning, P. Gregg Greenough, and Frederick M. Burkle Jr., "Hunger Strikers: Ethical and Legal Dimensions of Medical Complicity in Torture at Guantanamo Bay," *Prehospital and Disaster Medicine* 28 (2013): 616–24.
34 Ibid.
35 Michael L. Gross, "Force-Feeding, Autonomy, and the Public Interest," *The New England Journal of Medicine* 369, no. 2 (2013): 103–105.

I also think RYG's covenantal ethic of medicine can be very helpful in dealing with this complex topic. The crux of the issue is trying to determine the true wishes of the patient, who also happens to be a prisoner, which is exceedingly difficult given the cultural, language, and political barriers between the patient and physician. But even in this case, creating a covenantal relationship and partnership between the doctor and patient can help overcome these barriers. The focus should not be on coercion and power but on developing a relationship based on trust and mutual understanding. In these circumstances it might be easier to determine the true wishes of the patient and to reach an accommodation acceptable to both sides. For example, an agreement to take certain nutritional supplements such as vitamins as opposed to food or to accept fluids or feeding as their condition worsens. In the case of hunger strikers, the covenantal ethic of medicine tries to balance respect for the autonomy of the patient with the ethical principle of the sanctity of life and to walk the fine line between power and partnership.[36]

---

36 This paper was prepared before the publication in 2015 of a second important paper by RYG entitled "A Life of Halakhah or a Halakhah of Life?," in *Halakhic Realities: Collected Essays on Brain Death*, ed. Zev Farber (Jerusalem: Maggid, 2015), 265–314, in which he discusses his position on brain death. RYG comes out strongly in favor of brain death because of its potential to save lives through transplantation of donor organs. This paper is also due an extended discussion but in this limited space I would like to address briefly a central point of the paper. RYG writes "Over the years, I have come to understand two further implications of the Rav's teaching … When one asks a halakhic question, the criterion for the answer is not, primarily, precedent or existing norms. The prime criterion is to uphold life—or save it. This is why I'm convinced that the recognition of brain death as a halakhically valid criterion confirming the cessation of life is correct" (267–68). However, RYG does note, "Although my thinking on the religious importance of saving lives through science is drawn primarily from the writings of Rabbi Joseph B. Soloveitchik, and he is my model for a theology of halakhah dedicated to life. I acknowledge the gap between his theological forward thrust and his *pesaq* (adjudication). The Rav, in general, was less involved in *pesaq*" (313n122). Notwithstanding these comments, I think RYG's perspective on how halakhah should operate is a far cry from the traditional model of how a decisor should approach a halakhic query. The decision should be based on careful attention to the sources and with allegiance to legal precedent as opposed to focusing on desired outcomes, even if they are highly desirable. As I have discussed in previous forums (see, for example, Alan Jotkowitz, "On the Methodology of Jewish Medical Ethics," *Tradition* 43, no. 1 [2010]: 38–55), in situations where there is a lack of halakhic precedents related to the topic at hand, then theological concerns may play a dominant role in the decision-making process. It will be interesting to see if these different approaches to halakhic decision making will play a role in distinguishing the more liberal Open Orthodoxy from Centrist Orthodoxy.

CHAPTER 3

Irving Greenberg's Theology of Hybrid Judaism

DARREN KLEINBERG

INTRODUCTION: MOMENT JUDAISMS

In 1974, Rabbi Dr. Irving Greenberg presented a paper at the International Symposium on the Holocaust, held at the Cathedral of Saint John the Divine in New York City. The proceedings of the symposium were edited and published in *Auschwitz: Beginning of a New Era? Reflections on the Holocaust* (1977). Greenberg's chapter, entitled "Cloud of Smoke, Pillar of Fire: Judaism, Christianity, and Modernity after the Holocaust," is considered by some to be his "most important statement on the subject" of the Holocaust (Katz 62). In section four of the essay, subtitled "Jewish Theological Responses to the Holocaust," Greenberg introduced his original concept of "Moment Faiths." Extending Martin Buber's suggestion that we can only speak of "moment gods,"[1] Greenberg wrote that a full realization of the horrors of the Holocaust had to "end[ ] the easy dichotomy of atheist/theist," and that, in a post-Holocaust age, "We now have to speak of 'moment faiths,' moments when Redeemer and vision of redemption are present, interspersed with times when the flames and smoke of the burning children blot out faith—though it flickers again" (Greenberg, "Cloud of Smoke" 27). In a post-Holocaust era, Greenberg declared, faith in God could only be fleeting.

---

1 Greenberg interprets Buber in this way: "God is known only at the moment when Presence and awareness are fused in vital life. This knowledge is interspersed with moments when only natural, self-contained, routine existence is present" (Greenberg, "Cloud of Smoke" 27).

Today, more than forty years after the symposium and more than seventy years after the end of the Second World War, American Jews are in a different "moment." Rather than moment gods or moment faiths, the twenty-first century American Jewish reality is one of *Moment Judaisms*. In this coinage, the plural form "Judaisms" is intended to indicate the very real distinctions between the many different expressions of Judaism across the American Jewish landscape.[2] The sheer variety of Jewish behaviors, rituals, and cultural mores call for an acknowledgment of the plurality of Jewishness. Furthermore, the simple fact that some members of the Jewish community deny that other self-identified Jews are members of the same religion demands that we cannot but think of Judaism in plural terms.[3]

In addition to the plurality of contemporary American Jewish life, it is also the case that contemporary Judaisms are "momentary." For an increasing number of American Jews, the many Judaisms from which to choose are only some of the various identities that are available for adoption and that contribute to the complex identity politics of post-ethnic America. As David Hollinger has described, identity in the age of post-ethnic America is no longer inherited, singular, or fixed, but rather voluntary, overlapping, and dynamic. As such, post-ethnicity has very real implications for Jewish identity in the twenty-first century. Shaul Magid has written as well, in an era of post-ethnicity, "American Jews are multiethnic. For many of them, being Jewish is one part of a more complex narrative of identity" (Magid 11). These plural and momentary qualities call our attention to the fact that the nature and meaning of American Jewish identity—of American Moment Judaisms—is being renegotiated in the twenty-first century. It is in this context that I offer a consideration of Irving Greenberg's theology of what I call hybrid Judaism.

DEFINING PLURALISM

Greenberg's contributions to the field of intergroup and intragroup relations have generally been classified as expressions of pluralism. In fact, Greenberg's

---

2 To a lesser extent, the same might be said for world Jewry; however, my work addresses only the American Jewish experience.

3 For example, according to the interpretation of Jewish law (halakhah) recognized by most members of the Orthodox community, one can only claim Jewish status if one has a halakhically Jewish biological mother or if one has completed a religious conversion according to Orthodox standards. As such, those self-identified Jews that have a Jewish father and a non-Jewish mother, or that convert to Judaism according to non-Orthodox standards, are not considered Jewish by most members of the Orthodox community. As such, it is appropriate to describe these disparate Jewish communities as representing distinct Judaisms.

theology is more accurately understood as a proto–post-ethnic system that takes the notion of hybridity seriously. I refer to Greenberg's theology as proto–post-ethnic because it anticipated, in theological terms, much of David Hollinger's social-historical theory of post-ethnicity. Beginning in his earliest writings from the 1960s, Greenberg himself employed the language of pluralism; however, despite his self-identification with pluralism, a close reading of Greenberg's theological system reveals that his thinking extends beyond pluralism into the realm of post-ethnic thinking.

It is important to acknowledge at the outset that pluralism is a contested term that is often employed without clear definition. It has distinctive applications in ecclesiastical, philosophical, political, and sociological contexts. The earliest usage of the term pluralism dates back to the eighteenth century and referred to the simultaneous holding of two or more ecclesiastical offices by one cleric in the Church of England. In this sense it was seen as a corrupt institution in which "parishes, or benefices, could be bought and sold to the highest bidder" (Bender 7). Philosophically, pluralism has been used to mean "that the world is made up of more than one kind of substance or thing; (more generally) any theory or system of thought which recognizes more than one irreducible basic principle" (OED Online). This philosophical application of pluralism is most commonly associated with Harvard philosopher William James (1842–1910) and his 1909 Hibbert Lectures, which were later published in the volume *A Pluralistic Universe*. Politically, pluralism has been understood as a "theory or system of devolution and autonomy for organizations and individuals in preference to monolithic state power" or "a political system within which many parties or organizations have access to power" (OED Online).

For our purposes, I will turn to the sociological formulation of pluralism as a theory of identity and group life in America. The founding theorist of pluralism was Horace Meyer Kallen (1882–1974), who was born into a rabbinic family in Germany and immigrated with his parents to the United States in 1887. Settling in Boston, Kallen attended Harvard College, earning his bachelor's degree and a doctorate in philosophy. Following a seven-year teaching post at the University of Wisconsin–Madison, Kallen helped to establish the New School for Social Research in New York City and joined its faculty in 1919, where he taught until a year before his death. Despite thoroughly rejecting his father's Orthodoxy, Kallen became an influential leader in the American Jewish community. He played a significant role in the establishment of the Menorah Society at Harvard College and supported the growth of the Intercollegiate Menorah Association on other college campuses (Greene). These organizations promoted "Jewish culture as a means to foster pride" and their founders, Kallen among them, "hoped that their study as well as their fellowship would combat the 'indifference' and 'shameful ignorance of things Jewish'" (Greene 28–29). In addition, Kallen was a staunch supporter of Zionism, serving as a founding delegate to the American Jewish Congress (Pianko 302), and was often engaged in the cause for Jewish education, serving as vice president of the American Association of Jewish Education, among other roles (Kronish 142).

Kallen began writing about group identity and group life in America as early as 1906 and, in 1924, coined the phrase "cultural pluralism." In the closing paragraph of his important 1915 essay, "Democracy *versus* the Melting Pot: A Study in American Nationality," Kallen employed a now-famous simile:

> As in an orchestra, every type of instrument has its specific timbre and tonality, founded in its substance and form; as every type has its appropriate theme and melody in the whole symphony, so in society each ethnic group is the natural instrument, its spirit and culture are its theme and melody, and the harmony and dissonances and discords of them all make the symphony of civilization ... (Kallen, "Democracy" 116–17)

Here, Kallen used the simile of the orchestra to suggest that the different groups that make up a diverse society have fixed and distinct identities. The meaning of the orchestra as a metaphor for pluralism has been explained by Werner Sollors in this way: "[T]he stable quality of each instrument must be preserved. Kallen's definition of cultural pluralism rests on quasi-eternal, static units, on the 'distinctive individuality of each nation' ... on 'ancestry,' 'homogeneity of heritage, mentality and interest,' and mankind's 'psycho-physical inheritance'" (Sollors, "Critique" 260). David Hollinger has also written that, in employing the metaphor of the orchestra, Kallen "emphasized the integrity and autonomy of each descent-defined group" (Hollinger, *Postethnic* 92). Put simply, ethnic identity was, for Kallen, fixed. Kallen famously underlined this point at the end of "Democracy *versus* the Melting Pot" when he wrote that, "Men may change their clothes, their politics, their wives, their religions, their philosophies, to a greater or lesser extent: they cannot change their grandfathers. Jews or Poles or Anglo-Saxons, in order to cease being Jews or Poles or Anglo-Saxons, would have to cease to be ..." (Kallen, "Democracy" 114–15).

Kallen's point was twofold: first, individuals inherit a hereditary ethnic group identity that they cannot escape and, second, that the identities of each individual and group are, and should remain, distinct from one another.

According to Kallen, even as the orchestra of America includes a variety of instruments, the appearance and sound of each one is, and cannot but continue to be, fixed and distinct.

For Kallen, cultural pluralism was an essential characteristic of American democracy. In "Democracy *versus* the Melting Pot," Kallen presented a response to his Wisconsin–Madison colleague and nativist thinker, Edward Alsworth Ross (1866–1951), arguing that, rather than posing a threat to the United States, immigrants, and the cultural diversity they brought with them, supported the democratic ideals that defined America. Rejecting the conceptualization of America as a melting pot, Kallen claimed that, rather than melting into each other, immigrants could become American precisely as a result of *holding on* to their cultural particularity. In Kallen's words:

> ... the outlines of a possible great and truly democratic commonwealth become discernible. Its form is that of a Federal republic; its substance a democracy of nationalities, cooperating voluntarily and autonomously through common institutions in the enterprise of self-realization through the perfection of men according to their kind. The common language of the commonwealth, the language of its great tradition, would be English, but each nationality would have for its emotional and involuntary life its own particular dialect or speech, its own individual and inevitable esthetic and intellectual forms ... Thus "American civilization" may come to mean the perfection of the cooperative harmonies of "European Civilization" ... (Kallen, "Democracy" 116)

Kallen's vision was clear: if America was to remain a democracy, it could not be a melting pot, nor could it respond to its newest immigrants in Anglo-conformist or nativist terms.

Kallen returned to the subject of cultural pluralism (although not yet by that name) in an essay published in *The Menorah Journal* entitled "Nationality and the Hyphenated American" (1915). In this essay Kallen looked to Switzerland as a model for American democracy. Kallen observed that "... the nationhood of Switzerland is the most integral and unified in Europe today, because Switzerland is as complete and thorough a democracy as exists in the civilized world, and the efficacious safeguard of nationhood is democracy not only of individuals but of nationalities" (Kallen, "Nationality"). For Kallen, a country populated by a diverse citizenry could only be truly democratic if the multiplicity of nationalities present were distinct and protected. As such, Kallen believed that citizens of the United States should be empowered to carry dual identities. Kallen called this the "hyphenated American" and suggested that for "American nationhood … its democracy is its strength, and its democracy is 'hyphenation'" (Kallen, "Nationality").[4] A year after the publication of Kallen's two essays, the American philosopher and educational reformer, John Dewey, echoed Kallen's ideas and implored his audience at the National Educational Association that "the genuine American, the typical American, is himself a hyphenated character" (Gordon 139). Put differently, Kallen (and Dewey) did not simply believe that America had a responsibility to protect the diverse communities within its borders, but rather that those communities had a responsibility to hold onto their distinct ethnic and cultural identities to protect American democracy.

Although it did not have an immediate impact, Kallen's notion of cultural pluralism would become an influential theory of identity and group life in America. In his widely read "Protestant, Catholic, Jew" (1955), Will Herberg adapted Kallen's notion of cultural pluralism by turning his attention away from European ethnic groups and focusing instead on religious groups in America. By the last third of the twentieth century, cultural pluralism would be recast again, this time in the guise of multiculturalism. The multicultural rejection of "assimilation and the 'melting pot' image as an imposition of the dominant culture" and its calls for a society "in which each ethnic and racial element in the population maintains its distinctiveness" (Glazer 10) meant that it shared a great deal in common with cultural pluralism in its prescriptions for the importance of maintaining distinct individual and group identities in America. As Nathan Glazer has put it, the "new reality was once called cultural pluralism; it is now called multiculturalism" (Glazer, *Multiculturalists Now* 97). In other words, multiculturalism continued the legacy of cultural pluralism in America.

PLURALISM: A CRITIQUE

However, Kallen's original theory suffered from a critical flaw. In his book *Assimilation in American Life: The Role of Race, Religion, and National Origins*

---

4 W. E. B. Du Bois's notion of "double consciousness," while not identical, had much in common with Kallen's notions of cultural pluralism and hyphenation. As Daniel Greene has noted, "In 1897, just a decade before Kallen began to publish on pluralism, Du Bois famously asked, 'What, after all, am I? Am I an American or am I a Negro? Can I be both? Or is it my duty to cease to be a Negro as soon as possible and be an American?'" (Greene 8). As Greene has also pointed out, the question of race was a significant "blind spot" for Kallen.

(1964), The sociologist Milton Gordon wrote that, "If one inquires ... as to the specific nature of the communication and interaction which is to exist between the various ethnic communities and between individuals who compose them in the 'ideal' cultural pluralistic societies, the answer does not emerge clearly from Kallen's descriptions" (Gordon 148). Moreover, not only is Kallen's theory light on details, but Gordon also identified an inherent tension in Kallen's formulation of cultural pluralism: "On the one hand, he is opposed to 'ghetto' existence and group isolation and favors creative interaction. On the other hand, he is against the dissolution of the communities" (Gordon 148). As a result, Kallen's cultural pluralism did not account for what might actually happen "when peoples meet"[5] (Gordon 60) or, to put it in contemporary terms, it lacked a theory of change. For Kallen's cultural pluralism to manifest, it "demands keeping primary group relations across ethnic lines sufficiently minimal to prevent a significant amount of intermarriage, while cooperating with other groups and individuals in the secondary relations areas of political action, economic life, and civic responsibility" (Gordon 158). Put simply, Kallen failed to account for the importance, increasing likelihood, and implications of encounters across group lines.

A similar critique of pluralism, this time from the field of religious studies, indicates that pluralism fails to "adequately acknowledge the great diversity (and sometimes conflict) within particular religious traditions" (Bender and Klassen 12) and that, along similar lines to Gordon's analysis, "the doctrines and programs of pluralism that dominate the contemporary academic and public conversations do not constitute a theory of understanding religious interactions as they take place in the world" (Bender and Klassen 12). The result is a kind of pluralism discourse that projects and upholds a false image of the nature of ethnic and religious diversity and encounter in society.

POST-ETHNICITY

It is in this light that post-ethnicity stands as a compelling attempt to address the shortcomings of Kallen's theory of cultural pluralism and also to present a more accurate description of American society and the changing nature of identity. David Hollinger's book, *Postethnic America: Beyond Multiculturalism* (1995), turns away from pluralism and contrasts Kallen's work with Randolph

---

5 Gordon took this phrase from Alain Locke and Bernhard J. Stem, eds., *When Peoples Meet: Race and Culture Contacts* (New York: Hinds, Hayden & Eldredge Inc., 1942).

Bourne's important ideas about cosmopolitanism. The distinction between pluralism and cosmopolitanism is described in this way:

> Pluralism respects inherited boundaries and locates individuals within one or another of a series of ethno-racial groups to be protected or preserved. Cosmopolitanism is more wary of traditional enclosures and favors voluntary affiliations. Cosmopolitanism promotes multiple identities, emphasizes the dynamic and changing character of many groups, and is responsive to the potential for creating new cultural combinations. Pluralism sees in cosmopolitanism a threat to identity, while cosmopolitanism sees in pluralism a provincial unwillingness to engage the complex dilemmas and opportunities actually presented by contemporary life. (Hollinger, *Postethnic* 3–4)

It is these four characteristics of cosmopolitanism—voluntary affiliations, or communities of ascent (as opposed to descent); multiple identities; the dynamic and changing character of groups; and the potential for creating new cultural combinations—that Hollinger has emphasized in his theory of post-ethnicity.

Even as Hollinger claimed that group affiliations are voluntary and that communities of descent do not dictate identity, his theory of post-ethnicity did not call for a complete abandonment of inherited identity or identities. Recognizing that "many of the great cosmopolitans of history have been proudly rootless," Hollinger explained that, by contrast, "postethnicity is the critical renewal of cosmopolitanism in the context of today's greater sensitivity to roots" (Hollinger, *Postethnic* 5). This greater sensitivity is referred to as "rooted cosmopolitanism." In effect, "[a] postethnic perspective ... balances an appreciation for communities of descent with a determination to make room for new communities" (Hollinger, *Postethnic* 3). Whereas Kallen deemed communities of descent to be determinative, post-ethnicity honors their place, but only as part of what is a complex matrix of identity.

Unlike Kallen's cultural pluralism, which failed to appreciate the implications of social encounters across groups, post-ethnicity is predicated on the acknowledgment "that most individuals live in many circles simultaneously and that the actual living of any individual life entails a shifting division of labor between the several 'we's' of which the individual is a part" (Hollinger, *Postethnic* 106). In post-ethnic America, social mixing is simply part of the warp and woof of life, resulting in a high volume of cross-group encounters and, as a result, in the adoption of hybrid identities.

In this context, hybridity refers to the adoption of multiple, overlapping identities that are mutually influential. Specifically, hybrid refers to "[a]nything derived from heterogeneous sources, or composed of different or incongruous elements" (OED Online). Thus, Hybrid Judaism fuses the multiple with the singular. As such, "Judaism" is linked to "hybrid" to indicate the primary, rooted group identity while acknowledging that, in a post-ethnic reality, one is attached to and influenced by more than any one single identity group, both within and beyond the Jewish community.

GREENBERG'S THEOLOGY OF POST-ETHNICITY

Turning to Greenberg, we can now consider his proto–post-ethnic theology of encounter and appreciate the extent to which it advances beyond pluralism. Greenberg's writings on pluralism are spread throughout a half century of short articles, essays, monographs, and books. Although some of Greenberg's isolated writings on pluralism appear to fit neatly within Kallen's framework, when his entire corpus is considered and the culmination of his ideas is outlined, it becomes clear that his ideas inhabited a new space that is best described as proto–post-ethnic.

The two foci of Greenberg's theology are first his claim that, after the Holocaust, adherence to the biblical covenant between God and the Jewish people is no longer obligatory and, second, his understanding of the biblical notion that human beings are created in the image of God. In his 1982 essay "Voluntary Covenant," Greenberg addressed the theological implications of the destruction of Jewish life during the Holocaust. He posited that, as a result of the Holocaust, "The crisis of the covenant runs deep; one must consider the possibility that it is over." He continued:

> [M]orally speaking, God must repent of the covenant, i.e. do teshuvah[6] for having given his chosen people a task[7] that was unbearably cruel and dangerous without having provided for their protection. Morally speaking, then, God can have no claims on the Jews by dint of the covenant ... It can no longer be commanded ... If the Jews keep the covenant after the Holocaust, then it can no longer be for the reason that it is commanded or because it is enforced by reward or punishment. (Greenberg, "Voluntary Covenant" 34–35)

---

6 Repent.
7 I.e., the task of upholding the covenant.

Greenberg concluded: "What then happened to the covenant? I submit that its authority was broken" (Greenberg, "Voluntary Covenant" 35). The significance of this claim cannot be overstated. The suggestion that the obligatory nature of covenant between God and the Jewish people had ended represented a clean break with Jewish tradition.[8]

The implications of the voluntary stage of the covenant were significant for Greenberg's emerging theology of intra-Jewish pluralism. Later on in the essay, he wrote that

> *the voluntary covenant is the theological base of a genuine pluralism. Pluralism is not a matter of tolerance* made necessary by living in a non-Jewish reality, nor is it pity for one who does not know any better. It is a recognition that all Jews have chosen to make the fundamental Jewish statement at great personal risk and cost. The present denominations are paths for the covenant-minded all leading toward the final goal. (Greenberg, "Voluntary Covenant" 38)

Greenberg's conception of the voluntary covenant points to a form of intra-Jewish ecumenism that also includes within it the seeds of post-ethnicity. Recall that the first of Hollinger's four qualities of cosmopolitanism is that our affiliations are voluntary.

Turning to the second key aspect of Greenberg's theology, in his 1997 essay, "Seeking the Roots of Religious Pluralism," Greenberg offered his most complete theological treatment of pluralism. He wrote that "[m]odern culture made an initial sociological contribution to the growth of pluralism and the undermining of absolute (superiority) claims. Modern culture differentially created urban settings where everybody mixes. There the other is encountered" (Greenberg, "Religious Roots" 387). Thus, according to Greenberg, it is through contact—the very contact that Kallen failed to address in his conception

---

8 Addressing his concern that his readers might conclude that the Holocaust was a necessary stage in the unfolding of the covenant, Greenberg clarified that "the voluntary stage is implicit in the covenantal model from the very beginning" (Greenberg, "Voluntary Covenant" 37). Years later he would add that "the covenant model always pointed toward the idea that humanity would one day mature into full responsibility. Ideally, the development of modern culture with its concomitant explosion of human capacity should have been the occasion for humanity to take up a higher level of leadership in the covenant" (Greenberg, *For the Sake* 29). Greenberg's important clarification helped him avoid turning "the *Shoah* into the God of the system" (Greenberg, *For the Sake* 29).

of pluralism—that human beings can recognize the image of God in each other. The unprecedented opportunities for encounter in American society meant that "this has evoked a recognition of the other as no longer *other* but as the image of God" (Greenberg, "Religious Roots" 388). The meaning of this recognition was very clear to Greenberg:

> Because humans are in the image of God, they are endowed by their Creator with three intrinsic dignities: infinite value (the image of God is priceless); equality (there can be no preferred image of God; that would constitute idolatry); and uniqueness (images created by humans from one mold resemble each other, but God creates images from one couple or mold, and each is distinct for every other). All of society—economics, politics, culture—must be organized to respect and uphold these three fundamental dignities. (Freedman 31)

For Greenberg, the direct human encounter and the resultant recognition of the value, equality, and uniqueness of the other is the key to transforming our understanding and appreciation of one another.

Having established the theological importance of encounter, Greenberg postulated that "[p]luralism is the natural outgrowth of this experience. First comes the encounter, followed by the recognition and then by affirmation of the uniqueness and equality of the other" (Greenberg, "Religious Roots" 388). In coming to appreciate the image of God in each other, Greenberg stated that:

> The result is the coexistence in the believer's mind and experience of two (or more) religious systems whose claims and expressions are experienced as vitally (perhaps equally) alive and valid. This gives rise to the plurality of affirmations. (Greenberg, "Religious Roots" 388)

Greenberg is unequivocal in his interpretation of the potential power of encounter. As a direct result of his or her encounter with the other, he or she recognizes that person's inherent value as an image of God. In turn, they come to appreciate each other and their respective faiths as potentially equally valid and valuable religious systems. As a result, they can affirm the truth of that faith in addition to their own.

In a short piece published in the pages of the journal *Sh'ma*, Greenberg made explicit his most far-reaching conclusion. Returning to the theme of encounter, Greenberg wrote that,

> In appreciation of an open society and of the equality and uniqueness of others, I come to affirm the value of living and of teaching in the presence of other truths and systems. Other approaches teach me the limitations of my own views, preventing an imperialist extension of my truth/faith beyond its legitimate sphere into realms where it becomes a lie or is wrongly applied. And while I may come to refute or reject some contradictories, I may also learn from others' insights and may even integrate them, thus improving my own system. (Greenberg, "Principles of Pluralism" 5)

The importance of this claim cannot be overstated. Greenberg advanced the image of God idea to allow for the adoption of ideas from other religious systems as a way of improving one's own. It is in this statement that Greenberg presented the final version of his theology of religious pluralism. As he put it, "in our era of pluralism, we are living in an age of great religious breakthroughs" (Greenberg, "Religious Roots" 394). The result is nothing short of a post-ethnic understanding of religious identity.

Greenberg's theology is based on the sociological assumption that, in an open society, people will necessarily interact with each other as equals. His willingness to accept the implications of such encounters locates him not in the pluralist camp, but rather at the very cutting edge of post-ethnic thinking. As such, Greenberg's system is better described as a theology of Hybrid Judaism.

CONCLUSION

It is useful at this point to return to David Hollinger's conception of post-ethnicity to fully appreciate the similarities with Greenberg's theology of Hybrid Judaism. Hollinger described post-ethnicity in this way:

> Postethnicity prefers voluntary to prescribed affiliations, appreciates multiple identities, pushes for communities of wide scope ... and accepts the formation of new groups as a part of the normal life of a democratic society. (Hollinger, *Postethnic America* 116)

Greenberg's perspective with regard to religious group identity shares much in common with Hollinger's post-ethnic framework. Like Hollinger's post-ethnic preference for voluntary affiliations, Greenberg's covenantal theology identified the modern era as the era of the voluntary covenant.

The post-ethnic appreciation for multiple identities also has resonance with Hybrid Judaism. As we have seen, Greenberg's conception of encounter as a way of recognizing the image of God in one another leads to what he called "a plurality of affirmations." While Greenberg would certainly prefer that Jews remain rooted in Judaism and the Jewish community, it is also clear that Greenberg's theology of Hybrid Judaism contains within it the potential for Jews to be influenced by other religious traditions. And, as members of religious communities begin to integrate insights from other denominations and religions, the lines dividing one identity group from another necessarily become more porous. To put it in terms of Greenberg's own identity, to describe him simply as an "Orthodox Jew" would not do justice to the influence of non-Orthodox Judaisms, religions other than Judaism (specifically, Protestant Christianity), and those other intellectual traditions that have exerted such a strong influence on both his thought and his practice.

Next, the post-ethnic push "for communities of wide scope" is parallel to Greenberg's eager willingness to engage the open society and enter into dialogue with non-Orthodox Jews and non-Jews alike. Finally, the post-ethnic acceptance of the formation of new groups is implicit in Greenberg's covenantal theology. After all, if the covenant can no longer be commanded in the wake of the Holocaust, then, as Greenberg explicitly stated, any expression of Judaism, old or new, is theologically valid.

Greenberg's theology should be appreciated as a groundbreaking and profoundly honest appraisal of the implications of the American open society for Jewish identity. While some (many?) will balk at Greenberg's embrace of what happens "when peoples meet," others will appreciate his messianic vision of a time when, as a result of realizing the image of God in each other, we will have to be open to the possibility of transformation. In fact, if the results of the 2013 Pew Research Center's "A Portrait of Jewish Americans" are to be accepted, it appears that, at least to some extent, that time has already arrived. In an age of Moment Judaisms, the full implications of Greenberg's theology of hybrid Judaism provide important guidance as we attempt to navigate our contemporary situation.

BIBLIOGRAPHY

Berman, Lili Corwin. *Speaking of Jews: Rabbis, Intellectuals, and the Creation of an American Public Identity*. Berkeley: University of California Press, 2009.

Bender, Courtney and Pamela E. Klassen, eds. *After Pluralism: Reimagining Religious Engagement*. New York: Columbia University Press, 2010.

Beneke, Chris. *Beyond Toleration: The Religious Origins of American Pluralism*. Oxford: Oxford University Press, 2006.

Berger, Peter L. *The Heretical Imperative: Contemporary Possibilities of Religious Affirmation*. Garden City, NY: Anchor Press/Doubelday, 1979.

Bernstein, Louis. "Greenberg, Irving (1933–)." In *Encyclopaedia Judaica*, 904. Jerusalem: Keter Publishing House Ltd., 1972.

Freedman, Shalom. *Living in the Image of God: Jewish Teachings to Perfect the World*. Lanham, MD: Rowman & Littlefield Publishers, Inc., 1998.

Glazer, Nathan, and Daniel Patrick Moynihan. *Beyond the Melting Pot: The Negroes, Puerto Ricans, Jews, Italians, and Irish of New York City*. 2nd ed. Cambridge, MA: The MIT Press, 1970.

Glazer, Nathan. *We Are All Multiculturalists Now*. Cambridge, MA: Harvard University Press, 1997.

Goldberg, Harold. "Dr. Greenberg Discusses Orthodoxy, YU, Viet Nam, & Sex." *The Commentator* 28 (April 1966): 6, 8–10.

Gordon, Milton M. *Assimilation in American Life: The Role of Race, Religion, and National Origins*. New York: Oxford University Press, 1964.

Greenberg, Irving. "Cloud of Smoke, Pillar of Fire: Judaism, Christianity, and Modernity after the Holocaust." In *Auschwitz: Beginning of a New Era?*, edited by Eva Fleischner, 7–55. Brooklyn: KTAV Publishing House Inc., 1977.

———. "Seeking the Religious Roots of Pluralism: In the Image of God and Covenant." *Journal of Ecumenical Studies* (1997): 385–94.

———. "The Principles of Pluralism." *Sh'ma* (1999): 4–5.

———. "Voluntary Covenant." *Perspectives* October 1982: 27–44.

Greene, Daniel. *The Jewish Origins of Cultural Pluralism*. Bloomington: Indiana University Press, 2011.

Herberg, Will. *Protestant-Catholic-Jew: An Essay in American Religious Sociology*. Chicago: The University of Chicago Press, 1983.

Hollinger, David A. *Postethnic America: Beyond Multiculturalism*. New York: Basic Books, 2005.

Hutchison, William R. *Religious Pluralism in America: The Contentious History of a Founding Ideal*. New Haven, CT: Yale University Press, 2003.

Jakobsen, Janet R. "Ethics After Pluralism." In *After Pluralism: Reimagining Religious Engagement*, edited by Courtney Bender and Janet R. Jakobsen, 31–58. New York: Columbia University Press, 2010.

Kallen, Horace M. "Democracy Versus the Melting Pot: A Study of American Nationality. " In *Culture and Democracy in the United States*, 59–117. New Brunswick, NJ: Transaction Publishers, 1998 (1924).

Katkin, Wendy F., Ned Landsman, and Andrea Tyree, eds. *Beyond Pluralism: The Conception of Groups and Group Identity in America*. Urbana: University of Illinois Press, 1998.

Katz, Steven T. "Irving (Yitzchak) Greenberg." In *Interpretations of Judaism in the Late Twentieth Century*, edited by Steven T. Katz, 58–89. Washington, DC: B'nai B'rith Books, 1993.

Krell, Mark A. *Intersecting Pathways: Modern Jewish Theologians in Conversation with Christianity.* Oxford: Oxford University Press, 2003.
Kronish, Ronald. "John Dewey and Horace M. Kallen on Cultural Pluralism: Their Impact on Jewish Education." *Jewish Social Studies* 44, no. 2 (1982): 135–48.
Landsman, Ned, and Wendy F. Katkin. "Introduction: The Construction of American Pluralism." In *Beyond Pluralism: The Conception of Groups and Group Identities in America,* edited by Wendy F. Katkin, Ned Landsman, and Andrea Tyree, 110. Urbana: University of Illinois Press, 1998.
Landsman, Ned. "Pluralism, Protestantism, and Prosperity: Crevecoeur's American Farmer and the Foundations of American Pluralism." In *Beyond Pluralism: The Conception of Groups and Group Identities in America,* edited by Wendy F. Katkin, Ned Landsman, and Andrea Tyree, 105–24. Urbana: University of Illinois Press, 1998.
Leftwich, Joseph. *Israel Zangwill.* New York: Thomas Yoseloff, 1957.
Lichtenstein, Aharon. "Rav Lichtenstein Writes Letter to Dr. Greenberg/Rav Lichtenstein Answers Dr. Greenberg's Article." *The Commentator* (June 2, 1966): 7–8.
Newman, William M. *American Pluralism: A Study of Minority Groups and Social Theory.* New York: HarperCollins, 1973.
Obama, Barack H. *A More Perfect Union.* March 18, 2008. Web. October 6, 2013.
OED Online. S.v. "hybrid, n. and adj." March 2014. *Oxford English Dictionary.* Web. March 30, 2014.
———. S.v. "pluralism, n." June 2013. *Oxford English Dictionary.* Web. August 18, 2013.
Pianko, Noam. "'The True Liberalism of Zionism': Horace Kallen, Jewish Nationalism, and the Limits of American Pluralism." *American Jewish History* 94, no. 4 (2008): 299–329.
Putnam, Robert D., and David E. Campbell. *American Grace: How Religion Divides and Unites Us.* New York: Simon & Schuster, 2010.
Shapiro, Edward. "Will Herberg's Protestant-Catholic-Jew: A Critique." In *Key Texts in American Jewish Culture,* edited by Jack Kugelmass, 258–74. New Brunswick, NJ: Rutgers University Press, 2003.
Sollors, Werner. "A Critique of Pure Pluralism." In *Reconstructing American Literary History,* edited by Sacvan Bercovitch, 250–79. Cambridge, MA: Harvard University Press, 1986.
Zangwill, Israel. *The Melting Pot. A Drama in Four Acts.* New York: Macmillan, 1909.

CHAPTER 4

On the Meaning and Significance of Revelation for Orthodox Judaism

JAMES KUGEL

I wish to thank the organizers of the Oxford Summer Institute on Modern and Contemporary Judaism for having invited me to address the subject of revelation. I should make clear at the outset that I am not trying to speak in the name of Orthodox Judaism, or modern Orthodox Judaism; what follows is in no way intended as a manifesto. Rather, what I wish to do is describe what Jewish tradition seems to be saying on the subject of revelation—not only in words, but also in the underlying role that revelation exercises in Judaism.

THE MEANING OF REVELATION

First, about the meaning of the term *revelation*: in Judaism this refers to God revealing Himself and/or speaking to human beings. What we can know today about the "how" of this process is quite limited, but it seems clear to me that Judaism without revelation in this sense is impossible. To deny the phenomenon of divine speech is virtually to deny the existence of God Himself, at least from the standpoint of Jewish tradition. What sort of a God is it who is incapable of speaking to humans or unwilling to do so? Indeed, what sort of Judaism is it that denies that God spoke and gave us the Torah?

At the same time, we have this curious tradition that holds that God has somehow ceased to speak directly to Israel. Apparently, we have had all the divine speech that we need. So, at an early point we became a people of interpreters of divine speech rather than its direct recipients. (Of course, this is not altogether true: the same sages who denied the straight-line continuity of revelation into late biblical and postbiblical times nevertheless held out for the activities of the *bat kol*, the prophet Elijah, revelatory dreams, and the like, all of which continued in some form the basic act of divine-to-human communication; along with these, a robust mystical tradition on its own championed a way, or several ways, around the cessation of divine speech.) Still, this theme of the cessation of prophecy is one of the oddest features of the role of divine speech in Judaism.[1] We have no more prophets or other direct recipients of the divine word.

In fact, it is not just direct revelation that has ceased; by the same token, so has authoritative interpretation—at least as far as halakhah is concerned. By this I mean that no Jew, or at least no Orthodox Jew, is free to come up with a new, authoritative interpretation of the Torah's prohibition of work on Shabbat. He or she is obligated to be guided first by the thirty-nine categories of work listed in the Mishnah (Shabbat 7:2), and then by their further elaboration in the later chain of tradition: the Jerusalem and Babylonian Talmuds, Geonic writings, and so forth. Of course, a modern-day *posek* is free to opine on subjects previously untreated—microwave ovens, Shabbat timers, and the like—but even such a *posek* is obligated to follow (or at least to seem to follow) earlier traditions and guidelines; he cannot brazenly declare the past to be irrelevant. So, even the *interpretation* of divine speech is, in this regard, largely a thing of the past. (One might contrast this to the state of affairs in both Islam and Christianity, where direct, unmediated interpretation of sacred Scripture is very much the norm.) In short: while revelation—God speaking to man—played a central role in Judaism in the distant past, the great divine pronouncements to Israel's prophets have ceased; in fact, even the unmediated interpretation of divine speech is itself a thing of the past.

Yet, to say only this is, I believe, to miss something essential about the nature of revelation in Judaism. Here, I believe, help arrives from a rather unanticipated source, modern biblical scholarship—in fact, from two of that field's most challenging subfields, source criticism and textual criticism.

---

1 Further on this tradition: E. E. Urbach, "Matai Paskah ha-Nevuah," *Tarbiz* 17 (1946), 1–27; idem, "Halakhah ve-Nevuah," *Tarbiz* 18 (1947), 1–27; K. De Troyer and A. Lange, *Prophecy after the Prophets? The Contribution of the Dead Sea Scrolls to the Understanding of Biblical and Extra-Biblical Prophecy* (Leuven: Peeters, 2009).

SAGE #2

In general, I should say that the whole history of sacred texts in Judaism may be encapsulated in a brief exchange between two ancient sages. Sage #1 says: "My son, take this sacred scroll from my hands. It contains the very words that God whispered into the ear of His prophet." To which Sage #2 replies: "Thank you so much; this is indeed the word of God. But you know ... I'll bet I can make it *even better* with just a few little changes." The history of the development of different books of the Bible, as pieced together by modern source critics and text critics, is essentially an extended version of this exchange. There is scarcely a book of the Tanakh that has not undergone major editing and supplementation: "Move this over there, stick this in at the beginning, turn chapter 1 into chapter 6," and so forth.[2] This was still going on in the days of the Dead Sea Scrolls community at Qumran, in the closing two centuries BCE, when most of our biblical texts had been around for hundreds of years.

A question naturally arises about Sage #2's response: How dare he? And this question is of the greatest importance for understanding the true meaning of revelation in Judaism. So: How dare he? How dare this sage take the book of Isaiah and add some twenty-seven chapters onto the end of it? Indeed, how dare he, or more likely a different sage or sages, take the chapters preceding those twenty-seven and keep on tinkering with them, adding, for example, the "Isaiah Apocalypse" in chapters 24–27 (which arguably postdate the twenty-seven chapters added at the end of the book), and in general moving things around and interpolating all sorts of new material.[3] For that matter, how dare someone else come along and rearrange the order of the chapters in the existing book of Jeremiah, while also adding to the book roughly 2,700 words, the equivalent of some seven or eight chapters that were never part of the original? And how dare someone else, or a lot of someone elses, add to and/or rearrange the content of virtually every book in our Tanakh? "Oh, but not to our most sacred book,

---

2 On this subject, see the essays collected in H. von Weissenberg et al., *Changes in Scripture: Rewriting and Interpreting Authoritative Traditions in the Second Temple Period* (Berlin: De Gruyter, 2011).

3 The dating of Isaiah 24–27 remains a debated topic, some scholars locating it as late as Hellenistic times. On the overall process: J. Blenkinsopp, *Opening the Sealed Book: Interpretations of the Book of Isaiah in Late Antiquity* (Grand Rapids, MI: Eerdmans, 2006), esp. 72–77. Among surveys of the phenomenon of ongoing interpretation within the Bible itself: M. Fishbane, *Biblical Interpretation in Ancient Israel* (Oxford: Clarendon, 1985); Y. Zakovitch, *An Introduction to Inner-Biblical Interpretation* (Even Yehudah: Rekhes, 1992); M. Henze, ed., *A Companion to Biblical Interpretation in Early Judaism* (Grand Rapids, MI: Eerdmans, 2012).

the Torah," you might say. "No one would dare fiddle with that!" Well, you're wrong about that too, as we have learned from, among other sources, the Dead Sea Scrolls.[4] So really, *how dare he*?

I think I know pretty well the answers that sages from the closing three or four centuries BCE might provide: "There was an apparent inconsistency between what it says here in Deuteronomy and what was said in Exodus—so I had to change it"; "Ordinary people wouldn't understand this particular word/toponym/historical reference"; "I had to highlight what is really important in the prophet's words for us nowadays—so I did"; or sometimes, "We just don't think that way anymore," or "We don't do that anymore." But I believe that such answers would cover only the more limited sort of changes that sacred texts underwent in those centuries; they really can't account for much of the wholesale rearranging, reformulating, and supplementing that went on in earlier centuries. Actually, if you were to ask sages from this earlier period, I think—judging by the evidence—that they would be surprised by the question. "Why not?" they would ask. "Why shouldn't I change some things?" In other words, the real answer to the question "How dare he?" is: *he dares*. You may have a

---

4 See E. Tov and S. White, "Reworked Pentateuch," in *Qumran Cave 4.VIII: Parabiblical Texts Part 1* (DJD XIII), ed. H. Attridge et al. (Oxford: Clarendon, 1994), 268–71; E. Tov, "Rewritten Biblical Compositions and Biblical Manuscripts," *DSD* 5 (1998): 334–54, and S. W. Crawford, "The 'Rewritten Bible' at Qumran: A Look at Three Texts," *Eretz Israel* 26 (1999) (FS F. M. Cross): 1–8. On the Qumran roots of the Samaritan Pentateuch vis-à-vis the Masoretic text, R. Weiss, "Synonymous Variants in Divergences between the Samaritan and Massoretic Texts of the Pentateuch," in *Studies in the Text and Language of the Bible*, ed. R. Weiss (Jerusalem: Magnes, 1981), 63–189; J. Sanderson, *An Exodus Scroll from Qumran: 4QpaleoExod and the Samaritan Tradition* (Harvard Semitic Studies 30) (Atlanta: Scholars, 1986); Ursula Schattner-Rieser, "Der samaritanische Pentateuch im Lichte der präsamaritanischen Qumrantexte," *Qumran und der biblische Kanon*, in M. Becker et al. (Neukirchen-Vluyn: Neukirchener, 2009), 145–68; S. W. Crawford, "The Pentateuch as Found in the Pre-Samaritan Texts and 4QReworked Pentateuch," in *Changes in Scripture*, ed. H. von Weissenberg et al. (Berlin: De Gruyter, 2011), 123–36; also M. Bernstein, "What Has Happened to the Laws? The Treatment of Legal Material in 4QReworked Pentateuch," *DSD* 15 (2008): 24–49. On the Samaritan Pentateuch itself, see R. Pummer, "The Samaritans and Their Pentateuch," in *The Pentateuch as Torah*, ed. G. Knoppers and B. M. Levinson (Winona Lake, IN: Eisenbrauns, 2007), 237–69 and M. Kartveit, *The Origin of the Samaritans* SVT 128 (Leiden: Brill, 2009), 279–312. On the connection to "rewritten" Scripture: as P. Alexander, "Retelling the Old Testament," in *It is Written: Scripture Citing Scripture*, ed. D. A. Carson and H. M. Williamson (Cambridge: Cambridge University Press, 1988), 99–121; M. Bernstein, "Rewritten Bible" and George Brooke, "The Rewritten Law, Prophets, and Psalms: Issues for Understanding the Text of the Bible," in *The Bible as Book: The Hebrew Bible and the Judean Desert Discoveries*, ed. E. D. Herbert and E. Tov (London: British Library and Newcastle, DE: Oak Knoll, 2002), 31–40.

different idea of the significance of divine revelation, but if so, yours seems to be an ahistorical, anachronistic conception. Apparently, such freedom was simply part of the definition of what one does with a sacred text. So here is another, rather unique feature of revelation in Judaism: it's divine, but not inviolable.

THE GREAT FUNNEL

When did this freedom to alter divinely revealed words come to an end? Anyone who studies the textual history of the Bible knows that as time went on, the options for changing sacred texts gradually came to be limited. Back in the eighth century, our hypothetical Sage #2 had great latitude; by the third or second century BCE, he had less. Some minor insertions or deletions were still possible, a little transposition could be introduced here or there, a word or phrase could still be stuck in, but the heavy lifting of an earlier day was by and large no longer possible. And so, little by little, Israel's sacred library came to be standardized, not only as to the books to be included and excluded, but with regard to the very form of the texts, their every word. The once-green forest of Scripture was now petrified; no further changes were possible. Changing metaphors, one might say that the great funnel of possible alterations in a sacred text's meaning, which had started out wide at the top, gradually diminished; as time went on, the range of such possible changes came to be narrower and narrower, until, at the funnel's very bottom, there was no room left at all: henceforth, nothing could be changed.

But as a matter of fact, this great funnel is an illusion. Long before further modifications in the actual words of Scripture became impossible, another means of changing them had been developed, namely, ancient biblical interpretation.

When did ancient biblical interpretation start? The great works outside the Bible that bear witness to its existence and increasing importance—1 Enoch, the book of Jubilees, the Aramaic Levi Document, and others—go back to the third or early second century BCE, but some of the interpretive motifs that they contain surely go back earlier; indeed, the whole process of what is called inner-biblical interpretation leads us back to a considerably earlier date. Then, as the funnel of possible text alterations narrowed, the role of ancient interpreters came to grow correspondingly broader and more important. They continued to modify the meaning of sacred texts, but by different methods.

All ancient interpreters agree on this basic proposition: the words of Scripture may say X, but often what they really mean is Y. On this, scholars and sages of the most diverse schools and loyalties—Philo of Alexandria and Joshua ben Sira, the anonymous authors of the *Temple Scroll* and the Wisdom of Solomon, the *Testaments of the Twelve Patriarchs* and Josephus Flavius—all agree. For them, the Torah was full of hidden teachings: what the words *said* did not necessarily tell you what they *meant*. So, according to these ancient interpreters, God may have said to Adam that "on the day" that he ate from the forbidden tree he would die, but what He meant by *day* was actually "within a thousand years," the length of a single divine day; or else what He meant by *you will die* was not "you will keel over dead," but rather, "you will become a mortal being, a person who dies."[5] Jacob's sons may have spoken to Shechem and his father "falsely," but in this particular case that word (במרמה) really meant "with wisdom."[6] The law in Leviticus 18:21 that says, "You shall not give of your seed to pass over to Molech" might sound as if it is prohibiting the worship of the god Molech through child sacrifice, but what it was really intended to prohibit, according to ancient interpreters, was any marriage between a Jew and a non-Jew.[7] And so on and so forth, through hundreds and hundreds of examples. Thus, without changing a single word of Scripture, it became possible, toward the narrow end of that funnel, to introduce changes exceeding anything that text revisers, even at its wide end, could have dreamed of. In short, starting at least two or three centuries before the common era and continuing throughout the rabbinic period, scriptural texts continued to be modified, sometimes in radical ways. What began in divine revelation continually grew and changed.[8]

---

5 J. Kugel, *Traditions of the Bible* (Cambridge: Harvard University Press, 1998), 94–97, 127.
6 Ibid., 408–9.
7 Ibid., 425–27.
8 I am of course aware of the rabbinic doctrine of two Torahs, the written one that constitutes the books of Genesis through Deuteronomy, and an Oral Torah encompassing all those traditional interpretations and practices not found in the written one. This Oral Torah is said to have been given to Moses simultaneously with the written one, and although transmitted orally, it was ultimately committed to writing in the Mishnah, Tosefta, Jerusalem and Babylonian Talmuds, and so forth. It is not hard to see that this doctrine was designed to extend the canopy of divine revelation from Scripture itself to other traditional practices not mentioned in Scripture; it is, in this sense, the expression of an ideal, an attribution of equal authority to those unwritten practices. This notwithstanding, my aim here, as stated earlier, is to try to describe how revelation actually fits into the larger dynamic of rabbinic Judaism. The transmission of authority from the divine to the human seems to describe what is really there, and this in turn should help us understand the nature and function of revelation itself in Judaism.

THE SIGNIFICANCE OF REVELATION

The well-documented existence of the process that I have just described leads us to that second word in our assignment and a further question: what is the *significance* of revelation in Judaism? The answer is surprising. Obviously, it is not that what has been spoken by God to man is sacrosanct and therefore unalterable in Judaism: quite the opposite is true. To mention just two or three of the most striking examples: God said, "An eye for an eye," whereas rabbinic Judaism says that this verse refers to the obligation of the offender to give the victim monetary compensation for his lost vision, that is, the real meaning of "An eye for an eye" is "*Not* an eye for an eye." God says, "Do not seethe a kid in its mother's milk," whereas the adherents of rabbinic Judaism say, "Did you wipe that dairy dish with the wrong dishtowel?" Most significantly, God says, "You shall not add to what I have said or take anything away from it," whereas that is exactly what rabbinic texts do at almost every turn. So what is the significance of revelation in Judaism? Clearly it is not that the revealed text is always, or even usually, to be taken at its word; the text itself is not all-powerful. Then how are we to describe the true role of divine revelation in Judaism—both in general and in the biblical account of the revelation at Mount Sinai in particular?

I would say that Sage #2—and no less than him, Scripture's most ancient interpreters—conceived of divine revelation as a kind of beginning, the words that had been given by God to humans to guide them, and which were now to be explained and applied.[9] When it comes to *the* revelation, the great promulgation of law at Mount Sinai, its ultimate aim was announced from the start. "If you want to come close to Me," God says (I am rephrasing Exod. 19:5–6), "the only way is to become My employee, that is, to do what I command you." This is what is called in Hebrew *'avodat ha-Shem*, the service of God, and it is the great message of the Torah, I should say, its great *revelation*. But if this process starts in divine revelation, it must eventually make its way from highest heaven to right down here, to be interpreted and implemented on earth. As a famous rabbinic dictum asserted about the Torah (characteristically distorting the apparent meaning of a biblical verse), לא בשמים היא.[10] Although given on high, the Torah is *no longer* in heaven. To put it another way, the divinely revealed Torah is Volume 1 in a great, multivolume work entitled, *How to Serve God*. And while it is crucially important that Volume 1 will have come to us מפי הגבורה, from the very mouth of God, it is equally important to realize that Volume 1

---

9 An early snapshot of this process: Neh. 8: 7–8.
10 Deut. 30:12, as cited in b. Baba Metzi'a 59b.

is not the last word, but the first, the sacred beginning. What starts in heaven is ultimately given over into the hands of ordinary, or extraordinary, human beings. This handoff, from the divine to the human, is embodied in the compositional and textual history of various biblical books as well as in the emergence, and growing power, of ancient biblical interpretation in Second Temple times; but these are merely surface manifestations of what lies at the very heart of the Jewish conception of divine revelation, and far from being embarrassed by it, our rabbis championed it and celebrated it.

Thus, it is precisely this handoff that allowed rabbinic exegesis in a thousand places to overrule the plain meaning of the Torah's words; I do not believe that there is any other way to construe the evidence. But it is equally important to understand that what created this handoff was precisely the fact just mentioned, that from the start it was *'avodat ha-Shem*, the service of God, which was conceived to be the guiding purpose of the great revelation at Sinai. Even the Torah, our most sacred text, could thus be (and was) subordinated to it; time and again, its apparent meaning was modified in furtherance of this cause, to pin down the details of (and frequently, to elaborate and expand) the Torah's way for us to come before God as His servants. By the same token, it was this handoff that gave over to human authorities, and human frailty, the power to overrule not only Scripture, but also the divine voice itself.

There is no need here to repeat the famous Talmudic story of the dispute over the oven of Akhnai, whereby all manner of miraculous events and even a voice from heaven are overcome by a simple majority vote of rabbinic sages.[11] But an equally striking instance of this same principle is to be found in a matter rarely associated with it, namely, our Hebrew calendar.[12] Unlike the leaders of other forms of Judaism that existed in Second Temple times, the predecessors of rabbinic Judaism assigned the authority of determining the Hebrew calendar—and hence, of determining the start of each new month—not to eternal mathematical formulae or to the divinely established and unchanging cycles of the sun's movement through the sky, but to the altogether fallible testimony of any two witnesses who, having sighted the thin sliver of the new moon on the evening following the 29th day of the month, reported to a place called *Beit Ya'azek* in Jerusalem to be interrogated by a rabbinical court about what exactly they saw.

---

11 B. T. Bava Mezia 59b.
12 The Torah itself does not specify what sort of calendar it assumes when speaking of "the first month," "the seventh month," "the beginnings of months," etc. Some Second Temple–period Jews, such as the sectarians of the Dead Sea Scrolls or the author of the book of Jubilees, adopted a basically sun-based calendar in which months were arbitrary units with no connection to the phases of the moon.

Again, far from being embarrassed by this blatantly human process (and more pointedly, by this transfer of divine authority to mere humans), rabbinic Judaism actually glories in this fact, asserting on each Rosh Hodesh that God has established the laws of the New Month for Israel to apply on its own and without divine revelation, "Blessed are You, who have sanctified Israel and [so enabled us to sanctify] the beginnings of months." These are words worth pondering.

THE GREAT CHAIN OF TRADITION

To sum up, then: direct, divine-to-human revelation officially ended in biblical times, but it continues to be the basis on which all later Judaism stands. In particular, the Torah—the greatest instance of divine revelation in Judaism—is everywhere present today in Jewish piety: it is studied unceasingly by children and adults, cited daily in prayers, and read aloud from beginning to end in a yearly cycle of public readings. But the giving of the Torah, and as well the other acts of direct speech from God to Israel's prophets that followed, are all in the past; a new act of revelation can never exercise any normative role in Judaism. What is more, the Torah itself is read and understood through the lens of rabbinic exegesis, regarded as the definitive interpretation of its words. This interpretation is, like revelation itself, essentially closed nowadays, at least in regard to halakhic practice; it is subject to some further elaboration but may not be overthrown or ignored. In this respect, rabbinic interpretation may be said to have the same authority as divine revelation (indeed, even greater authority in practice, as I have explained).

In short: I believe that this "handoff" from divine to human authority has always been inherent in the very notion of revelation in Judaism. It is evidenced first in the textual history of different biblical books (whose history of development will lead us far back into biblical times) and later in the growing importance of biblical interpretation in the Second Temple period, which ultimately led to the great rabbinic corpus of Talmud and midrash. This interpretive tradition of the Torah is, as we have glimpsed, often at odds with the apparent meaning of its own words, freely modifying or supplementing their plain sense. Why should this be so? I believe that its authority ultimately derives from the underlying theme that characterizes both the Torah and its interpretive tradition, namely, the service of God; indeed, it is because this theme was from the beginning the highest goal of Judaism that the divine word could be, and was, willfully interpreted and supplemented, enabling the service of God to enter into nearly every aspect of human existence.

The closed-but-ongoing nature of both divine revelation and definitive interpretation is well captured in a particular bit of rabbinic midrash. The description of the Sinai revelation in the book of Exodus is reprised in Chapter 5 of Deuteronomy. But there, unlike the account in Exodus, the text of the Ten Commandments is followed by the assertion that God spoke those words to the people at Mount Sinai, "קול גדול ולא יסף—" in a mighty voice that …" Well, about the meaning this last word יסף there was some dispute among rabbinic sages. Some held that the word meant "add" or "continue," as if from the root *w-s-f*, whereas others held that it meant quite the opposite, "cease," as if from the root *s-w-f*. Which was right?[13]

> Said R. Isaac: That which the prophets in every generation were destined to prophesy they received at Mt. Sinai, for this is what Moses said to the people of Israel: "[Not with you alone am I concluding this covenant,] but both with those who are present here, standing with us today … and with those who are not present here with us today" (Deut 29:13–14). The latter [part of the verse] does not say "*standing* with us today," but merely "with us today," for these are the souls of those who were yet to be created; "standing" could not be said of them since they had no [physical] substance. Yet even though they did not exist at that time, every one of them received his portion [at Sinai] … And not only did all the prophets themselves receive their prophecies at Mount Sinai, but likewise all the sages who have been and who are yet to be, as it says, "The Lord spoke these words to all your assembly, a mighty voice that did not cease/continue." (*Shemot Rabba*, 28:6, cf. *Midrash Tanhuma*, *Yitro* 11)

As mentioned, a great ambiguity surrounds this last sentence, but I like to think that both senses of יסף were somehow to be kept in mind. That is, God spoke this one time and no more; the Sinai revelation was *the* one great act of divine

---

13 See Targum *Onqelos* on Num. 11:25 and Deut. 5:19, versus Targum *Onqelos* on Gen. 38:26, along with the discussion of יסף in b. Sota 10b, Sanhedrin 17a, and parallels. Each side of the debate had a point: if יסף meant "add" or "continue," then why should the Torah have said in the story of Eldad and Medad that when the spirit of God fell upon the seventy elders, they prophesied *and did not* continue [ויתנבאו ולא יספו] (Num. 11:25)"? Shouldn't it be that they prophesied *and did not cease*, as implied later on? On the other hand, after Judah discovered that he had had sexual relations with his daughter-in-law, why should the text have said that Judah "*did not cease* to have relations with her [ולא יסף עוד לדעתה] (Gen. 38:26)"? Shouldn't that be "*did not continue*"? Of course, each side had its counterarguments.

revelation, never to be repeated or equaled. In this sense, direct revelation ended when God "did not continue" but ceased speaking that very day at Mount Sinai. But the divine voice that started in heaven made its way down to earth, and all the words that followed, despite their coming *after* that one great revelation, nonetheless partook of its essence; they acquired their content and their authority from Sinai. To put it another way, since all future prophets and sages were present in spirit when the Torah was first given, what each of them said, however new or different it might appear, had been handed off to them at Mount Sinai. It is in this sense that one might also say that what began at Sinai has never ceased; in each generation, prophets and sages have arisen to attest to what they heard on that long ago day.

CHAPTER 5

Divine Hiddenness and Human Input: The Potential Contribution of a Postmodern View of Revelation to Yitz Greenberg's Holocaust Theology

TAMAR ROSS

The challenges that biblical criticism and the atrocities of the Holocaust pose, respectively, to traditional notions of revelation and theodicy are arguably the two greatest obstacles of our age to commonly accepted notions of Orthodox Jewish belief. Both involve the confrontation of metaphysical assertions with contrary empiric evidence of such scope or magnitude that all the usual tactics of religious apologetics appear inadequate. In the following essay, I would like to point to certain commonalities between an approach that I have been developing to the first issue and the response that Greenberg has been developing with regard to the second. I will then propose that some shortcomings in Greenberg's position (which he himself acknowledges) might be overcome if he were to adopt the implications of this parallelism in full.

I

Revelation has conventionally been understood in Judaism as the eruption of a transcendent God into the historic reality in order to convey a timeless message for humanity at large and the Jewish people in particular. The significance of this picture of revelation as emanating from an all-knowing God that stands over and above human weaknesses and fallibilities has been to bestow absolute authority to the way of life that has been developed on the basis of His original message.

Jewish thought has always provided some qualifications and nuances to an overliteral understanding of this statement, which left room for acknowledging the influence of shifting historical circumstances and subjective human input.[1] Loyalty to the system, however, especially in times of perceived threat, appears to mandate tying on our ideological loincloths more tightly. It is at such times that we most often hear strident statements of faith dogmatically professing commitment to an eternal and unchanging Torah with exhaustively predefined parameters.[2]

The latest instance of this dynamic can be perceived in the sharply dogmatic turn that Orthodox Judaism has taken since the nineteenth century. Previous to this, premodern Jewish society was secure in its unquestioning acceptance of tradition as no less a primary source of authority than its canonized texts. The more relaxed, pragmatic, and nonideological religious climate that then prevailed still characterizes traditional Sephardic Jewish communities less affected by modernity. In contrast, today's Orthodoxy represents a deliberate response both to a historicist approach, which views Judaism as shaped by external events and influences, and to the threat that the forces of modernity and its values have posed to the authority of halakhah.

Admittedly, Orthodox Judaism is not all of one ilk—in our day it encompasses segments continuing the legacy of Hungarian ultra-Orthodoxy, eastern European Hasidism and Mitnagdism, and German neo-Orthodoxy, as well as native American Orthodoxy of various stripes, Israeli religious Zionists,

---

1 For an extensive collection of sources substantiating this claim, see Yoshi Fargeon, "Wisdom and Science Is Granted unto Thee," in *Be-einei Elohim ve-Adam: He-Adam Ha-maamin u-Mehkar ha-Mikra*, ed. Yehuda Brandes, Tova Ganzel, and Hayuta Deutsch (Jerusalem: Bet Morasha, 2015), 17–162.

2 Jay Michael Harris has written a masterly historical survey of this dynamic: *How Do We Know This? Midrash and the Fragmentation of Modern Judaism* (Albany: SUNY Press, 1995).

etc. But, uniting all these groups, despite their differences, is the shift from traditionalism to modernity. The conscious, self-reflexive, conservative formulation of Judaism that constitutes Orthodoxy is—even in its anti-modernist formulations—a uniquely modern phenomenon.[3] Precisely because of this shift, it has come about that, especially since the nineteenth century, Orthodox spokesmen have typically promoted a view of revelation as the transmission of a rigid and static body of content, impervious to outside influences and considerations.

While a maximalist view of revelation was originally voiced only by the most extreme elements of Orthodoxy and eschewed by most learned traditionalists as oversimplified and, in some instances, simply false, at present it enjoys widespread support in more popular renditions of ultra-Orthodox ideology. This view has also been advanced in more moderate form even within the ranks of modern Orthodoxy, particularly as articulated in the United States. Thus we are told by Rabbi David Bleich, a Rosh Yeshiva at Rabbi Isaac Elchanan Theological Seminary (RIETS) and a prominent exponent of Centrist Orthodox ideology: "Normative Judaism teaches that Halakhah is not derived from any temporal 'worldview' or 'social situation' but expresses the transcendental worldview of the divine Lawgiver."[4] Because the Torah is not bound to any contemporary ethos, it "possesses an enduring validity which, while applicable to changing circumstances, is not subject to change by lobbying or by the exertion of pressure in any guise or form. Nor may independently held convictions, however sincere, be allowed to influence our interpretation of Halakhah."[5]

The widespread acceptance of this stance can be attributed largely to the powerful influence of the late Rabbi Joseph B. Soloveitchik. In a unique amalgam of "the Brisker method" founded by his grandfather, which viewed the development of the Oral law as a self-contained system shaped exclusively by its own internal logic and procedural rules, and neo-Kantian philosophy, which regards science as the product of a humanly formed system of categories, R. Soloveitchik understood the abstract concepts of Brisk as ideal categories

---

3 Michael Silber, "The Emergence of Ultra-Orthodoxy: The Invention of a Tradition," in *The Uses of Tradition: Jewish Continuity in the Modern Era*, ed. Jack Wertheimer (New York: Jewish Theological Seminary, 1994), 26n4; see also Jacob Katz, "Orthodoxy in Historical Perspective," in *Studies in Contemporary Jewry*, ed. Peter Y. Medding (Bloomington: Indiana University Press, 1986), 2, 3–6; Moshe S. Samet, "The Beginnings of Orthodoxy," *Modern Judaism* 8 (1988): 249–69.
4 David Bleich, *Contemporary Halakhic Problems*, vol. 1 (New York: Ktav, 1977), 83.
5 Ibid.

that serve as the only legitimate methodological tool for approaching the inner spiritual reality that halakhah is meant to render concrete. As in mathematics, these categories have a priori status. Their definitions are absolute, eternal, and not to be equated with historic, ideological, or moral interpretations that have accrued to them. Nor do they come to serve any value external to themselves. In subjugating himself to the norms of halakhah, "Halakhic Man" (the title of Soloveitchik's famous essay on this topic)[6] discovers and internalizes the ideal values and principles that are embedded in the Torah and realizes them to the best of his ability in the imperfect universe he inhabits. As R. Soloveitchik's son, Professor Haym Soloveitchik, concludes: "If law is conceived of as religious law must be, as a revelation of the divine will, then any attempt to align that will with human wants, any attempt to have reality control rather than to be itself controlled by the divine norm, is an act of blasphemy and is inconceivable to a God-fearing man."[7]

Such a pristine view of revelation breeds an ethos of unquestioning obedience to those elements of the Torah that are preordained and absolute. The ideal of religious behavior is epitomized most succinctly in the model of the *Akedah*, according to which Abraham unquestioningly subjected his natural human desires to the objectified standards of the divine will. This view comports with the assumption of rigid and stable notions of truth that are capable of being supported by a universal, neutral, and objective rationality that serves as their justification, an assumption that has characterized modernist thinking since the age of the Enlightenment.

II

The Soloveitchikian understanding of divine revelation has encountered increasing challenges over the past few decades, with the growing exposure of a younger generation of modern Orthodox students and scholars to the findings of biblical criticism. Critical readings of the biblical text are, of course, not unique to our times. Nevertheless, the intensity and depth of the problems these raise have increased exponentially in the wake of recent developments in science, technology, literary analysis, epistemology, and hermeneutic theory. Beyond the usual difficulties (erroneous or fallible content, questionable

---

6 Joseph B. Soloveitchik, *Halakhic Man* (Philadelphia: Jewish Publication Society, 1983).
7 Haym Soloveitchik, "Religious Law and Change," *AJS Review: The Journal of the Association for Jewish Studies* 12, no. 8 (Fall 1987): 205.

morality, and textual evidence of evolutionary historical development), the postmodern contention that all knowledge is "situated" (i.e., framed by the observer's prior values, expectations, and standards)—as evidenced, for example, in the feminist critique—has most recently problematized the very notion of divine revelation as verbal communication, given that language itself now appears to be so pervasively rooted in a particular perspective and cultural bias.[8]

While circles emanating from Yeshiva University that regard themselves as continuing the Soloveitchikian legacy have been overwhelmingly opposed to addressing such issues, the climate of discourse among religious academicians and even some of the more liberal Yeshiva circles in Israel has been more hospitable to efforts at candid confrontation.[9] This has partly to do with some obvious political differences between the situation of Orthodoxy in Israel and that of the Diaspora. For example, as opposed to Modern Orthodoxy in North America, its counterpart in Israel is more clearly demarcated from ultra-Orthodox circles and therefore less affected by its opinions. Moreover, official Orthodoxy in Israel is characterized by a weak rabbinate facing a religious literate laity that has greater confidence in its ability to make independent judgments. Another factor is the lack of urgency in Israel to create ideological borders between the Conservative and Reform movements. But a final element that might contribute to this openness is the difference between the submissive theocentric temper of Rabbi Soloveitchik's theology of divine–human relations that has dominated the American scene, and a more nuanced variety of monotheism promoted by Rabbi A. I. Kook, whose general worldview has had a dominant influence on the ideological orientation of religious Zionist circles in Israel.

Many elements in R. Kook's theology revive the more fluid views of revelation that were developed in premodern times. His immersion in the mystic tradition and its panentheistic image of God discourages positing God and His word as distinct from the flow of history and natural morality.[10] It also leads him to a view of truth which is remarkably sympathetic to the postmodern critique of sterile, fixed, and universal truths that purport to reflect a neutral and objective view "from nowhere," and to the celebration of conflict as a trigger to

---

8 For further elaboration, see Tamar Ross, *Expanding the Palace of Torah: Orthodoxy and Feminism* (Waltham, MA: Brandeis University Press, 2004), 139–42, 184–7.
9 As exemplified by *Be-einei Elohim ve-Adam*, and some publications produced by educators associated with Yeshivat Har Etzion.
10 See Ross, *Expanding the Palace*, 205–7.

spiritual advancement.[11] Such factors arguably place him in a better position when contending with the findings of biblical criticism and postmodern epistemology. While R. Kook did not set out these elements of his thought in the form of a systematic theology of revelation, a response that resonates various strands of his thought has greater chance of success in an age of increasing awareness of the human and fallible character of what is purportedly a divine text.

III

In some of my own writing, I have attempted to develop the bare bones of such a response.[12] Such a project, I suggest, involves two stages:

1. At the first stage, when viewing revelation from within tradition, we must try to achieve an understanding that is as coherent as possible on its own terms. This is accomplished by breaking down the distinction between divine speech and the natural historic process and recognizing that God does not speak through vocal chords but through the orchestration of history and the evolution of human understanding that develops in its wake. Aside from avoiding gross anthropomorphisms, if we are to understand God's word as conveying a message for all generations, its transmission cannot be limited to a one-time event, but must be understood as a process. This process began with the formal canonization of the Torah and its acceptance by the Jewish people as the primary filter through which the authorized beliefs and practices of Judaism are determined. It continues, however, with the cumulative interpretations that accrue to this text, inevitably informing and altering its meaning in light of the ever-changing historical contexts in which it is read. Viewed religiously, these contexts—no less than the original text—may likewise be regarded as an ongoing revelation of the divine word, constantly refining its meaning in light

---

11 Tamar Ross, "The Cognitive Value of Religious Truth Claims: Rabbi A. I. Kook and Postmodernism," in *Hazon Nahum: Jubilee Volume in Honor of Norman Lamm* (New York: Yeshiva University Press, 1997), 479–527.

12 See Tamar Ross, "Orthodoxy and the Challenge of Biblical Criticism: Some Reflections on the Importance of Asking the Right Question," available in English at http://thetorah.com/the-challenge-of-biblical-criticism, and in Hebrew in *Be-einei Elohim ve-Adam*, 242–88. An abbreviated version of this article was published in *Journal of Modern Jewish Studies* 14, no. 1 (March 2015): 6–26. For explication of this approach in a feminist context, see Ross, *Expanding the Palace*, 193–224.

of new surrounding circumstances. As a result, the Torah can be understood as all human (in terms of its literary and historical genesis) and all divine (in terms of its origin, value, and significance) at one and the same time.

Orthodox believers generally recoil from historical, sociological, anthropological, or psychological explanations of key customs and tenets. In their eyes, any suggestion of the influence of historical circumstances or comparison with surrounding cultures of the times is anathema. Yet this view of revelation through history manages to turn the reductionist conclusions of historicism and the external observer on their head, as if to say: "Of course revelation is influenced by history and the evolution of ideas (even when such ideas or their parallels are to be found in non-Jewish sources), but history and the evolution of ideas themselves are also the tools of revelation!"

As opposed to the more common attitude within Orthodoxy, R. Kook's acknowledgment of the influence of historical circumstances on Judaism takes into account not only the need to struggle against negative aspects of culture at large but also the absorption and refinement of whatever positive elements it has to offer. Indeed, a hallmark of R. Kook's positive attitude to secularism is the understanding that revolutionary and ostensibly destructive developments in the world of ideas are the most significant tools of all, for these are a clear indication that humanity has outgrown more primitive forms of spirituality and is ready for a new, more sublime level.[13] Taken in this spirit, we might conclude that even the challenges of biblical criticism in our day can be regarded as a rare privilege and a new revelation of the divine will. Divine providence itself has orchestrated the rise of serious problems with Torah as history so as to lead us, and all of humankind with us, to a new and more subtle understanding of the relationship between divine intent and human interpretation, which acknowledges the decisive role of human input. We do not doubt God when we walk through this threshold. We are listening to God as we go forward, for this too was from God.[14]

---

13 This idea appears in many of his writings. See, for example, A. I. Kook, *Orot ha-Emunah* (Brooklyn, NY: Langsam Associates, 1985), 48, 74–5.
14 History as a medium of revelation is a dominant theme in R. Kook's thought. For one example of contemporary writing, beyond my own, which builds on this view, see Daniel Shalit, *Ohr Shivat Yamim* (Jerusalem: Sifriyat Beit El, 1998). Although Shalit, a returnee to

2. Viewing our internal religious talk from a more universal perspective, however, leads to a second, more radical, stage in the development of a contemporary theology of revelation. Appropriating some of the insights of postmodern theory regarding language and its uses, we understand that equating professions of belief in divine revelation with factual descriptions entails a misconception of the role of such statements in the religious context. It is this misconception that has led to the bankruptcy of a modernist *Torah u-madda* approach, which regards religion as a rival source of knowledge vying with science. Instead, we now understand that the primary concern of such statements is not to discuss facts or establish history, but rather to function on an entirely different plane—appropriating a system of symbols and "picture" of reality that legitimate our most basic patterns of thought, feeling, and behavior, and signaling to our coreligionists that we share the same ultimate loyalties.

Despite his staunch traditionalism, this revolutionary shift from the conventional understanding of truth as corresponding to some objective reality "out there" also has significant parallels in R. Kook's writings, which reveal a remarkably tentative attitude to religious truth claims. R. Kook's skepticism is founded on the mystic's presumption of a built-in contradiction between finite human perceptions and God's monolithic all-encompassing infinity that transcends all definitions and distinctions.[15]

There is, admittedly, a deep divide between the mystic's call for epistemological modesty and a modern or postmodern rejection of metaphysics altogether. In R. Kook's thought, such modesty relates to a modern school of Kabbalah, known as the allegorical interpreters of the doctrine of *zimzum* (contraction), whose core idea provides an essential key to his entire worldview and

---

Orthodox observance, hardly mentions R. Kook explicitly, the intricate historic scheme which lies at the heart of his thesis reveals the pervasive influence of Kook's view of history and its application to feminism. See also Jerome Yehuda Gellman, *This Was from God: A Contemporary Theology of Torah and History* (Brighton, MA: Academic Studies Press, 2016), whose response to the historicist critique of biblical accuracy similarly reflects the influence of Kook's theology, capitalizing on the revelatory properties of history and on assumption of divine accommodationalism as important avenues of rapprochement with the critical insights of modernity.

15 A. I. Kook, "Suffering Cleanses," in *Orot* (Jerusalem: Mosad Harav Kook, 1963), 124–5.

its remarkably pantheistic thrust.[16] According to these latter-day mystics, the Lurianic assumption of God's need to contract His infinite being, in order to make space for a finite world that is other than He, is not to be understood literally, as an actual physical displacement and creation of a void. Instead, it should be taken as a metaphor for the concealment of an aspect of God's all-pervasive unity, thereby enabling an illusory realm of appearance. This understanding brings R. Kook to regard all truth claims as inadequate in principle and ultimately false, leaving them to be judged by a pragmatic spiritual standard that is very reminiscent of postmodern instrumentalism.[17]

While R. Kook employs the metaphysical language of tradition, the authority of revelation does not derive on his formulation from the "fact" that God gave us the Torah, but rather on strength of *kabbalat ha-umma*, which means the willingness of the Jewish people to accept it as such,[18] and the obvious spiritual benefits of this acceptance.[19] Even the notion of divine providence in the sense of an almighty God controlling affairs from above appears to be a "necessary truth,"[20] useful for developing our urge for perfection, rather than a "true truth" that exists independently of human needs. The realization that even such partial glimpses of the divine are encompassed in its infinite totality and provide us with indispensable tools for breaking down distinctions between the godly and the human, the holy and the profane, lends them their validity.[21]

---

16 For further elaboration, see Tamar Ross, "The Concept of G-d in the Thought of Harav Kook—Part I" [in Hebrew], *Daat* 8 (Summer 1982): 109–28; "The Concept of G-d in the Thought of Harav Kook—Part II" [in Hebrew], *Daat* (Winter 1983): 39–70; and "The Place of the Lurianic Doctrine of Zimzum in the Thought of Harav Kook" [in Hebrew], in *Mechkarim b'Hagut Yehudit*, ed. Moshe Idel and Sarah Heller-Wilensky (Jerusalem: Magnes Press, 1989), 159–72.
17 Ross, "The Cognitive Value."
18 A. I. Kook, *Eder ha-Yakar* (Jerusalem: Mosad ha-Rav Kook, 1985), 39; *Iggerot ha-Ra'yah I* (Jerusalem: Mosad ha-Rav Kook, 1985), 193–4; see also *Arpelei Tohar* (Jerusalem: Hamachon al shem Harav Zvi Yehuda Kook, 1983), 78, for a more essentialist twist to this argument.
19 A. I. Kook, *Iggerot ha-Ra'yah I* (Jerusalem: Mosad ha-Rav Kook, 1985), 48–9.
20 *Iggerot ha-Ra'yah I*, 106–7. For explication of Kook's understanding of necessary truths, see Ross, "The Cognitive Value," 491–6.
21 *Orot*, 124–5; *Iggrot Ha-Reayah I*, 47–8.

IV

Although Greenberg occasionally alludes to the challenge of historicism and biblical criticism,[22] the bulk of his thought is far more focused on the challenge to religious belief as epitomized by the Holocaust. The main question that he asks is not whether the Torah account of revelation as a divine message can be true in light of its human imprints, but rather: Can we still believe in the existence of a God who is omnipotent, benign, and just after the massive genocide conducted by the Nazis?

As Greenberg is well aware, post-Holocaust theology has produced a huge literature on the subject, ranging from the attempt to justify even the enormity of this evil as retribution for some deserved sin to foregoing any attempt at response, appealing to the limitations of human understanding.[23] Despite their virtuosity, each of these classic answers has evoked penetrating criticism.

Greenberg's ultimate solution to the problem appears to combine a notion of God's deliberate silence with the idea that such curtailment is the necessary means for a greater good. Similarly to David Hartman,[24] Greenberg suggests that God's abdication of responsibility in the case of the Holocaust signifies a critical rupture of His original covenant with the Jews. According to that covenant, God was committed to preserving the Jewish destiny in return for our commitment to observe His mitzvot as a means for progressing towards *tikkun olam*, liberation and redemption. However, Greenberg notes, ever since the original agreement established at Sinai, God's role has gradually diminished, shifting greater responsibility to the people of Israel in perfecting the world.

---

22 See, for example, Irving (Yitzhak) Greenberg, "Two Doors Rabbi Soloveitchik Walked Through but Did Not Open: The Future of Modern Orthodoxy," in *Rav ba-Olam ha-Hadash: Iyunnim be-hashpa'ato shel ha-Rav Soloveitchik al Tarbut, al Hinukh, ve-al Mahshava Yehudit*, ed. Avinoam Rosenak and Naftali Rothenberg (Jerusalem: Magnes/Van Leer, 2010), 245–77, available in English typescript at http://rabbiirvinggreenberg.com/wp-content/uploads/2014/06/Two-Doors-reduced.pdf.

23 For two anthologies surveying the range of theological responses, see: *Holocaust Theology A Reader*, comp. and ed. Dan Cohn-Shertok (Exeter, UK: University of Exeter Press, 2002); *Wrestling with God: Jewish Theological Responses During and After the Holocaust*, ed. Steven T. Katz, Shlomo Biderman, and Gershon Greenberg (Oxford: Oxford University Press, 2007).

24 See David Hartman, *A Living Covenant: The Innovative Spirit in Traditional Judaism* (New York: The Free Press, 1985), particularly 256–77. For a brief discussion of the similarities and differences between Greenberg's and Hartman's views regarding various stages in the development of the covenantal relationship between God and Israel, see Ehud Luz, "Zionism, History, and Demythologization," in *Mehuyavut Yehudit Mithadeshet: al Olamo ve-Haguto shel David Hartman*, vol. I, ed. Avi Sagi and Tzvi Zohar, 337–8.

Instead of understanding God's *hester panim* as a temporary punishment, it should now be understood as a necessary means for ensuring human freedom; our autonomy grows in direct proportion to God's hiding.[25]

In light of this claim, Greenberg traces the development of Jewish independence throughout history from the biblical era, in which God functions as the senior partner who responds directly to our behavior in terms of punishment or reward, to the withdrawal of divine intervention with the destruction of the Second Temple and the concomitant cessation of prophecy, and finally to the stage where God's absolute hiddenness shifts all responsibility for the destiny of creation to human initiative and freedom of choice. The Holocaust marks the culmination of this process. Now that God's presence has become totally hidden, the Jewish people must undertake full responsibility for the realization of history's Messianic goals. Such gradualism is manifested even in the nature of the Jewish festivals, which began with commemoration of the miraculous events of the desert, but morphed into celebration of the more naturalistic victories of Hanukkah and Purim, leading finally to the more "secular" accomplishments of Yom Ha-atzmaut and the founding of the Jewish state.[26]

V

Despite the difference in focus, some striking parallels arise from this initial sketch of Greenberg's treatment of the Holocaust and the approach I have suggested for resolving modern and postmodern challenges to the belief in divine revelation. In both cases, the solution appears to lie at the outset in dissolving the sharp dichotomy between the divine and the human by acknowledging the expanding role of human input. And in both cases, the form and degree of God's revelation appear to calibrate in accordance with the nature and pace of human maturation. Indeed, Greenberg's account of the various stages in the

---

25 See Irving Greenberg, "Cloud of Smoke, Pillar of Fire: Judaism, Christianity and Modernity after the Holocaust," in *Auschwitz: Beginning of a New Era? Reflections on the Holocaust*, ed. Eva Fleischner (New York: Ktav, 1977), 7–55, 441–6; "The Third Great Cycle in Jewish History," in *Perspectives* (New York: Clal-National Jewish Resource Center, September 1981); "Voluntary Covenant," in *Perspectives* (New York: Clal-National Jewish Resource Center, September 1982); republished in *Wrestling with God: Jewish Theological Responses during and after the Holocaust*, ed. Steven T. Katz, Shlomo Biderman, and Gershon Greenberg (Oxford: Oxford University Press, 2007), 499–523, 523–43, and 543–55, respectively.
26 Irving Greenberg, *The Jewish Way: Living the Holidays* (New York: Touchstone, 1988).

development of Jewish autonomy shares several features with a comparable periodization of Jewish history central to R. Kook's thought.[27]

Such resemblances testify to common ground between us with regard to my first move, in acknowledging the critical role that historical process and shifting contexts play in the effort of determining what the divine will is. However, I find it difficult to determine from Greenberg's current phrasing of the matter to what extent we continue to be in sync with regard to the second, more radical move that I make when attempting to view this internal religious narrative through more universal spectacles. In other words, I am not quite sure of the degree to which Greenberg regards his theological account (which views the gradual move from the supernatural to the natural as a deliberate, divinely initiated pedagogical device) as the unequivocal reflection of an inescapable, objective metaphysical truth, or as an optional narrative that *we*, as religious believers, are now free to develop in order to make some sense of it all.

Greenberg certainly does not appropriate the second, more radical, step of attributing his God-talk solely to human perceptions explicitly. In this connection, however, it is worth noting that Greenberg's notion of God's recession from history has undergone several revisions over the years. Initially (as formulated in "Cloud of Smoke") he characterized the status of his more conventional religious belief in God's omnipresence as "moment faith."[28] This was because his ability to sustain the traditional confidence in God's manifest presence in history and His fulfillment of the Messianic promise of redemption still functioned at least part of the time, although it was challenged by other moments in which this position no longer seemed credible.

The second stage of his thought (as evidenced in "The Third Great Cycle of Jewish History" and in "Voluntary Covenant")[29] was marked by a shift to the notion of voluntary covenant. At this point, Greenberg regarded God's nonintervention during the Holocaust more provocatively, as a blatant breach of His covenant with the Jewish people which released them from the obligation to uphold their share of the bargain. This led him to view continued operation of

---

27 See, for example, R. Kook, "Regarding the Ideational Development of Israel," *Orot* (Jerusalem: Mosad Harav Kook, 1963), 102–18; and *Orot ha-Emunah*, ed. Moshe Gurevitz (Jerusalem: Me-Alef ve-ad Taf and Langsam, 1985), 66–7, in which he views the historical development of Judaism as moving from submission motivated by fear of punishment to self-motivation and worship out of love. See a parallel development of this theme in Greenberg's *Triumph of Life*.
28 Greenberg, "Cloud of Smoke," 27, 33.
29 Supra, n25.

the broken covenant as merely a function of the Jewish people's willingness to voluntarily take over God's responsibility for preserving the Jewish future via their struggle to establish an independent Jewish state.

A third level of understanding comes to the fore in Greenberg's more recent thought, as developed during the past two decades in *Partnership for Life* and *The Triumph of Life*.[30] Instead of regarding God's nonintervention during the Holocaust as an inexplicable violation of His promise, he now regards God's original formulation of the covenant, as well as His subsequent behavior, more charitably—as an intentionally staged mechanism whose ultimate goal from the very beginning was to lead the Jewish people to a level of maturity that would allow them to assume full responsibility for *tikkun olam* (world repair) on their own. Such commitment from the human end would no longer be driven by hope of reward or fear of punishment. Divine retribution, as evidenced in the early period of our national history and typified by miraculous intervention on Israel's behalf, or even in later stages when such intervention was less obvious and concealed by convergence with natural causes, was—much like that of a benevolent parent—simply a pedagogic tool to wean His children off dependence and train them to be more active and mature in determining their destiny. Ultimately, the object of this exercise was to lead to Israel's assumption of full responsibility for their fate and for redemption of the world at large.[31] Such commitment would now be driven not by narrow calculations of self-interest, but rather by the nobler motive of love.

The point that strikes me most in Greenberg's theological trajectory is his painful awareness of some measure of inadequacy in each of his suggested solutions. Indeed, the tortured attempt of most Holocaust theologians to cover all bases has always conjured up for me the proverbial tale of the tailor, who responded to the complaint of his customer that the right sleeve of the suit he had ordered was too short by suggesting that he raise his left shoulder. When that resulted in exposure of the waist, the customer was advised hunch his back,

---

30 These two works, still in manuscript form, are currently being prepared for publication.
31 It is worth noting that similar ideas regarding the evolution from evident to hidden miracle as an educational device leading towards a more refined form of religiosity might be implied in Nachmanides's distinction between *nes galui*, *nes mefursam*, and *nes nistar*—see his commentary to Numbers 26:11, Exodus 13:16. (For further elaboration of this position, see Tamar Ross, "Miracle as an Added Dimension in Maharal's Thought," *Daat* [Summer 1986]: 84.) According to Nachmanides, however, the final lesson to be learned from the passage from blatant miracle to conduct of the world that is more compatible with natural law is not the obligation of humans to take independent control of their destiny, but rather that God lies even behind the ostensibly mundane and ordinary.

and so on. Eventually, when the customer left the shop, passersby whispered to each other: "Look at the beautiful suit the tailor produced. What a pity the customer is crippled!"

In a similar vein, the wish to avoid such contortions appears to move Greenberg to still retain something of his original notion of moment theology, even as he continues to fine-tune his earlier responses. On his own admission, the percentages he allocates to each type of moment belief shift from stage to stage.[32] Even in his most recent formulations, Greenberg can never bring himself to commit to one solution as comprehensive and absolute.[33] In retrospect, "the insight of the Holocaust taken at full blast" drives him to now generalize and conclude that "*all* truths are moment truths"[34] (emphasis mine), and that all the "human-implicated Absolutes" that typify the grandiose assumptions of modernity must now be reduced and made partial, or "broken."[35] But does this stance of epistemological modesty indicate a readiness on Greenberg's part to disassociate his theology from ontology altogether, and to link his commitment to its covenantal demands to a more "ironic" (in the Rortian sense)[36] view of their ultimate truth value?

bVI

Some support for the latter possibility may be teased out of a passage in Greenberg's introduction to his new book, *Partnership for Life*, where he makes a telling statement regarding a transformation that he underwent in his understanding of the value of ideas in general and religious doctrine in particular, once he left academia and entered the "real" world:

> For the first time in my life, I had to meet a payroll. I was stunned to discover how many brilliant ideas lost their luster in the daylight of reality. After a while, I concluded that a key measure of a truly great idea was how

---

32 Irving Greenberg, "Theology after the Shoah: The Transformation of the Core Paradigm," *Modern Judaism: A Journal of Jewish Ideas and Experience* 26, no. 3 (October 2006): 228.
33 Ibid.
34 Ibid., 227.
35 Ibid., 218.
36 See Richard Rorty, *Contingency, Irony and Solidarity* (New York: Cambridge University Press, 1989). An ironic stance in this sense does not imply cynicism, but rather a rejection of the understanding of truth claims as the mental mirroring of a mind-external world, preferring to view them in pragmatic terms.

it worked in real life. … I began to revise my criteria for judging the value of ideas.

When this insight became central to my understanding, I finally grasped that the Torah was not a book of intellectual reflections. Nor was it a law code or a set of doctrines. At its core, the Torah offers a vision of a paradise on Earth—and how to go about perfecting the real world in order to get there.[37]

Such reflections led Greenberg to conclude that "the message of the Jewish narrative is best described as a *hope*." Ultimately, the test of its "truth" is pragmatic:

> A hope is judged by whether it is realized and how it works in the reality. … Thus [Judaism] … showed great courage by stipulating that its truth or falsity, its success or failure, would be judged by whether humanity actually achieved the predicted goal.[38]

Greenberg then proceeds to apply this understanding to the concept of covenant, which he came to appreciate as the central idea in achieving the transformation of *tikkun olam*.

Stronger basis for assuming common ground between Greenberg and myself with regard to the questionable ontological status of our religious truth claims might, at first blush, be indicated by the fact that in his latest works[39] he too appropriates the classical notion of *zimzum* for his theological purposes. Closer scrutiny, however, reveals that the use we make of this concept is different. Following R. Kook and other latter-day kabbalists, I appropriate this paradigm in its metaphoric sense in order to identify the ultimate goal of our God-talk with a level of being which transcends the conventional division between realism and non-realism, or theology and ontology, and renders it superfluous. Greenberg, by contrast, employs the image of *zimzum* in its literal

---

37 Irving Greenberg, *Partnership for Life* (forthcoming).
38 Ibid., 6. This pragmatic turn is also evident in Greenberg's statement (in private communication—March 3, 2016) that instead of trying to explain suffering, he now prefers to stress the Soloveitchikian idea that our main response to evil must be to do something about it. Hence, the importance of restoring life and restoring the image of God (*tzelem elokim*) within us. "Upgrading the status of women and other marginalized groups, reformulating halakhah in order to remove discrimination, stereotyping, degradation and hatred, are more important than coming to an understanding."
39 See *Partnership for Life* and *The Triumph of Life*.

sense, in order to provide added gravitas to his shift from the notion of broken covenant and voluntary commitment to the notion of human autonomy as the pinnacle of a deliberately staged plan. This is done by relating the image of God's *actual* withdrawal in the act of creation to his understanding of covenant as the continuation of God's voluntary curtailment of His absolute power, gradually receding further and further from visible intervention in human affairs in a process leading us to full autonomy.

Despite this difference, Greenberg does seem to be groping for a more tentative understanding of faith claims that will take the postmodern critique of modernist absolutism and its confidence in universal meta-narratives into serious account. In the first instance, this leads him to assert that religion is not just about God, but rather about a divine–human partnership, as exhibited in the covenantal relationship. To the extent that the ultimate goal of this relationship is full acceptance of human freedom, its final form is inextricably bound by the degree and nature of human input. This leads him, even in some of his earlier work, to express sentiments faintly echoing the implicit pantheism of the allegorical interpreters of *zimzum* in his call to blur the distinction between the holy and the secular. On this understanding, the link between divine hiddenness and God's omnipresence can already be found in the "secularization insight" of the rabbis and their expansion of the realm of the holy through halakhic adjudication.[40] Paradoxically, it is precisely when the level of God's hiddenness reaches its highest level that the limitations of His transcendence as the ultimate "Other" are overcome and His presence inheres in all. Thus

---

40 "The Third Great Cycle of Jewish History" (*Wrestling with God*, 534–9). See also "Voluntary Covenant" (*Wrestling with God*, 554–5). The connection between divine hiddenness and a more encompassing religious life and its pantheistic overtones is again explicated (in private communication to me on March 3, 2016) as follows: "Although God is hidden, He is more present in the outcome of human actions—halakhah expands bringing holiness and the divine presence everywhere … Since God is totally hidden, God is everywhere. The religious is in the secular—but you have to drill to the right depth to encounter God and understand this process. Religion is not relating to a transcendent Other —as it is much more mysticism and God is in the all-in-all." It is worth noting here that Greenberg appears to be conflating the notion of *zimzum* as it first appeared in Talmudic sources with its later usage in the mystic tradition. While the Rabbis employed this term with reference to God's need to distill an aspect of His vastness in concentrated form, so that His presence, the Shekinah, could *enter into* a finite space *outside* of Himself (see *Bereshit Rabba* [Vilna edition], on *Bereshit, parsha* 5, *simman* 7; *Vayikra Rabba* [Vilna edition], on *Tzav, parsha* 10, *simman* 9), Lurianic kabbalists understood it in terms of God's need to contract and *withdraw from* a central point of His infinite being in order to make space *within* Himself for the creation of a finite being that is other than He.

one might conclude that so-called "ultimate truth" is achieved only when left entirely in the hands of humans.

In a later essay published in 2006,[41] Greenberg grasps the epistemological bull by the horns and grapples with the truth value of human formulations more directly. At this point, Greenberg expresses disillusion with the faith of modernism in the power of our inherited conceptual and ideological categories of thought to substantiate a religious worldview. As he puts it, "When the Holocaust is recognized as a touchtone, then the test of the validity of theologies is not just the criteria of intellectual and moral coherence but whether the position is credible in the presence of the Holocaust or in light of the implications of the event."[42] The difficulty that the Holocaust poses in upholding assumptions regarding "the essential goodness of human nature or that sickness and suffering are providentially inflicted on people because they sin … leads to a transformation of the categories that themselves are used to judge and to incorporate religious responses."[43] Rather than reject any previous paradigm outright, Greenberg's major response now appears to be recognizing the necessity for acknowledging "the brokenness of all worldviews and value systems."[44] Recognizing that "all narratives are grounded in specific groups (and that their authority is grounded in that factor),"[45] all "human-implicated Absolutes … ideas, values and forces" must be taken as partial.[46] Limits must be set in order to curtail cultural hegemony and moral centralization.[47]

Greenberg describes the alternative that he proposes to absolutism (i.e., setting limits and checks on the range of validity of any particular formulation of truth) as pluralism, rather than relativism (i.e., denial of objective truth completely).[48] On this understanding, "the drive to reach objective truth and to establish the existence of absolute values is not surrendered. It is only given its just limits and thereby protected against potential excesses."[49] This version of pluralism liberates Greenberg from his former existential torment, which rendered him torn between conflicting truths, and allowed him only "moment

---

41 Greenberg, "Theology after the Shoah," 213–39.
42 Irving Greenberg, "Theology after the Holocaust: The Transformation of the Core Paradigm," *A Journal of Jewish Ideas and Experience* 26, no. 3 (October 2006): 214.
43 Ibid.
44 Ibid., 215.
45 Ibid., 222.
46 Ibid., 218–19.
47 Ibid., 222.
48 Ibid.
49 Ibid.

faith." Instead of yearning for some global method of resolution between the memory of divine redemption in the Exodus and the divine indifference exhibited in the Holocaust, he now understands that until the coming of the Messiah, *all* truths are moment truths,[50] all must be balanced against each other, accompanied by the understanding that "insistence on certainty represents [a futile] nostalgia for restoration to a pre-expulsion, pre-Shoah Eden."[51] But the assumption that there *are* "objective truths and absolute values" still serves as the driving force behind the balancing process.

VII

Greenberg's latest tweaks to his theological response to the Holocaust are laudable and significant. On a moral plane, his advocacy of greater epistemological modesty certainly puts a damper on the perils of simplistic faith or any form of ideological fanaticism. But I believe that Greenberg would do well to take the implications of his *zimzum* paradigm one step further, and apply it (as I have, in developing the second stage of my response to biblical criticism) to his broader account of Jewish history as well.[52] This would involve abandoning the view of covenantal theology as an objective factual description of God and His intentions, and recasting it as a metaphysical narrative born of more pragmatic spiritual concerns, such as the need to grant life meaning or to deliberately cultivate human responsibility and an urge for the sublime.

I believe that this move, which stems from a general skepticism regarding the ontological status of all metaphysical claims, is as necessary for Greenberg's Holocaust theology, as it is for any contemporary Orthodox understanding of divine revelation. This is so, because any theological response to the Holo-

---

50 Ibid., 227, explicated in greater nuance on 238n64.
51 Ibid., 227.
52 In a lengthy footnote ("Theology after the Holocaust," 238n64) Greenberg comes very close to making this move with respect to revelation, when he suggests not only that "absolutist claims do not do justice to the dynamic relationship of the components of truth or to the interaction between the Divine and the human" (stage one of my theory of revelation) but "contrary to the claims of timeless truth, to the extent that revelation and Torah enter into human culture and discourse and into this broken world, they become moment (e.g., bounded) truths." But even at this stage, Greenberg still refers to truth as incorporating some reference to an "objective factuality," rather than as attempting to capture a preverbal undefined state of affairs in which the distinction between truth and reality is obliterated. And, more importantly, he does not examine the implications of this more nuanced view of truth for his Holocaust theology as well.

caust must take into account the same postmodern recognition of the role that human categories of thought play in the interpretation of events and phenomena that problematizes our understanding of revelation as the eruption of an external force into our historic reality.

Given the postmodern critique of absolutism, for example, can we accept Greenberg's sharp distinction between events of the past as "divine interference" and current events as *hester panim* as objective truth? Is there no place to attribute the difference between biblical and modern renditions of reality simply to the eyes of the beholders, and their differing views regarding the nature of the possible? That is to say, had we been part of the desert generation, would this have precluded our freedom in principle to view the miracles of that time as simply a "chance" convening of natural events? And if that generation were living in our day, would they not be equally prone to viewing the establishment of the State of Israel, along with its subsequent triumphs and setbacks as repeat performances of God's "repentance of the evil that He had inflicted,"[53] or as heaven-sent wake-up calls to the perils of hubris when "Jeshurun waxes fat"?[54] If so, the entire theory of God's gradually diminishing involvement in history loses its force as an indisputable statement of fact.

Over and above this objection, however, persisting with the claim of God's deliberately diminished presence leaves the theodicy question of the Holocaust unresolved. Even if we were to accept the notion that without evil, some positive values—such as autonomy and freedom of choice (as well as repentance, long-suffering, and empathy with the suffering of others)—cannot be maintained, not all instances of evil can be justified in this manner. Sometimes evil is so extreme, that no positive value in the world, even in the future, can compensate for the suffering it brings in the present. Was not the cry of six million worthy of penetrating the threshold of divine resolve? Moreover, even in purely practical terms, what value could there be to greater human autonomy, if this entails the possibility that no more players will be left on the field to maintain it? If humanity passes an unacceptable measure of destruction, will God never again intervene actively in history? Will a mother training her child to cross the street independently remain passive, even when he is about to be hit by a car?

Aside from the question whether declaring God's increasing abstention from intervention in human affairs intentional is the most hopeful message to be elicited from the Holocaust (although this may be so), leaving Greenberg's

---

53 As in Jeremiah 42:10–12.
54 As in Deuteronomy 32:15.

theory to stand alone, without the support of the mystic's ultimate safety net that all talk of divinely initiated human autonomy is in the last resort a provisional attempt to devise a plausible rather than necessary explanation from our human point of view, renders it wanting.

The mystic tradition, when functioning in accordance with its deepest premises, does not support an understanding of God's revelation in history as the eruption of a transcendent force into a reality that is other than itself. It is rather the culmination of a new constellation of forces *from within that reality*. According to the mystic tradition, God is not a person or an object that exercises agency on the world from without. Our personalist understanding is not to be belittled; it is a necessary pointer to that which in essence leaves no room for distinction between subject and object, or perceiver and the object of his perception.[55] Hence, revelation is a genuine vision of that totality as grasped by one of its aspects in a particular light. But because that totality is infinite, the potential meaning of revelation is also infinite, varying from generation to generation, building on and modifying previous understandings in accordance with the never-ending give and take between its seemingly discrete elements.

By the same token, so long as we experience ourselves as separate, independent beings and some measure of the personalist talk (i.e., talking about God as if divinity were a person) must be maintained, we speak—according to the mystic—*as if* God made a covenant and then rescinded. But while holding onto this picture for practical purposes, the realization that even this meta-narrative is not the full story allows us to understand that ultimately the theodicy problem is a nonissue. God cannot be held responsible for evil, for in an infinite monolithic reality where, in the words of R. Kook, "all that is imagined or capable of being imagined already exists" (כל המצויר והמדומה והאפשר להיות בציור באמת מצוי),[56] the category of justice is meaningless. This understanding is not to be equated with the view that our justice and God's are measured in different terms. Rather, the very category of justice makes sense only for created beings who live in a world of lack.[57]

---

55 A. I. Kook, "The Comprehensive Divine View," in *Orot ha-kodesh* II (Jerusalem: Mosad Harav Kook, 1985), 399–401; see also Eliyahu Dessler, *Michtav me-Eliyahu* III (London: Honig and Sons, 1955), 256–7.

56 A. I. Kook, *Arpelei Tohar* (Jerusalem: Hamachon al shem Harav Zvi Yehuda Kook, 1983), 5.

57 A. I. Kook, "The Ideal General Good," *Orot ha-Kodesh* II, 453: "The ideal world of the spirit does not recognize division at all, it recognizes only generality and unity; it surveys every detail only as part of the whole … Thus it comes to recognize that there is no general existence to evil. … It is corporeal matter that divides between objects in reality, and thereby also creates the distinctions between them" (translation mine).

Such a dissolution of the theodicy problem is not to be regarded as an excuse for belittling human suffering and promoting quietist resignation to whatever befalls us. Evil is real enough in our finite reality and needs to be eliminated.[58] But we are inspired by the believer who, like Job, though tormented by his experience, is willing to sing *Ani Maamin* ("I believe [in the Messiah's coming]") while being led to the gas chambers, or to worry about the minutiae of *hilkhot shehita* (the laws of animal slaughtering) under threat of his own slaughter, not because his affirmation of God is more *correct* than that of the Jew who now casts off his faith (or even worse, displays indifference), but because in this act he reinforces for us a response that bears promise of making sense of it all *from our point of view*.[59]

The conclusion we must now reach is that the meaning and significance of the belief in revelation, divine accommodation, and all religious doctrine making metaphysical claims, is best understood in light of its function in the life of the believer. The "truth" of such beliefs is substantiated not by appeal to external evidence or reinterpretation, but on the basis of their ability to inculcate spiritually meaningful attitudes and values, reinforcing the particular form of life on which such attitudes and values are predicated.

VIII

I am well aware that such blurring of distinctions between the divine and the human, and the justification of belief in revelation and divine providence in strictly pragmatic terms, are not without their own difficulties, at least on the psychological plane. Yet in medieval times, rationalist philosophers—as epitomized by Maimonides—generated an equally radical and problematic about-face from the biblical concept of God that nevertheless nurtures Jewish theology until the present day. I believe that contemporary Judaism, in confronting the turn from modernist to postmodern notions of truth, may now be on the brink of a comparable revolution in Jewish thought. While Orthodox theology has not yet caught up with these developments, popular grassroots initiatives—particularly among a younger generation of secular and religious Israelis—have

---

58 The same conclusion is drawn by Kook, ibid.
59 Kook makes a similar move when attempting to address the teleological question: the motive for creation—see *Orot ha-kodesh* II, "The Lack of Good and Its Purpose," 481–2.

already begun demonstrating the need to qualify a strictly heteronomous definition of Jewish spirituality and the naively objectivist approach that it has endorsed in the response to modernity. Such initiatives suggest that it may now be the task of the mystics to bridge the gap between religion and philosophy, and to teach us how to translate our new postmodern understandings into more profoundly experiential terms that will link us more firmly to our premodern roots.

CHAPTER 6

Modern Orthodoxy and Religious Truth[1]

MARC B. SHAPIRO

When the term Modern Orthodoxy is used, what does it mean? For some, it means getting a secular education and entering a white-collar profession. This need not have much impact on one's religious thought or practice, and there are indeed many such Modern Orthodox Jews whose theological outlook is little different than those to their right. There are other Modern Orthodox Jews who incorporate a modern scholarly approach into how they look at Jewish history and texts. Yet here too, this need not have much impact on their religious life. Other Modern Orthodox Jews are willing to make changes in Jewish practice, especially when it comes to matters concerning the role of women. For many of these people, the debate is simply around halakhic texts, and their theological assumptions are no different than more conservative Orthodox Jews.

Yet there is also a different sort of Modern Orthodox Jew. I do not want to refer to them as a group since their numbers are quite small. We are dealing with a few intellectuals, but as is often the case, what the intellectuals advocate often filters down to the community at large. For example, who could have imagined even twenty years ago that the position of women in Orthodoxy could change as much as it has? The Modern Orthodox intellectuals I will discuss have a different approach than the other groups mentioned, because they allow certain modern insights to enter into the very heart of Jewish theology. These thinkers deal with the nature of religious truth and how other religious traditions are to be regarded.

---

1 Although I have added a number of footnotes, the essay preserves the oral form in which it was delivered.

Rabbi Irving Greenberg has been central to this reevaluation of religious truth, but it is also important to put him into a broader context. The basic issue he and others have focused on is how open is Judaism to the notion that other faith communities are also recipients of religious truths by means of a revelation, that is, a divine–human encounter. Greenberg's thoughts appear in his 2004 book, *For the Sake of Heaven and Earth: The New Encounter between Judaism and Christianity*. This book contains essays written over a long period of time, so it gives us good insight into the development of Greenberg's ideas.[2]

In the post-Holocaust years, seeing how much of the Christian world had begun to repent for its anti-Jewish and antisemitic history, Greenberg saw a chance to correct the mistakes of Judaism in how it judged Christianity. In doing so he raised some controversial questions. For example, "Was there any way to allow for the possible legitimacy of Christians making such claims [Jesus's divine incarnation and resurrection] without yielding our firm conviction that Judaism is a covenant faith, true and permanently valid in history?"[3] "Could it have been God's purpose to start another religion alongside Judaism to bring the message of redemption to the world in accelerated fashion without breaking up the ongoing election and mission of the original covenanted children of Israel?"[4]

In the first chapter of *For the Sake of Heaven and Earth*, Greenberg explains how he came to develop his ideas. He also discusses his controversial essay in which he wrote that Jews should regard Jesus not as a "false messiah," but as a "failed messiah," that is, "one who has the right values, upholds the covenant but did not attain the final goal."[5] He also compared Jesus's failure to the "failures" of Abraham, Moses, and Jeremiah.[6] Greenberg notes that he intended the title "messiah" to be honorific, and he even thought that the adjective "failed" could be accepted by Christians since they too acknowledge that Jesus' task remains unfulfilled.

It is a little strange to me that Greenberg thought that this would be acceptable for Christians, since in their conception Jesus is not a failed messiah at all. He came into this world to die for humanity's sins and did exactly that, so where is the failure? The fact that Jesus's work remains unfinished has nothing to do with him being a failure. More surprising is that Greenberg thought that

---

2 For an Orthodox critique of this book, see David Berger's review essay in *Tradition* 39, no. 2 (2005): 66–78.
3 Irving Greenberg, *For the Sake of Heaven and Earth: The New Encounter Between Judaism and Christianity* (Philadelphia, PA: Jewish Publication Society, 2004), 31.
4 Ibid., 31–2.
5 Ibid., 32.
6 Ibid., 153.

Jews would also be prepared to accept the expression "failed messiah,"[7] and thus redefine their relationship to Christianity. When Greenberg was attacked in Orthodox circles for how he dealt with Jesus, he responded by toning down much of his original thought and daring ideas. Years later, when he wrote *For the Sake of Heaven and Earth*, he wondered if he should not have backed down but bravely defended his views.[8]

Once Greenberg was no longer concerned about being attacked on dogmatic grounds, he was able to develop a new theology, which he terms "Covenantal Pluralism." This refers to his notion that both Judaism and Christianity are part of a divine–human partnership operating so that our imperfect world will be brought to a state of perfection.[9] For Greenberg, Christianity is "another one of the particular covenants that God has called into being in order to engage more and more humans in the process of *tikkun olam*."[10]

Some might see this as an expansion of what Maimonides says about Jesus at the end of the *Mishneh Torah*.[11] However, what Greenberg is speaking about is really quite different than what Maimonides had in mind, since Greenberg is referring to an actual covenant between God and the followers of Christianity. Greenberg goes even further by arguing that it is a mistake for Jews to invalidate the truths of Christianity.

> Comfortable in the interpretation that the founding events of Christianity were meant to be accepted by Christians only and were not intended to undermine the ongoing validity of the Jewish way, Jews should understand that Resurrection and Incarnation were not putative facts to be argued over, they were signals intended for and recognized by the Christian community to bring them closer to God.[12]

This leads to Greenberg's most radical, that is, untraditional position, in that he accepts the possibility that the truths of Christianity can be factual.

> The claim that God became incarnated in a particular human body at a unique moment in history has always been denied by faithful Jews as

---

7   See ibid., 32.
8   Ibid., 34.
9   Ibid., 41.
10 Ibid., 44.
11 *Hilkhot Melakhim* 11:4.
12 *For the Sake of Heaven and Earth*, 45.

contradictory to God's essence and unjustified in light of the human capacity to turn to God directly. Similarly, Jews insisted that, to be valid, the messianic resurrection must include all of humanity. ... Why is it necessary for Jews (or other religionists) to insist that the truth of their historical experience with God extends into Christian communities and negates Christianity's claims? It is sufficient for Jews to affirm that they have no interest in restricting God's choice of tactics and methods of revelation. Exactly what happened in the first century is of limited import to Jews. They need not rule that the Trinity constitutes idolatry or degradation of pure monotheism. They need only insist that as open as they were, God did not give them the Christian signal—because God had another mission and purpose for them.[13]

Later in the book Greenberg repeats this basic point, stating that even with regard to the Incarnation, while it might be improbable and in violation of other biblical principles, "one can hardly rule out the option totally, particularly if it was intended for gentiles and not for Jews."[14] In this sentence the divinity of Jesus is offered as a possibility. In a rejection of another major aspect of historical Jewish thought, Greenberg even sees it as legitimate to advance the possibility that when the Messiah arrives and is asked if it is his first time here or his second, he will reply "no comment."[15]

As seen in the subtitle of Greenberg's book,[16] his focus is on Judaism and Christianity, and Christianity is of particular significance in that it was born out of Judaism. If you only read the early essays in the book—which are also the earliest in a chronological sense—it is unclear whether what Greenberg says about God having a covenant not just with Jews but also with Christians would

---

13 Ibid., 67–8.
14 Ibid., 156. See also 146. On 194–5, Greenberg writes:

> Did God then become incarnate to cross the covenantal divide in order to rescue humankind? Far be it from me as a Jew to prescribe to Christians or to God what happened in that religious experience. I can only suggest that the resurrection signal had to be so marginal, so subject to alternate interpretations, and the incarnation sign so subtle, as to be able to be heard in dramatically opposing fashions—one way by the band elected to start the new faith and another way by the majority of Jews called to continue the classical covenantal mission. Such a resurrection, such an incarnation, no Jew need fear or fight.

15 Ibid., 123.
16 *For the Sake of Heaven and Earth: The New Encounter between Judaism and Christianity.*

apply to adherents of other religions as well. In a later chapter, however, he is clear that all people can be seen as being in a covenant with God, as long as they act morally.[17] This latter point is relevant to Islam, which while adhering to monotheism, is excluded by Greenberg from covenantal pluralism. In making this judgment, Greenberg does not distinguish between mainstream Islam and its extremist varieties, since he claims that "the Muslim mainstream is, by and large, far from purging itself of supersessionism and hatred."[18]

One should not assume from what I have quoted up until now that Greenberg advocates religious relativism. On the contrary, Greenberg explicitly rejects relativism and says that the difference between pluralism, which he accepts, and relativism is that "pluralism is based on the principle that there still is an absolute truth."[19] For Greenberg, pluralism means that he affirms doctrines as true but recognizes that his truth might not be intended for others who have their own truth and even their own revelation.[20] Thus, even though the truths of different religions are in conflict, this does not mean that there is not room for all of them to exist together.[21] This must be distinguished from relativism, which for Greenberg means that there are no standards and no truth.[22] In Greenberg's words, "The essential difference between pluralism and relativism is that pluralism is based on the principle that there

---

17 See ibid., 213ff. See also ibid., 210, where the concept of idolatry is reinterpreted by Greenberg.

There is a real danger that the human version/understanding, which is by definition finite, will be extended by believers into an infinite claim that allows no room for the other. This human extension ends up with a pseudo-infinite; *this is the definition of idolatry*. Idolatry is the partial, created or shaped by finite humans, that claims to be infinite. … All human systems (even those that are given by divine revelation) that claim to be absolute, exercise no self-limitation, or leave no room for the other turn into idolatry, i.e., into sources of death. (italics in original)

18 Ibid., 41. In an early essay, Greenberg did equate Christianity and Islam, but he rejects this position in *Between Heaven and Earth*. See ibid. I think it is incorrect for Greenberg and others to use the term supersessionism with regard to Islam. This is because there is no notion of Islam superseding Judaism, or of Muslims replacing Jews as the focus of God's blessings. As far as Muslims are concerned, Abraham and Moses were themselves Muslims.
19 Ibid., 203.
20 Ibid., 205.
21 Ibid., 206.
22 Ibid., 196, 201ff.

still is an absolute truth. … Pluralism is an absolutism that has come to recognize its own limitations."[23]

Despite Greenberg's explanation, there are still ambiguities in his presentation. Raphael Jospe, who is himself an advocate of pluralism, has already pointed out a problem with Greenberg's position, since how can an acceptance of absolute truth leave room for limitations?[24] Greenberg states that "an absolute truth/value need not be absolutely right to be absolute."[25] This would appear to dilute the meaning of the word "absolute," for if an absolute truth incorporates imperfection, this means that it is not absolute truth after all.

As we have seen, Greenberg speaks of different truths for different people, which to my mind shows that he is not dealing with absolute or factual truth, or what we can call truth with a capital T. This also appears to be what Greenberg himself has in mind. Thus, the term "absolute" is inappropriate. It is precisely because modern thinkers have recognized the problems of speaking in terms of "absolute truth" that Rabbi Jonathan Sacks and Tamar Ross are led to their positions.

In 2002 Sacks published his book *The Dignity of Difference*. According to Sacks, in the post–September 11th climate we must do more than have tolerance for other cultures and religions, and do more than search for common values and give other religions basic respect. Rather, we must celebrate the diverse world we live in. Such a celebration of the diversity of God's world is more than tolerance and even more than pluralism; it is a recognition of the truth found in all religions.

More than fifty years ago, at the height of the ecumenical movement, a number of Jewish religious leaders were asked the following question: "Is Judaism the one true religion, or is it one of several true religions?"[26] It is significant that none of the Orthodox respondents were willing to grant that there is any truth in other religions, other than those truths which Mendelssohn would describe as the product of reason. In other words, everyone grants that if Christianity teaches that murder is wrong, then this is a truth,

---

23 Ibid., 203.
24 Irving Greenberg, "Pluralism Out of the Sources of Judaism," in *Jewish Theology and World Religions*, ed. Alon Goshen-Gottstein and Eugene Korn (Oxford: Littman Library of Jewish Civilization, 2012), 100.
25 Greenberg, *For the Sake of Heaven and Earth*, 205.
26 *The Condition of Jewish Belief* (New York: MacMillan Company, 1966), 7.

but it is not a religious truth particular to this faith, and it is not what Sacks has in mind.[27]

Sacks's predecessor as chief rabbi, Immanuel Jakobovits, was most adamant: "As a professing Jew, I obviously consider Judaism the only true religion, just as I would expect the adherents of any other faith to defend a similar claim for their religion."[28] This statement shows how much matters have changed in half a century. Today we are at a place where not only much (most?) of the laity, but also many religious figures are not prepared to claim that their religion is the only true one. Among my many Christian students, I do not believe that I have ever encountered more than a few who thought that their religion was the only true one.

Sacks is a child of a different era, one in which postmodern ideas are now prevalent, and this explains his alternative view of religion and truth. He attempts to locate "the celebration of [religious] diversity at the very heart of the monotheistic imagination."[29] He begins his book by describing an interfaith service that took place at Ground Zero in New York City, at which the Archbishop of Canterbury, a Muslim imam, and a Hindu guru recited prayers and meditations, and the Chief Rabbi of Israel read a reflection. This is a model of how religions should coexist, according to Sacks. He sees our era as one in which

> The great faiths must now become an active force for peace and for the justice and compassion on which peace ultimately depends. That will require great courage and perhaps something more than courage: a candid

---

27 In 1964 the Rabbinical Council of America, basing itself on R. Joseph B. Soloveitchik's essay "Confrontation," issued a statement dealing with interfaith relations that included the following sentence: "Each religious community is endowed with intrinsic dignity and metaphysical worth." The statement does not say that other religious communities have any "religious truth," only "intrinsic dignity" and "metaphysical worth." The complete statement appears in *Tradition* 6 (Spring–Summer 1964): 28. In 1950 Soloveitchik wrote: "However, this tolerant philosophy of transcendental univeralism does not exclude the specific awareness of the Jews of the supremacy of their faith over all others. ... The feeling of axiological equality of all faiths as a component of the individual religious experience is a *contradicto in objecto*." *Community, Covenant and Commitment*, ed. N. Helfgot (Jersey City, NJ: KTAV, 2005), 21–2.
28 *The Condition of Jewish Belief*, 112. He added: "The recognition of other faiths as 'equally true' is branded as apostasy in Jewish law (*Sanhedrin* 63a, based on Ex. 22:19)." The passage in *Sanhedrin* 63a does not say what Jakobovits attributes to it.
29 Jonathan Sacks, *The Dignity of Difference: How to Avoid the Clash of Civilizations* (London: Continuum, 2002), xi.

> admission that, more than at any time in the past, we need to search—each faith in its own way—for a way of living with, and acknowledging the integrity of, those who are not of our faith. Can we make space for difference? Can we hear the voice of God in a language, a sensibility, a culture not our own?[30]

In other words, Sacks is asking us to see God not merely in the peoples of the world, but even in their varying religions. He is asking us to make space for difference within the Jewish theological universe, without betraying the fundamentals of Jewish theology. Yet this is a very bold stance when one considers Judaism's historic tradition.

Sacks himself acknowledges, "I have not hesitated to be radical, and I have deliberately chosen to express that radicalism in religious terms."[31] As he puts it, our faith can give rise "to a generosity of spirit capable of recognizing the integrity—yes, even the sanctity—of worlds outside our faith."[32] In premodern times, "it was possible to believe that our truth was the only truth; our way the only way."[33] Today, the challenge is, "Can I, a Jew, hear the echoes of God's voice in that of a Hindu or Sikh or Christian or Muslim. ... Can I do so and feel not diminished but enlarged? What then becomes of my faith which until then had encompassed the world and must now make space for another faith, another way of interpreting the world?"[34]

Sacks's conclusion is to reject the notion that "one God entails one faith, one truth, one covenant."[35] In other words, while God's covenant at Sinai remains true for the Jewish people, other religions are expressions of alternative covenants with God, each of which represent their own truth. In Sacks's words, "God has spoken to mankind in many languages: through Judaism to Jews, Christianity to Christians, Islam to Muslims ... *God is God of all humanity, but no single faith is or should be the faith of all humanity.*"[36]

Sacks never explains what becomes of the liturgy, which in a number of places expresses a very exclusivist approach. He does not discuss whether he would be open to liturgical alterations in accord with his ecumenical vision. At

---

30 Ibid., 4–5.
31 Ibid., 17.
32 Ibid., 9.
33 Ibid., 10.
34 Ibid., 17–18.
35 Ibid., 200.
36 Ibid., 55 (italics in the original).

the very least, I do not see how it is possible for his vision to coexist with the (often excised) words of *Aleinu*: "For they bow to vanity and emptiness and pray to a god which helps not." Interestingly, these words are included in the Koren Sacks siddur, but they are placed in parenthesis.

Although Sacks claims that his position is *not* an endorsement of the legitimacy of polytheism,[37] and he would certainly also insist that he is not endorsing the legitimacy of idolatry, he never explains why not. Sacks himself tells us that truth on earth is not the whole truth: "When two propositions conflict it is not necessarily because one is true the other false. It may be, and often is, that each represents a different perspective on reality, an alternative way of structuring order. ... In heaven there is truth; on earth there are truths."[38] Who then is to say that an idolatrous or Trinitarian conception is not the truth of another culture—"a different perspective on reality"—while Jewish-style monotheism is the truth of the Jews? After all, as Sacks further notes, "God is greater than religion," and "He is only partially comprehended by any faith."[39]

I see no way to accept Sacks's basic propositions and at the same time to discount the legitimacy of *avodah zarah*[40] for those cultures that approach the divine in this fashion. Although Sacks himself apparently never intended to

---

37 Ibid., 65.
38 Ibid., 64.
39 Ibid., 65. Sacks does not mention Abraham Joshua Heschel's famous essay "No Religion is an Island," first published in the *Union Theological Seminary Quarterly Review* 21 (January 1966): 3–22. Yet Heschel's essay appears to have influenced Sacks. The following are some of Heschel's formulations that are very similar to what Sacks writes, from 14–15 in Heschel's essay.

> Is it not blasphemous to say: I alone have all the truth and the grace, and all those who differ live in darkness, and are abandoned by the grace of God? ... Is religious uniformity desirable or even possible? Has it really proved to be a blessing for a country when all its citizens belonged to one denomination? ... Does not the task of preparing the kingdom of God require a diversity of talents, a variety of rituals, soul-searching as well as opposition?
>
> Perhaps it is the will of God that in this aeon there should be diversity in our forms of devotion and commitment to Him. In this aeon diversity of religions is the will of God. ...
>
> No two minds are alike, just as no two faces are alike. The voice of God reaches the spirit of man in a variety of ways, in a multiplicity of languages. One truth comes to expression in many ways of understanding.

40 I intentionally use this term rather than idolatry, as *avodah zarah* need not have anything to do with worship of an idol.

go this far, he does say, with reference to religious truth, that "*each* culture has something to contribute."⁴¹ In other words, even societies that practice *avodah zarah* are included as making a positive contribution. Once Sacks is prepared to understand truth in a non-absolutist sense, then one cannot restrict the great circle of truth to only Christianity, Islam, and other monotheistic religions. It is worth noting that in the revised version of *The Dignity of Difference*, Sacks changed the passage quoted earlier in this paragraph to state that "each culture has something to contribute to the totality of human wisdom." Human wisdom is far removed from religious truth and is not what Sacks originally intended.

Although Sacks does not mention John Hick, a famous philosopher of religion, it appears to me that Sacks is following the path advocated by Hick in his influential book *An Interpretation of Religion: Human Responses to the Transcendent*.⁴² According to Hick, the truth formulations of all religions should be viewed as "incomplete attempts at expressing the ineffable, i.e., 'truths' only in a very weak sense of the term."⁴³ Using the terminology of Hicks, it appears that Sacks should be regarded as a "pluralist."⁴⁴ Here is Alan Brill's summary of "Pluralism."

> "*All world religions have some truth.*" Religious Pluralism ... accept[s] that no one tradition can claim to possess the singular truth. All groups' beliefs and practices are equally valid, when interpreted within their own culture. Thus, no one religion is inherently better or superior to any other major world religion. For pluralists, there may be differences in rituals and beliefs among these groups, but on the most important issues there is great similarity.⁴⁵

---

41 Sacks, *Dignity of Difference*, 64–5, italics added.
42 John Hick, *An Interpretation of Religion: Human Responses to the Transcendent* (New Haven, CT: Yale University Press, 1989).
43 See Tamar Ross, "Reflections on the Possibilities of Interfaith Communication in our Day," *Edah Journal* 1 (5761): 4, available at www.edah.org. The quote is Ross's summary of Hick's position.
44 See Alan Brill, *Judaism and Other Religions: Models of Understanding* (New York: Palgrave Macmillan 2010), pp. 144ff. Alon Goshen-Gottstein and Alan Jotkowitz also understand Sacks in this fashion. See Alon Goshen-Gottstein, "Arguing For/Over the Dignity of Difference" (paper presented at the Yale Center for Faith and Culture consultation on Respect and Human Flourishing), 8, available at faith.yale.edu/sites/default/files/files/Goshen-Gottstein.pdf; A. Jotkowitz, "Universalism and Particularism and the Jewish Tradition: The Radical Theology of Rabbi Jonathan Sacks," *Tradition* 44, no. 3 (2011): 53–67.
45 Brill, *Judaism and Other Religions*, 16. This is in contrast to "inclusivists" who believe that "[o]ne's own [religious] group possesses the truth; other religious groups contain parts of the truth." See ibid.

However, I find it doubtful that Sacks should be regarded as a complete pluralist, since I do not see any evidence that he would agree that "no one religion is inherently better or superior than any other major world religion." I think it is more likely that his position is that while Judaism and other religions only have part of the truth, Judaism still has more of the truth than do other religions.

Unlike Sacks, Tamar Ross does cite Hick, and her discussion, while covering much of the same ground as Sacks, is a philosophically more sophisticated analysis in which she reaches more radical conclusions.[46] She is not reticent about acknowledging that even those religions that Jews have regarded as idolatrous must be included in the great circle of truth when truth is understood with a lowercase *t*, that is, as a subjective portrayal of how we see the divine: "All religions are diverse symbolic objectifications of the same basic spiritual experience and intimation of Ultimate Being."[47] The corollary to this, as Ross makes clear, is that there can no longer be a hierarchy of religions, with Judaism at the top, containing Truth, and the other religions below it. As Ross puts it, "Because we are now talking of religions as different cultural-linguistic systems, they are incommensurable, and cannot even be graded hierarchically as part of a common effort."[48]

For Ross, the fact that we cannot make definite, objective theological truth statements is what leads her to what I would term a relativist position. For her, there is no truth with a capital *T*, only truth with a lowercase *t*, and "truth" does not mean the truth of propositional statements. Rather, something is true if it contributes to one's religious growth. As Ross explains, "truth is what is spiritually transformative."[49] Once truth is understood in this fashion, all religions that contribute to peace, goodwill, and personal spiritual growth have to be regarded as "true."

Ross's understanding of religious truth developed after she had masterfully explicated R. Kook's notion of tolerance.[50] I do not mean to say that Ross's views should be seen merely as a development of R. Kook's, as her outlook is

---

46 See Ross, "Reflections on the Possibilities."
47 Ibid., 5.
48 Ibid., 6.
49 Tamar Ross, "Religious Belief in a Postmodern Age," in *Faith: Jewish Perspectives*, ed. Avi Sagi and Dov Schwartz (Boston: Academic Studies Press, 2013), 211.
50 Tamar Ross, "The Cognitive Value of Religious Truth-Statements: Rabbi A. I. Kook and Postmodernism," in *Hazon Nahum: Studies in Jewish Law, Thought, and History Presented to Dr. Norman Lamm on the Occasion of His Seventieth Birthday*, ed. Yaakov Elman and Jeffrey S. Gurock (New York: Michael Scharf Publication Trust, 1997), 479–528.

heavily influenced by general philosophical concerns. It is, however, important for her to point out that her views are in line with what R. Kook was getting at. Thus, to support her own approach, Ross cites R. Kook, who states: "In relation to the highest Divine truth, there is no difference between formulated religion and heresy. Both do not yield the truth, because whatever positive assertion a person makes is a step removed from the truth of the Divine."[51] In other words, we can make no factual statements expressing absolute theological truth.

Yet Ross also notes that R. Kook cannot be seen as advocating a "pure relativism."[52] As she explains, when dealing with religious truth claims that are verbalized, not all of them are equally valid, as some are indeed more correct than others. "But since, in absolute terms, all are equally off the mark, the justification for preferring one alternative over another must now be based on criteria for truth which are not primarily cognitive."[53] This is an incredibly important point, as according to Ross, R. Kook entirely overturns the medieval understanding of truth and dogma.

In reading Ross I could not help but be reminded of Gandhi's famous words:

> I came to the conclusion long ago … that all religious were true and also that all had some error in them, and whilst I hold by my own, I should hold others as dear as Hinduism. So we can only pray, if we are Hindus, not that a Christian should become a Hindu. … But our innermost prayer should be a Hindu should be a better Hindu, a Muslim a better Muslim, a Christian a better Christian.[54]

As with Ross, when Gandhi speaks of all religions as being "true," he is not speaking about "truth" in any absolute sense.

I must also briefly note two other Orthodox thinkers who have offered new understandings of how Judaism should relate to Christianity. The first is Rabbi Eugene Korn, whose article, "One God, Many Faiths: A Jewish Theology of Covenantal Pluralism,"[55] adopts an approach quite similar to that of

---

51 Avraham Yitzhak Kook, *Orot ha-Emunah* (Brooklyn, NY: Langsam Associates, 1985), 46, translation in Ross, "Cognitive Value," 491.
52 Ross, "Cognitive Value," 493.
53 Ibid., 494.
54 Louis Fischer, ed., *The Essential Gandhi* (New York: Vintage, 2002), 184.
55 In Eugene Korn and John T. Pawlikowski, eds., *Two Faiths, One Covenant* (Oxford: Sheed & Ward, 2005), 147–54. See also Korn's more detailed essay, "The People Israel,

Greenberg and Sacks. Korn rejects the notion that all theological truth can be found in Judaism. He argues that "legitimizing different theological conceptions multiplies the possibilities for discovering God in our lives. ... When we grant religious validity to all moral faiths, we can find the Image of God in all religiously sincere people."[56]

While Korn speaks about "multiple sacred covenants," he also notes that the relationship between Judaism and Christianity is unique since they have a "shared spiritual patrimony" and a "messianic vision of history."[57] Korn, as with Greenberg and Sacks, is uncomfortable with traditional Jewish views of what can be termed theological exclusivity. These figures cannot accept, as traditional Jews in previous generations did, that all theological truth known to humanity can be found, and indeed originates, in Judaism. For Greenberg, Sacks, and Korn the matter also appears to be a question of justice, that the God of all humanity would not choose to limit his revelation to only one small people. This is a divergence from previous Orthodox thinkers, who had no difficulty at all with this assumption.[58]

I personally see the notion of "multiple sacred covenants" as opening up a can of worms, since if there are multiple sacred covenants shouldn't they be understood in accord with how the recipients of these covenants understand

---

Christianity, and the Covenantal Responsibility to History," in *Covenant and Hope: Christian and Jewish Reflections*, ed. Eugene Korn and Robert W. Jenson (Grand Rapids: Eerdmans, 2012), 145–72.

56 Ibid., 153.
57 Ibid., 154.
58 Regarding multiple revelations, after a groundbreaking interfaith gathering between representatives of the Israeli Chief Rabbinate and Hindu leaders, a lengthy declaration was issued. The first paragraph reads as follows: "Their respective traditions teach Faith in One Supreme Being who is the Ultimate Reality, who has created this world in its blessed diversity and who has communicated Divine ways of action for humanity for different peoples in different times and places."

This is a clear affirmation that it is not only the Jewish people who can claim a divine revelation, but even Hinduism and other unnamed religions have their origin in God. As Alon Goshen-Gottstein has noted, this is a "a revolutionary statement ... [that] accords with the finest of pluralistic theologies. ... By this understanding, Hinduism is as valid a revelation as Judaism, provided the recipients of the revelation are properly confined to their respective communities." Yet Goshen-Gottstein claims, and he is undoubtedly correct, that "the theological, let alone halachic, implications of this opening clause should be taken with a grain of salt." In other words, the Jewish signatories never intended their words to be taken literally, and perhaps were not even aware of the theological significance of what they signed. See Goshen-Gottstein, *The Jewish Encounter with Hinduism* (New York: Palgrave Macmillan, 2016), 186, 188, 198–9.

them, rather than through the lens of Jewish theological categories? Greenberg recognizes this, and I think this explains some of his formulations that I have already mentioned. Korn apparently also sees the implication of this, for he says that each group should call God by its own name, worship in its own way, relate to God with its own covenant, and understand God with its own religious insight. However, if that is the case, then what happens when these other sacred covenants affirm notions that Judaism cannot accept? It appears unavoidable that this will mean a legitimization of what Judaism has historically regarded as *avodah zarah*.

As I have already noted, this also appears to be the perhaps unintended implication of what Sacks wrote, what we can call Sacks #1. Sacks #2, after the revision of *The Dignity of Difference*, is a traditionalist according to whom all religions must be judged by their adherence to the Noahide Code. Sacks #1 does not mention anything about the theological restrictions of the Noahide Code, and for obvious reasons, since insistence on the Noahide Code in theological matters would be at odds with Sacks's major points that Judaism does not have the entire truth, that Jews must recognize the truth in other religions, and that God speaks to all people. If other religions are to be judged by their theological adherence to the Noahide Code, then Judaism has a theological veto over them.

It was the liberal approach of Sacks #1 that led to *The Dignity of Difference* being condemned as heresy and Sacks's rewriting of it.[59] It is worth noting that in 2004 Sacks won the prestigious Grawemeyer Award for *The Dignity of Difference*. Yet he won this award for the first edition of the book. According to the press release sent out by the award presenters, the prize-winning book challenges the view "that if one religion is true, all others must be false."[60] Needless to say, a Christian institution (Louisville Presbyterian Theological Seminary, which gives the award together with the University of Louisville) was not giving its highest honor to someone who thinks that Christianity is only acceptable and of value if it meets the standards of the Noahide Code as set forth by Jewish sages. This latter notion, which is behind the changes in the book's second edition, is completely at odds with what appears in the first edition.

---

59 See my "Of Books and Bans," *The Edah Journal* 3, no. 2 (2003): 1–16.
60 This press release can no longer be found on the internet. The phrase "if one religion is true, all others must be false" originates in Bertrand Russell's *The Problem of China* (New York: George Allen & Unwin Ltd., 1922), 40–41, where it is in fact identified as a Jewish concept: "The Chinese have not the belief, which we owe to the Jews, that if one religion is true, all others must be false."

Alon Goshen-Gottstein summarizes the difference between the two versions of Sacks's book as follows:

> The radicality of Sacks' pluralism is that he grounds it in God, thereby referring to differences of other religions as God-given, on a par with the particularity of the Jewish tradition. The later edition grounds pluralism in the human person and in human understanding and aspiration. Multiple revelations give way to multiple human understandings. If the earlier statement was open to multiple truths and to *religious* (as distinct from natural or human) diversity, the later position only recognizes human diversity as the source of differences between cultures, but has no room for religious foundations of the differences of different religions.[61]

Rabbi Shlomo Riskin is another Orthodox thinker who in a recent article has argued for religious pluralism of a sort.[62] While he indeed uses the term "religious pluralism," he really only deals with Christianity so it is not clear how far his position will go. On the one hand, he advocates R. Menahem Meiri's view "that idolatry is defined by ethical and moral abominations in the name of religion rather than with incorrect theological concepts."[63] Yet at the same time, Riskin speaks about the importance of the Noahide Covenant, which also forbids idolatry even for moral idolaters.

In seeking to make space in traditional Jewish theology for Christianity, Riskin adopts three approaches. One is that of Meiri, which I think is the most successful way to deal with the issue. The other approach is the argument that non-Jews are not obligated in what is known as *shituf*, that is, associating other beings (e.g., Jesus) with God. This idea has precedent in a long line of authorities. Riskin's third approach is, I think, quite strange considering the general thrust

---

61 Goshen-Gottstein, "Arguing For/Over the Dignity of Difference," 8. Goshen-Gottstein also analyzes at length the theological differences between the two versions of Sacks' book.
62 Shlomo Riskin, "Covenant and Conversion: The United Mission to Redeem the World," in *Covenant and Hope: Christian and Jewish Reflections*, eds. Robert We Jensen and Eugene Korn (Grand Rapids, Michigan: Eerdmans, 2012), 99–128.
63 Ibid., 125. Menachem Meiri agrees that idolatrous worship is forbidden for all. However, the implication of Meiri's statements is that such worship alone does not turn one into the "idolater" that is the focus of various harsh Talmudic judgments and laws. For this, one needs to also engage in thoroughly immoral behavior. See Moshe Halbertal, *Bein Torah le-Hokhmah: Rabbi Menahem ha-Meiri u-Va'alei ha-Halakhahh ha-Maimonim be-Provence* (Jerusalem: Magnes, 2000), ch. 3.

of his article. He relies on the Talmudic statement (*Hullin* 13b) that "Gentiles outside the Land of Israel are not idolaters but only follow the traditions of their fathers." The upshot of this statement for Riskin is that Christianity is an "illegitimate theology,"[64] but Christians are not worshippers of *avodah zarah*.

The reason I say it is strange to quote this text is that, applied to contemporary times, its meaning is that present-day Christians do not take their religion seriously and are just going through the motions. One cannot regard Christianity as a serious theology held by committed people—as Riskin indeed does—and at the same see the Talmudic statement as a valid categorization of these very people. The internal contradiction is simply untenable. Furthermore, while this approach might be helpful halakhically, it also raises the problem of paternalism, as it is Jews determining that Christians do not really take their religion seriously.

Riskin concludes his discussion by noting that everyone prays to "the same Divine Force who created and guides our world," and for the first time he mentions religions other than Christianity.

> Allah is another name for the one God ("El" or "Elohim"), the Trinity is mysteriously considered a unity by Christians, all the physical representations of the Buddha are meant to express the All in the All that is the god of the Far East.[65]

R. Joseph B. Soloveitchik was very concerned that when it came to interfaith dialogue that there would be a problem of quid pro quo. That is, the Christians revise their theology and in turn the Jews feel the need, even if only subconsciously, to do the same. It seems that this is what Riskin, and also Greenberg and Korn, have done (although they would claim that their new theological insights have nothing to do with quid pro quo but are instead the results of recent positive Jewish experiences with Christians). In recognition of the changes in Christian views of the Jews, Christians are now being told that their religion also shares in God's covenant.[66] Yet I do not see why one must concede this point,

---

64 Riskin, "Covenant and Conversion," 124.
65 Ibid., 126. Contrary to Riskin, Buddhists do not speak of a "Divine Force who created and guides our world."
66 In December 2015 a public statement appeared, signed by twenty-five Orthodox rabbis, stating that "Christianity is neither an accident nor an error, but the willed divine outcome and gift to the nations. ... Both Jews and Christians have a common covenantal mission to perfect the world under the sovereignty of the Almighty, so that all humanity

even from a purely political perspective. One can respect Christians, Muslims, Hindus, and others, treat them with dignity, and assume that they have a share in the world to come, without at the same time speaking of their religions as part of God's covenant and claiming that these religions have sanctity. If these religions make their adherents better people and the world a better place, then they are valuable and deserve great respect. However, this has nothing to do with whether the unique faith claims of these religions also have theological truth.

---

will call on His name and abominations will be removed from the earth." See "Orthodox Rabbinic Statement on Christianity," *The Center for Jewish–Christian Understanding & Cooperation* (Dec. 3, 2015), http://cjcuc.org/2015/12/03/orthodox-rabbinic-statement-on-christianity/. For a critical response, see David Berger, "Vatican II at 50," *Tablet* (Dec. 15, 2015).

CHAPTER 7

On Revelation, Heresy, and Mesorah—from Louis Jacobs to the TheTorah.com

MIRI FREUD-KANDEL

Academic biblical scholarship poses multiple challenges to Orthodox Judaism's concept of divine revelation. Historical and literary evidence pointing to such things as the composite nature of the Pentateuchal text, its multiple authors, the extended period of time in which it appears to have been compiled, and the sociocultural influences from the societies of the ancient Near East, have combined to raise questions regarding the Orthodox Jewish belief in *Torah min hashamayim*—"Torah from heaven."

Notwithstanding these problems, in 2013, Marc Shapiro presented a lecture in Oxford in which he reviewed some of the growing evidence within contemporary Orthodoxy of engagement with the range of scholarly challenges to the received account of *Torah min hashamayim*. He suggested that some of the fears associated with addressing this topic appeared to be breaking down.[1]

In this paper, I intend to expand on Shapiro's work by comparing two events between the 1960s and 2010s, exploring the extent to which greater flexibility within Orthodoxy regarding the findings of academic biblical scholarship can be discerned. The first event, the so-called "Jacobs Affair" in British

---

1 Marc Shapiro, "Is Modern Orthodoxy Moving towards an Acceptance of Biblical Criticism?," (lecture, Oriental Institute, University of Oxford, May 29, 2013). Shapiro's argument in this talk was subsequently published in a paper with the same title in *Modern Judaism*, 37, no. 2 (May 2017): 165–93.

Jewry, began in December 1961 and involved the successful ostracism from British Orthodoxy of Rabbi Dr Louis Jacobs, at the time viewed by many as a promising minister with strong prospects of becoming chief rabbi. Ostensibly, Jacobs's views on revelation were a key motivator in his exclusion from Orthodoxy. The second event is the establishment in 2013 of Project TABS (Torah and Biblical Scholarship) and its associated website, TheTorah.com. Designed to address rather than duck some of the challenges of biblical criticism, the willingness of contributors to this website to countenance the arguments of academic scholarship led to severe attacks from some quarters.

A key factor in this analysis is the role of geography in influencing theological flexibility, the scope for debate, and the assertion of controlling religious authority. The events of the Jacobs Affair were influenced by particular characteristics of British Jewry. By contrast, the development of web-based Jewish content on one level circumvents geography. As such, it points to some of the new challenges faced by Orthodoxy in an age of globalized communication and social media.[2] By crossing spatial and religious/denominational boundaries, the internet facilitates the dissemination of ideas that could otherwise be restricted in certain sectors. Yet the reception of themes disseminated in this way can remain bound by limits of geography as the assertion of local religious authority imposes limitations on what can be deemed religiously acceptable—or problematic.

Consequently, at the heart of the analysis here is the recurring question of religious authority and the manner in which it determines the contours of the debate over approaches to revelation in Orthodox Judaism. The increasing recourse to notions of *Mesorah* (tradition), used to empower those who seek to demarcate what is and is not acceptable within Orthodoxy, highlights a battleground pivotal in determining the future trajectory of Orthodox Judaism. The construction of a meta-argument that in certain respects seeks to function beyond any framework of critique offers a means of trying to protect the religious authority of those who seek to maintain what purports to be a Maimonidean approach to faith, drawing from the eighth of Maimonides's Thirteen Principles. However, the influence of political agendas emerges here as

---

2   Concerted efforts within Haredi sectors of Orthodoxy have sought to circumscribe access to computers or the internet, conscious of the threat they pose. Digital resources have also been harnessed in some sectors to further Jewish learning and outreach. See H. Campbell, ed., *Digital Judaism: Jewish Negotiations with Digital Media and Culture* (New York and London: Routledge, 2015). On Israeli Haredi responses, see Y. Cohen, "Haredim and the Internet: A Hate-Love Affair," in *Mediating Faiths: Religion and Socio-Cultural Change in the Twenty-First Century*, ed. M Bailey and G. Redden (Surrey: Ashgate, 2011), 63–74; K. Barzilai-Nahon and G. Barzilai, "Cultured Technology: The Internet and Religious Fundamentalism," *The Information Society* 21 (2005): 25–40.

significant, especially when considering the challenges that can be directed at Maimonides's own acceptance of all the tenets contained in this principle. This article will assess efforts presenting possible alternative positions.[3]

The first section offers a consideration of the experiences of Louis Jacobs in British Orthodoxy. At first glance, the lasting impact of the Jacobs Affair on the consciousness of British Jewry challenges Shapiro's thesis that Orthodoxy is increasingly making space for biblical criticism. In a British context, engagement with Jacobs's thought is circumscribed to exclude all bodies associated with the Orthodox religious authorities of the community.[4]

The following two sections consider increasing engagement with biblical scholarship within Orthodox Judaism beyond British shores in the period since the 1960s. Responses emerging following the launch of the website TheTorah.com reveal how contemporary interest in addressing the challenges of biblical scholarship to revelation have reignited controversy, heralding a return to similar charges of heresy to those expressed in some quarters in the 1960s and claims that Jewish faith is being undermined. Yet in important respects, the debate around these issues has been altered somewhat. The development of Open Orthodox Judaism, a strengthening of broader post-denominationalist impulses, and changing approaches to the types of answers that are even sought for theological questions can all be discerned. This suggests that a further examination of some of Shapiro's conclusions in regard to contemporary Orthodox attitudes toward biblical criticism can expand our understanding of the changing challenges facing Orthodoxy on institutional and theological grounds and the evolution it continues to experience.

LOUIS JACOBS AND THE JACOBS AFFAIR

Louis Jacobs's writings were driven by an effort to transmit the importance of theology to the life of a Jew. Jacobs urged individuals to undertake a "Quest" in

---

3 Alongside questions regarding the authority of revelation, feminism represents another area in which contemporary Orthodoxy has increasingly faced challenges. Examining Orthodox responses in both these areas highlights an instinct among those who perceive themselves as defenders of the tradition to make recourse to meta-arguments that can function above critique. See, for example, Adam Ferziger, "Feminism and Heresy: The Construction of a Jewish Metanarrative," in *Journal of the American Academy of Religion*, September 2009 (77): 3, 494–546.

4 For an example, see Elie Jesner, "I Was Silenced and You Need to Know Why," *Jewish Chronicle*, November 17, 2016.

order to try to make sense of their Judaism in contemporary terms that could resonate and help them, as he expressed it in the title of his most famous work, retain their "reason to believe." Noting the language of the blessing recited before Torah study, "Blessed are you … who has sanctified us with divine commandments and commanded us to busy ourselves with words of Torah," Jacobs argued: "The command to study the Torah is not a demand that we actually reach the full truth, only that we be honestly engaged in seeking it. The very involvement in the quest is the essential part of the mitzvah."[5] Jacobs did not shy away from acknowledging the marginal role that theology often plays in Jewish life. The importance of belief in influencing Jewish observance may well be questionable.[6] He nonetheless argued, "Judaism is not a form of behaviourism. All the practices of traditional Judaism are buttressed by faith. For the precepts to possess religious value they must be carried out as the Word of God."[7] Jacobs insisted that understanding how God could and did reveal a Divine Will was a critical question. Determining what divine revelation as the "Word of God" was to be understood to mean accordingly lay at the heart of his theology.

In *A Jewish Theology*, Jacobs explains that the task of the theologian should be differentiated from that of the historian. Rather than considering what Jews have believed in the past, "the theologian is embarked on the more difficult, but, if realised, more relevant, task of discovering what it is that a Jew can believe in the present."[8] For Jacobs, academic biblical scholarship had unequivocally demonstrated the impossibility of maintaining a literal understanding of Torah as the word of God, dictated to Moses at Sinai, and faithfully transmitted and captured in the Torah scrolls contained in contemporary synagogues. With a background in the yeshiva world and no preparation for the ideas he would study in university—in a manner somewhat comparable to the experiences

---

5   Louis Jacobs, *God, Torah, Israel: Traditionalism without Fundamentalism* (Cincinnati: Hebrew Union College Press, 1990), 48. The principle of the individual quest was central to Jacobs's thought, referred to across his many writings, and used as the name for the educational organization established by his New London Synagogue.

6   See, for example, Louis Jacobs, *Beyond Reasonable Doubt* (London: Littman, 1999), 51–2, 237, where Jacobs acknowledges the influence of factors other than belief in determining how Jews act and approach their religion. For an example of a sociological analysis of the factors influencing modern observance of Jewish ritual, see Arnold Eisen, *Rethinking Modern Judaism: Ritual, Commandment, Community* (Chicago: University of Chicago Press, 1999).

7   Louis Jacobs, *Principles of the Jewish Faith: An Analytical Study* (London: Vallentine Mitchell, 1964), x.

8   Louis Jacobs, *A Jewish Theology* (London: Darton, Longman & Todd, 1973), 1.

of Rabbi Yitz Greenberg prior to attending Brooklyn College—Jacobs experienced a radical clash with his beliefs.[9] Unable to countenance moving beyond and rejecting his belief in a personal, transcendent God capable of revealing a divine will, at the same time he could not dismiss the scholarly challenges to these beliefs that he encountered in his studies. Many of his writings consequently sought to reinterpret the meaning of revelation to construct new ways of approaching the concept to secure belief "in the present" and ensure that the mitzvot could retain their status as divine commands.

Jacobs first produced a detailed written account of this interpretation of revelation in his 1957 book *We Have Reason To Believe*.[10] The title of this work accurately reflected his expressed goal of applying reason to faith to produce an account of Judaism that could withstand a modernist critique. He attempted to defend the principle of "Torah from Heaven" while reinterpreting the meaning of the term "from" to incorporate human as well as divine elements. This dialectical theology, which Jacobs termed "Liberal Supernaturalism," built on a Buberian notion of encounter underpinning revelation. Despite questioning the precise divine content, he proceeded from there, in somewhat Rosenzweigian terms, to argue for a retention of the mitzvot contained in the Torah as divinely commanded.[11] In his retrospective work, *Beyond Reasonable Doubt*, Jacobs specified one of his aims to have been the identification of "the reasonable conclusions that result from 'scientific' investigation into the origins of the Bible and of Judaism itself."[12] In certain respects what emerges here is the manner in which his encounter with modernist ideas enthralled him, while his

---

9 Jacobs's family upbringing was not as thoroughly Orthodox as that of Greenberg; however, he became immersed in the yeshiva world so that he only encountered critical scholarship at university.

10 Louis Jacobs, *We Have Reason to Believe: Some Aspects of Jewish Theology Examined in the Light of Modern Thought* (New York: Vallentine Mitchell, 1957).

11 This draws from the distinction Rosenzweig identifies between law as *Gebot*—divine command—as distinct from *Gesetz*—specific laws. Observance of the latter, even in the absence of the perception of a direct sense of commandedness, offers a means of fulfilling the former, thereby securing an ongoing value for religious practice. See Franz Rosenzweig, *The Star of Redemption*, trans. William Hallo, (Notre Dame: University of Notre Dame Press, 1985), 176ff.

12 Jacobs, *Beyond Reasonable Doubt*, 25. See Louis Jacobs's *A Tree of Life: Diversity, Flexibility and Creativity in Jewish Law* (Oxford: Oxford University Press for the Littman Library, 1984) to appreciate Jacobs's understanding of revelation in relation to halakhah. For an intellectual biography of Jacobs's formative years, see Elliot Cosgrove, *Teyku: The Insoluble Contradictions in the Life and Thought of Louis Jacobs* (PhD diss., University of Chicago, 2008).

yeshiva background left him lacking the tools to understand the critique of its values that already existed when he was still trying to form a modernist Jewish theology. As Tamar Ross notes in a review of this later work,

> A major flaw in Jacobs' presentation is the fact that he still frames the question of valid criteria for distinguishing truth from dross in an early 20th-century modernist mode. That is to say, Jacobs is one of those who believe that there is a rock-bottom foundation of objective, neutral truth, and that "getting the right answer" is a matter of somehow ridding ourselves of the prejudices of fundamentalist religion in favor of an approach that takes into account reason and scientific inquiry. ... [He] fails to address the postmodernist notion that there is no neutral vantage point from which we may begin to discriminate between divine and human elements in the Torah. What postmodernism has taught us is that every act of observation is also an act of interpretation. The postmodern challenge to the divinity of the Torah is that no written or verbal medium can avoid the limitation of an all-pervasive perspective that both limits and biases its message.[13]

Examining the range of Jacobs's writings raises some challenges to this view. His appreciation of divine mystery and acknowledgment of the role of religious experience, building on a sense of revelation as divine encounter, allowed him space to argue that the divine and human elements of revelation could never be fully disentangled.[14] Ross's critique nonetheless highlights how many contemporary Jews raising theological questions are seeking different types of answers to those ostensibly offered by Jacobs. This could reflect changes in scholarship or be indicative of certain shifts within Orthodoxy as the location of its boundaries with Conservative Judaism have moved, creating greater flexibility in certain areas, which will be considered further below.

Regardless of how Jacobs's efforts to revise accounts of revelation were intended to defend a retained authority for the Torah and its mitzvot, the scope for his views to be countenanced within British Jewry was always limited. To the extent that British chief rabbis addressed theological matters

---

13 Tamar Ross, "Review," *Studies in Contemporary Jewry* 18 (2002): 303–4.
14 This argument is developed further by Paul Morris, "Torah min Hashamayim in Orthodox Theology: Disputes, Debates and Discourse," *Journal of Modern Jewish Studies* 14, no. 1 (2015): 27–39. See also the forthcoming Miri J. Freud-Kandel, *Theology and the Jewish Quest: The Religious Thought of Louis Jacobs* (Liverpool: Littman, 2020).

and gave consideration to interpretations of revelation, the findings of academic biblical scholarship were given little credence. During the chief rabbinate of Joseph Herman Hertz, between 1913 and 1946, the ideas associated with Higher Criticism were forcefully dismissed. Following the position of Solomon Schechter, it was characterized rather as Higher Antisemitism.[15] A quick scan of the popular commentary on the Pentateuch edited by Hertz, widely referred to as the Hertz Chumash, highlights the challenges posed by Jacobs's views.[16]

Also clear is how Jacobs's views did serve to alter the authority of the mitzvot contained within the Torah. By offering a reinterpreted account of revelation acknowledging human input, his position posed problems on a sociological level in addition to the theological questions it presented, since it could undermine the practical willingness to observe the mitzvot given their diminished divine sanction. Chaim Waxman has argued that it was this challenge, rather than charges of heresy, that led to Jacobs's ostracism from British Orthodoxy. In Waxman's reading, sociological concerns about standards of religious observance were of greater significance than theological matters.[17] While this account captures the marginal role theology often plays in the choices Jews make about religious observance, a point acknowledged by Jacobs, it also seems to overplay the role of observance within mainstream British Orthodoxy, reflecting the contemporaneous reality of the era of Orthodox nonobservance noted by Jeffrey Gurock in America too.[18] This was well-highlighted in the decision by one of Jacobs's key supporters, the former president of the mainstream Orthodox United Synagogue, Ewen Montagu, to be cremated following his death. In this context, an acceptance of literal accounts of revelation and

---

15 See Joseph Hertz, *The Pentateuch and Haftorahs* (London: Soncino, 1975), 554, 397; S. Schechter, "Higher Criticism—Higher Anti Semitism" in *Seminary Addresses & Other Papers* (New York: Burning Bush Press, 1960), 35–9. For additional accounts of religious disputes of British chief rabbis and the religious positions they sought to maintain, see Meir Persoff, *Faith Against Reason: Religious Reform and the British Chief Rabbinate 1840–1990* (London: Vallentine Mitchell, 2008).
16 See Eliezer Finkelman, "Torah from Heaven: Re-defining the Question," http://thetorah.com/torah-from-heaven-redefining/, which identifies the Hertz Chumash as an example of the entrenched views within Orthodoxy that view biblical scholarship as wholly incompatible with received accounts of revelation.
17 See Chaim I. Waxman, "Halakhic Change vs Demographic Change: American Orthodoxy, British Orthodoxy, and the Plight of Louis Jacobs," *Journal of Modern Jewish Studies* 14, no. 1 (2015): 58–71.
18 See Jeffrey S. Gurock, "Twentieth-Century American Orthodoxy's Era of Non-Observance, 1900–1960," *The Torah u-Madda Journal* IX (2000): 87–107.

the rejection of biblical criticism functioned as important boundary markers that helped to set Orthodoxy apart regardless of observance; this marked out Jacobs's position as challenging.

Beyond both theological and more practical sociological factors, Jacobs's outlook was further problematized by the nature of the institutional setup of British Jewry.[19] Influenced by the role of the established Church of England in British society, the Jewish community perceived a value in creating its own centralized umbrella institutions that could offer something of a parallel to church structures. The Board of Deputies of British Jews, the United Synagogue, the British chief rabbinate, and its Bet Din were all bodies that sought to consolidate authority and representation in British Jewry. This process reduced the scope for the development of independent bodies or innovative thinking.[20] The varied events that became known as the Jacobs Affair highlighted this centralized religious control.

The initial move that ignited the flames of the Jacobs Affair occurred in December 1961, when Jacobs resigned from his post at the Orthodox rabbinical seminary, Jews' College. Jacobs had taken up a position at this institution following assurances from a number of members of the college's governing body that he would shortly be promoted to the principalship. Reflecting the nature of Jewish institutional life in British Orthodoxy, formal ratification for this appointment lay in the hands of the chief rabbi, a position then occupied by Israel Brodie. Brodie's refusal to provide his approval led Jacobs to seek to force his hand by resigning. With Brodie subsequently under pressure to explain his decision, the London Bet Din jumped in to issue a statement identifying a "deep concern for the views expressed by the candidate in his writings and

---

19 For a detailed consideration of the institutional development of British Jewry, see Aubrey Newman, *The United Synagogue, 1870–1970* (London: Routledge & Kegan Paul, 1976); Raphael Langham, *250 Years of Convention and Contention: A History of the Board of Deputies of British Jews 1760–2010* (London: Vallentine Mitchell, 2010); Geoffrey Alderman, *Modern British Jewry* (Oxford: Oxford University Press, 1992); idem, "The British Chief Rabbinate: A Most Peculiar Practice," *European Judaism* 23, no. 2 (1990): 45–58; Todd Endelman, "The Englishness of Jewish Modernity in England," in *Toward Modernity, The European Jewish Model*, ed. J. Katz (Piscataway, NJ: Transaction, 1987), 225–67; Miri Freud-Kandel, *Orthodox Judaism in Britain Since 1913, An Ideology Forsaken* (London: Vallentine Mitchell, 2006).

20 Immanuel Jakobovits, prior to his appointment as chief rabbi, lambasted British Jewry for its predilection towards centralized institutions, which he argued had inhibited its scope for religious creativity. See "The Anglo-Jewish Contribution to Judaism, Tercentenary Reflections," *The Jewish Chronicle*, August 31, 1956, republished in his *Journal of a Rabbi* (London: W. H. Allen, 1967), 48–53.

addresses, which the Chief Rabbi considered to be in conflict with the fundamental beliefs of traditional Judaism."[21]

Prior to his appointment to Jews' College, Jacobs had served as minister of the United Synagogue's New West End Congregation. When this pulpit again became vacant around the end of 1963, a number of Jacobs's supporters, many of whom were prominent members of a sector of the lay leadership of British Jewry used to getting their way, sought to secure his reappointment to this post.[22] Yet again, however, the formal structures of British Orthodoxy intervened. The constitution of the United Synagogue recognized the chief rabbi as the religious authority over the institution as a whole, devolving only limited powers to the ministers serving each congregation. Formal approval from the chief rabbi was required before any rabbinic appointments could be made within the United Synagogue. Although Jacobs had received the necessary certification when first appointed to the New West End pulpit in 1954, Brodie was unwilling to provide his approval this time and insisted that without it, the post could not be filled. When the Board of Management of the New West End sought to circumvent the chief rabbi's authority, arguing that they wished to secure the appointment of the congregation's preferred candidate, Brodie had the committee removed from office.[23] This ultimately led to the formation of an independent congregation, the New London Synagogue. This community functioned outside the auspices of the United Synagogue and chief rabbinate. The instinct toward centralization ensured that it still required approval from the office of chief rabbi in order to be recognized by the Board of Deputies as a place of Jewish worship, a formal requirement if it was to be civilly registered to perform marriages. This certification was provided by Brodie's successor as chief rabbi, Immanuel Jakobovits, who hoped to calm communal relations somewhat by this act.

---

21 *Jewish Chronicle*, February 2, 1962. Coverage of the Jacobs Affair became a regular feature of *The Jewish Chronicle*. See, for example, *Jewish Chronicle*, December 29, 1961; January 6, 1962; May 11, 1962. See also Cosgrove's detailed account of the behind-the-scenes events that precipitated the events of the Jacobs Affair in Cosgrove, *Teyku*, 217ff. For the formal statement subsequently issued by Brodie explaining his position, see "Statement to Rabbis and Ministers," May 6, 1964, in *The Strength of My Heart: Sermons and Addresses, 1948–1965* (London: G. J. George, 1969), 343–55.
22 Chaim Bermant coined the term "Cousinhood" to refer to the interrelated lay leadership that dominated the hierarchies of Ashkenazi Jewry in Britain until around the mid-twentieth century. See his *The Cousinhood* (London: Eyre and Spottiswoode, 1971).
23 Jacobs offers his own perspective on this and other battles he faced with the Orthodox authorities in *Helping With Inquiries: An Autobiography* (London: Vallentine Mitchell, 1989), 160ff.

The events associated with the Jacobs Affair did not end there. Rather, they dragged on, further affirming the power of the chief rabbi, in consultation with his Bet Din, to exert religious authority over a significant sector of British Orthodoxy. During the chief rabbinate of Jonathan Sacks, around the turn of the twenty-first century, Jacobs was refused an *aliyah* (call up to the reading of the Torah) at the *aufruf* (pre-wedding *aliyah*) of his granddaughter's fiancé in a congregation under the auspices of the chief rabbi.[24] Jacobs's successful ostracism from British Orthodoxy allowed no leniencies.

When assessing both the opposition Jacobs faced and the support he received, the influence of broader concerns is manifest. There was a time lag of four years between the 1957 publication of Jacobs's *We Have Reason to Believe* and the eruption of the first stage of the Jacobs Affair. This was the period during which Jacobs took up his post at Jews' College, which could be taken to imply, as Jacobs and his supporters sought to do, that suspicions about his Orthodoxy were not fully formed as a consequence of the ideas expressed in his work.[25] Elliot Cosgrove's archival research has raised questions about this narrative. He has drawn attention to evidence of ongoing concerns regarding Jacobs's theology from both Brodie and members of his Bet Din.[26] Nonetheless, as Cosgrove also acknowledges, pointing to the argument Waxman subsequently developed, the extent to which theology can be identified as a driver in the events of the Jacobs Affair needs to be considered. This battle was about more than the arguments expressed in *We Have Reason to Believe*.

For many individuals on both sides of this clash, the specifics of Jacobs's argument for applying reason to Judaism and producing an account of revelation that could still retain a sense of divine authority were somewhat marginal. As has been suggested, among many of Jacobs's supporters, their approach to religious observance lagged some way behind their Orthodox affiliation. Consequently, questions about the divine origins of the Torah were of limited importance. What attracted them to Jacobs was an interest in supporting a rabbinical figure who had expressed a willingness to offer an account of Judaism that acknowledged some of the challenges faced by contemporary British Jews.

---

24 See *Jewish Chronicle*, August 1 and August 15, 2003. See also Meir Persoff, *Another Way, Another Time* (Brighton: Academic Studies Press, 2010), 258–9. The coastal Bournemouth Hebrew Congregation is not a member of the United Synagogue but nonetheless recognized the chief rabbi as its religious authority, highlighting the instinct toward centralized authority in British Jewry.

25 See *Helping with Inquiries*.

26 Cosgrove, *Teyku*, 221–37, 247–60.

Their perception, correct or not, was that the Orthodox establishment in British Jewry, influenced in particular by the chief rabbi's Bet Din, was moving to the religious right.[27] Through this process, support for the Britishness of British Jewry was seen to be diminished. Jacobs was seen to offer an alternative to this religious trajectory.

Rather than being a debate about interpretations of revelation, the Jacobs Affair was, then, in many respects an effort on both sides to influence who exerted control over the religious direction of the community. It was a battle over religious authority, but one that was precipitated more by political rather than theological concerns. The willingness Jacobs exhibited to question the received dominant account of revelation was interpreted by both his supporters and opponents to indicate a broader questioning approach to religious issues. Highlighting the influence of geographical factors, the nature of the institutional setup of British Jewry automatically weighted the scales in favor of the religious establishment.

---

27   The perception of a rightward shift in Orthodox Judaism received extensive consideration at the 2014 Oxford Summer Institute. The particulars of Jewish settlement in Britain influenced the types of shifts that can be identified in British Orthodoxy. Increased levels of religious observance, with an associated growth of kosher butchers, grocers, and restaurants, a rise in more strictly Orthodox communities, *mikvaot*, and rabbis only became manifest in the latter stages of the twentieth century. Notwithstanding the views of Jacobs's supporters in the 1960s, the explanation for these shifts is by no means due to the efforts of religious leaders alone. Rather, these moves can be seen to reflect changes more broadly observable in Modern Orthodox communities outside Britain—away from Orthodoxy's era of nonobservance. This was influenced by such factors as the development of multiculturalism and the increased role of Jewish education. See Charles S. Liebman, "Orthodoxy in American Jewish Life," *American Jewish Year Book* 66 (1965): 21–97; Samuel C. Heilman, *Sliding to the Right: The Contest for the Future of American Jewish Orthodoxy* (Berkeley: University of California Press, 2006); Jeffrey S. Gurock, "Twentieth-Century American Orthodoxy's Era of Non-Observance,"; M. J. Freud-Kandel, "Minhag Anglia: The Transition of Modern Orthodox Judaism in Britain," *PaRDeS, Zietschrift der Vereinigung für Jüdische Studien* 18 (2012): 35–49. See also Keith Kahn-Harris and Ben Gidley, *Turbulent Times, The British Jewish Community Today* (London: Continuum, 2010), which examines shifts in cultural Jewish identity among British Jews and related falls in United Synagogue membership. Chaim Waxman has argued that other factors challenge this narrative somewhat. Increased religious education and knowledge secured observance of practices that had previously been marginalized though always part of Orthodox teaching, while certain practices previously critiqued as outside Orthodoxy found their way into Modern Orthodox communities. See his "Halakhic Change vs Demographic Change"; Yehuda Turetsky and Chaim I. Waxman, "Sliding to the Left? Contemporary American Modern Orthodoxy," *Modern Judaism* 31, no. 2 (May 2011): 119–41; idem, *Social Change and Halakhic Evolution in American Orthodoxy* (Liverpool: Littman, 2017).

By successfully forcing Jacobs outside of Orthodox Judaism in Britain, the foundations came to be put in place for the subsequent creation of the Masorti movement in British Jewry. This functioned wholly beyond the control of the British chief rabbinate and outside Orthodoxy. The political battle for religious control of mainstream British Orthodoxy had been lost by Jacobs's supporters. Although Jacobs initially had sought to argue that his theological position could be presented as falling within the boundaries of an Orthodox account of Judaism, he later conceded that the space he and his supporters had come to occupy within British Jewry, with their questioning of the power of the religious authorities within the community, had resulted in their ostracism from this world. Jacobs accepted, albeit not necessarily willingly, a characterization of his views as Masorti.[28]

In certain respects, it is this last point that is worthy of further consideration as we turn our attention to more recent efforts within Orthodox Judaism to address the challenges to belief in divine revelation. The pushback against attempts to demarcate strict boundaries that would place certain individuals and ideas beyond the pale of Orthodox Judaism is a striking feature of contemporary battles. Feminist issues play a notable role here also. The growth in knowledge of the diversity of views countenanced within rabbinic Judaism—beyond what are presented as Maimonidean dogmatics—poses new challenges regarding the question of who is empowered to determine what is and is not acceptable within Orthodoxy. For those seeking to extend the boundaries, and those trying to guard them, efforts to define precisely how Orthodoxy is to be understood appear increasingly to be challenged.

POST-JACOBS

In the intervening years since the Jacobs Affair, there has been a marked growth within the Orthodox world of engagement with biblical scholarship. This is particularly manifest in three areas: within academic scholarship, in particular Israeli yeshivot, and on a popular level in certain educated circles of Orthodox Jewry. The examples offered below highlight rising challenges developing not only to the received interpretation of the Maimonidean account of how revelation is to be understood, but also regarding who gets to define these interpretations.

---

28 See, for example, his *Principles of the Jewish Faith*, x, and his later *Beyond Reasonable Doubt*, 14.

With increasing numbers of observant Jews entering the field of Jewish studies, not only have these individuals been engaging with the findings of scholarship, they have also been able to develop new fields of research from within a Jewish frame of reference. The planning of a Shabbat program for observant participants at the annual gathering of the Society of Biblical Literature (SBL) offers one indication of the increased profile of Orthodox Jews within the field of biblical scholarship. An example of the influence this is exerting beyond academic circles was a panel discussion on the subject of "Tradition and Scholarship, Tension and Complement," organized at the Orthodox B'nai Israel Synagogue in Baltimore to coincide with the 2013 SBL Conference. The suggestion at the end of this session that the *kaddish de'Rabannan* prayer be said, a prayer recited after religious study, indicated the sense not only that the scholarship undertaken was within the boundaries of Orthodoxy but also that it should ritually be acknowledged as such.[29]

The varied scholarship that has been pursued at an academic level has helped draw popular attention to the variety of ideas contained within rabbinic thought on how revelation can be understood.[30] This includes greater appreciation of Maimonides's own questioning of his Eighth Principle challenging what is meant by a Maimonidean position.[31] Widespread awareness of the questions raised by recognized medieval rabbinic authorities such as Abraham Ibn Ezra and Judah ha-Hasid on the nature and extent of divine revelation has also developed. Scholars such as James Kugel, Tamar Ross, and Norman Solomon, in significantly different ways, have disseminated some alternative views drawing from biblical scholarship within an Orthodox framework. While they

---

29 See Zev Garber, "Torah Thoughts, Rabbinic Mind, and Academic Freedom," TheTorah.com, http://thetorah.com/torah-thoughts-and-academic-freedom/. It should be noted that the Shabbat program was not solely aimed at Orthodox participants.

30 See, for example, Marc Shapiro, *The Limits of Orthodox Theology: Maimonides' Thirteen Principles Reappraised* (Oxford: Littman, 2004); Menachem Kellner, *Dogma in Medieval Jewish Thought: From Maimonides to Abravanel* (Oxford: Oxford University Press, 1986); idem, Kellner, *Must a Jew Believe Anything?* (London: Littman, 1999). As Shapiro notes in his 2017 *Modern Judaism* paper, "Is Modern Orthodoxy Moving towards an Acceptance of Biblical Criticism?," this growing popular knowledge has not disseminated to the masses but has spread among those interested in pursuing these issues.

31 See Daniel Rynhold, "Fascination Unabated: The Intellectual Love of Maimonides," *The Torah u-Madda Journal* 15 (2008–9): 257–82; Alfred Ivry, "The Image of Moses in Maimonides' Thought," 113–34 and Harvey Kreisel, "Maimonides on Divine Religion," 151–66, both in *Maimonides After 800 Years: Essays on Maimonides and His Influence*, ed. Jay M. Harris (Cambridge, MA: Harvard University Press, 2007). Marc Shapiro addressed this in *The Limits of Orthodox Theology*, 91ff.

have by no means escaped censure, critique, and explicit charges of heresy from some quarters, they continue to be invited to speak in Orthodox communities. Indeed Ross and Kugel both occupied faculty positions at the Orthodox-sponsored Bar Ilan University and, although there was opposition to their participation at events under the auspices of Yeshiva University, both were granted a forum there in which to speak. These scholars have contributed to efforts to demonstrate how, rather than challenging the authority of revelation, it is possible to identify the scope that exists within the tradition for addressing these ideas. The spaces that continue to be carved out for them to share their ideas indicate the Orthodox interest from certain sectors to learn more about this.[32]

The increasing influence of academic scholarship in certain Modern Orthodox Israeli yeshivot highlights another area in which perceptions of a challenge to received accounts of revelation are being reinterpreted in an effort to produce constructive responses rather than acceptance that these ideas are beyond the pale. Prominent yeshiva heads, like the late ShaGa"R (Shimon Gershon Rosenberg) and Yuval Cherlow, have applied tools of academic scholarship to Talmud study and acknowledged questions on the nature of revelation suggesting that alternative approaches can be valid. Rabbi David Bigman contributed an article to TheTorah.com outlining his approach to revelation. The article was an English translation of his contribution to a volume produced in Israel dedicated to addressing the challenge of scholarship to revelation, which brought together a group of broadly respected rabbis and scholars, who all locate themselves within the Orthodox world.[33] In a study of the varying ways in which certain

---

32 See James Kugel, *How to Read the Bible: A Guide to Scripture, Then and Now* (New York: Free Press, 2007); Tamar Ross, *Expanding the Palace of Torah: Orthodoxy and Feminism* (Waltham, MA: Brandeis University Press, 2004); Norman Solomon, *Torah from Heaven, The Reconstruction of Faith* (Oxford: Littman, 2012). On the critiques directed at Kugel and Ross, see *The Commentator* editions of January 7, 2009; February 11, 2009; February 18, 2009; or Orthodox blogs such as Hirhurim, January 1, 2009, http://hirhurim.blogspot.com/2008/12/considering-kugel.html; Aryeh Frimer, "Guarding the Treasure," *Bekhol Derakhekha Daehu – Journal of Torah and Scholarship* 18 (2007): 67–106. More limited controversy was directed at Solomon; see "A Book for the Thoughtful, 'Skeptical' Orthodox," *CJN*, January 7, 2013, http://www.cjnews.com/columnists/book-thoughtful-'skeptical'-orthodox; "When Orthodox Scholarship Is Neither," *CJN*, January 30, 2013, http://www.cjnews.com/opinions/when-orthodox-scholarship-neither; "Breaking: Toronot Vaad Excommunicates Rabbi Yehuda, Ibn Ezra, Others," DovBear, February 12, 2013, http://dovbear.blogspot.co.il/2013/02/breaking-toronto-vaad-excommunicates.html.

33 See Yehudah Brandes, Tova Ganzel, and Chayuta Deutsch, eds., *In The Sight of God and People: The Person of Faith and Biblical Criticism* [in Hebrew] (Jerusalem: Beit Morasha, 2015)

Israeli yeshivot are increasingly engaging with a range of ideas from scholarship, Lawrence Kaplan analyzed this greater willingness that appears to exist in some quarters to identify an alternative to a fear-driven response to the historicist challenge to Jewish texts, even as certain limits are retained.[34]

One of the contributory factors in the successful ostracism of Louis Jacobs from British Orthodoxy was that he raised his questions about revelation not as a scholar but as a rabbi seeking to take over the leadership of a rabbinical training institute. In contemporary Israel, the experience of rabbinical figures and respected Orthodox scholars engaging with these ideas has differed. Shapiro, noting some of these developments in his Oxford seminar paper, quoted an unnamed Haredi rabbinical leader, who anticipated that—like the eventual acceptance of Hasidism within the parameters of Orthodoxy, despite its former explicit exclusion—biblical criticism could also in time come to be accepted. The confluence of a rabbinic, scholarly, and educated cadre seeking to address the critique of biblical scholarship and demonstrate the possibility of constructing answers from within the Jewish tradition is certainly moving apace.

The significance of geography comes to the fore in these developments. The scope not just for academics but also rabbinical figures from certain Israeli yeshivot to engage with these challenges reflects important differences that demarcate the religious landscape of Orthodox Judaism in Israel. These differences distinguish it from both the British and American contexts. Among a variety of other factors, the weakness of Progressive Judaism in Israel offers a certain amount of freedom to engage with some of the questions emerging from academic scholarship, and a greater flexibility is consequently evident in certain Israeli Orthodox circles.[35]

---

and various essays on TheTorah.com. On ShaGa"R, see Miriam Feldman-Kaye,"Re-envisioning Jewish Theology: A Comparative Study of Harav Shagar and Tamar Ross" (PhD diss., University of Haifa, 2012). Also worth considering in this context, though it brings together individuals from a range of religious and secular backgrounds, is the website http://www.929.org.il, which offers a variety of approaches to the biblical text. At the 2017 World Congress in Jewish Studies at Hebrew University, Jerusalem, in a session on "Jewish Approaches to Bible Criticism," Adam Ferziger and Baruch Alster both gave papers considering some of the distinctive features of Israeli Orthodox engagement with biblical scholarship. See also Ferziger's essay in this volume.

34 Lawrence Kaplan, "Back to Zechariah Frankel and Louis Jacobs? On Integrating Academic Talmudic Scholarship into Israeli Religious Zionist Yeshivas and the Spectre of the Historical Development of the Halakhah," *Journal of Modern Jewish Studies* 14, no. 1 (2015): 89–108.

35 Tamar Ross addresses this phenomenon further in her article in this volume.

What is evident in these varied developments are the difficulties that have been experienced by those who have sought, in a manner reminiscent of Jacobs's treatment, to ostracize and place outside the boundaries of Orthodoxy those scholars or rabbinical figures who have been willing to countenance questions regarding the received accounts of divine revelation. Among the laity, in certain educated circles of Orthodox Jewry, there is evidence of a thirst for knowledge on the scope that exists within the rabbinic tradition of Judaism for addressing the challenges of biblical criticism.

The internet has been critical in the proliferation of this knowledge, as a resource and space for rapidly sharing and providing easy access to biblical scholarship through blogs and social media sites. The development of Project TABS and TheTorah.com fits within this newly developing framework. In examining below the backlash that has been directed against this initiative, it is clear that the influence of efforts to enforce boundary marking has by no means disappeared, which draws attention to comparisons with the events associated with the earlier Jacobs Affair.

THE TORAH.COM

The mission statement on the website of TheTorah.com states: "Project TABS (Torah And Biblical Scholarship) is an educational organization founded to energize the Jewish people by integrating the study of Torah with the disciplines and findings of academic biblical scholarship."[36] Rather than approaching the challenges of scholarship to revelation in negative terms, it is viewed as offering an opportunity. However, opponents of the website attempted to brand the initiative as heresy. The critique leveled against some of its key protagonists demarcated the engagement with academic biblical scholarship that characterized the website as beyond the boundaries of what was acceptable within Orthodoxy.[37]

Soon after the launch of the website, a series of essays was published by one of its founders, Zev Farber. While arguing that his Orthodox beliefs remained intact, he laid out here his acceptance of the findings of much of biblical scholarship: acknowledging the composite nature of the biblical text, the influence of mythologies from surrounding societies, and questioning the historical

---

36 See "About Project TABS – TheTorah.com," TheTorah.com, http://thetorah.com/about/.
37 This led to the resignation of three of the initial members of the Board of Project TABS.

reliability of the narrative and certain biblical characters.[38] Farber's associations with the burgeoning movement of Open Orthodoxy appeared to help draw ire to this initiative.[39] For its opponents, both Open Orthodoxy and receptivity to biblical scholarship challenge the pillars of religious authority understood to underpin any account of Orthodox Judaism.

Open Orthodoxy, though its name is being rethought by certain protagonists, represents a distinctive grouping on the left wing of the Orthodox spectrum. The term was developed by Rabbi Avraham (Avi) Weiss, the now retired Rabbi in Residence of the Hebrew Institute of Riverdale. He secured Open Orthodoxy with an institutional footing through its own rabbinical training college, Yeshivat Chovevei Torah (YCT), a sister institute training female religious leaders, Yeshivat Maharat, and its own rabbinical body, the International Rabbinical Fellowship (IRF).[40] Its development can be viewed as a response both to rightward shifts within Orthodoxy itself and the emergence of a space vacated by certain moves within the Conservative movement. During the approximately fifty-year period we have been examining, Conservative Judaism has taken a notable turn leftward, evident in its theology and decision-making on such issues as conversion, intermarriage, and advocacy of gay rights. The boundaries demarcating it from Orthodoxy have consequently become far

---

38 See Zev Farber, "Avraham Avinu Is My Father: Thoughts on Torah, History and Judaism," TheTorah.com, July 2013, http://thetorah.com/torah-history-judaism-introduction/. Earlier publications on the site by Farber included a two-part essay on Deuteronomy, which already incited criticism. See Zev Farber, "The Opening of Devarim: A Recounting or Different Version of the Wilderness Experience?," TheTorah.com, July 2013, http://thetorah.com/devarim-recounting-different/; Zev Farber, "The Opening of Devarim: Redaction Criticism and Modern Midrash," TheTorah.com, July 2013, http://thetorah.com/devarim-modern-midrash/.

39 The other two key figures involved in setting up Project TABS, Marc Zvi Brettler and David Steinberg, do not identify with Open Orthodoxy, though this has been ignored by the site's opponents.

40 See Avraham Weiss, "Open Orthodoxy! A Modern Orthodox Rabbi's Creed," *Judaism* 46, no. 4 (Fall 1997): 409–21. With attention on Open Orthodoxy heightened as a consequence of the battle over definitions of revelation and support for ordination of women rabbis, Weiss penned an updated popular summation of his position for *Tablet* magazine in June 2015: http://www.tabletmag.com/jewish-life-and-religion/191907/defining-open-orthodoxy. At the November 2015 gathering of the Agudath Israel of America, a proclamation by its guiding rabbinic council, the Moetzes Gedolei HaTorah of America, asserted that Open Orthodoxy did not represent an authentic form of Orthodox Judaism and graduates of its rabbinical seminaries were not to be recognized as Orthodox rabbis. The development of PORAT organization as a grassroots Orthodox pushback against right-leaning forces should also be noted, see poratonline.org.

clearer, facilitating engagement by Orthodox groups with certain issues previously associated with Conservative Judaism. In a 2014 furor over women wearing tefillin (phylacteries), it was instructive to see how supporters of this innovation were unafraid of the associations this ritual could conjure up with Conservative Judaism, secure in a sense of differentiation—while also driven by a growing consciousness of gender issues in Orthodoxy.[41] The development of Open Orthodoxy reflects, among other factors, the impact of intellectual engagement with contemporary thought among those sectors of Orthodoxy that continue to countenance this as a possibility.

Farber, a graduate of YCT and the first to receive *yadin yadin semikhah* (ordination as a religious judge), was coordinator of the conversion committee of the IRF. His involvement with TheTorah.com and the views he expressed in his opening essays were interpreted to represent Open Orthodox developments more broadly and lambasted accordingly. His critics presumed ostracism could successfully be achieved, as had been the case in the Jacobs's affair. In so doing, the opponents of TheTorah.com, who perceived a challenges to accounts of revelation to threaten the very structures of religious authority through which Orthodox Judaism was regulated, sought to reassert control. The intention was to attack and undermine the entire nascent movement with which Farber was associated and that he was seen to represent.

---

41 On changes in the Conservative movement, see J. Wertheimer, *A People Divided: Judaism in Contemporary America* (New York: Basic Books, 1993), 137–59; Daniel Elazar and Rela Mintz Geffen, *The Conservative Movement in Judaism: Dilemmas and Opportunities* (New York: SUNY Press, 2000); Jeffrey Gurock, "From Fluidity to Rigidity: The Religious Worlds of Conservative and Orthodox Jews in Twentieth Century America," in *American Jewish Identity Politics*, ed. Debrah Dash Moore (Ann Arbor: University of Michigan Press, 2009) 159–204; Jonathan Sarna, "The Debate over Mixed Seating in the American Synagogue," in *The American Synagogue: A Sanctuary Transformed*, ed. Jack Wertheimer (Hanover, NH: Brandeis University Press, 1987), 363–94. On the tefillin controversy, see Tully Harcsztark, "SAR Principal Explains Decision to Allow Girls to Wear Tefillin at School Minyanim," *The Jewish Star*, http://www.thejewishstar.com/stories/SAR-principal-explains-decision-to-allow-girls-to-wear-teffilin-at-school-minyanim,4665?sub_id=4665&print=1, January 26, 2014; Hershel Schachter, "On Women Wearing Tefillin" [in Hebrew], Theyeshivaworld.com, http://www.theyeshivaworld.com/wp-content/uploads/2014/02/rh.pdf; Steven Pruzansky, "The Real Story?," *Cross-Currents*, January 25, 2014, http://www.cross-currents.com/archives/2014/01/25/the-real-story. The Orthodox Rabbinical Council of America felt compelled to issue a statement affirming its approach to belief in revelation in response to the outcry that followed the launch of TheTorah.com: "RCA Statement on Torah Min HaShamayim," Rabbinical Council of America, July 31, 2013, http://www.rabbis.org/news/article.cfm?id=105768.

Many of these critiques were published in online publications such as the journal *Cross-Currents*. One such attack stated:

> Outright heresy is emanating from the heart of the YCT rabbinic world. No, this time we are not dealing with Open Orthodoxy … promoting yet another new brand of controversial inclusiveness or further blazing socio-religious trails that mainstream Orthodoxy and its halachic leadership deem as beyond the pale. This time, we are dealing with denial of the singular Divine authorship of the Torah–heresy of the highest order--publicly espoused in writing by one of Open Orthodoxy's most prominent rabbinic leaders. And we are also dealing with the rest of Open Orthodox rabbinic leadership refusing to condemn this heresy in its midst.[42]

Setting aside the blithe dismissal of the value of inclusivism, the criticism against Farber developed on two levels. First, his articles were damned as unquestionable heresy. Indeed, one response stated that the first reaction to encountering heresy of the sort espoused by Farber was to ensure that the boundary lines defining what is acceptable and what is heretical are clearly marked. It was acknowledged that people could benefit from the issues raised regarding biblical scholarship, yet it was tellingly noted that this "is the second order of business, not the first."[43] Beyond the identification of specific heresy, however, was a meta-halakhic argument charging Open Orthodoxy as a whole with representing "Mesorah-light Judaism." The nature of this critique was laid out in the following terms:

> This cavalier approach … denying that deference to Torah tradition and to greater Torah authorities are part of the bricks and mortar of Orthodoxy, has led to a total disconnect and the spinning off [of] a very foreign ideology under the term "Orthodox." Without a sense of connection, fidelity and reverence toward the Ba'alei Ha-Mesorah [guardians of the handed-down tradition] and their methodology, Torah study and theology become a free-for-all, such that radical and heretical approaches emerge.[44]

---

42 Avraham Gordimer, "From Openness to Heresy," *Cross-Currents*, July 18, 2013, http://www.cross-currents.com/archives/2013/07/18/from-openness-to-heresy/.
43 Yitzchak Adlerstein, "Is Heresy Horrible?," *Cross-Currents*, July 23, 2013, http://www.cross-currents.com/archives/2013/07/23/is-heresy-horrible/.
44 Gordimer, "From Openness to Heresy."

The focus on Mesorah involves an explicit move away from the possibility of individuals acquiring the knowledge and requisite skills to interpret Jewish teachings and construct theologies in opposition to those produced by the rabbinic figures identified as accepted and exclusive interpreters of tradition. It entrenches established views, secures control for recognized authorities, and removes the scope for change, unless sanctioned by those acknowledged as guardians of tradition: "the Ba'alei Ha-Mesorah." In certain respects, Mesorah functions as the antithesis of the academy, as a politically motivated tool that sidesteps theology and operates beyond any framework of critique. In another *Cross-Currents* article, the elusive nature of this construct was not only acknowledged but also celebrated:

> Mesorah is based upon halachic or hashkafic reasoning that often has not been popularized or formulated for mass consumption, thereby making it elusive save for those talmidei chachamim who have the requisite knowledge and insight ... Mesorah has been the bedrock of Jewish religious ritual and societal norms for millennia, and our occasional failure to appreciate it as a manifestation of Torah values does not permit us to dismiss its controlling role and its dispositive, defining function in all aspects of Torah life.[45]

The charge leveled against Open Orthodoxy was that it willingly failed to recognize the centrality of Mesorah in defining and determining how Jewish thought, practice, and belief were to be interpreted; it failed to accept limits on who was empowered in these spheres. More than that, the nature of Open Orthodoxy ensured that it would inevitably struggle to acquire an appreciation of Mesorah's role: "What is so obviously missing in all they [Open Orthodoxy] do is a sense of mesorah—that there are actions and attitudes that violate the spirit of Torah and are contrary to the way *ehrliche Yidden* (trans. honest Jews) have conducted themselves throughout the centuries. ... Open Orthodoxy has gone down the road of Judaism without mesorah."[46]

---

45 Avraham Gordimer, "Ordaining Women and the Role of Mesorah," *Cross-Currents*, June 3, 2013, http://www.cross-currents.com/archives/2013/06/03/what-about-mesorah-do-you-not-understand/.

46 Pinchos Lipschutz, "Non-Compromising Orthodoxy," *Yated Ne'eman*, October 16, 2013, http://www.yated.com/non-compromising-orthodoxy.3-1065-3-.html. The extent to which the recourse to Mesorah represents a contemporary replacement for the notion of *Daas Torah* is a topic worthy of further study beyond the scope of this paper. See Lawrence

Mesorah appears to be used when there is an effort to assert an authority that cannot be challenged. Yet in highlighting the manner in which prominent Modern Orthodox rabbis in Israel have come to engage with the challenge of possible reinterpretations of revelation, as indeed is the case on feminist issues too, the question arises as to whether there is a tipping point at which Mesorah can reasonably expect to be redefined by a changing rabbinic consensus from within? Open Orthodoxy stands accused of lacking "any sense of deference to Mesorah,"[47] and yet what the growing scholarship points to is the manner in which the Mesorah of Jewish tradition contains far more variety in interpretation than those who are recognized as "Ba'alei Ha-Mesorah" are willing to acknowledge. The call for deference builds on a presumption that received traditions have to be maintained and seeks to establish authority for affirming this view despite the evidence of alternatives.[48]

In the responses that emanated from within the ranks of the Open Orthodox leadership to the ongoing attacks directed against Farber, the website TheTorah.com, and, by association, against the movement and institutions he was perceived to represent, an important distinction that sets Open Orthodoxy apart from many opponents within Orthodox Judaism was highlighted. The instinct toward boundary marking is precisely something that the open stance of Open Orthodoxy is intended to challenge. Its conscious rejection of this approach represented one of the ways it sought to differentiate itself. The responses published by YCT faculty such as Rabbis Ysoscher Katz, Nathaniel Helfgot, and Asher Lopatin (Weiss's initial successor as head of YCT) all identify Farber's position as distinct from the account of revelation that is taught at YCT. Yet Open Orthodoxy demands an open tent approach, modeled on the home of the biblical Sarah and Abraham.[49] This ensured that explicit charges of

---

Kaplan, "Daas Torah: A Modern Conception of Rabbinic Authority," in *Rabbinic Authority and Personal Autonomy*, ed. Moshe Sokol (Northvale, NJ: Jason Aronson, 1992), 1–60. The role it has played in certain Orthodox attacks on feminist innovations has been examined insightfully in an article by Adam Ferziger. See Ferziger, "Feminism and Heresy."

47 Avram Gordimer, "The Open Orthodox Race to the Edge and Beyond: When Will It Stop?" *Cross-Currents*, October 1, 2013, http://www.cross-currents.com/archives/2013/10/01/the-open-orthodox-race-to-the-edge-and-beyond-when-will-it-stop/.

48 For a consideration of the role TheTorah.com can play in addressing these challenges, see Steven Bayme, "Embracing Academic Torah Study: Modern Orthodoxy's Challenge," TheTorah.com, http://thetorah.com/embracing-academic-torah-study-Modern-orthodox-ys-challenge.

49 See Nati Helfgot, "Torah Min Hashamayim: Some Brief Reflections on Classical and Contemporary Models," Morethodoxy.com, July 21, 2013, http://morethodoxy.

heresy leveled at Farber were limited within the Open Orthodox camp, exacerbating the critique from their opponents, who were precisely arguing for the necessity of drawing clear boundaries and conforming to the established model of ostracism.

Katz's response, as head of the Talmud department at YCT, is particularly noteworthy regarding the increasing necessity within Open Orthodoxy to address the questions posed by academic scholarship:

> Our students, congregants, and followers are turning to us less for help in halakhic matters. Increasingly they look to us for guidance on questions of faith, ethics and social mores. They are struggling with doubt and confusion that is an inevitable consequence of living in the modern world … Let it be clear YCT believes in Torah miSinai as it has been traditionally understood. At the same time, we see that it is our responsibility to graduate rabbis who can engage our community's doubts, and to do so by opening up, rather than closing down, conversation … A Chovevei student needs to be someone who is willing to grapple with the fundamental challenges modernity presents to the contemporary Jewish believer.
>
> Grappling is the key point. There is a segment in the observant community for whom פשוטה אמונה, simple faith, works. They are, however, not the majority. Large numbers of our community struggle with questions of faith, belief, authority, autonomy, ethics, morality and the like. The old methods of response are insufficient; they do not provide the solutions contemporary men and women are looking for.[50]

---

org/2013/07/21/torah-min-hashamayim-some-brief-reflections-on-classical-and-contemporary-models-guest-post-rabbi-nati-helfgot/; Asher Lopatin, "Revelation and the Education of Modern Orthodox Rabbis," Morethodoxy.com, July 26, 2013, http://morethodoxy.org/2013/07/26/revelation-and-the-education-of-modern-orthodox-rabbis/. Farber stood down from his position as head of the conversion body of the IRF in November 2013. For the IRF statement on approaches to revelation, see "IRF Confirms Commitment to Torah Min Hashamayim," International Rabbinical Fellowship, http://www.internationalrabbinicfellowship.org/news/irf-confirms-commitment-torah-min-hashamayim.

50 Ysosscher Katz, "Reflections on Torah Min Hashamayim and its Place in Jewish Thought and Life, from Yeshivat Chovevei Torah Rabbinical School," Morethodoxy.com, http://morethodoxy.org/2013/07/24/guest-post-by-rabbi-ysosscher-katz-. The "Modern Chasiddish" theology Katz espouses appears to reflect shifts in the types of Jewish practice that are enjoying increasing popular appeal. See his essay on Alan Brill's website, "Torat Chaim Ve'Ahavat Chesed," https://kavvanah.wordpress.com/2015/05/31/torat-chaim-veahavat-chesed-rabbi-ysoscher-katz. Significantly, perhaps under the weight of repeated attacks on Open Orthodoxy, Katz

One of the factors motivating Louis Jacobs to publish his views on revelation was a sense that he was not alone in encountering a cognitive dissonance between his Jewish faith and the scholarship he encountered at university. Some of the questions may have changed and the types of answers sought can differ too, but the underlying issues remain. Project TABS and Open Orthodoxy more broadly can be seen to be responding to a changing laity in certain sectors of Orthodox Jewry.

Some of these developments can be related to growing trends toward post-denominational or post-Orthodox attitudes. A state of flux can be identified here in accounts of how to approach God, how to interpret religious authority, and how to express a sense of religiosity. The willingness to be told what to do, how to believe, whom to include or exclude, and how to be religious are being reconsidered. The emergence of a movement toward Independent Minyanim points to the growing appeal of challenging the authority of religious institutions in moves toward post- or late-modernist approaches to Judaism. Individuals within these groups are less interested in rationalist explanations of Judaism, show signs of viewing God more in terms of a companion than as an authoritative, transcendent image, and explicitly seek those more expressive elements of Judaism that offer spiritual meaning regardless of any theological content about which certainty could never be established.[51]

---

did subsequently brand Farber an "apikorus" (heretic) in a radio interview with Dovid Lichtenstein, available at http://www.nachumsegal.com/jm-in-the-am/headlines-dovid-lichtenstein/. In response to repeated attacks, YCT has also sought, forcefully, to affirm its credentials regarding its teaching on revelation, see "Yeshivat Chovevei Torah's Position on Torah MiSinai and Partnership Minyanim," yctorah.org, http://www.yctorah.org/news/yeshivat-chovevei-torahs-position-on-torah-misinai-and-partnership-minyanim/. Worth noting in this statement is the manner in which some type of alignment appears to be established between the challenges presented regarding both feminism and revelation.

51 On this general phenomenon in religious identity, see for example D. Lyon, *Jesus in Disneyland: Religion in Postmodern Times* (Oxford: Blackwell, 2013); Paul Heelas, "De-Traditionalisation of Religion and Self: the New Age and Postmodernity," in *Postmodernity, Sociology and Religion*, ed. Kieren Flanagan and Paul C. Jupp (London: Macmillan, 1999), 65–82; Robert Wuthnow, *After Heaven: Spirituality in America since the 1950s* (Los Angeles: University of California Press, 1998). See also Ari Englenberg, "Modern Orthodoxy in Post-Secular Times: Jewish Identities on the Boundaries of Religious Zionism," *The Journal of Modern Jewish Studies* 14, no. 1 (2015): 126–39; Elie Kaufner, *Empowered Judaism: What Independent Minyanim Can Teach us About Building Vibrant Jewish Communities* (Woodstock, VT: Jewish Lights, 2012); Shaul Magid, *American Post-Judaism: Identity and Renewal in a Postethnic Society* (Bloomington: Indiana University Press, 2013); Steven M. Cohen, J. Shawn Landres, Elie Kaunfer, and Michelle Shain, "Emergent Jewish Communities and Their Participants, Preliminary Findings from

The growing phenomenon of types of Social Orthodoxy is noteworthy here as well, as it finds benefits in the religious life of Orthodox Judaism without perceiving a concomitant need to uphold the beliefs of Judaism. This can be seen to flow from both sociocultural factors and philosophical arguments.[52] J. David Bleich appeared to attack this development:

> While a generation ago the phenomenon of the non-observant Orthodox was the focus of consternation, in our time, it is the observant non-Orthodox that should be our concern. It may well be the case that, presently, the base level of educational attainment among Orthodox laity in the diaspora is greater than at any identifiable period of Jewish history. In that sense our educational endeavors have been crowned with unanticipated success. Not so with regard to transmission of Jewish belief.[53]

This critique of Orthodoxy, for transmitting knowledge of the strictures of the faith without a related understanding and internalization of Jewish faith, is not new. It was expressed in similar terms, albeit with a notably different underlying agenda and understanding, by Yitz Greenberg in the 1966 *Commentator* interview that led to considerable controversy at the time. Greenberg argued that Yeshiva University (YU) produced "secularly oriented students who are overlaid with an abundant practice of Orthodox ritual."[54] Greenberg's goal was imparting the ethical values of Judaism to the students of YU beyond adherence to halakhic practice. As such, it reflects a rather different critique than that

---

the 2007 National Spiritual Communities Study," Berman Jewish Policy Archive (Nov. 2007), http://www.bjpa.org/Publications/downloadFile.cfm?FileID=2784.

52 See Jay Lefkowitz, "The Rise of Social Orthodoxy," *Commentary* (April 1, 2014), https://www.commentarymagazine.com/articles/the-rise-of-social-orthodoxy-a-personal-account/. In a somewhat related vein see also Howard Wettstein, *The Significance of Religious Experience* (Oxford: Oxford University Press, 2012).

53 J. David Bleich, *The Philosophical Quest: Of Philosophy, Ethics, Law and Halakhahh* (Jerusalem: Maggid, 2013).

54 "Dr. Greenberg Discusses Orthodoxy, YU, Viet Nam, and Sex," *The Commentator* (April 28, 1966). On the Greenberg controversy at YU, see David Singer, "Debating Modern Orthodoxy at Yeshiva University: The Greenberg-Lichtenstein Exchange of 1966," *Modern Judaism* 26, no. 2 (2006): 113–26; Shlomo Danziger, "Modern Orthodoxy or Orthodox Modernism," *The Jewish Observer* (October 1966): 3–9; and Yitz Greenberg and Shlomo Danziger, "Orthodox Modernism—An Exchange," *The Jewish Observer* (December 1966): 13–20.

of Bleich. Both nonetheless highlight the manner in which Orthodoxy can become focused solely on ritual observance.

The controversy that Greenberg's views incited in the 1960s points to ongoing battles that have been occurring within both American and British Orthodoxy since the mid-twentieth century on the nature and direction of any type of Modern Orthodox Judaism. The emergence and recent strengthening in America of Open Orthodoxy indicate certain innovations in this struggle. The recourse to Mesorah to undermine these efforts reflects a corresponding attempt to assert authority and quash these developments. The validity of all alternative accounts of tradition are rejected with a vehemence intended to preclude their consideration.

That said, an important difference between the Jacobs Affair and current debates is the unwillingness of those within Open Orthodoxy who have been branded as heretics to accept the charge and rescind the right to define what can, or cannot, be included within an account of Orthodox Judaism. The assertion that alternative views, even in certain respects on interpretations of revelation, can have their place in Orthodoxy—as Shapiro noted, just as Hasidism has come to be accepted—indicates how certain shifts in the interpretation of religious authority are laboring to take hold, and beginning to influence who is empowered to exercise control.[55]

What should not be underestimated, however, is the extent to which political concerns over who has authority to make religious decisions drive efforts to defend Orthodox Judaism. The attacks on Farber and the Open Orthodoxy he is seen, rightly or wrongly, to represent highlight an ongoing effort within certain sectors of Orthodoxy to cling to an account of Mesorah and defend a belief in revelation that lies beyond the varied critiques directed at them. The inability so far to ostracize the likes of Ross and Kugel and the influence of the teachings of, for example, Rabbis Cherlow and ShaGa"R, among others, point to a significant shift in the contours of the debate regarding academic scholarship and its influence on Jewish theology.[56] Evidence of changing attitudes can certainly be found and developments on the internet and particularly in Israel

---

55 For a consideration in this context of the appeal enjoyed by TheTorah.com see Chaim Waxman, "Why Now? Toward a Sociology of Knowledge Analysis of TheTorah.com," TheTorah.com, http://thetorah.com/toward-a-sociology-of-knowledge-analysis-of-thetorahcom.

56 It should be acknowledged here that distinctions can be drawn between the particular positions adopted by each of these individuals on the extent of academic influence that should be permitted.

point to a broadening pushback over who controls Orthodoxy. Alongside questions on revelation, the role of feminism, though outside the spectrum of this paper to consider fully, has also been noted as a pivotal challenge in defining the future direction of Orthodoxy and the scope it contains for greater flexibility in both halakhic and hashkafic interpretation. The approach to questions such as those posed previously by Louis Jacobs is, then, in something of a state of flux; but the response continues to be driven by questions over who has the power to determine what is and is not to be retained or excluded from within the boundaries of Orthodoxy. Authority and revelation go hand in hand. A willingness to reinterpret the dominant account of revelation is perceived to hold out the prospect of challenging religious authority more broadly, ensuring this issue remains an ongoing battleground in the effort to define twenty-first century Orthodoxy.

Part Two

Past and Present

CHAPTER 8

What Is "Modern" in Modern Orthodoxy?

ALAN BRILL

What is "Modern" in Modern Orthodoxy? Over the last 240 years, "modern" has taken on many meanings because of the various stages and types of modernity. Some Jews practiced a modern religion at its inception in the 1770s, others after the pogroms of 1881, and others only entered modernity in the 1950s. The experience of modernity occurred at different rates, and forms varied among different countries and different groups. The term modern is associated with certain forms of Orthodoxy, yet frequently authors apply the term "Modern Orthodoxy" to diverse historical and contemporary phenomena that are not directly related to each other, such as autonomy, suburban aesthetics, feminism, speaking the vernacular, self-conscious choice, support for the state of Israel, and a college degree.

In light of the problematics of generalizing this term, what is the scholarly value in continuing to utilize it to analyze such a broad spectrum of phenomena? In this paper, I will present a number of examples of the history of this term, demonstrate the difficulties of using such a broad term, and show the need to rein in this conceptual spread. I will then put forward a theoretical construct that takes into account the need for greater awareness of the variety of usages of this term that does not tolerate essentializing of this term, but supports continued references to modern Orthodoxy.

The point of the article is to acknowledge that in the discussion of Modern Orthodoxy, the three moments of religious modernity, that of the

Enlightenment, twentieth-century modernism, and the late twentieth century return to religion, all became conflated and haphazardly mixed in the literature due to the definition of Modern Orthodoxy that developed in the 1960s. My goal is to acknowledge that the 1960s term American Modern Orthodoxy—with its emphasis on college and high modernist confidence in science and progress—has been mistakenly applied to other modernizing forms of Orthodoxy such as Religious Zionism, British United Synagogue, Hirschian Neo-Orthodoxy, and Centrism. There are multiple modernizing forms of Orthodoxy in many lands with separate, but overlapping, approaches. Yet, there is a commonality to the 240 years of modernizing forms of Orthodoxy.

This essay focuses on religion, not history and sociology. My interest in modernity is neither situated in the historical modern era, nor in how Judaism responded to the changes of the modern period. Rather, I am concerned with Orthodoxy as a modern form of religion. My question is not about the origins of the modern Jew, of which there are many fine historical explorations, or about the beginnings of modern reforms in the Jewish religion, but rather about the foundation of the various modern forms of the traditional religion. In other words, when and how did traditionalist religion engage with modernity?

USES OF THE TERM IN RECENT HISTORY

Many Orthodox Jews in the last 240 years have written works or created communities that contribute to the collective integration of modernity, called "modern Orthodoxy," with a lowercase *m*. The term "modern Orthodox"—with a small *m*—has been in use since the end of the nineteenth century to describe Orthodox congregations, rabbis, businesspersons, and Jews who were not old-fashioned; rather, they were Orthodox Jews who were modern and acculturated. Their modernity was usually based on and reflected in their dress, language, education, and attitude toward the broader world.

However, the Modern Orthodox movement, capital *M*, of the mid-twentieth century sought to embrace modernism and modernist issues. Modern Orthodoxy, as a specific movement, ranged from about 1940 until 1986 (or even until the start of the twenty-first century) and represented a specific response of a discrete group to modernity. In this latter sense of the term, Modern Orthodoxy was a distinct chronological and philosophical phase that arose from the integration of modernity and Orthodoxy, similar to the way that modern art or modernism in literature were particular phases in the histories of art and literature. Modern Orthodoxy, in fact, emulated and wanted to adapt this moment of high Modernism.

One of the first usages of the term Modern Orthodox (with a capital *M*) was in 1892, when the Reform scholar Claude G. Montefiore applied the term Modern Orthodoxy to the branch of Judaism with which his friend, and head of Jews' College, Michael Friedlander, affiliated.[1] The term did not, however, enter the British lexicon; rather, British Jewry continued to use the terms traditional, positive-historical, and United Synagogue Orthodox.

Reform rabbi Gotthard Deutsch used the term in 1898, when he published a tract called *Modern Orthodoxy*, in which he argued that the modernizing rabbis who founded the Orthodox Union were not true to Orthodoxy. These rabbis were only Modern Orthodox; hence, as modernizers they were not doing anything different from the Reform movement. In his *Jewish Encyclopedia* articles, Deutsch retrojected the term Modern Orthodoxy onto figures from the mid-nineteenth century like Jacob Ettlinger and Issac Bernays, who sought a worldly and nonsectarian Orthodoxy. In Deutsch's writings, the various Italian, British, German, and American rabbis who engaged in modernizing tendencies were categorized as Modern Orthodox because of their desire to be Orthodox despite their modern values and attitudes differing from those of official, mainstream Orthodox rabbis such as the Hatam Sofer.[2]

In the first half of the twentieth century, many congregations that later called themselves Conservative described themselves as modern Orthodox.[3] After World War II, these synagogues branded themselves as the new movement of Conservative Judaism, leaving a smaller group of synagogues with the adjective modern Orthodox. In the 1950s, Orthodoxy was seen by many leading sociologists as a vestige that would disappear. For example, in 1955, the late sociologist Marshall Sklare described Orthodox Judaism in America as a "case study in institutional decay."

American Orthodoxy sought to fight back and show the world that it could be modern, and not just the uneducated immigrant religion of the Lower East Side of Manhattan. Orthodoxy was associated in most people's minds

---

1 Claude Montifiore, "Dr Friedlander on the Jewish Religion," *Jewish Quarterly Review* IV (1892). Claude Montefiore, "Is Judaism a Tribal Religion?" *Contemporary Review* 42 (1882). I credit Michael Pitkowsky for these references.
2 Gotthard Deutsch, *Modern Orthodoxy in the Light of Orthodox Authorities* (Chicago: Bloch & Newman, 1898); Gotthard Deutsch, *Jewish Encyclopedia* s.v. "Bernays, Isaac," "Ettlinger, Jacob" (New York, 1901–6), http://www.jewishencyclopedia.com/articles/3118-bernays-isaac, http://www.jewishencyclopedia.com/articles/5899-ettlinger-jacob (accessed Dec. 27, 2017).
3 Marshall Sklare, *Conservative Judaism: An American Religious Movement* (Glencoe, IL: Free Press, 1945), 43.

with the teeming masses of non-American immigrants who were mostly poor and illiterate.

The proponents of Modern Orthodoxy during the post–World War II era had a more specific cultural goal: to show that they were not backward, uneducated, and ignorant of Western perspectives. They did not merely present themselves as sociologically modern; the modern rabbis presented themselves as intellectually modern. They made a specific choice to identity with high modernism, democracy, and science, as well as to advocate for liberal education. The modernization they adopted and advocated was that which granted ideological import to the rapidly changing America that was propelling itself forward toward urban growth, democracy, suburbia, automobiles, electric appliances, medical achievements, and mass education. Modern Orthodoxy thus sought to show that it was not outdated by highlighting that it could produce PhDs in literature, history, and biology; respond to modern issues from the pulpit; and fit into the American suburban landscape. One example of this was the sense of immense triumph when Yeshiva College made it onto the television show *College Bowl* in 1961. The team of three men and one woman led by a young Lawrence Kaplan, later the translator of Rav Soloveitchik's writings, showed that the young generation of Orthodox Jews could be polymaths in physics, poetry, and political science. By extension, it showed that Orthodoxy itself could indeed be modern and impressive.[4]

This moment, showing that one could be educated and Orthodox within the United States occurred more than a century after some Italian, German, and British Jews already entered the modern era and displayed erudition. Modern Orthodox rabbis proclaimed the 1960s as a new era for modern Orthodoxy, putting its *m* in lowercase as an adjective to indicate that it is not like the Ultra-Orthodox.

Charles Liebman (1934–2003), an American political and social scientist, and prolific author, started the study of Orthodoxy in his important essay, "Orthodoxy in American Jewish Life" (1965). Liebman depicts the "small-m" modern Orthodoxy of the post–World War II era as a church form of religion; he used the sociological distinction between a church attitude, which fosters a broad leeway of practices of beliefs, as opposed to the sectarian approach, which prescribes consistency and isolation. For Liebman, 1960s Ultra-Orthodoxy was an inwardly focused sect, while modern Orthodoxy was the outward looking and tolerant form of Orthodoxy. As a sociologist, he was weak in

---

4 Zev Eleff, "'Viva Yeshiva!' The Tale of the Mighty Mites and the College Bowl," *American Jewish History* 96 (December 2010): 287–305.

religious ideology, so Leibman's description of modern Orthodoxy is rather incomplete; he describes modern Orthodoxy as accepting the continued viability of the halakhah in the modern age and stressing what is common for all Jews. To illustrate this description, he invites his reader to study the writings of Emmanuel Rackman as an ideologue of modern Orthodoxy, and he occasionally notes Samuel Belkin on specific topics, such as the need to involve the laity.[5]

Liebman's personal view was that since modern Orthodoxy left theology mainly to personal beliefs, he chose not to discuss the theological elements or ideological construction needed to remain Orthodox and still accepted the selective integration of some modern elements. For Liebman, the ideology of those who wanted to create a theological modern Orthodoxy during the 1950s and 1960s was limited to what Rabbi Rackman termed "a coterie of individuals ... limited to a score of Rabbis whose interpretation of tradition has won the approval of Orthodox intellectuals"; they knew that their views did not reach the majority. This coterie including Rabbis Norman Lamm, Eliezer Berkovits, Emmanuel Rackman, Irving Greenberg, Walter Wurzbuger, Sol Roth, Shubert Spero, Isadore Twersky, and David S. Shapiro.[6] Liebman believed that the "modern" in the ideology of modern Orthodoxy was clearly an adjective.[7] Yet, the journal *Tradition*, which started in 1957 and which was the showcase of modern Orthodox thought for its first two decades, only called itself Orthodox without calling itself modern—that it was not ultra-Orthodox was self-understood.

By the 1970s, there was a burst of congregations, rabbis, and teachers who displayed this modern Orthodoxy and who saw themselves as the wave of the future. Like-minded individuals started to call themselves Modern Orthodox, with a capital *M*, to indicate that they were a separate sociological group than the Ultra-Orthodox, who were the non-Modern Orthodox Jews. The use of the term Modern Orthodoxy with a capital *M* to describe a social group and not an ideology only started to appear in newspapers around 1977, and it was notably spread by the journalist Ari Goldman, who was himself a proponent of a Modern Orthodox ideology.[8]

---

5 Charles Liebman, "Orthodoxy in American Jewish Life," *AJYB* vol. 66. (1965) 21–97.
6 Some of these figures will in later decades have internal differences between themselves and divide into modernist and Centrist forms of Orthodoxy.
7 Ibid.
8 For example, Ari Goldman, "Roslyn Synagogue Raising Spirits instead of Funds," *New York Times*, September 4, 1977. Prior mentions in the New York Times used lowercase. A 1966 precursor was Amitai Etzioni, *Studies in Social Change* (New York: Holt, Reinhart & Winston, 1966), 210–11.

Even as late as 1989, in the first full-length book dedicated to the sociology of the modern Orthodox community written by Samuel Heilman and Stephen M. Cohen, modern was still an adjective and the group studied was the demographic that was in the middle between traditional sectarians and nominal Orthodox.[9]

In the late 1970s, there were two changes that began a transformation of the "modern" from being a mere adjective to being an integral part of the compound noun "Modern Orthodoxy," in which the new capital *M* showed that the "Modern" was part of a noun that points to a specific sociological community. The first change was that Modern Orthodoxy came of age with a sense of triumphalism; its congregations started to become self-selected enclaves that openly called themselves "Modern Orthodox," and they applied the "Modern Orthodox" label to neighborhoods, day schools, summer camps, and educational institutions. The second change was that many of these congregations' leaders began to consider that Modern Orthodoxy's ideology was no longer designed for a "tiny articulate minority" (to use Rabbi Walter Wurzburger's phrase) but rather they began to understand it as central to the community's ideal of integrating modernity into a full observance of Orthodoxy.[10] These authors and practitioners started to capitalize "Modern" and began to consider it the ideal that would have a broader influence in their community. Even when they cited the older literature of the 1960s, such as the works of Liebman, the authors of the 1980s capitalized the *M* of "modern" because they retrojected their current ideal of a separate Modern Orthodox community onto the past two hundred years.

In response to this discourse, rabbis wrote many articles advocating Modern Orthodoxy, each offering their own individual definitions. Proponents of the view of Modern Orthodoxy as an eternal and stable ideology believed that Orthodox Judaism should be enriched by its intersection with modernity. For some thinkers, such as Rabbi Saul Berman, Modern Orthodoxy was defined as accepting the best analysis of Modernism, especially its rationalism, intellectualism, and use of the liberal arts.[11]

In the 1990s, by contrast, there was a rise of forms of modern Orthodoxy without the need for the prior high modernism, such as Centrism and

---

9 Samuel C. Heilman and Steven M. Cohen, *Cosmopolitans and Parochials: Modern Orthodox Jews in America* (Chicago: University of Chicago Press, 1989).
10 Alan Brill, "The Thought of Rabbi Walter Wurzbuger," *Tradition* 41, no. 2 (2008):1–35.
11 Saul Berman, "The Ideology of Modern Orthodoxy," *Shema*, February 1, 2001 (accessed June 16, 2017), http://shma.com/2001/02/the-ideology-of-modern-orthodoxy/.

Engaged Yeshivish, each of which had many aspects of modernity, but not others. Proponents of the liberal arts had to argue defensively for their position in the 1990s, unlike the relatively easy acceptance of modernism in the 1960s. Many leaders of Modern Orthodoxy still thought that attendance at college and professional school meant an acceptance of the philosophical modernism and mid-twentieth century liberal Modern Orthodoxy. They had no sense that, by that point, a majority of the American yeshiva world attended college but without any concern for philosophic modernism.

The original assumption of the term modern Orthodoxy—which implied that the attendance at college meant that one was in agreement with the broader concepts of Modern Orthodoxy—was incorrectly applied to these new trends. These new ideologies of Orthodoxy and modernity reveal a more complex series of ideologies and strategies than a simple before and after sequence of unenlightened and modern.

ANTHONY GIDDENS: THREE STAGES OF MODERNITY

At this point, we have many conflicting definitions of the term, creating the problems of using it in an academic context. There are multiple analytic frameworks to use to move the discussion forward, but in the context of this essay, I will briefly consider the distinction made by British sociologist Anthony Giddens of three stages of modernity: Enlightenment, Modernism, and Late Modernity as a way of teasing out the various meanings associated with modernity from 1770 to 2000. I am not attempting the major undertaking of producing an application of Giddens's theories to Jewish history; rather, I am using his three stages as a means to help define what is modern by dividing the use of the term *modern* into smaller units for the purpose of distinguishing the twentieth-century modern from the nineteenth and twentieth centuries.[12]

Giddens presents the Enlightenment as the first form of modernity, characterized by the eighteenth and nineteenth centuries' attempt to turn toward literacy, reason, science, and autonomy, as well as the fight against the old regime and traditionalism. In the first period of modernity, the goal of religion was to produce a rational and educated, cultured religion, such as the modern forms of Orthodoxy in England, France, and Germany.

---

12 Anthony Giddens, *Modernity and Self-Identity: Self and Society in the Late Modern Age* (Cambridge: Polity Press, 1991).

Modernism, the second form of modernity, is the enthusiastic embrace of the late nineteenth and early twentieth centuries' turn to urbanization, easy transportation, individuality, and new understandings of humanity and society. The goal was to cultivate a religion that grapples with modernist challenges and accounts for individuality. Modernist expert knowledge—such as expertise in science or attending a university—during this period was authoritative.

Late modernity, the third form of modernity, is an attempt at risk management that acknowledges the fragility and complexity of a world reflected in globalization, consumerism, spirituality—as well as the specter of genocide, and fundamentalism—while also embracing the new materialism and post-secularism. During this period, there was a loss of trust in the expert authority of modernity, which resulted in the emergence of multiple forms of authority.

THE PREMODERN

Before we turn to the modern era, we must note Giddens's definition of the premodern. This is important because many prior discussions of the difference between premodern and modern Orthodoxy often assume modernist individuality as the division between the eras, and use the second period of modernity as the crucial divide between eras.[13] Giddens, following prior thinkers such as Max Weber and Karl Mannheim, contends that tradition largely structured premodern society. In such traditional cultures, people did not have to think much about how to act in any given social setting because their actions had been handed down to them and prescribed by longstanding customs and traditions.

However, Giddens adds that in the premodern era their sense of space and time was different from ours. According to Giddens, in the premodern era, reality was believed to be divinely arranged into an ordered universe with an otherworldly component. There was a clear map of reality with preordained eschatology, afterlife, and cyclical time.[14] There was also a need for spiritual intermediaries guiding one through this universe. In the Jewish case, this was the cosmology of the Kabbalah.

Amplifying Giddens's approach, Doreen Rosman opens her work, *The Evolution of the English Churches: 1500–2000*, with a bold statement about her

---

13 David Kettler and Volker Meja, "Karl Mannheim's Jewish Question," *Religions* 3, no. 2 (2012): 228–50.
14 Giddens, *Modernity and Self-Identity*, 17, 31, 83, 87; Anthony Giddens, *The Consequences of Modernity* (Cambridge: Polity Press, 1990) 6, 17, 56–7.

starting point in early modern Europe. She asserts, "People's passage from this life to the next and their entry to heaven were ... matters of major concern."[15] Inherent in the premodern worldview is that people thought that most believers did not enter heaven; they had to work very hard to earn their eternal reward by belonging to confraternities, appealing to saints and to the beyond, engaging in magical rites, and practicing esoteric wisdom. However, modernity changed that major preoccupation.

The negation of early modern forms of religion initiated modern discussions about religion. In the case of Judaism, the negation of the past began specifically with the generation that followed the Enlightenment. For example, Rabbi Shmuel David Luzzatto (also known as Shadal, 1800–1865) was a scholar, poet, and biblical exegete who produced prolific correspondence and writing. A child of the Enlightenment era, he rejected the early modern world and therefore the kabbalistic worldview of his forefathers. Shadal's autobiography recounts the moment when Shadal turned his back on his father's type of premodern orthodoxy: "In Nissan 1814 ... his mother lay fatally ill ... His father, a believer in Kabbalah, prayed in the appropriate kabalistic manner; however, he saw that his prayers were to no avail." Assuming that his son shared his sense of tradition, "he instructed his son in the appropriate manner of prayer, to raise the soul through various Worlds, then to the Sefirot, and eventually to the Creator himself." Shadal, however, refused to pray in such a way—even though this was a request from his father concerning a life-threatening condition of his mother. Shadal explained that "I no longer believed in this creed and therefore could not pray in that manner [that his father wished]."[16]

Shadal and his contemporaries offer the clearest examples of Giddens's description of the shift from of the premodern to the modern—no more focus on death, on the world to come, on esotericism, or on ritual.[17] Starting in the early nineteenth century, an acceptance of modern scientific cosmology became the major category for entrance into modern society. Shadal would not have called himself a practitioner of modern Orthodoxy; in his era, Orthodoxy was reserved for those opposed to the Enlightenment. However, he was modern

---

15 Doreen Rosman, *The Evolution of the English Churches, 1500–2000* (Cambridge: Cambridge University Press, 2003), 1.
16 Samuel D. Luzzatto, "Autobiografia di S.D. Luzzatto (Autobiography of Samuel David Luzzatto), Translation into English by Sabato Morais," *The Jewish Record*, August 3–10, 1877.
17 Isaiah Tishby, *Messianic Mysticism: Moses Hayim Luzzatto and the Padua School* (Oxford: Littman Library of Jewish Civilization, 2008).

and he had a perspective that in later decades would be called Orthodox since he was opposed to changes in traditional practice.[18]

PHASE ONE

Using Giddens's outline of the emergence of modernism, its first phase was characterized by a process by which, in many countries, many Jews came to separate the core values of their Judaism from what they considered contingent beliefs and practices of the premodern; however, they still thought of themselves as following ritual practices and Talmudic traditions. There were modern forms of Orthodoxy in France, England, Italy, Russia, Romania, Algeria, Egypt, and Germany among others. While these communities had separate trajectories and made different decisions during this process, all of them sought a religion without superstition, fanaticism, and supernaturalism. All of these Jews sought to speak the vernacular, to attain western education, to integrate into Western culture, and, when applicable, to understand Judaism using historicism. Many practitioners of forms of nineteenth-century Orthodoxy with modern tendencies thought that their approach embodied both the true enlightenment and the restoration of a pristine Judaism, unlike the shallow approach of those who threw off religion.[19]

It is helpful to use factors such as the community's entrance into the middle class and the bourgeois public sphere to categorize different modern Orthodoxies of the late nineteenth century. Their entrance into the middle class was accompanied by urbanization, increased basic education, subscription to mass media, and political activity. Religion was no longer just about the elite—whether priests, rabbis, or holy men—but about ordinary people. Books, essays, and newspapers about religion were now written for the laity. The middle class preferred domestic activities and community engagement such as schools, journals, and social services. Education and commodities served as tools for identity formation, helping community members strike a balance between comfort and culture. The home represented serenity and moderation in all things and a refuge from work. To thrive, the middle class needed the resources of both secularization and tradition, the former to allow for material success and the latter to create a cohesive

---

18 Jeffrey C. Blutinger, "So-Called Orthodoxy: The History of an Unwanted Label," *Modern Judaism* 27, no. 3 (October 2007): 310–28.

19 For more on these mediations of creating an enlightened Orthodoxy, see Ulrich L. Lehner and Michael Printy, eds., *Companion to the Catholic Enlightenment in Europe* (Leiden and Boston: Brill, 2010); Ulrich L. Lehner, "What Is Catholic Enlightenment?," *History Compass* 8 (2010): 166–78.

value system. This group however, was not overly progressive, liberal, or secular, so forms of traditional religion flourished.[20]

Many of the forms of modern-oriented Orthodoxy in western continental Europe, such as those in Germany or Italy, were aimed at businessmen in order to create a family-oriented Orthodoxy with religious literature for the family. In contrast, British modernizing Orthodoxy, under the influence of wealthy donors such as Moses Montefiore, presented an aspirant model that promoted high church and upper-class values. This model only gave way to middle-class values after many decades, giving a unique flavor to the British United Synagogue.

Russia represents the opposite end of entering the public sphere from the upper- and middle-class values of Western Europe. Modernizing Orthodoxy in Russia produced religious Zionism, in which the term *modern* meant answering the needs of a post-1881 society, including basic education for the masses, economic concern for the laity, and a growing sense of nationalism. Therefore, Religious Zionism was oriented toward the common person, focusing on productivity and employment combined with some progressive social elements. Rather than seeking integration into the host country as in Western Europe, Religious Zionism formed a nationalist theory with a mission for the people of Israel and a purpose in Jewish history.[21]

MODERNISM: MODERNITY PHASE TWO

The term *Modern* also applies to the period that began in intellectual circles between 1870 and 1910; more generally, it refers to the changes of the 1910–70 period. This era occurs after the Enlightenment period and includes the emergence of social science, scientism, psychoanalysis, existentialism, and evolutionary thinking in geology, biology, politics, and sociology. Within this modernism, rationality meant the growing disenfranchisement of religion from the established institutions toward a sense of personal subjectivity.

Communities affiliated with the American Modern Orthodoxy of the post–World War II era had a goal to show that they were not backward, uneducated, and ignorant of Western perspectives. The modern rabbis did not merely present

---

20 Giddens is relying on the seminal work of Jurgen Habermas, *The Structural Transformation of the Public. Sphere: An Inquiry into a Category of Bourgeois Society*, trans. Thomas Burger, with the assistance of Frederick Lawrence (Cambridge, MA: MIT Press, 1989).
21 Joseph Shapira, *Hagut, Halakhah ve-Tsiyonut: al Olamo ha-Ruhani shel ha-Rav Yitshak Yaakov Reines* (Tel-Aviv: ha-Kibbutz ha-Meuhad, 2002).

themselves as sociologically modern; they also presented themselves as intellectually modern. They made a specific choice to identify with high modernism, democracy, and science, as well as to advocate for liberal education. Samuel Belkin, president of Yeshiva University, optimistically sought to embrace the best of American values and the American education system. There were already important antecedents to this approach in the early years of Yeshiva College, most notably by Bernard Revel and Pinchas Churgin, but Belkin devoted his life to its articulation.[22] Belkin believed that the hybrid of the modern world and Orthodoxy would serve as an entrance into America for first-generation college students to study the best of Western civilization. Belkin advocated liberal arts education and a democratic freedom of inquiry. Belkin and those under him used the word "synthesis," where the "individual has absorbed the attitudes characteristic of science, democracy and Jewish life and responds appropriately in diverse relations and contexts."[23] Belkin pointed out that it was natural for observant Jews to attain college degrees in Spain, Italy, England, and Holland.

Belkin's modernization, while not philosophically or historically complex, advocated the modernity of universalism of religion, the brotherhood of mankind, and, above all, the need for democracy. Nevertheless, as the historian Arnold M. Eisen noted, Belkin spoke like a universalist, as would a Reform or Reconstructionist Rabbi; however, his particularism and Orthodoxy remained in place. For Belkin, "modernity" was not an adjective or a modifier but one of two parallel paths both actively pursued.[24]

A defining moment of Modern Orthodoxy occurred in the late 1950s, when there was a theological turn in American religion, encouraging several rabbis with PhDs who wanted to create a theological modern Orthodoxy. According to Rabbi Rackman, that group which called itself "modern Orthodox" knew that their views did not reach the majority. Alternately, Rabbi Walter Wurzburger wrote that only a limited "tiny articulate minority" sought "the art of combining our Jewish particularity with openness to the values of modernity."[25]

---

22 Bernard Revel, "The American Yeshiva," in *The Jew in the Modern World. A Documentary History*, 3rd ed., ed. Paul Mendes-Flohr and Jehuda Reinharz (Oxford and New York: Oxford University Press, 2010), 504–6; Pinchas Churgin "Meeting Again," *Masmid: Published by the Student Organization of the Yeshiva College* (June 1932) 35.
23 Samuel Belkin, "The Truly Higher Education: An Inaugural Address," *Essays in Traditional Jewish Thought* 1 (New York: Philosophical Library), 9–17.
24 Arnold M. Eisen, *The Chosen People in America: A Study in Jewish Religious Ideology* (Bloomington: Indiana University Press, 1983), 99–109.
25 Brill, "The Thought of Rabbi Walter Wurzbuger," 1–35.

American Modern Orthodoxy, which adopted the name Modern Orthodoxy as its own despite its own reservations about the term, was a specific movement based on a specific response of a specific group to modernity. It was a specific phase in modern Judaism that arose from the integration of modernity and Orthodoxy, just as Modern Art or Modernism in Literature were particular phases. The term signaled the break between the Orthodoxy of the older immigrant generations and the new Orthodoxy of the college-educated generation. Some members of this group wrote articles embracing a broader vision of modernism that would fully embrace modernism's autonomy and subjectivity.[26]

Modernism also played itself out on other modernizing forms of Orthodoxy. For example, some members of German Neo-Orthodoxy embraced twentieth-century modernism. They notably later became leaders of the fledgling religious kibbutz movement in Israel, offering an intellectually progressive yardstick definition of modernizing Orthodox compared to mainstream Religious Zionism during this period, which was generally more concerned with building a state and army than with modernist thought.[27]

LATE MODERNITY

The third use of the term modern is for the current era of "late" modernity. In late modernity, intellectuals no longer see a meta-narrative of progress and improvement over the last centuries. Moreover, intellectuals see more fragility than progress, and they place more emphasis on one's social experiences and cultural contexts, rather than on autonomy.[28] Late modernity "has the feeling of riding a juggernaut" in which modernity itself has gone in an "erratic runaway" direction.[29] We strive to manage the risk and uncertainty the best we can. One of the means of risk management is to turn to religion as a personal choice. The loss of acceptance of the authority of modern expert knowledge opens up a realm for other sources of authority.

---

26 Liebman, "Orthodoxy in American Jewish Life"; Benny Kraut, *The Greening of American Orthodox Judaism: Yavneh in the 1960s* (Cincinnati: Hebrew Union College Press, 2010).
27 Mordechai Breuer, *Modernity within Tradition: The Social History of Orthodox Jewry in Imperial Germany* (New York: Columbia University Press, 1992); Aryei Fishman, *Kibbutz Judaism and Modernization on the Religious Kibbutz* (Cambridge: Cambridge University Press, 1992).
28 John Micklethwait and Adrian Wooldridge, *God Is Back: How the Global Revival of Faith is Changing the World* (London: Penguin Press, 2009).
29 Giddens, *Modernity and Self-Identity*.

This loss of the acceptance of authority, together with the emergence of new authorities has been helpful for religious practice. As noted by many social observers, postmodernity has been kind to evangelicals, Fundamentalists, Mormons, Orthodox Jews, and most other forms of highly committed religion—since modernity and religion are now each considered sources of authority.[30] The current era is one of post-secularization in which religion has returned and defines itself in contrast to modern ideas, even as it simultaneously ever embraces late modern society and consumerism.

The goal of the Enlightenment, to replace irrational dogmas and superstitions of traditional societies with rational certainty, has failed in that the irrational and superstitious has returned to an unusual extent.[31] For many, personal spirituality and seeking has replaced twentieth-century modernity. In the new spiritual marketplace, people can now choose to follow Rabbi Nachman of Breslov, practice yoga, believe in the prosperity gospel, or spend a year in a traditional seminary—or do all of these things together or in turn. Perhaps the one characteristic that distinguishes late modern religious life is diversity. More charitably, the philosopher Charles Taylor points out that in the current age people are seeking individual meanings and moral order in religion.[32] New issues such as the essence of life, feminism, gender, globalization, and media are replacing the concerns of earlier decades.[33]

The most successful theologies today are those similar to the engaged evangelical Christians, who choose to practice a limited modernism combined with a more literal faith and personal spirituality. They were the fastest growing Protestant group in America, and they seemingly offer an answer for contemporary needs. Evangelicalism combines modernist autonomy with strong religious content, selections from popular culture, and family values. They use rock music, embrace popular culture revivalism, and find God in the values of suburbia.[34] People in this age can be lawyers and doctors with superior educations having mastered much of the nineteenth-century sense of modernity, but at the

---

30   Ulrich Beck, *A God of One's Own* (Cambridge: Polity Press, 2010).
31   Amanda Porterfield, *The Transformation of American Religion* (Oxford: Oxford University Press, 2001).
32   Robert Wuthnow, *After Heaven: Spirituality in America Since the 1950s* (Berkeley: University of California Press, 1998); Charles Taylor, *A Secular Age* (Cambridge MA: Harvard University Press, 2007).
33   Peter Berger corrected his prior views; see Peter Berger, *The Many Altars of Modernity: Toward a Paradigm for Religion in a Pluralist Age* (Berlin: De Gruyter Mouton, 2014).
34   Jose Casanova, *Public Religions in the Modern World* (Chicago: University of Chicago, 1996).

same time come home to the strong engaged religion of the evangelicals, Pentecostals, and Orthodox Judaism.[35]

Some Modernists, including many who use the term Modern Orthodoxy, misunderstand the return of strong forms of religion as hampering the progress of modernity. These movements, however, need to be understood on their own terms as being traditional and modern at the same time, but in a new configuration.

These late-modern changes led to the rise of Centrism and Engaged Yeshivish in the twenty-first century as new forms of modern Orthodoxy, which are configurations with many aspects of modernity, but lacking the need for high modernism. Modern Orthodoxy, as Centrism, emerged through a greater commitment to learning, observance, and rabbinic authority. The community entered the fields of law and medicine with a professional success that dwarfs the modern Orthodox Jews of the modernist age, and they sought formal halakhic guidance through legal, business, and medical halakhah. Centrism effaced the agenda of modernity in favor of a rhetoric of Mesorah (continuity of rabbinic leadership), unchanged and continuous. They could do this since college education, entrance into the middle class, and acceptance in the professional workplace was already a universal given within the community.

At the same time, graduates of traditional yeshivot also entered into the professions and suburbia as pragmatic decisions rather than ideological ones. This shift in self-identification created what I am terming "Engaged Yeshivish," or the rise of professional and suburban Yeshivish, a group who are yeshivish but also graduate-school educated lawyers, doctors, or therapists. This group adheres to the sages regarding Torah, but on matters of American common-sense science or psychology, they accept the suburban worldview.[36] The Engaged Yeshivish are outward looking, providing Orthodox content attuned

---

35 Christian Smith, *American Evangelicalism: Embattled and Thriving* (Chicago: University of Chicago Press, 1998).

36 The term "Engaged Yeshivish" is based on the terminology in the study of American evangelicals. In the 1990s, there was a backlash against University of Chicago's Fundamentalism Project. Many started to explain evangelicals not as fundamentalists, or sectarian, but as actively engaged in the wider world. In his 1996 book *American Evangelicalism*, Christian Smith used the phrase "engaged Evangelicals," and by 2000 it was regularly used in the press. At that point, the term could equally be used to describe similar Jewish phenomena.

to media, self-help books, suburbia, and other products offering meaning for everyday life.[37]

The ignoring of high modernism does not mean it is not modern. Rather, Centrism, Engaged Yeshivish, and certain aspects of Chabad are modern even without an emphasis on modernism and higher education. They give more credence to Torah authority, but this Torah can often itself be in the aforementioned popular forms.

When many advocates speak of Modern Orthodoxy, they tend to think of the progressive modernism of the 1960s, with a sense of supersessionalism believing that the twenty-first century will culminate in the era of modernism they envisioned. From the perspective of late modernity, there is no longer any progress, evolution, or supersession of one era by another, just a passage of eras and centuries—each with its own concerns.

THE UTILITY OF MODERN ORTHODOXY AS FAMILY RESEMBLANCES

So what remains of the category Modern Orthodoxy after we account for all these differences in era, country, and emphasis? Can it still be used?

Ludwig Wittgenstein, the Austrian-British philosopher, posited that having ideological commonalities meant that those who adhere to the ideology share common rules and language. Wittgenstein argues, that even within a set of rules there could be "family resemblances"—sets of features that are broadly similar without being identical in all respects, or features that possess some overlapping characteristics of a special kind among members of the same group. Ideological family members would not necessarily have all the features, but in a large family, any member could share something in common with other members, thereby also allowing the possibility that two members could have nothing in common. For example, liberalism (or conservatism, or Marxism) contains internal variants that share a range of overlapping as well as distinct properties. In the case of liberalism, all proponents may promote individuality, but they may vary over ideas of property, history, rationality, and social change.

All modern Orthodox Jews are modern—in a religious sense as opposed to a temporal one—in that they have modernizing tendencies wherein they

---

37 Adam S. Ferziger, *Beyond Sectarianism: The Realignment of American Orthodox Judaism* (Detroit: Wayne State University Press, 2015).

accept at least some of the tenets of modernity to create a modern form of observance. These Jews, for example, tend to accept science, literacy, technology, social mobility, the lack of an autonomous community, and the need for an education. The acceptance of a scientific worldview and, more importantly, the rejection of the premodern kabbalistic worldview—of magic, otherworldly focus, and concern with the afterlife—is a cross-ideological commonality existing between all groups, as is the acceptance of a this-worldly approach to religion. In practice, they reject the traditional Judaism of the eighteenth and nineteenth centuries and the Yiddish-speaking folk culture of Eastern Europe, but they differ in their practical, quotidian acknowledgment of these changes. Only some accept westernization, embourgeoisement, and suburbanization. In the case of Israeli forms of modern Orthodoxy, citizens accept the need to become part of the state-building project.

The term *Modern Orthodoxy* encompasses many divergent ideologies and theologies; they are distinct, though related, philosophies that in some combination provide the basis for all variations of "Orthodox yet modern" ideologies today. There were different forms in France, Italy, Algeria, Britain, and Turkey that often are overlooked in discussions that only focus on the Russian, German, and American forms of modernizing Orthodoxy. These variations break down into specific subunits, and, depending how you count, you can list five, twelve, or over twenty subgroups and variants.

This approach, while widespread in the study of modern Christianity, especially for demarcating the variety of Protestant denominations, is not the common approach for the study of Orthodoxy in modernity. Many Jewish scholars persist in arguing that the modern approach to Judaism began at a moment when an idealized traditional society gave way to a new society based on inevitable secularization.

Literary historian Jacques Barzun provides a model, similar for our purposes to Wittgenstein, for explaining the variety of types of modern Orthodoxy. Barzun presented the wide varieties of Romanticism in different countries, compared their similarities and differences, and even acknowledged how in some of the cases they would not have recognized the label or seen the similarity in other varieties.[38]

For those wedded to an understanding rooted in denominational history, I repeat that I am not claiming the eighteenth century as the start of Modern Orthodoxy—nor even as the source of Modern Orthodoxy's ideas. I am claiming that there are varieties of modernizing tactics and strategies that started

---

38 Jacques Barzun, *Classic, Romantic and Modern* (New York: Doubleday, 1961).

with the beginnings of the modern era, however defined, that influenced various groups in their combination of a theologically non-liberal Judaism with selective adaptations of modernity. These points of theological modernity are neither infinite in possibility nor entirely contingent on circumstance; rather, they are a set body in which many were still useful and interchangeable for aiding the self-definition of other cultural constructions of Modern Orthodoxy.

All forms of modern Orthodoxy seek to embrace some secular studies, citizenship, and integration into the broader culture. They tend to speak the vernacular, dress closely to Western attire, conform to the leisure patterns of the host country, and attend events with nonreligious Jews. They reject those who seek isolation from the broader culture as well as those who merely passively tolerate the secular culture. The sociologist Samuel Heilman uses the term "syncreticist" for the modern Orthodox position, which tries "to uncover and retrieve what from his Orthodox perspective seem[s] to be valuable elements of modernity and fit them into the framework of traditional Orthodoxy … supplementing the latter with the 'riches' of modernity." Heilman points out that for some, the two realms of Judaism and modernity remain separate, while others seek a creative synthesis while retaining "strict limits on [their] willingness to transform halakhah." They overcome the distance between their modern lives and the textual traditions with "legitimations from the distant past which are nevertheless presented as continuous with the present."[39]

The most important criterion to define Modern Orthodoxy is the sense of the conjunctive, the need to combine acculturation with Torah. Beyond the obvious desires to combine Western knowledge with Torah and have a strong secular education in school, the goal is to attempt to have the best of both worlds. To display to oneself and others that one has a reasonable faith, one needs to show a desire to combine the best of both cultures. Modern Orthodoxy accommodates its goal in diverse ways, by reinterpreting tradition in light of contemporary values, understanding contemporary values in light of tradition, or compartmentalizing competing systems. On a deeper level, there is dialectic, oscillation, or synthesis between revelation and reason, revelation and man's consciousness of authority—and human feeling, reason, and morals. Modern Orthodoxy seeks to be located in a conceptual middle. It has a strong conviction that God had "accommodated" the Torah life to humanity's limited understanding by using language, imagery, and stories suited to particular ages and cultures.

---

39 Samuel C. Heilman, "The Many Faces of Orthodoxy: Part I," *Modern Judaism* 2, no. 1 (1982): 23–51; Samuel C. Heilman, "The Many Faces of Orthodoxy: Part II," *Modern Judaism* 2, no. 2 (1982): 171–98.

Unlike this self-perception, I must note that recent research, beyond the scope of this paper, treats modern secularity and religion as separate variables allowing for greater bifurcation in which one can combine as contradictory elements the modern and the Orthodox.[40]

DIFFERENCE FROM EACH OTHER AND FROM OTHER FORMS OF ORTHODOXY

Nevertheless, despite these commonalities we need to be more cautious in our use and understanding of the term and appreciate the differences between groups.

Modern Orthodox communities as a whole generally do not mix and match between these various approaches. Just because one community has a certain approach to an issue of modernity, that does not mean that all of them do, or even that they should. For example, the historical approach to Talmud was accepted in the Berlin Orthodox seminary; however, this historical acceptance in Berlin does not mean that it was accepted by those who have as their emphasis the Eastern European *beit midrash*. Similarly, just because American Jewry placed emphasis on secular liberal education as the criteria for integration, it does not mean the same was true for Israeli Religious Zionists, who were concerned with army and state and were likely to have a collective statist approach to integration. If the Religious Workers Party and Kibbutz Hadati rejected the need for a yeshiva as part of its agenda, it does not mean the other formulations agreed. A full history of the last 200 years of modernizing forms of Orthodoxy, both theological and social, would be needed to present all of the diversity and differences between the various forms of modernity.

Each approach developed in its own interpretive community with a specific narrative of decisions and factors leading to the modernist strategies it accepted; in turn, each interpretive community validated its own method. The varieties of modern Orthodoxy each have separate sources of authority, and any given formulation of modern Orthodoxy does not necessarily have authority in the other group. Each group was usually not informed sufficiently about the other groups to have responded to positions, even if it knew about the other

---

40 Saba Mahmood and Talal Asad, "Modern Power and the Reconfiguration of Religious Traditions," *SEHR* 4, no. 27 (1996), https://web.stanford.edu/group/SHR/5-1/text/asad.html.

options. Finally, the implementation of other positions would not necessarily resonate with the practitioners and community life of a given approach.

Modern Orthodoxy is ideologically counterbalanced by trends toward traditionalism, conservatism, and separatism—usually referred to with the evaluative description ultra-Orthodox, which was called Hyper-Orthodox in the nineteenth century and which is now referred to with the more neutral term Haredi in Israel. They too encompass many separate ideologies and should not be amalgamated since this group includes diverse ideologies in many countries over two centuries.

The traditionalist groups, each in their own way, oppose various aspects of the family resemblance of modern Orthodoxy. This opposition, however, should not be seen as a drive to reject modern Orthodoxy as much as it should be seen as an attempt for these groups to develop their own internal ideologies including a life of purity, intensive Torah study, a need to be *haimish*-following the in-group customs of the Haredi culture, or to create closed community enclaves. Modern Orthodox is not an inverse of Haredi values or vice versa; both groups have separate and nonadjacent value systems.[41]

From the perspective of Wittgenstein's family resemblances, the scholar Aviezer Ravitzky already noted that the relationship between the two diverse groups—the modern Orthodox and ultra-Orthodox—can also be treated under the rubric of family resemblances. Yet, the two groups should be seen as similar to the distinction between liberals and conservatives. To use an example from the tradition of American political ideology, American political conservatives are overwhelmingly not monarchists, unlike many conservatives elsewhere, and despite their "conservative" approach, they work within the political liberalism and democratic ideals of the American founding fathers. Ultra-Orthodox groups and modern Orthodox groups create different divisions in different countries.[42]

---

41 Hebrew University professor and specialist in Haredi ideology Benjamin Brown lists the following ten fundamentals of non-modern Haredi thought: (1) belief in the Sages in all matters; (2) decline of the Generations, hence the need for conservatism; (3) rejection of changes and modernizations in the law; (4) simplicity of belief and rejection of theological investigation; (5) rejection and struggle against modernity and secularism; (6) struggle against Zionism; (7) closed society making a fortress against culture; (8) a curriculum of all Torah, or as close as possible; (9) essential hierarchies of people, Jews, and genders; (10) stringencies in Jewish law (Chumrot). Benjamin Brown, "Ten Fundamentals of Haredi Haskafa," *Eretz Acheret* 56 (1997): 56–65.
42 Aviezer Ravitzky, "Introduction: On the boundaries of Orthodoxy," in *Orthodox Judaism: New Perspectives* [in Hebrew], ed. Yosef Salmon, Aviezer Ravitzky, and Adam S. Ferziger (Jerusalem: Magnes Press, 2006).

MODERN ORTHODOXY: TERMINABLE AND INTERMINABLE

In conclusion, despite the differences, there remain useful family resemblances of the varieties of modern Orthodoxy, especially the universal need to come to terms with modern existence. It also remains useful for differentiation with Ultra-Orthodoxy.

In contrast, modern Orthodoxy remains differentiated from medieval and premodern thinkers who were integrated within the intellectual climate of their cultures, such as Maimonides or one of the many similar voices of Gaonic Baghdad, Al-Andalus culture, Provencal thinkers, or Italian Jewry. They each dealt with medieval and early modern cultural categories and problems, providing answers for their own age. Medieval, Renaissance, and Enlightenment forms of rationalism are distinct. Hence, it takes specific intellectual acts of reading and adaptation by modern authors to overcome the historic difference between those prior texts and the modern era.

In summary, modern Orthodoxy is both terminable and interminable. All constructions of modern Orthodoxy are culturally situated, geographically located, and ever bound to a specific time. Even a single denomination consists of many trends, sub-movements, and cultural shifts. All varieties of modern Orthodoxies have commonalities based on ideology, people, institutions, and texts, yet they are all terminable in that the resources, concerns, needs, and connections to other movements are situated in a specific era. Modern Orthodoxy cannot return to the premodern world of the early eighteenth century, even if it returns to many of its texts, because of the broad changes in cosmology, politics, and worldview. So too, modern Orthodoxy will continue to use many of the ideas and formations of earlier formulations of modern Orthodoxy from the nineteenth and twentieth centuries, even if it cannot return to the original conditions of construction.[43]

---

43 It is important to note that in contemporary newspapers and on television that the word "modern" is currently being used to mean "up-to-date" and "stylish," as in "you need more modern shoes." This was confirmed by the Macmillan dictionary listing as its second meaning for the word modern "using the most recent methods, ideas, designs, or equipment." It also cited the correct usage: "These techniques are not used in modern medicine. We should replace the equipment with something more modern," http://www.macmillandictionary.com/us/dictionary/american/modern (accessed May 19, 2016).

CHAPTER 9

Can Modern Orthodoxy Survive?*

JACK WERTHEIMER

On the current American Jewish scene, one group stands out for its seemingly successful integration of traditional religious behavior and belief with full participation in modern society. Consider the landscape. On the liberal side of the religious spectrum, Conservative Judaism, until recently the largest of the denominations, identifies itself as traditional, but only a minority of its adherents strive to observe the dictates of Jewish law (halakha). As for more liberal movements, most of their members make no claim to be exemplars of traditional

---

* This essay, a significantly revised version of a paper presented at the Oxford Summer Institute in Modern and Contemporary Judaism, appeared online at *Mosaic* as the monthly essay in August 2014. It is available at http://mosaicmagazine.com/essay/2014/08/can-modern-orthodoxy-survive/. My thanks to Neal Kozodoy, the editor of *Mosaic*, for permission to reprint the essay. I have added footnotes to the original to substantiate points raised. This essay draws on interviews I conducted with observers of Modern Orthodoxy. I am grateful to the following rabbis who spoke with me: Saul Berman, Avi Bossewitch, Yonatan Cohen, Zev Farber, Jeffrey Fox, Kenneth Hain, Yosef Kanefsky, Bob Kaplan, Dov Linzer, Yechiel Poupko, Steven Pruzansky, J. J. Schacter, Uri Topolosky, Kalman Topp, and Daniel Yolkut. I also interviewed Maharat Ruth Balinsky and Elana Stein Hain. And I benefited from conversations with Rabbi Yitz Greenberg, Professor Benjamin Gampel, Dr. Larry Grossman, Jay Lefkowitz, and Ruthie Simon. What I learned in these rich interviews is not attributed by name to my interviewees because the ground rules we set defined the interviews as "on background." My fellow participants in the Oxford Summer Institute in Modern and Contemporary Judaism commented on an earlier draft of this essay. Their thoughtful critiques and suggestions inform this revised essay in many ways. Special thanks to Professors Adam Ferziger and Miri Freud-Kandel, the organizers of the seminar for organizing a rich weeklong discussion and pressing all participants to sharpen our thinking.

Judaism but rather regard themselves as advocates of—to invoke the names of the best-known movements—reform, reconstruction, or renewal. Meanwhile, at the opposite end of the continuum, one finds Orthodox groups that, while punctiliously observant, self-consciously insulate themselves to one degree or another from Western culture or explicitly reject the assumptions of modernity.

This leaves the sector known as Modern Orthodoxy. Relatively small in number, making up just three percent of American Jewry as a whole—and by no means comprising all who identify themselves as Orthodox—it alone seems to have found the sweet spot: a synthesis of the modern with traditional Jewish observance. Recent surveys, including Pew's *Portrait of Jewish Americans*,[1] make clear just how well the Modern Orthodox have combined both parts of their name.

WHO ARE THE MODERN ORTHODOX?

Organizing their family lives far more traditionally than do their liberal counterparts, the Modern Orthodox tend to marry earlier and to maintain a fertility rate well above replacement level; only small percentages intermarry. In order to insure the transmission of their religious commitments, they enroll nearly all of their children in the most immersive forms of Jewish education. Their synagogues, unlike most of those in the Conservative or Reform orbit, are teeming with regular worshippers every day of the week. Many sizable ones offer multiple prayer services every morning, afternoon, and evening, accommodating the busy schedules of individual worshippers. They also report rising numbers of men and women participating in study classes, and even of teenagers seeking out opportunities to learn on Sabbath afternoons. In a reinforcing loop, as one rabbi notes, "more intensive learning has created greater levels of observance."

Synagogue life is further reinforced by the life of school and summer camp. Day-school attendance from early childhood through high school has become de rigueur for Modern Orthodox families. According to Pew data, 90 percent of those between the ages of eighteen and twenty-nine have attended a day school for at least four years—a much higher figure, incidentally, than the one for their parents or grandparents. The figures for summer camps are comparably impressive.

---

1 Most of the numbers from the Pew study cited in this essay do not appear in the published report but were run for me by Professor Steven M. Cohen, whose help proved indispensable. I deeply appreciate his generosity. Subsequent to the appearance of this essay, the Pew Research Center issued its own report on the subject, "A Portrait of American Orthodox Jews: A Further Analysis of the 2013 Survey of U.S. Jews," August 26, 2015, http://www.pewforum.org/2015/08/26/a-portrait-of-american-orthodox-jews/.

None of this would be feasible without financial resources. Nationally, according to Pew, thirty-seven percent of Modern Orthodox households have incomes of over $150,000, a figure not matched by any other Jewish denomination. In the metropolitan New York area, home to the largest concentration of Orthodox Jews of all stripes, the Modern Orthodox contingent shows the largest proportion earning $100,000 or more and $150,000 or more.[2]

This relative affluence makes it possible for some in the community to support key institutions with generous donations, including scholarship assistance for day-school families. It also means that a large majority are able to shoulder the costs of Jewish living. Only those with resources—and commitment—can afford to live within walking distance of synagogues, purchase kosher food products, pay membership dues and building-fund assessments to synagogues, and, most expensive of all, cover K–12 tuition costs in day schools and send their children to Orthodox summer camps. Despite this heavy financial burden, there is no evidence that significant numbers have opted for public schools—or decided to limit the size of their families.

Finally, none of this comes at the expense of active participation in American society. Just like their counterparts elsewhere in the Jewish community, the Modern Orthodox attend college and earn advanced degrees at far higher rates than most other Americans. Both men and women go on to work, as we have seen, in the more lucrative sectors of the American economy. Some rise to positions of great distinction in their fields of endeavor, including in American public life (e.g., a secretary of the treasury and US attorney general; and Joseph Lieberman, once the Democratic nominee for the vice presidency).

In short, Modern Orthodoxy in America appears healthy and vibrant, with functioning communities not only in large metropolitan areas but also in nearly every midsize Jewish community and even some smaller cities like Indianapolis; New Orleans; Bangor, Maine; and Worcester, Massachusetts. Given the movement's successes—and the cachet of dynamism that attaches to it—one might expect its leaders to be in a mood to congratulate themselves.

And yet that is not the case. A close reading of what Modern Orthodox leaders are saying publicly, and even more bluntly in private, reveals a great deal of anxiety about current trends within their communities. (In what follows, I will be relying in part on interviews conducted on the understanding that quotations would not be attributed.)

---

2   UJA-Federation of New York, *Jewish Community Study of New York, 2011*, 220.

The anxieties being voiced have partly to do with numbers. Although the majority of those raised Modern Orthodox remain in that camp, the community does suffer defections, leading to worries about the possibility of demographic decline. But it is not only the potential erosion of its population that agitates the movement. A battle now rages for its soul—a tug of war over both practices and ideas that is pitting rabbis against each other even as some lay people work to push their synagogues onto new paths. At bottom, this internal struggle is over nothing less than the foundational assumption of the movement: that it is indeed possible to combine fidelity to traditional Judaism with modern values and understandings.

PRESSURE FROM THE RIGHT

To grasp the dynamics of the current struggle, it is critical to understand that it is playing out against challenges from both the "traditional" and the "modern" side of the equation. (Specialists on Orthodoxy have subdivided it into many more groupings than two, but these are the major ones.) I'll begin with the traditionalist challenge, which derives from the increase and growing self-confidence of another sector within the larger Orthodox world itself. That sector comprises the Haredim, often known in English as the "ultra-Orthodox."

The Haredi camp encompasses both a number of Hasidic sects and the spiritual descendants of their no less pious historical antagonists: the mitnagdim, or opponents of Hasidism, since that movement's emergence in the eighteenth century. In the metropolitan New York area, Haredim tend to cluster in enclaves like Williamsburg, Boro Park, and Crown Heights in Brooklyn and certain neighborhoods of Queens, as well as Lakewood, New Jersey, and a couple of upstate New York counties. Haredi communities also exist in such cities as Baltimore, Los Angeles, and Chicago. Wherever they are, the Haredim have distinguished themselves not only by their aloofness from much of Western culture and learning, or by the wary distance they maintain in social interactions with Gentiles, but also by their self-segregation from their fellow Jews, emphatically including the Modern Orthodox—and precisely because of the latter's accommodation of American mores, openness to the wisdom of the Gentiles, and willingness to interact with non-Orthodox Jews and their leaders.[3]

---

3 I have discussed the Haredim in "What You Don't Know about the Ultra-Orthodox," *Commentary*, July 2014, https://www.commentarymagazine.com/articles/what-you-dont-know-about-the-ultra-orthodox/.

Historical antecedents to the current standoff between the modern and Haredi sectors of Orthodoxy are easy to find. During the mass migration of Eastern European Jews at the turn of the twentieth century, some rabbis strove to recreate the all-embracing religious culture of Eastern Europe in the New World setting. Jeffrey Gurock, the foremost historian of American Orthodoxy, labels these rabbis "resisters"—the main object of their resistance being the intrusion of American ways into their lives. Against them stood more moderate immigrant and native-born rabbis, whom Gurock labels "accommodators." Each group established its own rabbinic organization (or, in the case of the resisters, three separate organizations).[4]

As the immigrant population adapted to America, the accommodating or Modern Orthodox position triumphed. Symptomatically, Modern Orthodox rabbis played an outsized role as chaplains during World War II;[5] in the postwar era, the dominant face of American Orthodoxy was that of Yeshiva University–trained rabbis (and their counterparts at the Hebrew Theological College in Skokie, Illinois), who were joined together in the Rabbinical Council of America (RCA). The Modern Orthodox ideal was conveyed by the motto of Yeshiva University (YU), *Torah U'madda*, usually translated as Torah and secular knowledge or, more broadly, Western culture and learning. For second- and third-generation American Jews attracted to this synthetic ideal, the figure they looked to was Rabbi Joseph B. Soloveitchik, who embodied the ideal through his mastery of rabbinic texts and his broad knowledge of and continuing engagement with Western philosophy.

But even as Modern Orthodoxy reached the peak of its influence, an influx of Holocaust-era refugees from both Nazism and Communism gave a powerful boost to the resisters' cause. The newcomers came with an ideology of separatism that had developed in Europe and found institutional expression in the Agudath Israel movement established in the early part of the century. As the Haredi Rabbi Yaakov Weinberg of Baltimore's Ner Israel yeshiva put it: "there is an 'otherness' to us, a gulf of strangeness that cannot be bridged, separating us from our compatriots."[6]

---

4 Jeffrey Gurock, "Resisters and Accommodators: Varieties of Orthodox Rabbis in America, 1886–1983," *American Jewish Archives* (November 1983), 87–100. Reprinted in *The American Rabbinate: A Century of Continuity and Change, 1883–1983* (New York: KTAV, 1985), 10–97.

5 On the chaplains, see Daniel Bronstein, "Torah in the Trenches: The Rabbi Chaplains of World War II, 1940–1946" (PhD diss., Jewish Theological Seminary, 2009).

6 Quoted in Samuel C. Heilman, *Sliding to the Right: the Contest for the Future of American Jewish Orthodoxy* (Berkeley: University of California Press, 2006), 32.

During the second half of the twentieth century, the key lines of division hardened. The resisters were intent on rejecting much of "enlightened" Western culture—whose bankruptcy, in their view, had been exposed in the depravity of the Holocaust—and no less bent on insulating themselves from what they saw as the corrupting morals of secular modernity. The accommodators, for their part, while recognizing that not everything condoned by modern fashion was in sync with traditional Judaism, were open to absorbing "the best that has been thought and said," regardless of its source. They flocked to universities and entered the professions, working side by side with non-Jews. They also maintained connections with Jews who were not traditionally observant but with whom they were prepared to work toward common ends. The most noteworthy common end was Zionism, which they embraced despite its largely secular leadership—a step shunned by the resisters, many of whom remain staunchly non-Zionist to the present day.[7]

In the face of withering criticism hurled at them by their critics among the resisters, Modern Orthodox Jews insisted on the legitimacy of their way of life—stressing, in addition to the embrace of Zionism, the value of what Jews can learn from Gentiles; full participation in the larger society (bounded only by strict adherence to Jewish ritual observance); and the provision to girls and women of the same kind of Jewish education received by boys and men (though not necessarily in mixed-sex settings). As we have seen, this insistence paid off handsomely.

Now, however, several developments have combined to give rise to a well-founded anxiety. One source of concern, alluded to above, is demography. Just a few decades ago, the modern sector constituted the large majority of Orthodox Jews; in our time, it has become vastly outnumbered by the Orthodox resisters and is on track to decline even further. As compared with the 3 percent of American Jews who (according to Pew) identify themselves as Modern Orthodox, 6 percent identify themselves as Haredi. In absolute numbers this translates into an estimated 310,000 adult Haredim compared with 168,000 adult Modern Orthodox.

---

7 Yitzchak Blau itemizes the key areas of continuing differences between the Modern Orthodox and Haredi camps: beyond the question of secular education and attitudes toward the state of Israel "other dividing lines include issues pertaining to women, attitudes toward gentiles and other Jewish denominations, ... the role of the rabbi ..., the credence given to ethical intuitions, ... and the willingness to include communal and personal needs as a factor for halakhic leniency." "Contemporary Challenges for Modern Orthodoxy," in *The Next Generation of Modern Orthodoxy*, ed. Shmuel Hain (New York: The Orthodox Forum, 2012), 299.

The disparity only widens when we look at younger age cohorts. Whereas those raised Modern Orthodox constitute 18 percent of American Jews over sixty-five, they represent slightly under 3 percent of those between eighteen and twenty-nine. Something closer to the reverse holds among those raised Haredi, who constitute 1.6 percent of Jews aged sixty-five and older but rise to 8 percent of the eighteen to twenty-nine year olds.

And then there are the children. A 2011 population study of Jews in the New York City area estimated the number of Haredi children at 166,000, roughly four times the number of Modern Orthodox children.[8] Marvin Schick, who used different categories in a 2009 national census of day schools, counted 125,000 children in Haredi schools versus 47,000 in Modern Orthodox and so-called Centrist Orthodox schools.[9] (The latter subgroup eschews coeducation in its middle schools and high schools.) Since then, by all accounts, the numbers of Haredi children have only increased.

To be sure, this is not the only circumstance depleting the numbers of Modern Orthodox Jews in the United States. Another one, ironically, stems from the movement's great success in imbuing its young with Zionist values. Precise numbers are lacking, but by some estimates as many as twenty percent of Modern Orthodox youngsters who spend a year or more in Israel during the "gap" between high school and college end up making their homes there for at least some period of time.[10] Needless to say, settling in Israel is socially and religiously approved behavior within the Modern Orthodox world, but that does not diminish its demographic impact on the community as a whole.

Still another worrying sign is the not insignificant rate of defection to more liberal movements. Thus, among those between the ages of thirty and forty-nine who have been raised Modern Orthodox, fully 44 percent have

---

8 *Jewish Community Study of New York*, 216.
9 Marvin Schick, *A Census of Jewish Day Schools in the United States, 2008–2009* (New York: Avi Chai Foundation, 2009), 6–7.
10 Theodore Sasson claims that young Orthodox families have been overrepresented among *olim* for quite a while both because of their religious and ideological motivations, as well as in response to the high costs of Jewish living in the US. *The New American Zionism* (New York: New York University Press, 2014), 112. Heilman estimates the aliyah figure for Modern Orthodox youth who spent a gap year in Israel at twenty percent. *Sliding to the Right*, 120. I have not found comparable information on Aliyah by Haredi Jews. On the dimension of this emigration that represents a brain drain, Jonathan Sarna has written, "This may be terrific from an Israeli perspective, but can a movement that sends its most illustrious sons and daughters there truly expect to triumph here?" *Sh'ma*, Februbary 1, 2001, http://shma.com/2001/02/the-future-of-american-orthodoxy/.

moved religiously leftward; among those between eighteen and twenty-nine, 29 percent no longer identify as Orthodox. (The commentator Alan Brill may have been the first to coin the term "post-Orthodox" for this population.)[11] True, as noted above, Modern Orthodoxy is much more successful than liberal denominations at retaining its members, and it continues to attract from them as many as it loses; but the losses hurt.

If the relatively static size of their community, and the sheer demographic heft of the Haredim, afford grounds for worry about the long-term viability of the Modern Orthodox way of life, beyond this concern lies another, related one: what some Modern Orthodox rabbis describe as a crisis of confidence among their laity. A salient symptom of that crisis, visible even among some otherwise highly acculturated Modern Orthodox families, is the decision to gravitate rightward toward Haredi or semi-Haredi schools and synagogues. Such families are driven, contends one of their rabbis, by "religious insecurity and feelings of guilt about that insecurity." This rabbi therefore sees his role as twofold: insisting on the validity of Modern Orthodoxy even as he encourages his congregants to intensify their commitment and practice. As he admits, it is a difficult balance to negotiate, and for some it does not suffice. Another rabbi, voicing exasperation over the rightward drift in his community, musters sarcasm to describe his congregants' perceptions: "If you are not [religiously] serious, you go to my shul; if you are more serious, you go to more right-wing shuls because there are communal advantages to being there."

As it happens, the Pew data suggest that the movement rightward may be balanced by a movement of Haredi Jews traveling in the opposite direction. Moreover, those joining "right-wing shuls" do not generally move into Haredi communities. It would thus be more accurate to see the so-called "slide to the right" as a matter less of massive defections to the Haredi camp than of a shift *within* Modern Orthodoxy, led in this instance by those inclined to adopt aspects of Haredi life while remaining nominally Modern Orthodox.

In some cases, the "slide" takes merely symbolic or token form, as when men wear black hats during prayer and women adopt Haredi-style head coverings while otherwise continuing to maintain their very modern style of life. More significant, and much more distressing to stalwarts of Modern Orthodox

---

11 Alan Brill, "Is there a Post-Orthodox Judaism that Corresponds to Post Evangelical?," *The Book of Doctrines and Opinions*, blog post, November 19, 2009, https://kavvanah.wordpress.com/2009/11/19/is-there-a-post-orthodox-judaism-that-corresponds-to-post-evangelical/.

values, has been the assimilation—some would say infiltration—of a "neo-Haredi" worldview into some of the movement's key institutions.

Since the passing of Rabbi Soloveitchik from the scene some thirty years ago, the Yeshiva University world has lacked an authoritative figure who personifies for the broader public the synthesis proclaimed in YU's motto of *Torah U'madda*. Meanwhile, a neo-Haredi group of *roshei yeshiva*—the term, often translated as deans of Talmudic academies, more accurately connotes advanced teachers of rabbinic texts—has planted its flag at YU's Rabbi Isaac Elchanan Theological Seminary (RIETS), which educates, ordains, and shapes the religious and halakhic worldview of Modern Orthodox rabbis.[12] In addition, Modern Orthodox day schools often employ Haredi teachers who likewise communicate their ideology to impressionable students and may encourage them after graduation to attend an Israeli yeshiva or girls' seminary where neo-Haredi perspectives predominate. Of late, some long-time Modern Orthodox synagogues have also taken to hiring Haredi or neo-Haredi rabbis to fill their pulpits. And the community as a whole has become dependent on Haredim who fill certain ritually critical roles, including as scribes who write Torah scrolls and other religious documents, kosher slaughterers, and supervisors of kosher food production.[13]

Most subversive of all has been the internalization of the idea that Haredi Judaism represents the touchstone and arbiter of Orthodox authenticity, period. This has placed Modern Orthodoxy on the defensive, handcuffing it to a way of thinking at odds with its founding assumptions. Willy-nilly, by absorbing the resistant mind-set, important sectors of the movement have thereby undermined Modern Orthodoxy's accommodative ideology and, worse, have made it more difficult to help their members navigate as observant Jews who embrace modern culture.

---

12 On the emergence of these forces at YU in the period after the death of J. B. Soloveitchik, see Jeffrey Gurock, *Orthodox Jews in America* (Bloomington: Indiana University Press, 2009), 267–72.

13 A detailed accounting of this capitulation by Modern Orthodox institutions to Haredi personnel appears in Yehudah Turetsky and Chaim I. Waxman, "Sliding to the Left? Contemporary American Modern Orthodoxy," *Modern Judaism*, 31, no. 2 (2011): 10. The admission of Haredi or neo-Haredi religious functionaries into the Rabbinical Council of America has been cited by some observers as the prime explanation for the implacable hostility displayed by that organization toward more "open" versions of Modern Orthodoxy.

PRESSURE FROM THE LEFT

If the challenge represented by the Haredim exerts pressure on Modern Orthodoxy from one direction, another and equally great challenge makes itself felt from the opposite direction. To Rabbi Yitz Greenberg, speaking at a recent forum on the Pew study, Modern Orthodox Jews live "on the same [cultural] continuum" as their non-Orthodox counterparts, being no less "exposed to the attractions of modernity and the acids of skepticism/historical criticism/social mores," and no less likely to succumb to those twin forces, both the "attractions" and the "acids," than are Conservative, Reform, or for that matter nonaffiliated and secular Jews. Rabbi Greenberg even attributes the "demographic decline" of the movement primarily to this factor.[14]

Actually, as we have seen, the problem is not (or not yet) one of serious decline but rather of demographic stasis. But there can be no doubt that Modern Orthodox Jews have become at least as alert to the most controversial issues roiling their movement from the Left as from the Right. To adapt Jeffrey Gurock's nomenclature of resisters versus accommodators, which he applied to the struggle within the larger Orthodox world between the Haredim and the Modern Orthodox,[15] we may say that Modern Orthodoxy itself is now beset by a no less bitter or momentous struggle: between its own internal resisters attracted by Haredi Judaism and accommodators more willing to adapt Jewish law to twenty-first-century ethical sensibilities.

Undoubtedly, the most hotly debated set of issues concerns the status of Orthodox women. Sexual equality is now taken for granted in most Modern Orthodox homes, and holding males and females to different standards is increasingly unthinkable. Under the circumstances, why should it not occur to some girls that they too might don tefillin (phylacteries), traditionally the accoutrements of male worship?[16] How much Torah and Talmud ought girls and women be encouraged to study? May women serve as synagogue

---

14 Rabbi Greenberg elaborated on his views in a personal correspondence with me, dated May 15, 2014.
15 This is the theme of Turetsky and Waxman, "Sliding to the Left?"
16 On controversies over girls donning tefillin, see Amanda Borschel-Dan, "Orthodox Girls Fight for the Right to Don Tefillin," *Times of Israel*, January 21, 2014, http://www.timesofisrael.com/modern-orthodox-girls-fight-for-the-right-to-don-tefillin/; Tully Harcsztark, New Jersey *Jewish Star*, January 26, 2014, http://thejewishstar.com/stories/SAR-principal-explains-decision-to-allow-girls-to-wear-teffilin-at-school-minyanim,4665; and for a scathing denunciation of the policy, *Rabbi Pruznansky's Blog*, January 26, 2014, https://rabbipruzansky.com/2014/01/26/the-real-story/.

presidents?[17] May they conduct their own prayer services, lead parts of mixed services, or wear tefillin during public worship? And, drawing the greatest heat: what are rabbis prepared to do to release "chained" women (*agunot*), whose husbands have refused to grant them a proper writ of divorce?[18]

Other debates center on the proper treatment of homosexuality and homosexuals in the Orthodox community; how the community should relate to non-Orthodox Jews; the authority exercised by the Israeli chief rabbinate in matters pertaining to American Orthodox Jews; the authority of congregational rabbis vis-à-vis that of roshei yeshiva; the latitude, if any, for interpreting the theological category of "Torah from Heaven" (i.e., the belief that the Torah was dictated verbatim by God to Moses); and more. In short, the same culture wars that have engulfed non-Orthodox Jews, Catholics, and Protestants now rage in the Modern Orthodox world.

This is not the place to discuss the complex legal and theological arguments on these issues advanced by different rabbinic authorities. Suffice it to say there are deep differences over who is credentialed to issue legal rulings and how flexible is Jewish law. On one side, Modern Orthodox resisters argue they are constrained by halakhic precedent even when it comes to mitigating the

---

17 For a consideration of some halakhic dimensions of this question, see Aryeh Frimer, "Women in Communal Leadership Positions: Shul Presidents," *Text and Texture Blog*, June 2, 2010, http://text.rcarabbis.org/women-in-communal-leadership-positions-shul-presidents-by-aryeh-frimer/. On the ways these questions have been resolved differently in Modern Orthodox synagogues, see "The First Women Shul Presidents in Orthodox White Plains," JOFA, February 15, 2013, http://www.jewfem.com/easyblog1/entry/from-the-jofa-blog-the-first-women-shul-presidents-in-orthodox-white-plains; Stuart Ain, "Young Israel Movement in Turmoil over Upstate Shul," *Jewish Week*, June 29, 2010, http://www.thejewishweek.com/news/new_york/young_israel_movement_turmoil_over_upstate_shul; and Josh Nathan–Kazis and Shuly Seidler-Feller, "Rabbi of Historical Orthodox Synagogue Overturns Decision to Let Women Lead," *Forward*, June 30, 2010, http://forward.com/news/129105/rabbi-of-historic-orthodox-synagogue-overturns-dec/

18 The struggle to free *agunot*, women "chained" to recalcitrant husbands who refuse to divorce them or extort huge sums of money as the price of a get, a Jewish writ of divorce, has agitated Orthodox communities for many decades. It has led to the creation of special courts to free such women, which predictably have been denounced by prominent rabbis, including Joseph B. Soloveitchik in the past, and today by sectors of the Rabbinical Council of America; and it has led to the approval of prenuptial agreements permitting courts to dissolve a marriage under certain circumstances. The literature on these controversies is immense. In the present context, what is more important is how damaging the failure of Orthodox rabbis to resolve these tragic circumstances has been to their own credibility and the respect accorded to them.

suffering of *agunot*. On the other side, accommodators tend to interpret Jewish law as in some degree subject to historical circumstances; Blu Greenberg, the preeminent leader of Orthodox feminism, has encapsulated this view tersely, declaring that "where there's a rabbinic will, there's a halakhic way." Many advocates of new thinking see the principal driver of change as the larger Orthodox community, with rabbis lagging behind.

While such disagreements on matters of Jewish law occupy the foreground, a series of cultural forces in the background are seen by all as shaping current debates.

Rabbinic authority is waning. Rabbis across the spectrum of Modern Orthodoxy, resisters and accommodators alike, point to a community that has absorbed American understandings of the sovereign self. "What rabbis say does not matter" is a refrain I have heard repeatedly. "Authority is in retreat," declares one rabbi; says another, "People like traditional davening (prayer) and singing; but when it comes to halakha impinging on them, then they resist." In one Haredi school, the head of Jewish studies states without any prompting, "In today's age, the model of rabbinic authority does not exist. We don't live in ghettoes anymore, so you have to reach students where they are. Saying 'because it is so' no longer works."

In private conversation, the same lament recurs regardless of ideological position, although some go on to lay the blame for the loss of rabbinic authority on their opponents. On the accommodative side, the prevailing sentiment is that hidebound rabbis have brought this situation on themselves because, when it comes to the demands of modernity, they are "oblivious and clueless." From the resisters, one hears that the accommodative wing has undermined the authority of recognized legal decisors by running to peripheral figures who are only too willing to approve innovations. Many sense their loss of authority so keenly that they shy away from asserting their views on the major cultural issues of the day even when they personally feel strongly about them.

Accelerating these trends is the new reality of the internet. Thanks to it, states one rabbi, "Everybody has a right to have a position; everyone has a *de'ah* [opinion] about everything." Educated Jews can look up answers to their own questions and choose from the answers available online. Many feel empowered in this role simply by dint of their day-school education and by the time they have spent studying in Israel, even as they are also encouraged by modern culture's stress on individual autonomy to act according to the dictates of their conscience.

In this connection, day schools themselves are faulted by some for inadequately preparing their students to cope with the intellectual and moral challenges they encounter once they enter college. Rabbis on both sides agree that the failure lies in the deliberate neglect of questions of belief, theology, and the "why" of observance. From my own visits to Orthodox day schools, I question this critique. To me the problem seems more fundamental: there is no way fully to prepare Orthodox young people for the transition from their insular and homogeneous environment to university, where the reigning values are so at odds with traditional Judaism. Be that as it may, however, efforts to remediate the situation are being made by rabbis in both the resistant and accommodative wings who are undertaking to teach their congregants about what is relevant and meaningful in Judaism rather than focusing solely on the study of texts. "I used to give heavy-duty classes on *rishonim* and *aharonim*," one rabbi on the side of the accommodators informed me, referring to classical rabbinic commentators. "Now I teach about *derekh eretz* [proper behavior], women and ritual observance, and *tz'dakah* [Jewish giving]."

One thing is certain: an estimated 70 percent of Modern Orthodox college students are enrolled in secular institutions of higher learning,[19] and the impact of their experience there cannot be ignored. True, many of the parents and grandparents of current students also attended secular colleges, but it can be postulated that academic values and assumptions have changed since then, or that they are instilled far more explicitly than they were in the past, or both. On every campus today, incoming students are required to attend an intensive orientation program during which they are exposed to strongly formulated judgments about diversity, tolerance, and correct thinking. In this hothouse atmosphere, how is it possible for Orthodox students to argue in defense of the unequal treatment of women in the domain of religious observance? Can one conceivably emerge from a college experience today without having encountered attitudes toward sexual behavior at odds with traditional Orthodox beliefs?

Making it still harder to shelter today's Modern Orthodox Jews is that they have strayed beyond the commuter colleges favored by an earlier generation. Once on campus, moreover, they are also less likely to shy away from courses on sexual roles, psychology, comparative religion—or modern biblical criticism—that will challenge views they absorbed during their day-school years and from their elders.

---

19 This estimate appears in Michelle Waldman Sarna, "An Emerging Approach to Emerging Adulthood and Modern Orthodoxy," in *The Next Generation of Modern Orthodoxy*, ed. Shmuel Hain (New York: The Orthodox Forum, 2012), 255.

As with the challenge from the Haredim, so with the challenge from "modernity," one can trace the effects on the institutional level as well as the personal. Acknowledging the seriousness of both challenges, some among Modern Orthodoxy's accommodative leaders and activists, male and female alike, have been pushing to reinvigorate and reinforce the movement's founding ethos from within. To generalize, one might say that these efforts are aimed simultaneously at fending off the inroads of Haredization and at incorporating, to some unspecified degree, the "open" ethos of modern liberal culture.

In 1996, an organization, Edah, was founded with just that dual purpose in mind. Its leader, Rabbi Saul Berman, issued a pamphlet spelling out "a variety of Orthodox attitudes to selected ideological issues"—with the emphasis on "variety." The issues ranged from the treatment of women in Jewish law to the meaning of *Torah U'madda*, from pluralism and tolerance within Orthodoxy to outreach aimed at non-Orthodox Jews. A year later, Edah was joined by the Jewish Orthodox Feminist Alliance (JOFA), whose declared mission is to advance "social change around gender issues in the Orthodox Jewish community."[20]

Although Edah folded after a decade, JOFA continues with its work. And in the meantime, a number of other institutions and initiatives have arisen, each dedicated to fostering change in the Modern Orthodox world. They include Yeshivat Chovevei Torah (YCT), an accommodative rabbinical seminary competing with YU's RIETS, and Yeshivat Maharat, which styles itself as the "first institution to ordain Orthodox women as clergy"; both of these institutions are associated with a camp that has come to be called Open Orthodoxy.[21] Allied with them is the International Rabbinical Fellowship, whose announced aim is to stand up for "the right, responsibility, and autonomy of individual rabbis to decide matters of *halakhah* for their communities."[22]

In the same orbit, if not necessarily of the same mind, are women-only prayer groups as well as "partnership minyanim" where men and women share

---

20 Saul. J. Berman, "Diverse Orthodox Attitudes," Edah, 2001. JOFA's mission statement appears on its website.
21 These institutions and the title were associated with Rabbi Avraham (Avi) Weiss. See "Open Orthodoxy! A Modern Orthodox Rabbi's Creed," *Judaism* 46:4 (Fall 1997): 409–21. Since the original publication of this essay, Weiss has retired and new leaders are distancing themselves from the term "Open Orthodoxy."
22 Gurock describes the emergence of these groups and some of the skirmishes of the 1990s and early twenty-first century in *Orthodox Jews in America*, Chapter 10, especially 285–31.

the responsibility of leading different parts of the prayer services in a manner deemed acceptable to select rabbinic authorities.[23] To disseminate new thinking, Modern Orthodox bloggers have been busy putting forth more "progressive" perspectives. One of them, the website *TheTorah.com*, grapples with the findings and conclusions of modern biblical scholarship, long regarded as inherently inimical to the teachings of traditional Judaism.[24]

It is not unusual for some Modern Orthodox Jews and their rabbis to pick and choose among these activities. Members of women's prayer groups, for example, may confine themselves to that initiative alone. Some students at YCT may support partnership minyanim while others do not. Some students at YCT and Yeshivat Maharat decline to identify themselves personally with Open Orthodoxy. Interestingly, it has been estimated that as many as 40 rabbinical students at RIETS itself would participate in a partnership minyan, even though several of the leading Talmudists at that institution have unequivocally proscribed such prayer services.

In sum, it is problematic to assume that individuals, even if they share a willingness to stretch the boundaries of Orthodoxy, form part of a common accommodative camp. Nor is it possible to quantify the number of Modern Orthodox Jews sympathetic to any of these efforts, though most observers assume it is relatively small and limited to a few centers of liberal thinking in New York, Washington, Boston, and Los Angeles. Still, just as it means something that Modern Orthodox congregations in, for example, St. Louis and Kansas City have sought out women to serve in a quasi-rabbinic role, it seems safe to assume that the 120 or so rabbis ordained so far at YCT and now occupying positions on campuses, in day schools, in chaplaincies, and in pulpits all around the country have had an impact of their own. The same can be said for

---

23 On the controversies over so-called "partnership minyanim," see Uriel Heilman, "'Partnership Minyan' Spreads among Orthodox—and Rabbis Fire Back," *Forward*, March 5, 2014, http://forward.com/news/193860/partnership-minyan-spreads-among-orthodox-and-ra/. On Women's Tefilla, Batsheva Marcus, and Ronnie Becher, "Women's Tefillah Movement," *Encyclopedia*, Jewish Women's Archive, http://jwa.org/encyclopedia/article/womens-tefillah-movement; and for the grounds for opposition as laid out by an Orthodox rabbi, "Michael J. Broyde, "Women Only Torah Reading," *Torah Musings* blog, October 15, 2012, http://www.torahmusings.com/2012/10/womens-only-torah-reading/.

24 The appearance of *TheTorah.com* with its more questioning and open-minded approach to biblical criticism has stirred new controversies. For a powerful critique of this new trend within Modern Orthodoxy by a sympathizer with Open Orthodoxy, see Yoram Hazony, "Open Orthodoxy?," *Torah Musings*, May 27, 2014, http://www.torahmusings.com/2014/05/open-orthodoxy/.

the ideas making their way into every corner of the Modern Orthodox community through the reach of the internet.

TOWARD A NEW SYNTHESIS?

The most basic consequence of these cumulative changes is an increased awareness that the ground is shifting. As one observer has put it, "everyone knows the lines are moving." The same individual notes how, "in shuls, people talk about how far to the Right Modern Orthodoxy has gone." Meanwhile, for those opposed to Open Orthodoxy, the ground is similarly perceived to be shifting, albeit in a distinctly different if not heretical direction.

The discomfort has led some rabbis to speak of a widening chasm within the movement and the inevitability—if not the desirability—of a schism. On the resisters' side, those insisting that lines must be drawn have mostly limited themselves to fighting against new practices rather than ostracizing people, although, in a few synagogues, men who participate in partnership minyanim have been banned from leading services in their home congregations, and there are concerted efforts to bar YCT graduates from being hired by major Modern Orthodox synagogues. Some resisters have also taken to dismissing their opponents as closet Conservative Jews; to one prominent rabbi, the Open Orthodox should be known as "the observant non-Orthodox."[25]

For their part, advocates of Open Orthodoxy have shown little hesitancy about castigating their traditionalist opponents as reactionaries. Resentment toward Yeshiva University boils over in statements that the institution has fallen under the sway of rabbis with no understanding of today's world and has become intellectually bankrupt. By contrast, Open Orthodox rabbis pride themselves on their hospitality to those who are not Orthodox. "We create an open space and do not say 'no,'" one leader declares. Another draws the distinctions differently: "YU is modernist; [its people] think they are right. They draw lines in the sand. YCT people are post-modern. We see no conflict between intellectual openness and using critical tools, even as we remain committed to *halakhah*."

---

25 For a few examples, see Ari Soffer, "'Open Orthodox' or 'Neo-Conservative'?," *Arutz Sheva*, April 1, 2014, www.israelnationalnews.com/News/News.aspx/179142; and *Rabbi Steven Pruzansky's Blog*, "Open and Closed," November 15, 2013, http:/rabbipruzansky.com/2013/11/15/open-and-closed/. "With the demise of the Conservative movement, there is that niche to be filled [by the Open Orthodox]—but wouldn't the ultimate consequences be the same?"

And then there are those in the middle who feel sympathy for both sides and want a peaceful resolution that will keep everyone in the same camp. At a celebration of recent RIETS ordainees, a keynote speaker emphasized a single theme: we at YU are open; we have always stood for openness. Was this a peace offering to the progressive side of the spectrum, another salvo in the battle over legitimacy, or perhaps both? Others watch in embarrassment as "the hotheads" denounce each other. In most quarters, there is a sense that the current situation is unsustainable.

Of course, it is possible to view the factionalism within Modern Orthodoxy as a sign of vitality. Thus, one might say that differences have arisen because those on each side, equally committed to the Jewish future, are alarmed by the unhelpful ideas or policies being promoted by their counterparts on the other side. One might even remark that, in the fastidiously "non-judgmental" climate prevalent today in the rest of the American Jewish community, it is refreshing to encounter Jews prepared to stake a claim to what they see as true, necessary, and obligatory.

Worth noting, in any event, is that the programs and institutions spawned by rival factions are stimulating a welcome spirit of creativity. As Yehuda Sarna, the rabbi of New York University's Bronfman Center, has observed, "There are multiple Torah and college options, multiple rabbinical schools, multiple forms of Orthodox Zionism, multiple ways of engaging with modernity, multiple entry and exit points to the community."[26] One merely has to cite the range of Orthodox websites issuing commentaries on the weekly Torah portion, and compare those offerings with the paucity of non-Orthodox counterparts, to appreciate the dynamism. The same can be said about bloggers in all sectors of the Modern Orthodox community who address everything from matters of theology to preparing brides for their wedding night.

Moreover, despite conflicts over practices, Modern Orthodox Jews of all stripes observe the same religious common core—daily prayer, kosher food restrictions, laws of family purity, Sabbath and festival celebrations. In fact, one of the contentions of the accommodators is that they are in no danger of going the way of Conservative Judaism precisely because, whereas the Open Orthodox live and work in religiously observant communities, Conservative rabbis historically made legal decisions for communities that did not observe Jewish law. Open Orthodoxy can experiment with new ideas and interpretations, they

---

26 Yehuda Sarna, "The End of the Middle of the Road," in *The Next Generation of Modern Orthodoxy*, ed. Shmuel Hain (New York: The Orthodox Forum, 2012), 345.

contend, because the commitment to Jewish law will keep them and their followers in check.

In "The Rise of Social Orthodoxy," an essay in *Commentary*, Jay Lefkowitz put this perspective succinctly: "I imagine [that] for many others like me, the key to Jewish living is not our religious beliefs but our commitment to a set of practices and values that foster community and continuity."[27] Assumed in this formulation is that practices and values will remain unaffected by changing beliefs. But is that right? In fact, as we have seen, a whole set of core Modern Orthodox assumptions is under assault both from forces outside Modern Orthodoxy and from the partisans of those forces within, and there is considerable evidence that some practices, and even some values, are changing as a result.

Thus far, the Modern Orthodox world has managed to flourish and persist by creating a community of practice and by focusing most of its intellectual energy on intensified Talmud study. This is not to be minimized. The movement's vibrant communal life, high levels of observance, and serious engagement with traditional texts are monumental achievements. But, caught as Modern Orthodoxy is between the absolutism and insularity of Haredi Judaism and the realities of an open and radically untraditional American society, are those achievements sufficient to retain a population well integrated into American life and profoundly influenced by its mores, assumptions, and values?

The urgent question for Modern Orthodoxy is which values can be accommodated without undermining religious commitment and distorting traditional Judaism beyond recognition—and, conversely, what losses will be sustained if Modern Orthodoxy should undertake more actively to resist the modern world in which its adherents spend most of their waking hours.[28] The same urgent question, mutatis mutandis, has confronted other Jewish religious movements in the past, and has continued to haunt their rabbis and adherents long after they made their choice of a path forward. That is one reason why today's unfolding culture wars within Modern Orthodoxy carry far-reaching implications not only for that movement but for the future of American Judaism as a whole.

---

27 Jay P. Lefkowitz, "The Rise of Social Orthodoxy," *Commentary*, April 2014, 37–42.
28 This first question is central to Rabbi Haskel Lookstein's response to "social Orthodoxy." "The Rise of 'Social Orthodoxy:' Is it Good or Bad for the Jews?," sermon delivered at Kehillath Jeshurun, April 26, 2014. Lookstein asks whether the burdens of observance will be shouldered in the absence of belief in the divine origin of the mitzvot. But the reverse is also important for Modern Orthodoxy to address: if it does not find ways to accommodate some aspects of what passes for advanced Western culture, will it continue to be relevant to its adherents and will it heighten the cognitive dissonance they may feel?

CHAPTER 10

Where Have All the Rabbis Gone? The Changing Character of the Orthodox Rabbinate and its Causes

SAMUEL C. HEILMAN

INCREASED LAY LEARNING LEADS TO A DECLINE OF THE RABBINIC MONOPOLY ON TORAH KNOWLEDGE

One of the key accomplishments in the resurgence of Orthodoxy after the Holocaust has been the near universal acceptance among its adherents of the idea that in order to be a truly Orthodox Jew one must be educated Jewishly and increasingly that such Jewish education does not stop after the high school years but should be an ongoing adjunct to life as a committed Jew. The days when one could comfortably call oneself an Orthodox Jew simply by virtue of communal affiliation or synagogue attendance but remain largely ignorant of the great corpus of Torah learning are mostly over, except in the case of those who are newly Orthodox, and for them, at least in principle, only temporarily. In the case of such neophytes, the assumption is that they will mark their movement into Orthodoxy not only with increasing religious ritual observance but also and no less with an active commitment to engage in ongoing Jewish study at whatever level suits them. Indeed, the increasing number and variety of translations of classic or even obscure Jewish texts, vernacular commentaries, weekly Torah-portion sheets, community learning centers (including kollel outreach), and Torah lectures available either in one's geographic vicinity or via the internet are now an integral element of Orthodox Jewish life, no less than a day school and yeshiva education. Extended time spent in Israel in a full-time learning setting is also increasingly a part of all this, frequently during adolescence but also more and more during young adulthood. Institutions like Pardes and Matan, as well as a variety of study trips sponsored by various organizations, and daylong seminars on Torah topics have expanded this sort of Israeli Jewish study opportunities to adults.

The tremendous popularity of the "Daf Yomi," an idea originally floated by Rabbi Meir Shapiro of Sanok, Poland at the August 1923 World Congress of Agudath Israel, for Jews to all review the same folio of the Babylonian Talmud each day until they had completed the entire Talmud in seven and a half years is perhaps the most stunning measure of this expanded Jewish study. For years taken up by a barely noticeable few, by the late 1990s it had become an activity taken up by Orthodox Jews of all stripes and the *siyum* came to be attended by tens of thousands. Today there is barely an Orthodox community that does not have one or more groups engaged in Daf Yomi. Clearly, the generations of Orthodox Jews for whom Talmud study was a basic curricular element have turned it into a continuing presence if not an essential ritual in their lives.

The net result of this merging of obligatory Jewish study with contemporary Orthodox identity—a Jewish ideal of the Talmudical sages but historically limited to a small elite—is an extraordinarily learned laity, at least when compared to earlier generations. The general Orthodox assumption of התקטנות הדורות, the doctrine that believes in the so-called "decline of generations," in which "each succeeding generation, or each succeeding epoch, is in some significant and religiously relevant sense inferior to preceding generations or epochs," argues we in these days are religious pygmies when compared to our forebears who were giants. Notwithstanding, the days when the Orthodox rabbi in town was the only Jewish scholar or even the preeminent one whose Jewish learning and erudition towered over all the laity in the community, who were in comparison Jewishly ignorant and underdeveloped, would seem to be long gone.[1] Indeed, for an Orthodox rabbi to be considered a Jewish scholar today the ante has been raised significantly, and what might have been enough learning at earlier times to affirm his Jewish scholarly status is not necessarily enough today in many Orthodox communities. In many places today—especially in North America, the United Kingdom, Australia, and Israel—where an educated Orthodoxy is flourishing, there are lay Jews (and not only the males among them) who at least on the surface can comfortably navigate a page of the Talmud

---

1 Chaim I. Waxman, "Toward a Sociology of Psak," *Tradition* 25, no. 3 (Spring 1991): 13.

and many of its commentaries—to be sure often with the help of the Artscroll or Steinsaltz editions—with much the same ease as a rabbi. They are also familiar with Bible (and often can chant it from the Scroll), can steer their way through some Maimonides and other medieval and modern commentaries, including the codes such as the *Shulchan Aruch* and the Rema's (Moses Isserles) glosses on it. They even know once obscure commentaries, which they have on their well-appointed bookshelves. Even the ChaBaD house Orthodox, where Judaism-lite is commonly the norm, are expected to learn about Orthodoxy, albeit through the prism of the Rebbe and his interpreters' version of it (admittedly not the standard but quickly supplanting it in many places).

This is really in sharp contrast to life among the Orthodox of pre-Holocaust Europe—when Talmud study and Jewish literacy was really limited to a relatively small elite (as indeed it was for generations). Moreover, after the lost years of the Holocaust, when Torah learning was essentially suspended for the generation that survived, this new unexpected and broad-based Jewish literacy stands in sharp contrast. When I was growing up Orthodox during the 1950s and early 1960s in northeastern America, Jewish literacy in the Orthodox communities was still the exception rather than the rule. Who even heard of the Daf Yomi?

Moreover, for all that today's Jewishly educated Orthodox Jews do *not* know in the Jewish corpus, they now know where and how to find out about it—albeit sometimes with the assistance of Google or other internet resources, but also with the help of their friends. The day when a local rabbi was the only one who could understand or teach Torah is gone in much if not most of the Orthodox world of today. The rabbi may be the only one who pursues it as a vocation, but by no means is he the only possible teacher in town. The community of the faithful are also the community of the Jewishly informed and informing. They may not be the "scholars society" that Menachem Friedman has described for whom study is a way of life (if indeed it truly is among the Haredim and not just a placeholder until they find something else), but they are far from a society of boors or *am ha'artzim* that was once a very large, if not the dominant, segment of Orthodoxy. As for the rabbi, if he seeks a position as a Torah teacher, he may have to stress his tutoring abilities for the children, for still today more than ever Orthodox parents relegate Torah study to rabbis more than to themselves.

To be sure, most *non*-Orthodox Jews today know far less Jewishly than their forbears did, and in a sense this has added to the gap that increasingly separates the contemporary Orthodox from all other Jews—but that is another story in the contemporary Jewish world, about which I have written elsewhere.

The popularity of the Daf Yomi and the tens of thousands who participate in it is only the most prominent of the examples of how the credo עשה תורתך קבע that has become inherent to Orthodoxy is today expressed in practice. The sight of a heavily used *beit midrash* in the synagogue, the growing presence of community kollels in which laity participate, the explosion in the publishing of so-called Torah literature, the large personal libraries of Torah texts (rivalling those held by those of the great yeshiva of Volozhin)—are all evidence of the integration of Torah study with Orthodox identity.[2] And it is not just limited to males.

If once women did not share in this Jewish learning and way of life, those days are gone too in the contemporary Orthodox world. With the nearly universal commitment to providing their daughters with a day-school education—or in the Haredi domains, years in a girls' seminary—the Orthodox have created a cadre of Jewish women who also feel the ongoing obligation to engage in Jewish study, who know texts once limited only to men and can look to women among them who are familiar with even some of the most recondite Jewish Torah matters, and who often can make their ways through the paths of Jewish learning with some of the same as or even greater ease than the men. Anyone who spends time at the all-night Jewish study in Orthodox congregations during the Shavuot holiday will likely not be surprised to see girls and women both in attendance and often as instructors. Although some Orthodox rabbis might wish otherwise, because they consider women's Torah study in general and Talmud learning in particular as undermining Orthodoxy, by encouraging egalitarianism and feminism, Orthodox women Torah scholars and their supporters "argue that rather than undermining the foundation of the Orthodox community, opportunities for women to learn in a real and serious way are strengthening it."[3] They too are as often as not more engaged by Torah study than the men. They too do not need a rabbi to teach them, often preferring women scholars, and some of those women seek to join the ranks of those who study Torah as a vocation.

There is even a growing halakhic literature expressly targeted to women that is, to borrow from the title of Tamar Ross's book, "expanding the palace of

---

2 On the library in Volozhin, see Gershon Hundert, "The Library of the Study Hall in Volozhin, 1762: Some Notes on the Basis of a Newly Discovered Manuscript," *Jewish History* 14, no. 2 (2000): 225–44.

3 Rachel Rosenthal, "What's Wrong with Women Studying Talmud, Rabbi Willig?," *The Forward*, August 17, 2015, http://forward.com/sisterhood/319262/an-open-letter-to-rabbi-mordechai-willig/?utm_content=sisterhood_Newsletter_TopSpot_Title_Position-1&utm_source=Sailthru&utm_medium=email&utm_campaign=Sisterhood+Redesign+2015-08-18&utm_term=Sisterhood (accessed August 19, 2015).

Torah," as seen especially in such volumes as Deena Zimmerman's *A Lifetime Companion to the Laws of Jewish Family Life* that address halakhic issues pertaining to women.[4] Ironically, among the so-called Modern Orthodox women who embrace general culture, this knowledge and active engagement with Torah may be even greater and more enthusiastic than in the Haredi world, where traditional gender role models that claim women should not invade the realm of Torah study have become a part of the culture war between the Haredim and all other Jews, forcing some women to downplay what they know of Torah learning for fear that if they do not, they might be seen as challenging the traditional dominance of men in that world and as such as ideological renegades.

In some ways, this growing Jewish competence and learning among today's Orthodoxy is not simply a reflection of changes in the Jewish world. It may also be understood as a reflection of the growing emphasis in modern western culture on individual competence and accomplishment, at first for men but increasingly for both genders. That was largely the goal of a liberal education, which at its best not only transmitted a lot of knowledge to all people regardless of who they were but also and more crucially empowered individuals to learn how to study on their own. Education is after all the engine of a meritocracy, and creates conditions for giving power to knowledge rather than ascribed status. What was once a goal of liberal arts and science education is now also such in Torah education—even in the precincts of Orthodoxy.

Jewish education, and even Orthodox Jewish education (particularly the day-school version of it), developed in consonance with that value and out of the same social and cultural roots. Among those who encouraged this engagement, even and especially among women, was no less a Modern Orthodox rabbinic giant than Rabbi Joseph Dov Soloveitchik, who already in a May 27, 1953, letter wrote: "Not only is the teaching of *Torah she-be-al peh* [the Talmud] to girls permissible but it is nowadays an absolute imperative." He went further endorsing a "uniform program" of such Torah learning in the day school "for the entire student body."[5] That was how women—and often the college educated among them—increasingly became included in Jewish learning, in spite of a long tradition that excluded them from it by virtue of their birth and gender, arguing their competence lay elsewhere. All this was the inevitable complement

---

4 Deena Zimmerman, *A Lifetime Companion to the Laws of Jewish Family Life*, 2nd rev. ed. (Jerusalem and New York: Urim Publications, 2006).
5 Joseph Dov Soloveitchik, *Community, Covenant and Commitment: Selected Letters and Communications* (New York: KTAV, 2005), 81–2.

to accentuating "the importance of the individual person," that emerged in the last three centuries of Western civilization.[6] *All this has clearly challenged the idea of the rabbis having a monopoly of Torah learning and the special authority that comes with it.*

SHTIBBELIZATION OF ORTHODOXY AND DEMOCRATIZATION

There has been another development in Modern Orthodox life that has had an important impact on the rabbinate that is not, strictly speaking, purely Jewish in its origins. The embrace of democratic principles from the political environment in which Modern Orthodoxy has found itself for the last two generations, coupled with the fact that rabbis are often seen as employees rather than autonomous leaders in the modern world, has in many cases led to the rise of the laity over the rabbinate. When combined with the already described empowerment of individuals in modern life, a correlate has been a downplaying in the importance of authority, including frequently clerical authority. As both Aaron Kirschenbaum and Adam Ferziger have noted, the modern world has taken a toll on the authority on the modern clergy and the local rabbi.[7] Add to that the aforementioned growing ability of the Orthodox to do-it-yourself in Torah learning and the special importance of the rabbi evaporates. In fact, as all this was happening, the Jewish Orthodox attachment to large synagogues with a series of rabbis heading them was being exchanged for what some have called "the *shtibbelization* of Orthodoxy." This was a process in which the educated Orthodox preferred small congregations led and governed by the lay leadership where the rabbi, if there was one, was at best a kind of first among equals or missing altogether. Some claimed this movement was the result of the Modern Orthodox rejecting the high-church style of the large synagogue or looking for a congregation on the cheap—and those motives surely have been part of the process. But the fact that an Orthodox laity existed that knew how to provide for themselves Jewishly without the ongoing input of an onsite rabbi surely was a prerequisite for such *shtibbelization*. These shitibbels were not the prewar shuls of the unlearned; they were instead face-to-face gatherings of those who saw themselves as the sufficiently learned.

---

6 Marvin Perry, *Western Civilization: A Brief History*, vol. 2 (Boston: Houghton Mifflin, 1981), 186.

7 Aaron Kirschenbaum, "Mara de-Atra: A Brief Sketch," *Tradition* 27, no. 4 (1993): 39; and Adam Ferziger, "Between Outreach and 'Inreach': Redrawing the Lines of American Orthodox Rabbinate," *Modern Judaism* 25, no. 3 (October 2005): 237.

IMPACT ON RABBINATE

Not necessarily among the Orthodox but at least among American Jewry, the number of incoming students in rabbinical seminaries has fallen by about twenty-eight percent in the last decade.[8] In the Orthodox world, according to a recent JTA report, Yeshiva University, an important source of the rabbinate, claims that only twenty-five percent of its newly minted rabbis find work in congregations, and twenty percent go to secular professions. Many shuls have only part-time rabbis. Moreover, as the JTA report notes, "most American rabbinical schools are placing more emphasis on leadership and professional training, not just Talmud and Torah study." If among the non-Orthodox this is because the laity is not interested, among the Orthodox it is because the laity can do it on their own.

Yet even in the face of these developments, rabbis have surprisingly not disappeared (although the classic synagogue pulpit is not where they will always be found) and Orthodoxy, even at its most modern, has not so easily broken out of what Philip Rieff once called "the enclosing circle of authority" or thrown off completely "the yoke of traditional discipline."[9] For Orthodoxy historically defines itself by discipline and surrender to religious authority, even when its practitioners feel a modern person's sense of competence and attachment to democratic principles. Thus in spite of their growing familiarity with Jewish texts and Torah learning, there remains within the community and many of its texts what Aviad Stollman has described as "a consistent policy of directing the reader to a halakhic authority," a sense that in the final analysis one needs a rabbi to make the all-important judgments about what is and is not to be done.[10] Stollman calls this "a conservative, if fashionable [among the Orthodox] policy."[11] What its source is we shall see in the next section.

Thus, the "orthodox" trumps the "modern" when the community highlights the residual power of the rabbinate. On the other hand, the "modern" trumps the "orthodox" in the decision by most contemporary Orthodox Jews not to make use of one's Torah learning as a pathway to become a rabbi as a vocation.

---

8 Uriel Heilman, "So You've Decided to Become a Rabbi," JTA, March 14, 2014, http://www.jta.org/2014/03/14/life-religion/so-youve-decided-to-become-a-rabbi (accessed March 15, 2014).
9 Philip Rieff, *Charisma: The Gift of Grace and How It Has Been Taken Away from Us* (New York: Vintage, 2008), 148.
10 Aviad Stollman, Review Essay in *Meorot: A Forum of Modern Orthodox Discourse* 6, no. 1, (2006): 5, http://www.yctorah.org/component/option,com_docman/task,doc_view/gid,313/ (accessed April 17, 2014).
11 Stollman, Review Essay, 6.

One might hypothesize that those who do emphasize the "orthodox" above the "modern" are more likely to choose to become rabbis. This often comes with what I have elsewhere called the Orthodox "slide to the right." The less modern one is willing to be, the more one is likely to be a rabbi and at the very least defer to the rabbi's authority. The exception here of course is among women, where the more modern option for them is indeed to try to become a rabbi. That would be because such a tendency emerges out of a modern sensibility, a willingness to buck tradition and entrenched rabbinical and Orthodox norms.

Paradoxically, then, even as it improved the Jewish learning of all people, making them as informed as many of those rabbis who lead their congregations, the culture of Torah learning in Modern Orthodoxy has at one and the same time freed itself of the need for a local rabbi to direct it and yet at least among some of its adherents stubbornly maintain a fixed belief in the role of the *mara d'atra*, the master of the locality, though increasingly that locality's boundaries become stretched to include a yeshiva.[12] That there still exist such local rabbinic guides can at least in part be explained by the lingering traditional view of the role of the rabbi in Torah learning and the element in Orthodoxy that has been sliding to the religious right.

DAAS TORAH AND THE AUTHORITY OF THE RABBI

From at least the days of the Mishnah, Judaism (under the tutelage of the rabbis themselves) has always enshrined the superior position of the Rabbi as Master Teacher—one looked on not only as learned but also as being the heir of the prophets, the person whose stature and honor reflects the importance and veneration of the Torah itself. For those who reached the apex of rabbinic authority, the right to be a decisor of Jewish law was part of his superiority. He had the ability to choose "between conflicting precedents and opinions" of what Jewish law and practice required and apply it to concrete conditions.[13] His (always "he") knowledge could even become tantamount to *Daas Torah*, an understanding that in effect was believed to bestow on him the power to intuit the deeper meaning of the Torah and therefore share in the authority of the Torah

---

12 Aaron Kirschenbaum, "Mara de-Atra," 35. To be sure, as Kirschenbaum notes, there is an opinion *hilketa k'batrei* that "the law follows the opinion of the later halakhic scholars," ostensibly because they knew the reasoning of the earlier ones as well as their own and took it into consideration (37).

13 J. David Bleich, *Contemporary Halakhic Problems* (New York: Ktav and Yeshiva University Press, 1977), xvii.

itself and be able to extend it into domains that might seem extracurricular or beyond its reach. *Daas Torah* made a rabbi's ex cathedra opinions and interpretations about what was permitted and what prohibited resonate with the authority of the Torah even on matters not apparently considered by it, which in a sense made the rabbi share (as did the prophets) the authority of God.[14] That remains a legacy not easily discarded.

No one accepted the sort of expansive rabbinic authority of *Daas Torah* more than those who are students in the yeshivas and seminaries. Thus, the very people whose learning might put them ahead of others in the Jewish world and might have therefore positioned them knowledgeably to challenge the ultimacy of the authority of their teachers did not. While the Talmudic Rabbi Channinah might have remarked, "I have learned much from my teachers, more from my colleagues, and the most from my students" (B.T. Ta'anis 7a), those very students were always urged "Make for yourself a Rabbi" (Avot 1:6). No matter how much you may have taught your rabbis, they were also told, they always remain your superiors. That instruction, if followed, would of course counteract any revolutionary throwing off of authority that increased learning might have stimulated. The idea of *Daas Torah* structured into Orthodoxy that the rabbi could get inside the Torah the way a lay student of it never could.

In the Haredi world, with its cultural and ideological emphasis on the idea of *yisrael sabbah* (the superiority of the ways of old), these countervailing forces of increasing Jewish education and the empowering knowledge it brings versus the imperative of accepting the ultimate authority of the rabbi have for generations worked to maintain a curb on individuality or Jewish autonomy and discourage challenges to the dominance of the rabbi. Indeed, in its ritualized learning, the yeshiva and its worldview of *hitkatnut hadorot* affirms the continuing need to look up and defer to rabbis and elders.[15] In this world, rabbinic authority is doing quite well and remains intact.

In the Modern Orthodox world, however, where one might have expected the countervailing forces to be more powerful because modernity by its nature always considers the new as improved, sees tomorrow as superseding yesterday, and empowers the young to "do-it-yourself" and move beyond their elders, that has not been the case. This is because in most instances, the sources of the

---

14 See Jacob Katz, "Da'at Torah—The Unqualified Authority Claimed for Halakhists," in *Jewish History* 11, no. 1 (Spring 1997): 41–50; and Alfred Cohen, "*Daat Torah*," *Jewish Law*, http://www.jlaw.com/Articles/cohen_DaatTorah.pdf (accessed May 12, 2014).

15 Menachem Kellner, *Maimonides on the "Decline of the Generations" and the Nature of Rabbinic Authority* (New York: SUNY Press, 1996), 3.

knowledge among the most learned of the Modern Orthodox Torah have been authorities—rabbis and teachers—who share the Haredi worldview in which the conservative position that we live in a Torah world of descending authority and generational decline dominates. In this world, a growing knowledge of Torah is not meant to free one from the yoke of tradition or the enclosing circle of authority but rather powerfully to reaffirm it. Even when one knows what the tradition requires and what the halakha is, one needs to find a rabbi to confirm it. This is in spite of the fact, as Aviad Stollman points out, "when both facts and *halakhah* are known to a person, there are very few instances where he or she is required to acquire an explicit specific ruling from an independent halakhic authority," and "nowhere do we find in the *Mishnah*, in Maimonides' *Mishneh Torah* or in the *Shulkhan Arukh* a ruling that ends ... 'ask a rabbi' or 'ask your local rabbi.'"[16]

The common explanation within rabbinic circles and the traditional world for this practice is the variety of customs and the diversity of local practice as well as the broad latitude of rabbinic interpretations for the precise conditions that frame behavior. Yet today the *mara d'atra*, master of the locality, is often outshone by the yeshiva rabbi or the Hasidic rebbe who are viewed as superior because all too often the local leader himself seems hardly a match for the Torah-educated Orthodox laity. Those local rabbis who do seek to hold onto the traditional mantle of *mara d'atra* often try to appear (dress and talk) like these *roshei yeshivas* or even a Hasidic *rav*—a stance that may at times appear in sharp contrast to their modernist congregants (though more in harmony with their yeshiva-educated offspring who have slid to the religious right).

Where does this all leave us? The modern Jew is convinced he can autonomously choose what to do and how to do it by him or herself, but the Orthodox person still lives in the shadow of a superior rabbinic authority.[17] In a way, then, this contradictory and paradoxical state of affairs—where laity can do quite well without rabbis and often do but where it still often defers to and expresses a need for them—is perfectly emblematic of contemporary Orthodoxy, which stands midway between do-it-yourself, sometimes antinomian Judaism and traditional Orthodox deference to clerical authority.

---

16 Stollman, Review Essay, 8.
17 Haym Soloveitchik, "Migration, Acculturation, and the New Role of Texts in the Haredi World," in *Accounting for Fundamentalisms*, ed. M. Marty and R. S. Appleby (Chicago: University of Chicago Press, 1994), 197–235.

Given this paradox, we find a variety of approaches among the Modern Orthodox to their rabbis. On one edge of the spectrum are those who choose their rabbis on the basis of how they want to live their lives, examining his religious proclivities and halakhic opinions before designating him as their authority. They have taken the Mishnaic mandate to make for themselves a rabbi as predicated on their first choosing for themselves an ethos and worldview with which such a rabbi will be in tune. This may not be exactly in line with what Yisrael Meir Kagan, the Hafetz Hayim, had in mind when he noted that "our generation is different from previous generations where every generation had a tradition to follow the path of the Torah," but no statement could better describe the modernist ethos.[18] These are the people whose rabbi must be a mirror that reflects the kind of Jews they want to be. One might say theirs is a literalist interpretation of the famous dictum: עֲשֵׂה לְךָ רַב, וּקְנֵה לְךָ חָבֵר "Make for yourself a rabbi and acquire for yourself a friend" (Avot 1:6). Let the rabbi you make be able to share your worldview like a friend.

Given such a constituency, rabbis, especially those who sought to be *mara d'atra*, understood that to find a following, they had to "appeal to as many Jews as possible."[19] Such rabbis needed to shape themselves to the needs and views of their laity, which grew increasingly self-confident that they knew the Torah well enough and the modern world better to challenge the rabbi, who did not adapt himself to their understandings of what Judaism demands in the contemporary world. In such a community, the younger rabbis, better educated secularly and more comfortably acculturated—but with a solid Torah knowledge—were the ideal spiritual guides.[20]

At the other end of the range were the Orthodox, who have consistently enlarged their numbers as the twentieth century gave way to the twenty-first and tended toward the Haredi. Educated in traditional yeshiva environments that acknowledged a priori the supremacy of the teacher and the outstanding wisdom of the Torah sage, they allow him to determine "proper behavioral norms."[21] Exposed

---

18 "Letters to the Supporters of Torah in the City of Pristik," quoted in Waxman, "Toward a Sociology," 15.
19 Ferziger, "Between Outreach," 237.
20 See, for example, comments about the late Rabbi Tony Ozer Glickman: http://yucommentator.org/2018/03/rabbi-ozer-glickman-yu-rosh-yeshiva-dies-suddenly/ (accessed March 21, 2018), who is described as "An active user of Facebook and social media, Rabbi Glickman was seen by many students as a role model for and avid advocate of *Torah UMadda*. He regularly spent time meeting with students about Torah, Jewish philosophy, and networking advice."
21 Waxman, "Toward a Sociology," 17.

to rabbis who inhabit a world in which one is expected to shape oneself according to *their* demands and the idea of received authority, they have held on to this ideal, even in the midst of the modern world they still often inhabit. In such a cultural space, the older rabbis, those often at the top of the yeshiva or heading the Hasidic court who remain steeped in the eternal yesterday and venerated for their distance from the up-to-date and profane, are considered the ideal spiritual guides and "arbiter of the values of the entire community."[22] Moreover, in their judgment, the best guidance is the one that is most demanding and stringent.[23] As Orthodoxy has slid to the religious right, these rabbis have enhanced their positions, and there are those in the Orthodox world—even in the Modern Orthodox world—who defer to them, and by doing so depreciate the extent of their own Jewish knowledge. The master always knows better.

It was not always thus. In the United States, and especially in the 1950s and 1960s when Orthodoxy was reestablishing itself after the Holocaust, the years of my youth, and the leading age of the observant Jewish community, Yeshiva University's Rabbi Yitzchak Elchanan Theological Seminary (RIETS) was its primary training ground. It dispatched rabbinic graduates armed with a college degree and Orthodox ordination (often from Rabbi Dr. Joseph Soloveitchik), who tried to shape a new kind of Orthodoxy. Replacing the old-style yeshiva-trained rabbis, many from Europe, who lacked the modernist credentials and worldview that were desired, they entered the scene ready to listen and learn from their constituency and share a lifeworld with them, aware that they needed to understand rather than dictate to their community. If they did not, they feared they would not stem what had for generations been the flow away from Orthodoxy.

I can still recall, when as a young boy growing up in Brookline, Massachusetts, how my synagogue awaited, with great anticipation and enthusiasm, our new, albeit part-time weekend rabbi. He had a BA 1953 from Brooklyn College and ordination that he received the same year, and was working on a doctorate at Harvard University while also serving as chaplain at Brandeis. Yitz Greenberg was his name, and he was replacing an old-line Hungarian immigrant with a Satmar background (who would himself later feel the pull of modernization and go on to get his own PhD from Brandeis). We were all certain this rabbi in his twenties, who spoke in an unaccented English and appreciated a university education, would understand our congregation better, filled as it was with other people whose educational background and aspirations were similar. Indeed, he did, fitting perfectly

---

22 Jacob Katz, *Tradition and Crisis* (New York: Schocken, 1971), 198.
23 Waxman, "Toward a Sociology," 16.

into the blend of Modern Orthodoxy that the community reflected. He inspired the youngsters like me as well as our parents, many of them Holocaust survivors or children of immigrants, with the idea that we could and should be a part of the modern culture in which we found ourselves yet still remain loyal and attached to our Jewish commitments. His belief, articulated in his sermons and attitude when he was my congregational rabbi, but committed to writing many years later, was that "beyond my world there is another realm of discourse and truth that may coexist with mine."[24] It was a sentiment that animated the Modern Orthodoxy he represented and which inspired me and those who shared our community. It affirmed "the value of living … in the presence of other truths and systems … and learning from others' insights … and thus improving" my way of life.[25]

But as I have pointed out elsewhere, this generation of rabbis has by and large not managed to replicate itself. The laity these rabbis inspired religiously did not generally choose to be rabbis. They were satisfied to be a committed and Jewishly educated laity, hoping but not seeing to it that there would other Yitz Greenbergs emerging to lead them. Hope, however, turns out not to be enough. By choosing to remain overwhelmingly among the laity, my generation effectively left the rabbinic role to those who wanted to be all Jewish all the time. People who generally slid to the religious right, who chose Judaism as a vocation, who in their training to become rabbis accepted the notions of *Daas Torah* and the eternity of clerical and very Orthodox authority.

While there are some challenges to this state of affairs—whether through *shtibbelization* or the emergence of modernist training programs for rabbis (like Rabbis Avi Weiss's and Dov Linzer's *Yeshivat Chovevei Torah*) and even the movement for a female rabbinate—it remains to be seen whether the current generation will produce rabbis like Yitz Greenberg who can shift the balance away from the right. One senses that if there is to be a reinvigorated Modern Orthodox rabbinate that refuses to slide to the right, it will be one led by women for whom any slide to the right would mean their own vocational demise. This means that the future for Modern Orthodoxy must anchor itself to the aspirations of women who study Torah and the men who support or are willing to share the rabbinate with them. Yitz Greenberg understood this when he found his life partner Blu Greenberg, whose own contribution to that future and to Orthodox women inspires all who hope for a Modern Orthodoxy that stops the slide to the right. Only time will tell what the generation of the current century chooses.

---

24 Irving Yitz Greenberg, "The Principles of Pluralism," *Shma*, April 1999, 4.
25 Greenberg, "The Principles of Pluralism," 5.

CHAPTER 11

Modern Orthodox Responses to the Liberalization of Sexual Mores[1]

SYLVIA BARACK FISHMAN

INTRODUCTION

One of the most compelling Jewish voices speaking to the great moral challenges of the twentieth and twenty-first centuries is Rabbi Irving Greenberg—"Yitz" Greenberg as he is almost universally known. Rabbi Greenberg's thoughts on issues such as theology, war and peace, and Orthodox responsibilities to human history have influenced every stream of Judaism, as well as secular Jews and non-Jews. Less well-known to many, Yitz Greenberg's prescient views on sexuality played an important role that is sometimes overlooked today. Half a century ago, in the 1960s, concepts of gender role construction and attitudes toward sexual values and behaviors underwent sweeping societal and attitudinal transformations. In the American Orthodox community, as in other religious groups, some responded with openness and creativity, and others with repression, reaction, and punitive measures. Yitz Greenberg launched a conversation from within the Modern Orthodox realm on how Orthodoxy might respond to the challenges of changing sexual mores and provide useful guidance. He bravely and prophetically urged original, thoughtful approaches to this quotidian human

---

1 Some of the materials in this chapter are discussed in a different context in Sylvia Barack Fishman, ed. and intro., *Love, Marriage and Jewish Families: Paradoxes of a Social Revolution* (Waltham, MA: Brandeis University Press/University Press of New England, 2015).

activity, with its capacity for producing joy and delight, or misery and destruction. Decades before most of his peers, Yitz Greenberg realized, in the words of Jay P. Lefkowitz's recent article on "The Rise of Social Orthodoxy,"[2] that "the two great cultural fault lines of our generation" are clustered around gender and sexuality. Greenberg saw that it is not only issues of "women's rights and gay rights," which Lefkowitz invokes, that make it incumbent on us to examine Modern Orthodoxy's approach to sexuality, but a broader area of profound changes.

After his bold wrestling with sexual challenges in the 1960s, Yitz Greenberg focused his attention primarily on other issues for several decades, commenting about sexual matters only from time to time. Yet over the decades, both those who shared Greenberg's struggle for innovative Orthodox responses to gender and sexual challenges and those who rejected it have been influenced—knowingly or unknowingly—by his advocacy. Yitz Greenberg played a key role in nurturing change within American Orthodoxy by breaking the Orthodox public silence on fraught subjects. The very fact that he discussed gender and sexuality, along with his unconventional suggestions about sexual attitudes and behaviors, broke taboos and created a (sometimes intermittent) conversation which gave later Modern Orthodox innovators increased freedoms. His comments in the 1960s and in the following years have been salient and inspirational to some Orthodox Jewish leaders, thinkers, and laity who, like Greenberg, have grappled creatively with these issues. He was influential within the Orthodox world not only for those Orthodox Jews who shared many of his values but also for those who did not approve of his statements. Greenberg's words about sexuality often evoked pushback and reaction from Orthodox Jews who condemned changing societal mores in areas such as extended singlehood and premarital sexual activity, the increased prominence of the observant homosexual community, and expectations for more open expression of sexuality within marriage.

Today, increasing segments of the Modern Orthodox world participate in open discussions of gender and sexual issues about which Yitz Greenberg was a trailblazer. A growing cadre of Orthodox professionals work to help Orthodox Jews understand their bodies better and have more satisfying and meaningful sexual experiences, and to make personal choices with integrity and yet live deeply committed to Jewish law and tradition. This essay analyzes Greenberg's and other Modern Orthodox responses, within the contexts of what one might consider the Orthodox left and the right—open American societal approaches,

---

2 Jay P. Lefkowitz, "The Rise of Social Orthodoxy: A Personal Account," *Commentary Magazine*, April 1, 2014.

including more liberal or "Open" Modern Orthodoxy, and increasingly reinforced boundaries within Haredi streams of Orthodoxy. This chapter draws from print materials (some of them based on various early interviews with Greenberg) and also excerpts from my own recent interviews with him. Quotes without citations are drawn from my interviews, and were approved by him for publication.[3]

"SEX IS A RELIGIOUS ACTIVITY"

Our discussion begins in the mid-1960s, which some of us remember vividly as an era of social and political unrest and high passions. Americans debated involvement in the Vietnam War, with many participating in vigorous protests against the war. American Jews were particularly active in the American Civil Rights Movement. Not least, the overtly tranquil surface of 1950s middle-class conformity, gender-role clarity, and family-centeredness was disrupted by intersecting and interrelated forces: Serious younger Americans confronted their elders and demanded that they approach the burning social, political, and economic challenges of the day with moral gravitas. Jewish young adults as well turned to their religious and communal leaders demanding answers. Some young Americans accused their elders of hypocritical external adherence to bourgeois proprieties, while neglecting authenticity and the inner life; conventional marriage and families were also sometimes the target of these attacks. Some men were influenced by the *Playboy* philosophy that urged men to enjoy their sexual freedom fully for many years before capitulating to the demands of marriage and family.[4]

Betty Friedan's *The Feminine Mystique* (1963), followed by the well-publicized rhetoric of Second Wave Feminists, raised the consciousness of America's middle-class women, telling them they lacked economic and psychological preparation to function independently and to fulfill their own needs. These male and female "liberation" movements grew out of the ready availability

---

[3] Interview with Rabbi Irving "Yitz" Greenberg by Sylvia Barack Fishman, Jerusalem, June 1, 2014. Fishman and Greenberg conferred subsequently to verify the accuracy of all quotations, concluding with a final text on December 9, 2014.

[4] Barbara Ehrenreich, *The Hearts of Men: American Dreams and the Flight From Commitment* (New York: Anchor Press/Doubleday, 1983) asserts that the ideology of the 1950s that steered women into housewifery steered men into supporting wives and families; her theory is that this constellation was rejected by men before it was rejected by women, as the Playboy philosophy preceded feminist critiques of the middle class family.

of birth control and the concomitant separation of sexual activity and reproduction. That combination of birth control and the liberation movements had a profound impact on the life choices of individual men and women, precipitating an evaluation of middle-class American gender role construction and sexual mores. A seismic and ongoing social change was underway that affected Modern Orthodox Jews along with other Americans. Today we are still trying to understand its dimensions and implications.

As Yitz Greenberg remembers the 1960s, they presented an enormous opportunity to Modern Orthodoxy: "In hindsight, Modern Orthodoxy was at the peak of its influence. Modernity was still the dominant process. Haredim were still considered marginal—by themselves as well as by other American Jews." If Modern Orthodox leaders at that point "had faced the questions of modernity," he says, they would have "earned and maintained their influence." However, rather than taking the approach of Rabbi Joseph Soloveitchik that "Torah can function in every society," and that "we can shape and conquer current challenges with religious values," Greenberg asserts that Modern Orthodox leaders "backed away" from that moment of opportunity and its challenges.

Three factors led to the intimidation and disheartening of Modern Orthodox leadership at the very time they should have been strong and courageous, according to Greenberg's recollection. First, the 1960s were a time of "revolution." American Jews were rocked by "the sexual revolution, the shift in relations with Gentiles, i.e., the complete acceptance of Jews in American society—and the intermarriage that went with that." As the percentage of Jews who went to college skyrocketed, the spread of *new* ideas through college education, including biblical criticism and the historical development of Jewish religious culture, shook up Modern Orthodox leaders. They were frightened that the new freedom and the attractive modern trends were out of control. They feared that neither they nor their students could handle these threats. Second, the arrival of greater numbers of European Haredi (ultra-Orthodox) Jews and the growth of diverse Haredi communities, affected them. They were intimidated by the "aggressive" behavior of rabbinical figures from those communities who tried to impose their norms on the Modern Orthodox—such as prohibiting Orthodox congregations and Orthodox rabbis from membership in the Synagogue Council of America, to prevent Orthodox clergy from joining denominationally mixed local Boards of Rabbis. Third, a growing awareness of the moral and spiritual implications of the Holocaust led the Modern Orthodox to become more leery of modernity. There was a weakening of the assumption that "what is modern is right." As for the Ultra-Orthodox world, the Holocaust "gave them the moral and spiritual authority to reject modernity." In the past, they fought modern culture but often felt it was unstoppable. Now they aggressively attacked it and believed they could roll it back. In the face of what seemed like passionate and unambivalent pressure from the religious right, many Modern Orthodox leaders felt that Modern Orthodoxy itself was compromised while the others were pure and valid—so they "backed down on their principles," Greenberg asserts.

In the 1960s, the growing cultural search for a more expressive lifestyle, as well as the sexual revolution, made him aware of the importance of finding guidance from within Jewish law and culture for what was obviously a major social change. He posed a challenge to Modern Orthodoxy: "Do you want to be relevant in this culture?" Observing at the time the changing environment around him, he noted, "The negative phenomenon of promiscuity is real. But people have real sexual needs as well." There is a religious value to expressing love in sex, and the new situation presented a chance to assert an ethic of relationship—as against the *Playboy* philosophy and growing promiscuity. Given the fact that American Jews no longer married at the early ages prescribed in some Talmudic texts and rabbinic codes, how was Modern Orthodox Judaism going to respond to the actual conditions of Jewish lives? Total denial of any contact between the sexes constituted a demand to repress emotions. This would lead to permanent emotional distortion and diminution of the ability to develop relationships and positive emotion in sexuality.

Yitz Greenberg articulated some of his developing thoughts on sexual mores in a series of interviews with Hillel Goldberg, who utilized this ongoing conversation to create a written, edited interview; Yitz Greenberg approved the text before it was transcribed onto the pages of the Yeshiva University student newspaper, *The Commentator*, appearing on April 28, 1966, under the headline: "Orthodoxy, YU, Viet Nam, & Sex." Most of the article was devoted to the first three topics. Greenberg's thoughts on sexuality, although only three paragraphs long, were articulated in language that many could have—and did—consider provocative. Greenberg had previously dealt with Orthodox responses to the liberalization of sexual mores at a Yavneh convention in 1964, and in his Yeshiva University class, entitled "Ethical Thought in the Nineteenth Century," but this was the first time his ideas on sexuality appeared in print for a broader reading audience. Rabbinic authorities were directly accused of unresponsiveness or worse in a statement at the end of the second paragraph: "Sex has come to be considered as a secular activity only because the *Poskim* have abdicated their responsibility in examining its true meaning." At fault, according to Greenberg, were rabbinic leaders who simply repeated laws that stemmed from now defunct sociological assumptions, and neglected to give contemporary Jews religious guidance.

Greenberg's example of such unreal prescriptions were the prohibitions against unmarried men and women touching each other: "The prohibition of *negiah* is based upon a technical *halacha*—that a girl is in a state of *nidah* until she performs *t'vilah* in the *mikvah*," Greenberg asserted, explaining that the reason that unmarried girls were not allowed to immerse in the mikvah by the medieval rabbis was their fear concerning "the looseness of morals of many, who, having gone to the *mikvah* would feel free to do anything."[5] Rather than continuing the medieval emphasis, Greenberg declared, "sex is a religious activity, it is the expression of relationship and caring for the other, we abuse it by ignoring it." He urged contemporary Orthodox rabbinic authorities to create laws that reflect peoples' real religious choices, and he proposed a structure for those choices grounded in "the depth" of the interpersonal "encounter":

> Today the *Poskim* should recognize that there is nothing wrong with sex per se, and should promulgate a new value system and corresponding new *halachot* about sex. The basis of the new value system should be the concept that experiencing a woman as a *tzelem Elokim* is a *mitzvah*, just as much as praying in Shul. The *Poskim* should teach people that the depth of one's sexual relationship should reflect the depth of his encounter. ... This new approach to sex, even with its problems, would be much better than our present suppression of such a deep and meaningful activity. Indeed, I believe that more people would end up observing, for they would see relevance and rationale in the new *halachic* categories.[6]

Reaction from both students and colleagues was swift and outspoken. Rav Aharon Lichtenstein, then a Rosh Yeshiva at RIETS and a former professor of English literature at Stern College, wrote a lengthy response. As David Singer points out in his masterful article, "Debating Modern Orthodoxy at Yeshiva College,"

> In 1966, Yeshiva College was very much a modern Orthodox institution, seeking to create a bridge between Jewish tradition and the modern world ...

---

5 "Dr. Greenberg Discusses Orthodoxy, YU, Viet Nam, & Sex," *The Commentator*, Thursday, April 26, 1966, 6–10.
6 "Dr. Greenberg Discusses Orthodoxy," April 26, 1966.

[through] synthesis, and Greenberg and Lichtenstein were seen to embody it to the full. Both men were rabbis and Harvard PhDs, a magical combination that propelled them to the front rank of the Yeshiva faculty. To the students who flocked to their classes, Greenberg and Lichtenstein were living proof that it was possible to be Orthodox and modern at the same time.[7]

Lichtenstein asserted that by saying that "*Tanach* doesn't look upon sex as an evil," yet "the *Poskim* have abdicated their responsibility," Yitz Greenberg had "driven a wedge" between *Torah SheBichtav* and *Torah She'b'al Peh* (the written and oral traditions). Greenberg clarified his views on the pages of the same newspaper on May 12, 1966. His clarifications focused on those areas of his original statements that had aroused the most reaction. *Taharat hamishpakha* (Jewish family law) was often neglected even by contemporaneous Orthodox Jews, Greenberg asserted, and he had meant his comments about new *halakhot* to be directed at improving the performance and the meaningfulness of Jewish family law within a marital context. Traditional Judaism included strands which were negative and mistrustful of marital sexuality, Greenberg pointed out, and those elements sometimes interfered with Orthodox couples experiencing the full depth, power, and religious dimensions of sexual activity. Greenberg insisted he had been misinterpreted by those who saw his comments as referring to premarital sexual activity—a rather curious assertion, given his several references to unmarried girls.[8]

David Singer notes that Greenberg's articulation of his beliefs run "to some 8,000 words," while Lichtenstein "was able to mount 5,000 words in rebuttal" in *The Commentator's* last issue for that academic year. Singer comments: "Lichtenstein zeroed in on Greenberg's handling of the issue of sexual behavior. Greenberg's critics were convinced that his call in the interview for a 'new value system and corresponding new *halachot* about sex' referred to a premarital situation. Greenberg, in his letter to the editor, vehemently denied this."

Today, however, reflecting on that episode, Greenberg acknowledges that he had premarital and well as marital sexual concerns in mind when he gave the original *Commentator* interview. He says that he retreated from his original

---

7 David Singer, "Debating Modern Orthodoxy at Yeshiva College: The Greenberg-Lichtenstein Debates," *Modern Judaism* 26, no. 2 (May 2006): 113–26.
8 Letters to the Editor, "Greenberg Clarifies and Defends His Views," *The Commentator*, Thursday, May 12, 1966: 8–9.

intention for several reasons. First was his realization that if he pursued the area of sexual liberalization that it would attract intense opposition and he would have no further opportunities to make a difference regarding all his other interests. He was, at the time and for many years, deeply committed to creating a dialogue and a new set of understandings between Jews and Christians. He was wrestling with the moral implications of the Holocaust. These issues felt more compelling to him. He believed that openly presenting his views on premarital sexuality would close off any willingness to listen to him on any other issues, and so he made a choice. After the shocked responses to his statements about sexuality in the *Commentator*, "I've stayed away from the whole area. If I would have continued, I would have lost that argument anyway and I would have been finished in the community." And, for the most part Greenberg has seldom returned to the subject of sexuality, despite publishing and speaking extensively about other issues. He explains, "I didn't think I had enough halakhic authority to change opinions on that subject" in that world. Today, almost fifty years later, Yitz Greenberg's thoughtful and coherent reflections on a contemporary Modern Orthodox sexual ethic are summarized in the conclusion of this paper.

CONTEMPORARY SINGLE ORTHODOX JEWS AND THEIR PERSONAL LIVES

Since the initial dramatic stirrings of the 1960s, sexual attitudes and behaviors have undergone profound transformations, as increasing numbers of American Jews marry late, or not at all. This extended singlehood—often accompanied by sexual activity outside of marriage—has not been typical of previous Jewish life in most historical communities, where Jewish societies made married adults and their families central, while it marginalized the unmarried. Indeed, most historical Jewish societies encouraged marriage with "carrots"—communal celebration of and support for the newlyweds—and "sticks"—communal mistrust of unmarried adults, especially of unmarried men. As a result, unmarried Jews seldom found a comfortable niche in traditional communities. In contrast, few contemporary Jewish communities are cohesive enough to implement either carrots or sticks. Easily available birth control has made cohabitation without marriage logistically simple for the vast majority of American Jews in their twenties, thirties, and beyond.

Some assume that later marriage is primarily related to the fact that American Jewish women and men ubiquitously attain at least a college education, and well over a quarter earn advanced degrees. However, the pursuit of higher education in large numbers has long been one of the identifying characteristics of American Jews; previous generations only delayed marriage until after college. As Stephanie Coontz recounts concerning Americans as a whole, in the 1950s college attendance actually enhanced marital prospects because the four years of college served as a virtual marriage market: "For men, going to college was the way to get a good job. For women, it was the way to get a good husband." Middle-class Jewish women typically worked for a few years, married, had children, and became homemakers, partially because they "understood the likelihood of social censure if they pursued" careers.[9]

Today, aspirations for high levels of career achievement, much more than education, contribute to delays in romantic commitments and marriage. American Jewish men and women today report that they postpone permanent commitments until after they have completed their education and certain benchmarks in their careers.[10] Over recent decades, college has largely ceased to be a forum where large numbers of American Jews identify enduring romantic partners. Even Orthodox students who do not participate in casual sexual encounters often choose friendship groups rather than pairing off leading to permanent commitments. Except for religiously observant students, undergraduates commonly report themselves "not ready" to recognize potential marriage partners. American culture encourages them to consider all available options in every arena, encouraging graduating college students to take a year or more off to explore the world before getting on with the rest of their lives.

Orthodox Jewish young adults' lives and choices reflect American expectations, but often moderated in response to traditional Jewish expectations. As Harriet and Moshe Hartman note: "On average, Orthodox men marry about a year earlier than non-Orthodox men, and Orthodox women marry about two years earlier than non-Orthodox women."[11] Extended years of singleness among Orthodox American Jews are both symptomatic and symbolic of the extent to which American Orthodox attitudes and behaviors reflect a blending,

---

9   Stephanie Coontz, *A Strange Stirring: The Feminine Mystique and American Women at the Dawn of the 1960s* (New York: Basic Books, 2011), 108.

10 Daniel Parmer, "What's Love Got to Do with It? Marriage and Non-Marriage among Younger American Jews," in *Love, Marriage and Jewish Families: Paradoxes of a Social Revolution*, ed. Sylvia Barack Fishman (Waltham, MA: Brandeis University Press/University Press of New England, 2015), 33–54.

11 Harriet Hartman and Moshe Hartman, *Gender and American Jews* (Albany: State University of New York Press: 1996): 154.

or coalescence, of contemporary American and historical Jewish values.[12] For example, some Orthodox single males have slenderness on their list of desirable attributes not because it is a Jewish value but because of the influence of the American media-created construction of beauty. However, on the same person's lists, religious attributes come directly from the world of Jewish tradition, and can include minutely calibrated, boutique levels of religious observance, such as—she will/won't cover her hair when married, will/won't wear slacks, will/won't sing at the Shabbat table. This list-making activity arises both out of Jewish culture and out of American culture, and the attributes on the list juxtapose both American and Orthodox societal norms.[13]

EXTENDED ORTHODOX SINGLEHOOD AND SEXUALITY

Extended singlehood has implications for the sexual mores of contemporary Orthodox Jews for very obvious reasons: avoiding premarital sexual activity is less challenging when one is only single and living as an independent adult for a short time before marriage. Today, the sexual mores of Modern Orthodox American Jews are diverse: Some Orthodox singles strictly avoid any physical contact with the opposite sex before marriage, an approach often described as *shomer negiah* (guarding against touching). Numerous Orthodox singles avoid sexual intercourse but do not attempt the total avoidance of physical affection in dating situations—very much like the broader American middle-class expectations of "good girls" in the 1950s culture. Some—especially Orthodox singles no longer in their early twenties—are sexually active, as are their non-Jewish peers.

As Steven Bayme comments in his "Biographical Introduction" to Greenberg's seventy-fifth birthday *Festschrift*, the proportion of Modern Orthodox singles aspiring to *shomer negiah* status today is no doubt higher than it was in the 1960s. In the 1960s, Modern Orthodox singles "prioritized the imperative of developing a long term relationship with a would-be partner over certain dictates of halakha." In contrast, the sexual ethos assumed by some single Modern Orthodox Jews has been transformed by the year or two in serious Israeli yeshivot in gap-year programs. "By the late 1970s," comments Bayme,

---

12 Sylvia Barack Fishman, *Jewish Life and American Culture* (Albany: State University of New York Press, 1999), 10.
13 Sylvia Barack Fishman, "Perfect Person Singular," in *Orthodox Forum: Gender Relations In Marriage and Out*, ed. Rivka Blau (New York: Michael Scarf Publication Trust, 2007).

"most YU students adhered to more restrictive modes often neglected in the 1960s."[14] At the same time, the phenomenon of the "tefillin date"—when a single Orthodox man brings phylacteries with him on a date because he assumes he will be spending the night with his date—was already a topic of conversation in the 1960s. Testimony to the fact that this behavior still endures was seen in an episode of the Israeli television sitcom, *S'rugim*, when one of the characters forgets to bring his tefillin but doesn't want to borrow them from a female Reform rabbi because he feels it is inappropriate for women to use them.

The proportion of Modern Orthodox singles who try to maintain a *shomer negiah* avoidance of physical contact when they date may actually have grown over the past few decades—or at least devotion to this law is more talked about. At a Yeshiva University Orthodox Forum conference on "Men and Women Inside and Outside of Marriage," which took place April 3–4, 2005, a panel of four young Modern Orthodox singles described the dating situation which they observed around them. As luminaries such as Rabbis Aharon Lichtenstein ZT"L and Yossi Blau listened in horror, these young people said that many of the Modern Orthodox singles they knew were so worried about "being *over* on *shomer negiah*" (transgressing the laws of *shomer negiah*, that is having physical contact with their date) that when they really started to like each other and be attracted to each other, but did not feel ready to make a permanent life commitment, they broke off the relationship with that person when it got too intense to resist. They would rather terminate the relationship—which might eventually have led to marriage—rather than have physical contact with that person outside of marriage. At this point, a prominent and highly regarded rabbinic authority spontaneously spoke from his corner of the room: "Why are you all so obsessed with *shomer negiah*? Everyone knows that singles aren't going to be very good at observing *shomer negiah*. Why don't you all focus on a mitzvah that's more appropriate for you, that you can keep well?" No doubt this spontaneous utterance in the closed environment of a gathering of rabbinical and academic colleagues articulated an idea he was unwilling to share in a more open environment, such as classes with the young men he routinely educates.

---

14 Steven Bayme, "Dr Irving Greenberg: A Biographical Introduction," in *Continuity and Change: A Festschrift in Honor of Irving Greenberg's 75th Birthday* (Lanham, MD: University Press of America, 2010), 3.

LOVE AND MARRIAGE

For some time after the 1966 articles and letters in *The Commentator*, much written conversation about sexuality under Modern Orthodox auspices avoided discussion of premarital sexual activity. Instead, Orthodox venues focused on marital sexual activity and how to come to terms with contemporaneous sexual mores within the Orthodox family context. In the early 1980s, Blu Greenberg published *On Women and Judaism: A View from Tradition* and Maurice Lamm published *The Jewish Way in Love & Marriage*. Blu Greenberg's memorable book deals movingly with many aspects of the experiences of Orthodox Jewish women, including the impact of feminism, but erotic yearning outside of the context of marriage was not one of its subjects. Maurice Lamm's book declared that it would deal with "premarital" sexual attraction; it did so—briefly—by explaining Jewish understandings of common law marriage, *yadua batzibbur*, and by condemning any sexual activity outside of "the boundaries of monogamous marriage."[15]

At Stern College in 1981, Stern College Speech Arts Forum and American Mizrachi Women presented a symposium on "Love and Marriage," with participants Rabbi Norman Lamm, Rabbi Saul Berman, and Mrs. Blu Greenberg, with Rabbi Kenneth Hain serving as the moderator. Rabbi Berman focused on the tension between two laws that "require postponed gratification," the *Issur Hirhur* and the *Issur Yichud*, on one hand, and the precepts, "Love your neighbor like yourself," and "Your brother shall dwell with you," on the other hand. "It is precisely this dialectic, between the restraint of the first two laws and the openness of the latter two that forms the key to the Jewish perception of ethics in dating and courtship, and serves as the basis of a successful marriage and family," Berman declared. As for the pain of yearning for what one cannot have, "You don't die from wanting," Berman dryly commented. Blu Greenberg explained the laws of niddah, how they are observed, and how difficult they are to observe. She said preparing for the talk taught her a lesson: "Just as we make an ongoing commitment to observe niddah, so we must learn to maintain a firm and unswerving commitment to build a marriage. ... [W]e do not walk away from a marital relationship whenever it hits an impasse." Blu Greenberg also said that "niddah teaches us something about the selfhood of women," that is, a woman must develop "a sense of self autonomy, of being in control of herself."

---

15 Blu Greenberg, *Women and Judaism: A View from Tradition* (Philadelphia: Jewish Publication Society of America, 1981); Maurice Lamm, *The Jewish Way in Love & Marriage* (Middle Village, NY: Jonathan David Publishers, 1980).

Finally, Rabbi Lamm, who had authored *A Hedge of Roses* about traditional Jewish marriage in 1966, warned about the perils of careerism—with words that seemed to focus only on the dangers of women paying too much attention to "self-realization," but not men doing the same:

> A special effort must be made to reestablish that priority of family and children. ... Women who feel that their major commitment is not to family and children, but to a career that demands total commitment, will feel put upon. We have got to be very careful about overdoing the contemporary emphasis on self-realization. ... We must not fall prey to that narcissism, whether we are men or women. ...[16]

Contrary to Lamm's warning against careerism, today's Modern Orthodox younger couples have emerged as positive models of how to build strong families on a basis of partnership and shared responsibilities. Surprisingly for some observers, recent research shows that homogamous educational and occupational patterns are most pronounced among Modern Orthodox couples. Among such couples "there is an especially high proportion of women in professional occupations (55 percent) compared with women in the other denominations and in the broader population of white women."[17] An evolving test case of blended American liberal male and female gender role construction and Jewishness may be provided by Modern Orthodox communities, which juxtapose aspects of the Haredi and secular American worlds: In Modern Orthodox synagogues Judaic maleness is gradually indoctrinated and socially approved in ways very similar to the Haredi model, but girls and boys socialize together before and after services, at home, at school, and in their leisure time. Modern Orthodox parents expect high performance both in Judaic and secular subjects at school from both boys and girls. Moreover, involvements with American cultural maleness via participatory and spectator sports, for example, are often encouraged or even facilitated by Modern Orthodox communities.

These high proportions of Modern Orthodox two-career families and highly educated professional wives are consistent with findings in the Pew study that American Modern Orthodox Jews have higher percentages of college graduates (65 percent) than Conservative (62 percent) or Reform Jews (61 percent), and the highest percentages of household incomes over $150,000 as

---

16 Norman Lamm, *Seventy Faces: Articles of Faith*, vol. 2 (Jersey City, NJ: Ktav, 2002), 189.
17 Hartman and Hartman, *Gender and American Jews*, 88–9, 184.

well (37 percent, 23 percent, and 29 percent, respectively).[18] These marriages of homogamously well-educated dual-earner couples are also unusually stable. Thus, the gendered patterns prevalent within today's Modern Orthodox partnership marriages are illustrative of what one observer calls, *An Unfinished Revolution*.[19] Rather than conforming to an older pattern whereby women, even those working full-time at demanding jobs, were delegated an unwieldy and notorious "second shift" of unpaid household and child care responsibilities,[20] in today's American culture, gender and status hierarchies have attained unprecedented porousness, and unheralded "shadow work" is arguably distributed widely among high-powered professionals regardless of gender.[21] Changing gender patters have also given rise to new findings about male capacities for effective parenting: In dramatic contrast to the assertions of Carol Gilligan and her followers that women are differently hard-wired for empathy, compassion, and better parenting,[22] sociologist Barbara Risman's study found that both actively parenting married fathers and single fathers demonstrate parenting skills similar to those of mothers.[23] A national study of the changing American workforce found that working mothers spent slightly less time with their children and working fathers slightly more on workdays than they had in the past; on non-workdays both mothers and fathers spent increased time with children, with the increase among fathers slightly greater than among mothers.[24]

CONTEMPORARY INNOVATIVE ORTHODOX ENTERPRISES DEALING WITH SEXUALITY

In 2004, almost forty years after the *Commentator* discussions of sexual activity, Yitz Greenberg returned again in his book *For the Sake of Heaven and*

---

18 "A Portrait of Jewish Americans, Findings from the Pew Research Center Survey, 2013," 43.
19 Kathleen Gerson, *An Unfinished Revolution: How a New Generation is Reshaping Family, Work, and Gender* (New York: Oxford University Press, 2010).
20 Arlie Russell Hochschild and Anne Machung, *The Second Shift* (New York: Viking Adult, 1989).
21 Craig Lambert, "Our Unpaid, Extra Shadow Work," *The New York Times*, Sunday, October 30, 2011, SR 12.
22 Carol Gilligan, *In a Different Voice: Psychological Theory and Women's Development* (Cambridge, MA: Harvard University Press, 1982).
23 B. J. Risman and D. Johnson-Sumerford, "Doing It Fairly: A Study of Postgender Marriages," *Journal of Marriage and the Family* 60 (1998): 23–40.
24 T. Bond, E. Galinsky, and J. Swanberg, *The National Study of the Changing Workforce* (New York: Family and Work Institute, 1998).

Earth to a discussion of the two opposing strands of rabbinic attitudes toward sexuality, primarily within a marital context.[25] In the ensuing years, Greenberg has more often articulated thoughts about contemporary Jewish lifestyles. But whereas his earlier comments were seen as transgressive and isolated him because he broke the silence on many topics connected to personal choices, gender, and sexuality, in recent years Greenberg's comments have found broader, more receptive audiences, for at least two reasons: first, the lives of the majority of contemporary American Modern Orthodox Jews are quite different than in the 1950s and 1960s. Second, and not least, today other significant Orthodox voices also advocate for change, and have helped to create new facts on the ground. While the tone of these responses spans a wide range, what unites them is the attempt to incorporate the best of contemporary liberal approaches to sexuality from within firm commitments to Orthodox Jewish life and values. Some of these public leaders and innovators clearly remember Yitz Greenberg's much-discussed *Commentator* views, while others do not, but they are certainly continuing a conversation that he helped to initiate.

In contrast to the Orthodox Forum's rabbinic stance of private acknowledgment but avoidance of public statements about changing gender roles and sexual expectations, a limited but significant number of Modern Orthodox rabbis, leaders, and educators increasingly and publicly acknowledge and deal with changing attitudes and behaviors. Their responses include educational and advocacy organizations, books, public statements, open symposiums and webinars, and the creation of educational curricula. A whole category of innovative classes has been created in the United States and Israel for men and women who will be married shortly, often called *Kallah* (bride) and *Hatan* (groom) classes.

Educational and advocacy organizations to promote innovative Orthodox responses to the sexual needs and experiences of Orthodox Jewish women and men have been established both in the United States and in Israel. For example, in the United States, Yeshiva University's Center for the Jewish Future has initiated an organization called Tzelem, which produces curricula for educators, and runs conferences for Orthodox pre-marriage counselors. Tzelem also develops and promotes a pilot curriculum designed for elementary school students, "Life values and intimacy education." It has been taught in two Orthodox

---

25 Irving Greenberg, *For the Sake of Heaven and Earth: The New Encounter between Judaism and Christianity* (Philadelphia: Jewish Publication Society of America, 2004).

day schools, SAR Academy in Riverdale, the Bronx, and Yeshivat Noam in Paramus, New Jersey. Tzelem was created in 2005 by the 2005 Orthodox Forum singles' panel members Dr. Jennie Rosenfeld (who has since married) and Koby Frances, and is now directed by Rosenfeld. The curriculum was originally created in 1999 by Yocheved Debow, then associated with the Fuchs Mizrachi School, outside Cleveland, Ohio, and Anna Wolosky-Wruble. Dr. Rosenfeld feels strongly that the education of tomorrow's Orthodox Jews is one of the most important tasks facing educators who want to create healthy attitudes toward the body, sexuality, and intimacy, saying: "Everything Tzelem does with older educators and with rabbis, those are all Band-Aid measures. But when you take a third or fourth grader … we really have the potential to stop problems before they start."[26]

In Israel, social worker Dr. Michal Prins and Gush community activist Rabbi Raffi Ostroff have formed what some characterize as a "revolutionary organization" called *Merkaz Yahel*, the Center for Jewish Intimacy, dedicated to enhancing intimate sexual relationships in the Orthodox community through education. In addition to a program that educates Orthodox women to understand their own bodies, *Merkaz Yahel* reportedly "founded a specialized training center for men and women comprised of social workers, marriage counselors, and therapists to prepare professions … about the delicate balance of dealing with intimacy issues within the Orthodox community."[27]

Books, articles, and other publications are also an important vehicle for educating the Orthodox public and promoting social change. Two recent books in particular are deserving of note: Rabbi Elyashiv Knohl published a book in Hebrew, *Ish Ve-Isha* in 2002, which appeared in English as *The Marriage Covenant* in 2008. The table of contents reveals that it deals with weddings, marital relationships and sexuality, and aspects of childbirth and parenthood. The *Jerusalem Post* reviewer called the book a "toolbox for building healthy husband-wife relations" and noted that the book's discussion of "foreplay techniques, positions, even the proper use of lubricants" are included out of "a desire to help fellow Jews better serve God," since "Judaism obligates the husband to provide his wife with sexual pleasure."[28]

---

26 Sarah Kricheff, "Orthodox Schools Test the Waters with 'Intimacy Education' Classes," *The Forward*, January 16, 2008.
27 Lea Speyer, "Taking the Taboo away from Sexual Intimacy," *Israel Prophecy News*, May 16, 2014.
28 Mathew Wagner, "Don't Scream, 'Oh My God,' but Sex Is a Mitzvah," *The Jerusalem Post*, April 3, 2009.

Dr. Rosenfeld and David S. Ribner's *The Newlywed's Guide to Physical Intimacy*[29] is a slender volume, written with respect for Jewish law, enhanced with graphic clarity about all aspects of sexual expression, including an envelope with pen-and-ink drawings. Rosenfeld and Ribner note that the fear of transgressing *shomer negiah* sometimes results in married Orthodox couples feeling fearful or anxious, often ignorant of the sexual potential of themselves and their partners. They feel it is their religious obligation to lift that curtain of ignorance: "At every step in the creation of this manual, we keenly felt the presence of the *Borei Olam*," the authors write. "This manual is written to ease the transition to marriage for Torah-observant couples," they explain. "Shared sexual activity, helped along by hormones, nerve endings, and your five senses, can help you achieve a level of physical pleasure not possible elsewhere in your life." Observations such as, "Your enjoyment as sexual partners is more than just physical; it can bring you to a place of closeness with another person that no other experience can provide," are examples of the book's clarity about emotional factors and insecurities as well as about physical sensations.

This viewpoint articulated by these and other Modern Orthodox authors, that God creates the human body to experience physical pleasure, and that pleasure can have a spiritual dimension and can intensify caring bonds between a couple, is very much in harmony with Yitz Greenberg's insistence in the 1960s that "sex is holy," and that sexuality can provide opportunities for an appreciation of *b'tzelem Elokim*. But life is lived locally, as many observers have noted, and the information that sexual pleasure has religious potential has not reached large numbers of ordinary women within Orthodox and especially within Haredi (Ultra-Orthodox) communities. In a vivid episode from Samuel Heilman's masterful ethnography of Haredi Jews, *Defenders of the Faith*, Heilman describes the almost unbelievable ignorance of some yeshiva boys prior to marriage, in which some find the idea of sexual intercourse outlandish and repulsive; in the most extreme cases these negative attitudes interfere with the consummation of the physical relationship.[30] Like the men whom Heilman describes, many Haredi women are utterly ignorant of their own bodies, some of them despite repeated childbirth. For some, this results in sexual dysfunctions of various kinds and severities, including an inability to

---

[29] Jennie Rosenfeld and David S. Ribner, *The Newlywed's Guide to Physical Intimacy* (Jerusalem and New York: Gefen Publishing House, 2011).

[30] Samuel Heilman, *Defenders of the Faith: Inside Ultra-Orthodox Jewry* (New York: Schocken Books, 1992).

tolerate intercourse and a consequent inability to conceive. For others, it has meant a life without the concept—never mind the reality—of sexual pleasure.

Several Modern Orthodox pioneers in the United States and Israel, including Dr. Bat Sheva Marcus, Rabba Sarah Hurwitz, and Dr. Naomi Marmon Grumet have been working to upgrade the sexual satisfaction of Orthodox women and men through therapy and education. They work both with individual clients who require a series of therapeutic conversations and remedial activities to help them heal their sexual dysfunctions, and also with other professionals who need to upgrade their comprehension of the physical and psychological struggles their own clients encounter. The mere fact that such topics are discussed within Orthodox frameworks symbolizes and reflects transformations in Orthodox culture—a far different situation than Yitz Greenberg's prescient comments encountered.

These projects, focused on women becoming educated about their own bodies and their potential, are built in some ways on the American cultural phenomenon that began with the publication of *Our Bodies, Ourselves*. However, Orthodox therapists' tasks are complicated by the fact that Haredi (and some Modern Orthodox) women worry that taking specific physical steps to increase their own pleasure may run counter to halakhic guidelines. For these clients, halakhic authority resides in their rabbis; any suggestion from their therapist—no matter how seemingly benign or how deeply private—must first be submitted to the rabbi for his approval. In a recent interview in *The New York Times* naming Dr. Marcus "The Orthodox Sex Guru," she movingly describes the plight of numerous clients. The article also recounts that rabbis who initially forbid the use of particular strategies are sometimes won over when Dr. Marcus helps them understand the transformative positive impact they can have on the couple's being able to fulfill religious prescriptions for marital sexuality.[31]

Sexual information with a Modern Orthodox interpretive framework is also extended to broader audiences through projects such as "The Joy of Text," a monthly podcast supported by JOFA, the Jewish Orthodox Feminist Alliance, and Yeshivat Chovevei Torah Rabbinical School, YCT. "The Joy of Text" is co-hosted by Rabbi Dov Linzer and Dr. Marcus, and moderated by Ramie Smith, and it deals in very frank detail with numerous topics connected to Orthodox lifestyles and sexuality which at one time were seldom discussed in public forums in the general public, let along Orthodox programs.

---

31 Daniel Bergner, "Flesh of My Flesh: The Orthodox Sex Guru," *The New York Times Magazine*, January 25, 2015, 24.

HOMOSEXUALITY AND GENDER IDENTIFICATION DIVERSITY IN MODERN ORTHODOX COMMUNITIES

If the changing sexual attitudes of heterosexual Jewish men and women, more fluid gender roles, and the open discussion of sexuality and its manifestations have posed a challenge to Orthodoxy—or at least to many Orthodox leaders, the increased prominence of observant homosexual Jews pose another kind of challenge. Male homosexual activity is widely understood by most Orthodox rabbinical authorities—and many Orthodox Jews—to be prohibited by biblical law. Female homosexual acts are strongly discouraged in Talmudic discussions. Many Orthodox rabbis (including some Modern Orthodox rabbis like Norman Lamm and Barry Freundel)[32] have articulated the idea that homosexuality is a "choice" and thus can be avoided through willpower, motivation, and medication—despite powerful scientific evidence to the contrary.

However, the status of homosexual Jews within Orthodox religious communities is now the subject of lively debate. Some Orthodox voices have urged a more realistic and compassionate approach. Many Orthodox minds were opened and changed by the 2001 film "Trembling Before God," which vividly portrayed the heart-wrenching struggles of gay and lesbian Jews to reconcile—or at least juxtapose—their homosexual and Orthodox lives. That film, produced by Sandi Simcha Dubowski, put real faces and souls to what had been for many Orthodox leaders an abstract and somewhat alienating issue. That process of personalization, and making the Orthodox homosexual issue feel immediate, rather than distant, was furthered by Orthodox gay Rabbi Steven Greenberg in his 2004 book, *Wrestling with Man and God: Homosexuality in the Jewish Tradition*. That book precipitated a review in the *Edah Journal* (the journal of the Modern Orthodox organization whose motto was—Edah: the Courage to be Modern and Orthodox) by Asher Lopatin, now the president of Yeshivat Chovevei Torah, who is widely perceived as being "liberal" or "open" Orthodox; Rabbi Lopatin came to the conclusion that the book was a "brilliant work of creativity and research," which yet could not "enter the Orthodox bookshelf" because it does not include sufficiently traditional Orthodox thinkers and their attitudes.[33] Stern

---

32 Barry Freundel, "Homosexuality and Judaism," *Journal of Halacha and Contemporary Society* (RJJ) XI (1986): 70–87; Norman Lamm, "Judaism and the Modern Attitude to Homosexuality," *Encyclopedia Judaica Year Book*, 1974.

33 Asher Lopatin, "What Makes a Book Orthodox? *Wrestling With God and Men* by Steven Greenberg (Madison: University of Wisconsin Press, 2004)," *The Edah Journal* 4, no. 2 (2005): 1–11.

College of Yeshiva University continued to employ Joy Ladin, who "was hired and tenured as a male instructor of English" but "returned from leave as a female professor, and "recounts her transition from male to female in *Through the Door of Life: A Jewish Journey Between Genders* (2012)."[34]

At the more traditional end of this phenomenon of Orthodox public discussion, British rabbi Chaim Rapoport published a book on *Judaism and Homosexuality: An Authentic Orthodox View*. While firmly situated from within the Orthodox world—Rabbi Jonathan Sacks wrote an approving forward to this book—there is no doubt that Rapoport has been quite influenced by his readings of scientific research on human sexuality. For example, he strongly rejects the idea championed by some Orthodox rabbis that homosexuality can be reversed through medication, therapy, or willpower, or that all Orthodox homosexuals should marry heterosexually and bear at least a son and a daughter, regardless of their lack of sexual interest. Instead, Rapaport emphasizes the emotional and companionate aspects of marriage which would be compromised by a lack of physical desire: "The duty to provide the emotional security afforded by meaningful intimacy is written into the very marriage contract as an essential component. ... It would therefore be wrong for him to enter the institution of marriage with the knowledge that he could not 'gladden his wife' ..." However, Rapaport also insists, conforming to traditional understandings of the biblical prohibition against male homosexual activity, that Orthodox homosexuals must not engage in sexual activity or marry persons of their own gender.[35]

Another discussion situated—at least physically—within the traditional Modern Orthodox world took place when the Yeshiva University Tolerance Club and Wurzweiler School of Social Work hosted an event entitled, "Being Gay in the Orthodox World: A Conversation with Members of the YU Community," on December 22, 2009. Four male YU students were panelists and Rabbi Yosef Blau, then YU's *Mashgiach Ruchani* (Spiritual Advisor), served as the moderator of the conversation. About 800 people attended, according to one observer, and a transcript was made of the proceedings although Rabbi Blau had asked that no recordings be made. The event was reported to be very moving and informative—and not surprisingly the very fact that it had taken place created an enormous stir in the Orthodox community, with a broad spectrum of opinions.

---

34 Dinah M. Mendes, "Is There a New Judaism for Gender Identity?," *Moment Magazine*, September 3, 2013.
35 Chaim Rapoport, *Judaism and Homosexuality: An Authentic Orthodox View* (London: Vallentine Mitchell, 2004), 94–5.

In Israel, Tova Hartman and Irit Koren authored a study, "Between 'Being' and 'Doing': Conflict and Coherence in the Identity Formation of Gay Orthodox Jews." They came to the conclusion that true resolution of these two identities is often impossible, but that resolution of conflicts ceases to matter for many gay and lesbian Jews:

> Instead of abandoning the valuative framework that rejects their sexual identity, or vice versa, the Orthodox gay men and women we interviewed allowed their religiosity to push them to understand their homosexuality as an integral element of their religious destiny, which in turn has required them to delve into it all the more profoundly. ... This evolving relationship between these two mutually-exclusive, highly defining aspects of identity ... in turn serves as a source of inspiration, consolation, and strength ... [36]

Thus, when Yitz Greenberg was asked to write an imaginary letter to an imaginary homosexual son, which was published in *Moment* Magazine in 2011, the issue of Orthodox homosexuals was already prominent on the American Orthodox radar screen. Unlike some public figures—even outside of Judaism—who didn't articulate compassion until they had an actual homosexual child who "came out," Rabbi Greenberg's letter was loving and compassionate, as well as sober and realistic. First, he stipulated that a declaration of homosexuality should only be made by a "mature" person who had "considered" fully the implications of his "decision." Greenberg then proposed what I would argue are his first principles or holy commandments regarding sexual activity. He framed nonmarital sexuality within ethical and cosmological beliefs that are central to Greenberg's worldview, and to his profound belief in sexuality as sacred expression. I have bolded that section below:

> My heart goes out to you. As you were raised as an Orthodox Jew, you already know that since the time of the Torah, homosexuality has been condemned in our community, especially in more traditional circles. While treatment is improving, I fear that you will face much rejection and hostility, and I wish that I could prevent it or protect you. Nevertheless, if

---

36 Tova Hartman Halbertal with Irit Koren, "Between 'Being' and 'Doing': Conflict and Coherence in the Identity Formation of Gay Orthodox Jews," *Identity and Story: Creating Self in Narrative*, ed. D. P. McAdams, R. Josselson, and A. Lieblich (Washington, DC: American Psychological Association, 2006).

you live your life this way, I would hope that you would apply the Torah's other guidelines for sexuality to your own practice. **Sex should not be casual or promiscuous. It should never be exploitative or abusive. Sexuality should express relationship and love; the deeper the sexuality, the deeper the relationship that it should express. You should try for the Jewish ideal, which remain family and creating/nurturing life via children (by conception or adoption). This is a great joy and a fulfillment in life.** Your mother and I love you very much as a total person. This feeling has not changed with your announcement.[37]

In the 2013 international conference of the Jewish Orthodox Feminist Alliance (JOFA) several enthusiastically received panels further explored Orthodox homosexuality. Among other speakers, Rabbi Steven Greenberg discussed the various issues that arise as he and his (male) partner are raising observant children.

Public statements advocating inclusive treatment for gay and lesbian Jews in the Orthodox world have become a powerful strategy for building communal support on a grassroots level. In July 2010, a group of Orthodox rabbis and educators in the United States originally published in a "statement of principles on the place of our brothers and sisters in our community who have a homosexual orientation." The original statement was prepared by Rabbi Nathaniel Helfgot; subsequently, revisions to this statement were implemented based on feedback from Talmud scholars, educators, rabbis, mental health professionals, and homosexual Orthodox Jews. Rabbi Aryeh Klapper and Rabbi Yitzhak Blau contributed to a significantly revised version of the document, most recently updated in April 2016. This statement, whose signatories include more than 200 well-known Orthodox rabbis, professors, thinkers, and educators as well as a few *roshei yeshiva* (rabbinical seminary headmasters),[38] demands that homosexual Jews be treated with "dignity and respect." It argues that halakha

---

37 Yitz Greenberg, "A Rabbi's Advice: How to Respond to Your Gay Child," *Moment Magazine*, November 16, 2011.
38 Signatories included, for example, Israeli Rabbi Binyamin (Benny) Lau, community rabbi at the Ramban synagogue in Katamon, Jerusalem and founder of Beit Morasha's Beit Midrash for Social Justice; and American rabbis Shmuel Goldin, former president of the Orthodox Rabbinical Council of America and senior rabbi emeritus of Congregation Ahavath Torah in Englewood, New Jersey; Haskel Lookstein, rabbi emeritus of Congregation Kehilath Jeshurun in Manhattan and principal of the Ramaz Orthodox day school from 1966–2015; and Marc Angel, rabbi emeritus of Congregation Shearith Israel, the historical Spanish and Portuguese Synagogue in Manhattan.

prohibits only "homosexual acts; it does not prohibit orientation or feelings of same-sex attraction." Like several other books and statements, this statement of principles affirms "the religious right of those with a homosexual orientation to reject therapeutic approaches they reasonably see as useless or dangerous." It acknowledges the "great pain and suffering often experienced by homosexual Orthodox Jews," and urges that "rabbis and communities need to be sensitive to that reality." Like Rapoport's book, the statement urges that homosexual Jews should be welcomed as synagogue and community members. Also like Rapoport's book, the statement urges that those with "an exclusively homosexual orientation should under most circumstances not be encouraged to marry someone of the other gender, as this can lead to great tragedy." When it comes to institutional policies however, the statement is more complicated: Significantly, the statement clearly leaves it for individual synagogues and rabbis to "establish its own standard with regard to membership for open violators of halakha"—which is the way "members who are openly practicing homosexuals and/or living with a same-sex partner" are characterized. Moreover, "Jewish religious same-sex commitment ceremonies and weddings" are viewed as being outside the pale of halakhic Judaism. At the same time, the statement urges that "the adopted or biological children of homosexually active Jews in the synagogue and school setting" be accepted and "embraced."[39]

Similarly, in Israel the Beit Hillel organization, an Israeli Modern Orthodox rabbinic group, published a letter in 2016 urging Orthodox communities and congregations to show "social inclusion" to homosexual Jews, allowing them to "serve as prayer leaders in the synagogue and carry out all public functions." The letter emphasizes that "according to the Torah and halacha, the acts are forbidden but not the proclivities, and therefore people with same-sex tendencies, men and women ... are obligated by all the commandments of the Torah, they can fulfill an obligation on behalf of the public and carry out all of the community functions just like any member."[40]

In thinking about the ways in which Orthodox Jewry has responded to homosexual Orthodox Jews, it is useful to review the situation of homosexual Jews in general in contemporary Jewish communities. Today, gay, lesbian, bisexual, transgender, and queer (LGBTQ) Jews comprise about 7 percent of

---

39 Statement of Principles NYA, Wednesday, July 28, 2010, List of Signatories updated April 2016, http://statementofprinciplesnya.blogspot.com/.
40 Stuart Winer, "Dozens of Orthodox Rabbis Call for Accepting Gay Congregants," *The Times of Israel*, April 11, 2016.

American Jews, according to a recent study by Steven M. Cohen, Caryn Aviv, and Ari Kelman. The same study reported that 31 percent of self-reported LGBTQ Jews are married or partnered, and another 9 percent are raising their own children.[41] National studies of American populations have repeatedly shown that Jews are extraordinarily liberal regarding societal acceptance of homosexual individuals and families. The Pew *Portrait of Jewish Americans* (2013), for example, reported that 82 percent of America's Jews say homosexuality "should be accepted by society": that percentage increases to 89 percent of Jews age 18 to 49 and 89 percent of Jewish college graduates. The Pew authors note, "compared with Jews, the general public is far less accepting of homosexuality (57 %)." In the general population, Republicans are much less accepting than Democrats, but "Jewish Republicans are more accepting of homosexuality compared with other Republicans (51 % vs 39 %)."[42]

Increasingly the partnerships, marriages, and families LGBTQ Jews create are being acknowledged by and incorporated into American Jewish institutions. The Reconstructionist movement and the Reform movement's Central Conference of American Rabbis (CCAR) approved the marriages of LGBTQ Jews in the mid-to-late 1990s. The Conservative movement's Rabbinical Assembly (RA) Committee on Jewish Law and Standards affirmed in 2006 that marriage between two Jewish men or two Jewish women "have the same sense of holiness and joy as that expressed in heterosexual marriages." Two formal ceremonies to sacralize such marriages were proposed by that committee in 2012. These Conservative-authored same-sex wedding ceremonies are based on traditional Jewish wedding ceremonies but omit some of the language and blessings, and these ceremonies are not called *kiddushin*,[43] the ancient ceremony consecrating the contract whereby a Jewish bridegroom acquires a bride.

In Jonathan Krasner's new study of American Jewish homosexual couples with children, he found Jewish communal acceptance drew many of his subjects closer to Jews and Judaism, and was influential within intermarried LGBTQ Jewish households as well. As Krasner summarizes: "a significant minority of non-Jewish subjects stated that their [own] religion's negative attitudes toward homosexuality made them more receptive to their Jewish partner's arguments in favor of raising their children as Jews." However, not surprisingly, "those

---

41 Steven M. Cohen, Carol Aviv, and Ari Kelman, "Gay, Jewish, or Both? Sexual Orientation and Jewish Engagement," *Journal of Jewish Communal Service* 84 (2002): 154–66.
42 Pew, *Portrait of Jewish Americans*, 101.
43 Ben Sales, "Conservative Rabbinic Group Issues Guidelines for Same-Sex Wedding Rituals," *JTA*, June 4, 2012.

families who attempted to find a home within the Orthodox community generally had a more negative experience."[44]

BACKLASH AGAINST CHANGES IN GENDER ROLES AND SEXUAL MORES

To the extent that Orthodox Judaism is truly "sliding to the right," in Samuel Heilman's memorable phrase, that rightward slide is often organized around and expressed by prescriptions concerning gender and sexuality.[45] Religious leaders in some religious societies discourage women from working outside the home. Of course, economic issues are complicated in those Haredi societies where women are often the only wage earners in the family. Where Haredi women are expected to work, other measures are employed to ensure women's compliance with expected social behaviors, goals which are often articulated in the language of modesty to prevent any incidents of—or even the appearance of—improper sexuality. Women's workplaces are carefully supervised, especially with regard to internet access.[46] Opposing the loss of traditional gendered lifestyles (as well as loss of their own power) some Haredi rabbis have ruled that Orthodox women should not pursue higher secular education, use the internet without supervision, or drive cars, and that they should strictly avoid taking on new religious obligations or public roles.

Another strategy for maintaining sexual distinctiveness within Orthodox societies is to place ever-increasing emphasis on female modesty, which has the side effect of erasing individualism in wardrobes. Some Haredi women internalize these prescriptions and ratchet them up a notch, inventing new expressions of "modesty" beyond those required by the rabbis of their communities, eagerly separating themselves from the world of men. Indeed, this value has been so thoroughly internalized by pious women in Haredi Jewish societies that women have often gone beyond the directives of male clergy, taking on themselves an exclusively black-and-white wardrobe, voluminous shape-hiding cloaks,[47] and in a few cases even burqas. As Lea Taragin-Zeller demonstrates,

---

44 Ibid. [ed. Most recently, see *Homosexuality, Transsexuality, Psychoanalysis, and Traditional Judaism*, ed. Alan Slomowitz (New York: Routledge, 2019).]
45 Samuel Heilman, *Sliding to the Right: The Contest for the Future of American Jewish Orthodoxy* (Berkeley: University of California Press, 2006).
46 Rivka Neriya-Ben Shahar, *Haredi (Ultra-Orthodox) Women and Mass Media in Israel: Exposure Patterns and Reading Strategies* (PhD diss., The Hebrew University, 2008).
47 Sima Zalcberg Block, "Shouldering the Burden of Redemption: How the 'Fashion' of Wearing Capes Developed in Ultra-Orthodox Society," *Nashim: A Journal of Jewish Women's Studies and Gender Issues*, Special issue on Gender and Jewish Identity 22 (Fall 2011): 32–55.

for many Haredi young women today *tzniut* (modesty) has become the new female virtue of choice.[48] This preoccupation with modesty has made inroads in certain segments of the Centrist and Modern Orthodox communities as well. Responding to this trend, Modern Orthodox artist Andi Arnovitz, decries the sexualization of very young children that is implicit in exaggerated Haredi demands for "modest" dress that suggest that three-year-old children should be covered up for modesty's sake.[49]

Fearing social chaos, some religious Christians and Muslims—and some Orthodox Jews—reject a liberal ethos in which, in American politician Rick Santorum's words, "it comes down to freedom and it comes down to sex." Reactionary men and movements discourage freedoms such as women's access to birth control and young people's access to secular education, and campaign against legalizing gay and lesbian marriage.[50] Thus, perceived transformations in understandings of gender, love, and the family precipitate pushbacks by stakeholders fearful of losing power and also by grassroots lay people, who find the societal shifts and changes around them deeply disturbing. These areas of economic and political—as well as religious—anxiety certainly play a role in the ever-escalating emphasis in Haredi circles on silencing women's voices via *kol ishah* (women's voices) strictures; the erasure of women's faces from public posters, magazines, and illustrations; and insistence that women not share public spaces or be prominently featured in public programs because of putative sexual enticements.

MODERN ORTHODOXY AND SEXUALITY: YITZ GREENBERG'S CONTEMPORARY APPROACHES

The demonstrable success of many Modern Orthodox families in negotiating the competing value systems of Orthodox Judaism and American society, along

---

48 Lea Taragin-Zeller, "Between Modesty and Beauty: Reinterpreting Female Piety in the Israeli Haredi Community," in Sylvia Barack Fishman, ed., *Love, Marriage and Jewish Families: Paradoxes of a Social Revolution* (Waltham, MA: Brandeis University Press/University Press of New England, 2015), 308–26.
49 Chavie Lieber, "Great Fashion Advice Comes From Israel," JTA, January 2, 2013, reports that Rav Shlomo Aviner authored a long discussion of appropriate clothing for girls and women in the weekly pamphlet, *B'Ahavah U've; Emunah*.
50 Richard W. Stevenson, "Social Issues Return to Dominant Role in National Debate," *The New York Times*, February 5, 2012; and Charles M. Blow, "Santorum and the Sexual Revolution: At War with the 1960s," *The New York Times*, March 3, 2012.

with the demands of personal life, family, and career are striking. Although they may no doubt feel out of control on a day-to-day basis, married Modern Orthodox men and women seem to have found viable models for balancing their American and Jewish lives. This sense of viability and balance seems to stand in marked contrast to experiences of Modern Orthodox singles in the now often extended years before marriage. Some of the difficulties experienced by both unmarried and married Modern Orthodox Jews today are linked to confusion about Modern Orthodox approaches to changing sexual mores. The outside culture often appears chaotic or heartless, and provides little sustenance for those wishing to construct a personal sexual ethic. On the other hand, many do not find classic rabbinic constructions of *shomer negiah* or niddah strictures feasible, appealing, or supportive of their approach to life.

Returning to the challenge that he posed in 1966, "Today the *Poskim* should … promulgate a new value system and corresponding new *halachot* about sex," Yitz Greenberg today is planning to write a comprehensive approach to sexuality, which he hopes to publish in the future. He builds his system upon the axiom, "Sexuality is the most powerful language for expressing the relationship between two human beings, and for expressing their love." Sex gives expression to nonverbal as well as verbal forms of communication, and is a central aspect "of the human condition." Sexual activity should be "authentic," by which Greenberg means that "the level of behavior should be congruent to the level of commitment," and sexual activity should be an expression of deep emotion and affection. "The depth of emotional attachment should dictate the extent of physical involvement," he emphasizes. "Sexual intercourse says, 'I love you completely.'" Sexual activity that is not accompanied by commitment and deep feeling "is a lie," says Greenberg. The lie represents the gap between what the sexual partner wants and imagines he or she is getting and what the physical techniques, when not backed by real emotions, are actually expressing. The partner seeks confirmation of self, of being intrinsically valued, of being respected. This is what engaging in sexual intercourse communicates: you are desirable, both in body and soul. I am totally focused on you and all of me is responding to you with excitement and pleasure. I value you as you are and seek to please you. But when the emotions aren't there then intercourse is a "lie" and the sex is just a physical exercise which leaves the partner "empty." Put another way, promiscuity is a failed search for confirmation. Casual sex trivializes sex, implying that sexuality carries no deeper message. It is just another bodily activity like playing sports.

Both unmarried and married Jews today face challenges in terms of halakhic prescriptions concerning sexuality—for singles, concerns about physical contact and expression of affection before marriage, and for married couples, similar concerns during times when a woman is officially in the state of niddah and thus sexually unavailable. Greenberg asserts that some historical rabbinic sources, including the rulings of Rav Yosef Karo, but not R. Moses Isserles, employ what might be called a "scorched-earth policy" toward sexuality. They are so worried about possible infringements of the prohibition of sexual activity during niddah that they proscribe many normal interactions between the couple and thus remove all possibility of physical contact. Karo in particular also "codifies every Talmudic negative attitude toward sex done in a state of ritual purity," reducing it to a halakhically mandated chore that should be accomplished as quickly and with as little passion as possible.[51] But those severe restrictions—which do not allow for any physical contact in situations where full sexual contact is prohibited—have their own negative consequences, according to Greenberg. They objectify women and reduce their status as partners in a rich and sanctified relationship. They often distort the relationship between potentially loving couples, depriving their relationship of the nonverbal signals and expressions which are vital to healthy emotional life. In so doing, he says they "negate the *tzelem Elokim*" of the sexual partner.

In contrast to those rabbinic sources permeated with mistrust of sexuality and emphasis on restraint, Greenberg cites rabbinic sources to show precedents for his emphasis on the positive emotional bonds between the couple established by sexuality rather than on the negative potential for sinful contact.

Yitz Greenberg concludes that it is time that the *harchakot* that brake all possible contact with the niddah should be recalibrated by the *poskim*. The decisors and the couples should be guided by R. Akiva's principle that it is better to err on the side of behavior that sustains loving relationships, even if that behavior poses possible challenges to current norms of *harchakot*.

Rigid Haredi restrictions of gender contact or of sexuality may work for their societies, because the vast majority of their young people are paired off in safe sexual unions at an early age, Greenberg notes. But for Modern Orthodox Jews, a strict adherence to *shomer negiah* strictures may be experienced as inappropriate and may lead to mistaken, even tragic decisions:

> The total restriction of sexuality may be successfully achieved by warping—or even permanently crippling—the capacity to express affection and deeper relationship through sexual connection. It can also lead to decisions to marry

---

51 See R. Yosef Karo's rulings in *Shulchan Aruch, Orach Chayim*, chapter 240, paragraph 1, 2, 4, 8, 9, 14. (There is a softer tone in his rulings, op. cit., paragraphs 3, 10.) The restrictive rulings in *Orach Chayim* are paralleled by Karo in Shulchan Aruch. Even HaEzer, chapter 25, paragraphs 2, 5.

when the individual and/or the couple may not yet be mature enough to handle the daily care, emotional give-and-take, and behavioral compromises needed to make a marriage work. Negative fallout of such decisions that grow out of frustrated hormonal urges included failed marriages, battered capacities for relationship, and loss of years of connection and emotional growth. Sometimes the price paid is conditioning one's self to lie about the true state of one's emotions or to dull or spoil the capacity to know one's real feelings. A better policy would be that *poskim* affirm the legitimacy of sexual exploration in a growing relationship but regulate it to meet halachic ideals. This could include going to *mikvah* to remove the issue of violation of their niddah state when they make contact. The *poskim* should offer an ethic of relationship in which sex is never casual, promiscuous or purely physical. Rather it is an authentic expression of feeling, meant to honor—and deepen—the existing level of relationship and commitment.

In the absence of action from *poskim*, Greenberg suggests what he ironically calls the "power of positive sinning":

> If a single man or woman finds another appropriate individual to whom they are attracted and with whom they want to deepen the connection, they proceed. The term positive sinning is an acknowledgement that they are going beyond what is currently permitted and is in that sense a violation. On the other hand, it is positive in that it reflects a desire to meet the Torah's values and goal of sexuality that is the expression of being a *tzelem elokim* who works to get to know another person as *tzelem elokim*. It is not a casual or exploitative or abusive contact. All interaction is for connection, relationship building with an implied goal of becoming a permanent, stable commitment which enables lifetime marriage and family creation.
>
> Laws regulating sexuality (indeed, all *halakhot*) are not some electrified barbed wire fence which means that to try to go beyond the current boundary is to be instantly electrocuted. Rather the couple should realize that ultimately they stand before God who will judge their behavior. If they have judged passions rightly, they will find that God's judgement recognizes that the *mitzvah*—the good—in knowing a *tzelem elokim* and confirming it in the other and deepening it in one's self in part through sexual expression outweighs the negative in breaching a norm that is not constructive, often counterproductive, in an age of extended years of singlehood.

The goal is covenantal sexuality—in which the pleasure and self-expression is nurtured by relationship and commitment and enhances the *tzelem elokim* of each of the partners. The interaction and the pleasure grow out of appreciating the value, uniqueness and equality of the other and is never exploitative or promiscuous. Such sexuality only deepens the relationship and widens the range of communication and sharing. By the same token, the pleasure given or taken is not hedonic or selfish but is part of a deeper embrace of life and of the other. Precisely because marriage is covenantal, the *halakhah* assumed that marriage is the standard locus of sexuality. Such a value-driven sexuality can be applied towards behavior in both marriage and single status. In the end, this criterion should be applied in judging any form of sexuality. This positive halakhic approach also means that the holiness dimension in sexuality is not expressed in withdrawal and restriction only. After all, the state of niddah is generally the shorter part of the month. In the covenantal approach the holiness is deeply infused into the sexual expression which is permitted in the state of *taharah* period which is most of the time. Carried out in this spirit, sexuality and intercourse articulate love and deepen it. Then giving pleasure, expressing love, enriching the relationship between one *tzelem elokim* and another is recognized for what it is—one of the highest forms of encountering *Shekhinah*—of recognizing God's presence and increasing it in the world.

CONCLUSION: INNOVATION AND INFLUENCE

The world of Modern Orthodoxy has changed in subtle and overt ways since Yitz Greenberg first articulated his thoughts on how Orthodox Jews might navigate a world of changed personal expectations. As this chapter has shown, topics concerning gender and sexuality that were taboo when Greenberg broached them are now discussed thoughtfully and in detail—at least in certain Modern Orthodox circles. But the conundrums that Greenberg struggled with remain problematic, and Greenberg's vision remains useful as well as inspirational. His sexual ethic is a deep, centered, and nuanced approach much needed in what often appears to be the utter confusion and chaos of today's world, in which great personal unhappiness is generated by both shallow sexual exploitation and violent sexual oppression and repression. One can only hope—along with Yitz Greenberg—that such a sexual ethic can compete for loyalty in an open society—and win.

CHAPTER 12

"The Road Not Taken" and "The One Less Traveled": The Greenberg–Lichtenstein Exchange and Contemporary Orthodoxy

ADAM S. FERZIGER

> Dear Yitzchak,
>
> ... As I understand it, you sought ... to stir up discussion [on a number of issues], to rescue them from the tundra of obscurity, to which a conspiracy of apathy and silence had consigned them ... Well, I agree wholeheartedly with the aim—but I take issue with your mode of pursuing it ...
>
> With best personal wishes,
> Sincerely,
> Aharon[1]

I am grateful to an anonymous reader, and especially to both of my coeditors for their rigorous readings and comments on an earlier draft. Notwithstanding their disagreements with aspects of my analysis, they shared insightful critiques and suggestions that contributed substantially to the final product.

1 Aharon Lichtenstein, "Rav Lichtenstein Writes Letter to Dr. Greenberg," *The Commentator* June 2, 1966, 7–8 [reprinted in Zev Eleff, *Modern Orthodox Judaism: A Documentary History* (Philadelphia: Jewish Publication Society, 2016), 179–82].

These introductory lines were part of a lengthy public letter penned by Rabbi Dr. Aharon Lichtenstein (1933–2015) to his Yeshiva University (YU) colleague and friend, Rabbi Dr. Irving "Yitz" Greenberg (b. 1933), that appeared in the student newspaper *The Commentator* on June 6, 1966. They set the tone for a critical assessment of a wide-ranging interview of Greenberg printed six weeks earlier in the same publication as well as his subsequent clarification statement in a latter issue.[2] In general, Lichtenstein objected to Greenberg for not being more careful in facilitating the publication of an open-ended examination of "matters about which you or I have no business issuing manifestos … The point is simply that we must, collectively, develop a much keener sense of responsibility as regards the discussion of Halachic and theological problems … the Mishna advises, '*chochomim hizaharu be-divreichem*' [sic: "Sages be careful with your words"]."[3] More specifically, Lichtenstein expanded on a list of elements in Greenberg's comments that he found most troubling.

To date, research on this interchange has highlighted a growing chasm that it projected within American Modern Orthodox Judaism, and its role in the public and ideational alienation of Greenberg from the sector. In a thoughtful analysis, David Singer records Lichtenstein's admission that he shared some of the same concerns that Greenberg raised. Nevertheless, Singer focuses on their sharp disagreements. As he summarizes, "… a messy affair that brought into view a deep fissure within the ranks of modern Orthodoxy … it quickened a

---

2 Hillel Goldberg, interviewer, "Dr. Greenberg Discusses Orthodoxy, YU, Viet Nam, and Sex," *The Commentator*, April 28, 1966. A scanned version of the *Commentator* edition, as well as Greenberg's subsequent letter to the editor, "Greenberg Clarifies and Defends his Views, *The Commentator*, May 12, 1966, and Lichtenstein's letter, are available at http://rabbiirvinggreenberg.com/wp-content/uploads/2013/05/Commentator-articles-YG-and-AL.pdf. The original newspaper texts were copied precisely into clear type by Joshua Meir Feigelson in "Relationship, Power, and Holy Secularity: Rabbi Yitz Greenberg and American Jewish Life, 1966–1983" (PhD diss., Northwestern University, 2015), 214–35 (Appendices A, B, C). Since it is available for perusal or download by open access via internet, I will henceforth cite from the rendition in its pages under the following titles: "Greenberg Interview," "Greenberg Clarifies," and "Lichtenstein to Greenberg." (https://search.proquest.com/openview/0333b1b9def72caf9815b6529af89447/1.pdf?pq-origsite=gscholar&cbl=18750&diss=y).

3 "Lichtenstein to Greenberg," 230. All citations maintain the transliteration styles of the original documents. On the importance that Lichtenstein placed on reverence for *gedolim*—great rabbinic authorities, see Aharon Lichtenstein, *Leaves of Faith* 2 (New York: Ktav, 2004), 290. See the discussion in Alan Brill, "An Ideal Rosh Yeshiva: By His Light: Character and Values in the Service of God and Leaves of Faith by Rav Aharon Lichtenstein," *Edah Journal* 5, no. 1 (2005): 16.

process of polarization that in a few short years brought Greenberg to Orthodox avant-gardism and Lichtenstein to Orthodox centrism."[4]

Singer and others are, no doubt, correct that the ideological gaps between these two Harvard-educated, intellectual and religious rising stars of 1960s YU and American Modern Orthodoxy, widened much further in the following decades.[5] That said, by bringing some of the key areas of the 1966 conflict into dialogue with positions expressed by Lichtenstein in later years, as well as those of his students, which he did not necessarily fully endorse but set into play, a more intricate evaluation of the original encounter unfolds. In some cases, Lichtenstein himself subsequently articulated outlooks that could coexist or even buttress those first asserted by Greenberg. In others, institutions identified with Lichtenstein and prominent disciples, pushed beyond their teacher's own comfort level, but for the most part in ways that today are considered within the spectrum of contemporary Orthodoxy, especially in Israel.

While the specific personal and theological trajectories of these two figures digressed in fundamental ways, this does not contradict the ongoing development of a multilevel proximate ideational "conversation" between them. Bringing to light and examining these interfaces more closely offers insight into the

---

4 David Singer, "Debating Modern Orthodoxy at Yeshiva College: The Greenberg-Lichtenstein Exchange of 1966," *Modern Judaism* 26, no. 2 (May 2006): 122 (113–26). See also: Alan Brill, "Modern Orthodoxy #15 [from minute 60]," YU Undergraduate Lecture (March 21, 2005), http://www.yutorah.org/lectures/lecture.cfm/710497/Rabbi_Alan_Brill/Lecture:_Modern_Orthodoxy_15; and "Modern Orthodoxy #16," YU Undergraduate Lecture (March 23, 2005), http://www.yutorah.org/lectures/lecture.cfm/710544/rabbi-alan-brill/lecture-modern-orthodoxy-16/; Feigelson, "Relationship, Power, and Holy Secularity," 38–74; Lawrence Grossman, "Rabbi Yitz Greenberg and American Orthodoxy: The Crisis of 1966–67," in *A Torah Giant: The Intellectual Legacy of Rabbi Dr. Irving (Yitz) Greenberg*, ed. Shmuly Yanklowitz (Hoboken, NJ: Urim/Ktav, 2018), 279–94. I thank Dr. Grossman for providing me with an advanced copy of his perceptive article. See also Samuel I. Heilman, "Review: *Modern Orthodox Judaism: A Documentary History* (Philadelphia: JPS, 2016)," *American Jewish Archives* 69, no. 1 (2017): 135–6. Jeffrey S. Gurock, *The Men and Women of Yeshiva* (New York: Columbia University, 1988), 224–6, focuses on the distinctions between Greenberg and Lichtenstein's visions for YU's Orthodox student involvement in broader societal issues.

5 In 2005, another interchange between Greenberg and Lichtenstein appeared in the pages of *The Commentator* that offers profound testimony to the widening of the personal chasm between them over the ensuing years since 1966. This material was republished in *My Yeshiva College: 75 Years of Memories*, eds. Menachem Butler and Zev Nagel (New York: Yashar, 2006). See Irving Greenberg "Yeshiva in the 60s," 179–87; Aharon Lichtenstein, "The 60s," 374–7; Irving Greenberg, "Response to 'The 60s,'" 377–81. Scanned versions are available at http://rabbiirvinggreenberg.com/writing/debates/.

evolution of Modern Orthodoxy since the 1960s, and especially since the early twenty-first century. I will begin my discussion by pointing to biographical elements shared by Greenberg and Lichtenstein that have received minimal attention, and are deserving of consideration in an essay that highlights their analogous if unequivocally incongruent routes. I will then concentrate on three issues that were central to their 1960s exchange: relations with non-Orthodox and nonobservant Jews, Bible scholarship, and Orthodox attitudes toward sexual behavior.[6]

INSIDER-OUTSIDERS

In comparison to Greenberg, who only arrived on campus in 1959 when he was hired to teach history, Singer portrays Lichtenstein as an "YU insider." To be sure, Lichtenstein's association with the institution dated back to 1949, long before he began to teach literature in YU's Stern College for Women in 1957 and afterwards Talmud on the men's campus. I suggest, however, that both should be considered "Insider-Outsiders," who had robust connections to YU and Modern Orthodoxy prior to their appointments to its faculty, but also shared critical molding experiences that set them apart from the institution and its ideological constituency.

Lichtenstein's scholastic and personal association with YU was more extended and direct. He arrived there at the age of sixteen, received his undergraduate degree from Yeshiva College, and after many years of Torah learning in YU's study halls under the tutelage of its master teacher, Rabbi Dr. Joseph B. Soloveitchik, was granted rabbinical ordination by the YU-affiliated Rabbi Isaac Elchonon Theological Seminary (RIETS). A few years later, Lichtenstein married the daughter of his teacher, Tova Soloveitchik.[7] Yet Greenberg too had a prior extended link to YU through four years of attendance at the high school it sponsored, the Brooklyn Talmudical Academy (BTA). This educational choice was reflective of the immigrant Borough Park home in which he grew

---

6 Additional areas regarding which Lichtenstein took issue with Greenberg already in the 1960s, included: YU students entering a Methodist church in Washington DC, to join a caucus of Jewish groups protesting the Vietnam War (unlike for civil duties such as voting, Lichtenstein did not think the circumstances warranted entering a church); Greenberg's critique of the focus of YC's Torah education; Greenberg's minimizing the respect due Torah scholars; the need to set limits on involvement in American society.

7 Shlomo Zuckier and Shalom Carmy, "A Brief Introductory Biographical Sketch of R. Aharon Lichtenstein," *Tradition* 47, no. 4 (Winter 2014): 6–16. The entire volume is dedicated to Lichtenstein's life and thought. See also Ari Kahn, "The Life and Learning of Rav Aharon Lichtenstein," *Explorations* (June 6, 2016), http://arikahn.blogspot.co.il/2016/06/the-life-and-learning-of-rav-aharon.html.

up. His parents were deeply religiously committed but also intent on enabling the secular intellectual development and acculturation of their son.[8] Greenberg was also a counselor in a summer camp that facilitated Orthodox observance, but celebrated the Americanization of the attendees, who were mostly children of European immigrants.[9]

Lichtenstein's father possessed a European doctoral degree and taught in BTA and at YU's girls high school division "Central," but he and his wife—the daughter of the secretary of the Telz yeshiva who grew up among Lithuanian Orthodox "royalty"—sent their budding Talmud scholar son to the more traditionalist (Haredi) Yeshiva Rabbi Chaim Berlin.[10] There he was mentored by the younger brother of his future father-in-law, Rabbi Aaron Soloveitchik,[11] and came under the influence of the powerful yeshiva head and a central ideologue of the post-Holocaust renaissance of Lithuanian Orthodox culture in America, Rabbi Yitzchak Hutner.[12] Lichtenstein attested throughout his life that these two figures had profound influence on him, particularly regarding issues of faith and moral fortitude.[13] He also acknowledged his serious consideration, at a certain point, of pursuing advanced Talmud studies in the burgeoning bastion of American Haredi culture, Beth Medrash Govoha of Lakewood, New Jersey. In the end, he felt that Soloveitchik's creativity would be more beneficial to his development as

---

8   See Irving (Yitz) Greenberg, "Modern Orthodoxy and the Road Not Taken: A Retrospective View," in this volume. See also the insightful discussion of Feigelson, "Relationship, Power, and Holy Secularity," 45–53.

9   Phone conversation with my mother, Sandra Ferziger Gottlieb, November 6, 2017, who attended Camp North Star in New York's Adirondack mountains during the summer of 1950, where Greenberg was a counselor and color war general.

10 On his mother, Bluma Lichtenstein, see Aharon Lichtenstein "Ima," trans. *Jewish Action* vol. 79, no. 1 (Fall 2018): 46–7. The Hebrew original is available at http://asif.co.il/?wpfb_dl=5818.

11 For alternative biographical accounts, see Shmuel Marcus, "The Indomitable Spirit of Rabbi Ahron Soloveichik," *Jewish Action* (2001), https://jewishaction.com/tribute/indomitable-spirit-rabbi-ahron-soloveichik/; "The Amazing Story of Rav Ahron, ZTL," *Emes ve-Emunah Blog*, February 7, 2006, http://haemtza.blogspot.co.il/2006/02/amazing-story-of-rav-ahron-ztl.html.

12 Lawrence Kaplan, "Rabbi Isaac Hutner's 'Daat Torah Perspective' on the Holocaust: A Critical Analysis," *Tradition* 18, no. 3 (Fall 1980): 235–48.

13 Aharon Lichtenstein, "The Source of Faith Is Faith Itself," *Jewish Action* 53, no. 1 (Fall 1992), reprinted in *Tradition* 47, no. 4 (2014): 188–91; idem, "My Education and Aspirations: Autobiographical Reflections of Rav Aharon Lichtenstein ZT"l (2007), oral presentation transcribed posthumously by Marc Herman and Dov Karrol and adapted for print by Reuven Ziegler and Yoseif Bloch, http://etzion.org.il/en/my-education-and-aspirations-autobiographical-reflections-rav-aharon-lichtenstein-ztl.

a Talmudist.[14] Here too, Greenberg's path offers a parallel. After graduation from BTA, instead of continuing to Yeshiva College, at his father's advice he chose to attend the local Beis Yosef (Navaredok) Yeshiva, and enroll simultaneously in Brooklyn College. Greenberg, received his rabbinical ordination from Beis Yosef, and drew deep inspiration from the passion of this traditionalist-oriented institution and its unique focus on spiritual growth, profound ethical contemplation and behavior, and service to the people of Israel.[15]

Thus, when Lichtenstein and Greenberg arrived at YU's Washington Heights, New York campus in the late 1950s, it was not only their years in Boston and their Harvard PhD's that distinguished them. Along with their considerable Modern Orthodox credentials, they both had been nurtured at crucial stages in Haredi-style yeshivas that did not idealize American life nor the efforts of YU to integrate Jewish and secular learning under the roof of one institution. Neither Greenberg nor Lichtenstein accepted their Haredi yeshivas' full worldviews. But nor can they be considered classic YU insiders with minimal exposure to alternative approaches. On the contrary, their prior backgrounds separated them from other veterans, and may have contributed to their decisions to detach themselves when the environment ceased to be congenial to their independent and original thinking about contemporary Jewish life.

Within a year of each other, both these "Insider-Outsiders" left YU.[16] The roots of Greenberg's official 1972 exodus from YU to set off on a public career focused on the broader Jewish community can certainly be identified in the events of spring 1966; in fact, from 1968 he lowered both his teaching load and his campus profile considerably.[17] Yet it would also be mistaken to completely divorce these texts from Lichtenstein's own leave-taking from YU one year before in 1971, to create an independent path for himself as coleader of Yeshivat Har-Etzion in Israel. Notably, already in his 1966 response letter to Greenberg, Lichtenstein acceded, "I [also] think that your diagnosis of the current state of YU is fundamentally sound."[18]

---

14 He shared this with me during a private meeting that took place in his Yeshivat Har Etzion in July 1984, a few days before I completed a year of study there.
15 Greenberg, "Modern Orthodoxy and the Road Not Taken." (in this volume) On the Eastern European roots of the Navaredok approach, see David Fishmam, "Mussar and Modernity: The Case of Novaredok", *Modern Judaism* 8, 1 (February 1988): 41–59.
16 Among the other young and dynamic figures who overlapped with Greenberg and Lichtenstein on the YU faculty and eventually settled in Israel were: future Israel Prize–winning scholars Gerald (Ya'akov) Blidstein and Charles S. Liebman, and Rabbi David Hartman.
17 Greenberg, "Modern Orthodoxy and the Road Not Taken."
18 Lichtenstein, "Lichtenstein to Greenberg," 233. Soloveitchik opposed the decision of his daughter and son-in-law to move to Israel and others deemed it, "foolhardy and

Inasmuch as Lichtenstein remained affiliated officially with YU through his position as principal lecturer at its Gruss Institute in Jerusalem, it was in the context of his primary role as head of an Israeli Religious-Zionist *yeshivat hesder* that he opened original vistas within Orthodoxy—both for his locally bred students and the many who came from abroad to study under his aegis. In point of fact, parallel to Greenberg's estrangement from the American Orthodox establishment, for many years Lichtenstein was considered an outlier by the dominant voices of Israeli Religious Zionism,[19] and his yeshiva had a distinctly unconventional reputation.[20] Yet it is not only within the Israeli milieu that Lichtenstein's voice digressed from the consensus. The approaches that became dominant in YU since their nearly simultaneous departures were certainly patently different from those of Greenberg, but by no means did they reflect Lichtenstein's either.[21] Indeed, be it vis-à-vis the dominant Religious Zionist yeshiva milieu or the YU environment, some of Lichtenstein's most prolific students would certainly qualify as "avant-garde."[22] Actually, in certain cases their outlooks share a great deal in common with those expressed by Greenberg in 1966.

---

irresponsible." See the eulogy for her husband delivered in New York by Dr. Tova Lichstenstein in June 2015, https://vimeo.com/129696529. For a stimulating counter-historical narrative, see Zev Eleff, 'What if Rav Aharon Had Stayed? A Counter-History of Postwar Orthodox Judaism in the United States, *Lehrhaus*, March 13, 2017, http://www.thelehrhaus.com/scholarship/2017/3/9/what-if-rav-aharon-had-stayed-a-counter-history-of-postwar-orthodox-judaism-in-the-united-states#ftnt_ref19.

19 This was clearly Lichtenstein's self-understanding. See, for example, Moti Levi, "Rav Lichtenstein to Zionist Rabbis: 'Some Humility Please,"' *Walla News*, March 17, 2011, http://matzav.com/rabbi-lichtenstein-to-zionist-rabbis-some-humility-please/. The original Hebrew publication that same year (2011) of Haim Sabato, *Seeking His Presence: Conversations with Rabbi Aharon Lichtenstein* (Tel Aviv: Yedioth Ahronoth, 2016), exposed a much broader Israeli audience to Lichtenstein's core outlook. The increasingly prominent role of his students in Israeli religious, public, and academic life were also key factors in the expansion of his influence upon Israeli Religious Zionism. Nonetheless, it remains far from the dominant mainstream political and ideological outlook.

20 Adam S. Ferziger, "Religious Zionism, Galut, and Globalization: Exploring 'Gush' Exceptionalism," in *That Godly Mountain*, ed. Reuven Ziegler (Alon Shevut: Etzion Foundation, 2012), 109–21; Yair Kahn and Kalman Neuman, "A Rabbinic Exchange on the Disengagement: A Case Study in R. Aharon Lichtenstein's Approach to Hilkhot Tzibbur," *Tradition* 47, no. 4 (2014): 157–87; Dov Schwartz, "Haguto shel ha-Rav Aharon Lichtenstein: Tadmit u-Mezi'ut," *Da'at* 76 (2014): 11–12.

21 Adam S. Ferziger, *Beyond Sectarianism: The Realignment of American Orthodox Judaism* (Detroit: Wayne State University Press, 2015), 114–29, 211–24. Aspects of Lichtenstein's independent outlook are highlighted in Alan Jotkowitz, "'I am in the Middle': Rav Aharon Lichtenstein's Vision of Centrist Orthodoxy," *Hakirah* 22 (2017): 49–66, www.hakirah.org/Vol22Jotkowitz.pdf.

22 Yoel Finkelman, "On the Irrelevance of Religious-Zionism," *Tradition* 39, no. 1 (2005): 32–9.

ATTITUDES TOWARD NON-ORTHODOX AND NONOBSERVANT JEWS

In the first section of the 1966 *Commentator* interview, Greenberg spoke at length about his approach to contemporary Jewish identity, and the relationship of Orthodox Jews to their non-Orthodox brethren. He first posited that the central theme of Judaism is the covenant with God, "… the definition of a Jew is one who takes the covenant idea seriously … It doesn't matter to me whether one calls oneself Orthodox, Conservative, or Reform."[23] While he confirmed that he was linked on a personal level to Orthodoxy, and that he surmised that Orthodox Jews have the highest percentages of those who engage God earnestly, he also pointed to crucial areas in which the non-Orthodox approaches are preferable. "Orthodoxy refuses to come out of its European ghetto psychology … Conservative and Reform have taken the risk and dealt seriously with the problem of Judaism's relevance to modern life, but I believe they have come up with wrong answers … Orthodoxy's escape is the belief that the Torah cannot stand up to the challenge of contemporary civilization … This attitude reflects our cowardice … Our desire to withdraw is an indication of our unwillingness to admit that our beliefs are shallow …"[24]

In his ensuing clarification letter, Greenberg responded to those who saw his initial statement as suggesting that the "ideal Jew" is not necessarily one fully committed to halakhic Judaism, by offering a less vociferous articulation. All the same, he reiterated that both Orthodox and non-Orthodox streams contain those who "struggle to keep the covenant," and others who exert little effort in this direction. "Ideas," he declares, should not be "ignored simply if labeled Conservative or Reform. They should be judged on their merits … I would concede that I exaggerated by ignoring the differential Orthodox obedience to *halachah* [sic], but I did so in the belief that we are far too self-congratulatory and fail to recognize how, in our own way, we work out our own equivalents—'leaving out' or neglecting many *halachot* … I am convinced that … dropping our self-righteousness and empathetically understanding our fellow man's motivations, would increase our own religious depth and our influence on others."[25]

In later years, Greenberg advanced the concept of "voluntary covenant" that challenged the obligatory foundation of the traditional understanding of the

---

23 "Greenberg Interview," 214.
24 Ibid., 214–15.
25 "Greenberg Clarifies," 222.

halakhah,[26] and advocated a more unequivocally pluralistic approach to legitimization of non-Orthodox denominational theology and worship.[27] Certainly, inklings of these positions can be read into his 1966 *Commentator* expressions. Yet at that juncture, his main claims were that there is much positive that can be discerned within the Conservative and Reform efforts to navigate head-on the interface between Judaism and modern ideas and social realities. As such, the Orthodox would do well to cease proclaiming their own "righteousness" and polemicizing against their seeming adversaries. Instead, they ought to devote themselves to identifying the numerous areas in which they stand to learn from fellow movements.

In his critical response, Lichtenstein disagreed emphatically with Greenberg's original statement that taking the covenant seriously, regardless of one's denominational affiliation, is the basis for defining an "ideal Jew." As to Greenberg's moderated version, however, Lichtenstein found much with which he shared common ground. Like his overall evaluation, he took issue primarily with his counterpart's strategy:

> I would … disagree with your tactical approach to Conservative and Reform Judaism. Of course, I agree that there are individual Reform and Conservative Jews whose religious experience, viewed as a subjective phenomenon, must be regarded seriously as a genuine striving for *kedusha* which therefore has value … However, if we shift to another plane and ask what is the objective character of Conservatism or Reform [Judaism] … the answer is that it is wholly invalid … In dealing with this area, therefore, we need stress two points concurrently: that the subjective experience of the non-Orthodox Jews may have genuine religious content and value but that their interpretation of the Torah is in error and must be rejected outright.[28]

While Lichtenstein advocated addressing both aspects of the non-Orthodox, he assumed that Greenberg would prefer to focus purely on the encouraging sides.

---

26 Irving Greenberg, "Voluntary Covenant," *Perspectives* (New York: National Jewish Center for Learning and Leadership [CLAL], 1987), http://rabbiirvinggreenberg.com/wp-content/uploads/2013/02/2Perspectives-Voluntary-Covenant-1987-CLAL-2-of-3.pdf.

27 Irving Greenberg, "Theology after the Shoah: The Transformation of the Core Paradigm," *Modern Judaism* 26, no. 3 (October 2006): 213–39, http://rabbiirvinggreenberg.com/wp-content/uploads/2013/02/Theology-After_Modern-Judaism_redpr.pdf.

28 "Lichtenstein to Greenberg," 234.

Tactical distinctions duly noted, the common evaluations of Lichtenstein and Greenberg regarding the "genuine religious content" of the non-Orthodox placed both of them at odds, even with the relatively "tolerant" approaches that had gained traction among nineteenth- and twentieth-century Orthodox rabbinical authorities—including Soloveitchik. Figures such as the Rabbi Jacob Ettlinger of Altona (1798–1871) and the "Hazon Ish" (Rabbi Avraham Yeshayahu Karelitz, 1878–1953), the Lithuanian-born leader of the nascent Haredi (traditionalist) sector in mid-twentieth century Israel, undermined traditional sanctions on religious deviants by claiming that their actions stemmed from ignorance, "infants taken captive," rather than spite. But Karelitz made clear that in as far as Jewish content was concerned, even the non-Orthodox Zionists who did not tamper directly with traditional religious interpretations, were an "empty wagon" in comparison to the "fully stocked" Orthodox. Rabbi Abraham Isaac Kook (1865–1935), the first Ashkenazic chief rabbi of Palestine, also offered a dispensation to his fellow sinners due to being "coerced by the force of modernity," but pushed further by pioneering a mystical-Zionist interpretation of the deviation of secularization as a necessary instrumental step toward redemption. Soloveitchik emphasized the "fate" shared by all Jews, but made clear that as to matters of "faith," non-Orthodox Judaism was completely counterfeit. In each of these cases, allowances were raised that neutralized premodern categories and emphasized ethnic and national solidarity. None of them, however, recognized the inherent religious merit of non-Orthodox Jewish behavior and institutions, and they certainly did not indicate that the Orthodox had anything of value to learn from their fellow brethren.[29]

After leaving YU and settling in Israel, Lichtenstein's appreciation for the positive values that he identified among non-Orthodox Jews became even more pronounced. Moreover, over time his statements demonstrate closer affinity to Greenberg's 1966 expressions, both regarding the important role that the non-Orthodox play in contemporary Jewish life, the lessons that can be learned from them, and the value in certain situations of direct cooperation.

Writing for a 1982 forum on "The State of Orthodoxy" that appeared in *Tradition* magazine, he admonished his compatriots for their triumphalist overfixation on the increasingly evident "resurgence" of American Orthodoxy in light of prior predictions of its demise by prominent mid-century social

---

29 For an expanded discussion, see Adam S. Ferziger, "On Fragmentary Judaism: "On Fragmentary Judaism: The Jewish 'Other' in the Worldview of R. Dr. Aharon Lichtenstein," *Tradition* 47, no. 4 (2015): 34–68.

scientists. Their self-satisfied euphoria, he protested, prevents them from addressing the overall dire condition of American Jewry: "With intermarriage running close to 50 percent, when studies indicate that three-fourths of our brethren do not enter *any* house of worship *any* day of the year, while the fabric of the Jewish family is impaired ... can anyone rest content because several thousand *benei Torah* ... are now more committed?"[30] Under such circumstances, it would be wrong to focus on the negative aspects of any Jewish framework that could draw Jews toward increased involvement—even those religious streams whose theological legitimacy was highly suspect:

> Nor do I share the glee some feel over the prospective demise of the competition. Surely, we have many sharp differences with the Conservative and Reform movements, and these should not be sloughed over or blurred. However, we also share many values with them—and this, too, should not be obscured. Their disappearance might strengthen us in some respects but would unquestionably weaken us in others. And, of course, if we transcend our own interests and think of the people currently served by these movements—many of them, both presently and potentially, well beyond our reach or ken—how would they, or K'lal Yisrael as a whole, be affected by such a change? Can anyone responsibly state that it is better for a marginal Jew in Dallas or Dubuque to lose his religious identity altogether than drive to his temple?[31]

Such an acknowledgment of the intrinsic religious value of non-Orthodox houses of prayer would have been a complete anathema to Soloveitchik. The latter referred to them as "Christianized" synagogues that do not justify being characterized as "bona fide Jewish religious institutions,"[32] and famously advised a young man to stay home rather than hear the shofar blowing on Rosh Hashanah in a sanctuary with mixed pews. No doubt Soloveitchik's statements must be understood within the heated context of mid-twentieth century Orthodox–Conservative polemics.[33] All the same, Lichtenstein does not just

---

30 Aharon Lichtenstein, "The State of Orthodoxy: A Symposium," *Tradition* 20, no. 1 (Spring 1982): 47–50. Reprinted in *Leaves of Faith* 2: 334 (331–6).
31 Lichtenstein, *Leaves of Faith*, 334.
32 Joseph B. Soloveitchik, "Message to a Rabbinic Convention," in *The Sanctity of the Synagogue*, ed. Baruch Litvin (New York: The Spero Foundation, 1959), 109–14.
33 Joseph B. Soloveitchik, "On Seating and Sanctification," *Jewish Day-Morning Journal*, November 22, 1954 (translated from Yiddish and reprinted in Litvin, *The Sanctity of the*

neutralize the pejorative. He actually buttresses the importance of sustaining non-Orthodox religious institutions. Furthermore, there is certainly no doubt that Lichtenstein did not support the landmark Conservative responsum from 1950 that permitted congregants to drive to synagogue on the Sabbath.[34] That notwithstanding, in the quotation just cited he essentially expressed his appreciation for the pragmatic logic that led to this decision: otherwise most American Jews would not attend synagogue at all.

Notably, while Lichtenstein was expressing appreciation for the positive elements in non-Orthodox synagogue life, other Modern Orthodox–affiliated figures fixated on an impending irrevocable split between the Orthodox and the liberal denominations. As Rabbi Reuven Bulka proclaimed in 1984, "a cataclysmic split within the North American Jewish community … may result in the total renunciation of a significant number within the Jewish community by another group, and the separation-cum-divorce of these two movements into a mainstream Judaism and a new religion …"[35]

Lichtenstein's most extensive and for that matter far-reaching statements regarding his views of nonobservant and non-Orthodox Jews, surfaced toward the end of the first decade and at the beginning of the second decade of the twenty-first century. In 2010, he published an article entitled "Beyond the Pale? Reflections regarding Contemporary Relations with Non-Orthodox Jews." On the one hand, he remained adamant in his opposition to offering any level of official legitimacy in areas related to Jewish law to non-Orthodox denominations and their clergy.[36] On the other hand, he did not feel that these provisions should

---

Synagogue, 114–18). Seth Farber has demonstrated compellingly that R. Soloveitchik did express appreciation for individual non-Orthodox rabbinical figures and the roles their synagogues played in their locales as a means for "communal organization and unification." See Seth Farber, "Reproach, Recognition and Respect: Rabbi Joseph B. Soloveitchik's Mid-Century Attitude Toward Non-Orthodox Denominations," *American Jewish History* 89, no. 2 (2001): 193–214. Nonetheless, there is no clear literary evidence to suggest that R. Soloveitchik valued their activities from a religious perspective.

34 Morris Adler, Jacob Agus, and Theodore Friedman, "Responsum on the Sabbath," *Proceedings of the Rabbinical Assembly of America* XIV (New York: Rabbinical Assembly, 1950): 112–37.

35 Reuven P. Bulka, *The Coming Cataclysm: The Orthodox-Reform Rift and the Future of the Jewish People* (Oakville, ON: Mosaic Press, 1984), 13.

36 Aharon Lichtenstein, "Beyond the Pale? Reflections regarding Contemporary Relations with Non-Orthodox Jews," in *The Relationship of Orthodox Jews with Believing Jews of Other Religious Ideologies and Non-Believing Jews*, ed. Adam Mintz (New York: Yeshiva University Press, 2010), 187–223. The essay was republished in Aharon Lichtenstein, *Varieties of Jewish Experience* (New York: Ktav, 2011), 129–65.

undermine a position of respect and appreciation for the valuable work done within non-Orthodox frameworks.

> And does anyone imagine that if every non-Orthodox temple were to shut down forthwith, that on the morrow the membership would flock, en masse, to the nearest *shul* or *shtibel*? If indeed temple attendance and affiliation are waning, and on the assumption that the absentees are beyond the reach of our own message, is there not, beyond competition, as much cause for dismay as for gratification ... [37]
>
> Non-Orthodox movements often provide a modicum of religious guidance, of access to Jewish knowledge and values, of spiritual direction and content. Moreover, they provide it for many beyond our own pale and reach. In such situations, the contribution to Jewish life is real and meaningful.[38]

Together with counseling careful navigation of such cooperation, Lichtenstein was strident in his repudiation of those within the Orthodox spectrum who emphatically oppose these efforts. "In our world, there are those who subscribe to the thesis that under no circumstances is it permissible or advisable to advance the cause of deviationists ... For them, the answer to our question is as straightforward as the query. However, I find this view wholly untenable, on moral, national, and, quite frequently, *halakhic* grounds."[39] Extending his "moral" perspective a step further, Lichtenstein revealed that there are areas that even override long-held bans against formal ceremonial cooperation. Thus, he was stunned by a student's query concerning a controversy within an American Orthodox synagogue in regard to participation in a joint communal Holocaust Remembrance Day convocation with non-Orthodox congregations, "Shocked, I responded that, as far as I knew, the Nazis had not differentiated. Could we?"[40]

Lichtenstein's independent approach to involvement with the non-Orthodox in religiously charged arenas received keen expression in a March 2013 discussion of the controversies surrounding permission for such groups to pray

---

37 Lichtenstein, "Beyond the Pale," 195.
38 Lichtenstein, "Beyond the Pale," 208.
39 Ibid.
40 Ibid., 207.

collectively at Jerusalem's Western Wall (Kotel). He encouraged all groups who go there to "come to the Kotel deferentially, reverentially, respecting what the Kotel means to a great many people," and "I would want to maintain halakhic standards; I don't think that having mixed congregations, men and women together, that that's the place to fight it out." What appeared to be most troublesome to him, however, were those on both sides who turn this *terra sancta* into a venue either for "political demonstration" or "power struggles." In parallel, he was deeply cognizant of the symbolic importance of the Kotel to all Jews: "When I'm there, I sometimes see someone with a makeshift yarmulke, standing at the Kotel itself, at the outer wall, crying his heart out, experiencing that which many people more devoted, more halakhically disciplined, perhaps don't feel. I don't think that by challenging the sincerity of Conservative or Reform individuals, or as groups, we gain very much religiously or even, for that matter, politically." Therefore, his practical advice was, "I don't believe … that there's so much to be gained by barring people from having access to the Kotel … I don't think we should try to have every possible restriction in place in order to manifest and to demonstrate our authority and our power."[41] This would be the case "even if they would have their own *minyanim* [quorums] and their mode of *tefillah* [prayer]."[42]

No doubt Lichtenstein was adamant in maintaining Orthodox standards of Jewish law, but he made considerable effort to accommodate non-Orthodox groups and enable them to experience Judaism's holiest space in a manner which was at least to some degree on their own terms and not those dictated purely by the Orthodox hegemony over Israeli sacred sites. Most profound in this regard was Lichtenstein's consent to a clear non-Orthodox presence—apparently including the use of their own prayer books and rituals—as long as men and women remain physically separated during the service.

The volume *Mevakshei Panekha* appeared in 2011 and presents extensive excerpts from a series of conversations and interviews on key topics between rabbi and novelist Haim Sabato and Lichtenstein.[43] In the chapter on

---

41 *Pages of Faith*, March 5, 2013, http://pagesoffaith.wordpress.com/2013/03/05/5-non-orthodox-prayer-groups-at-the-kotel/ (accessed March 21, 2014). The blog is the work of long-time YHE student and personal assistant to R. Lichtenstein, Dov Karoll. On its purpose, see: http://pagesoffaith.wordpress.com/about/ (accessed March 21, 2014).
42 Ibid.
43 Haim Sabato, *Mevakshei Panekha: Sihot in Ha-Rav Aharon Lichtenstein* (Tel Aviv: Yedioth Ahronoth, 2011). Regarding the 2016 English translation, see note 18. Citations here are translated from the original Hebrew version.

"relationship to secular Jews," Lichtenstein declares forthrightly that the positions advanced during the twentieth century by the Hazon Ish and Kook were unacceptable to him, for they each embody a "judgmental" and "totalistic definition" of an entire population. Regarding the Hazon Ish's portrayal of the nonobservant as an empty wagon or boat, Lichtenstein understood that by presenting secular culture as vacant depravity, such a pejorative discourse serves the defensive goal of "protecting" the religious public from the attractions of the outside environment. This description of nonobservant Jewry, however, was simply inaccurate:

> The spiritual and ethical portfolio of portions [of this group] contains lofty and important matters of [significant] moral meaning ... to say 'empty wagon' implies that they have nothing, nothing which isn't better than we have. This is something that I believe to be factually false, and I also have no interest in reaching such a situation.[44]

Similarly, Hazon Ish's adoption of *tinok she-nishbah* (an infant taken captive) as a fitting halakhic category for excusing contemporary nonobservant Jews for their behavior due to their lack of knowledge, may be useful for solving certain technical problems such as the prohibition against drinking wine touched by a public Sabbath desecrater. Lichtenstein's concern was with the broader connotations of this terminology. Like the empty wagon, "If we relate to such people as infants taken captive, we do not give them any credit. We do not find any aspect of them deserving of imitation, we assume that there is nothing about them that is spiritually meaningful."[45]

Lichtenstein lamented that this nomenclature moreover projects an "infantilization" of the nonobservant collective as if to say, "nebukh, they are not to blame for their situation."[46] From this perspective, Kook's seemingly more beneficent evaluation of the unconscious but constructive role played by secular Zionists in the redemptive process is even more perturbing. For it is essentially saying to them that "you think this and this, but we know that deep inside you there is another world ... A day will come when this hidden world will be revealed, when you shall shed a layer of the outer peel."[47] Such

---

44 Sabbato, *Mevakshei Panekha*, 142–3.
45 Ibid., 143.
46 Ibid., 144.
47 Ibid., 145.

expressions infuriated Lichtenstein, "This is how they relate ... like to an onion that has one peel removed after another. Such engagement is condescending, I would not want to be addressed in this manner and I don't think they [nonobservant Jews] should be related to this way either ... [T]o me it dwarfs them, it is not the appropriate level of respect for the divine essence in every human being, even if he/she is not exactly as we might like."[48]

Lichtenstein's reticence towards "totalistic" perceptions of Jewish others informed his approach to pragmatic issues of cooperation with non-Orthodox leaders and groups as well. As he noted throughout much of his career, he recognized the potential pitfalls of working together, but he vehemently disagreed with those within Orthodoxy who advocated a sweeping prohibition against such contacts. The alternative position that Lichtenstein advanced was to accept and appreciate the reality of "fragmentary Judaism" as a fundamental principle:

> I think that the [proper] Jewish-ethical-religious position is to be capable of recognizing and appreciating things that are fragmentary (partial) ... I say to my students, if you think of becoming a rabbi, go to the rabbinate with a recognition and appreciation of fragmentary things.[49]

While ideologies are in principle purist and demand full commitment, in reality individual acts of Jewish involvement or expressions of positive connection need to be cherished—even if they will never lead to observance or to provision of support for the interests of the Orthodox. At the same time, Lichtenstein stressed that even if he appreciated the ethics and creativity of the secular, as well as the spiritual quests and religious acts of Conservative and Reform Jews, he was by no means an egalitarian pluralist like those who maintain that "No one is perfect ... they don't keep Shabbat, and we are not careful in other matters."[50] Lichtenstein was absolute in his belief that Orthodox interpretation of Jewish law is the correct one and that upholding an observant lifestyle is the only ideal form of Jewish living. But this did not prevent him from extolling the positive Jewish elements found among others, acknowledging those areas in which these groups and individuals excel beyond his own constituency, and, as such, encouraging his followers to learn from even their sharpest ideological adversaries.

---

48 Ibid.
49 Ibid., 151–2.
50 Ibid., 152.

Regarding non-Orthodox and nonobservant Jews, then, in the years after their departures from YU, both Greenberg and Lichtenstein moved beyond the positions that they expressed in the 1966 *Commentator* exchange. Greenberg turned toward more unequivocal pluralism, which contributed to the perception that he had veered from the accepted Modern Orthodox way. Lichtenstein remained unabashed in his pronouncements regarding the fundamental correctness of the Orthodox way, but he also digressed from accepted outlooks. In doing so, he actually sustained and advanced a stance that was very close to Greenberg's 1966 presentation. Indeed, at that time, Lichtenstein criticized Greenberg for not offering a more balanced view that, along with appreciating the good, also set in bold the problematic aspects of the non-Orthodox. Subsequently, Lichtenstein himself adopted a similar but not identical tactic through his "fragmentary" approach that highlighted the positive elements in the ideals and practices of each Jewish faction, and what others stood to learn from them.

BIBLICAL SCHOLARSHIP

In his pioneering 1965 study entitled, "Orthodoxy in American Jewish Life," social scientist Charles S. Liebman, who at the time was a colleague of Greenberg and Lichtenstein at YC, opined:

> ... the modern Orthodox ... [make] no serious effort ... to engage in biblical criticism, and thereby [rule] out the development of any outstanding Orthodox biblical scholars in the United States. Modern Orthodoxy pays lip service to the notion that something ought to be done in this area and that aspects of biblical criticism can be incorporated into the Orthodox tradition, but no one is prepared to undertake or even encourage the work.[51]

Indeed, in Greenberg's *Commentator* interview, which appeared the following year, he listed the lack of serious engagement with the methods and conclusions of modern biblical criticism among the core examples of YU's unwillingness to confront the intellectual challenges of the era. He, therefore, advocated the training of Orthodox experts in this field. Their entrance into the YU classroom, he asserted, was not simply in order to provide the students with alternatives to the heretical notions arising from the academy. Rather, he sought a

---

51 Charles S. Liebman, "Orthodoxy in American Jewish Life," *American Jewish Year Book* 66 (1965): 47 (21–97).

synthesis that would affirm the positive and illuminating perceptions of the critics, without eliminating faith in God from the picture: "We should acknowledge a debt to Bible critics. They have shown that the Torah is not toneless, but has elements in common with the temporal experience of the ancient Near East ... We need to understand Biblical scholarship in order to more fully understand our own revelation." He further indicated that there is a broader spectrum of theologically tenable definitions of revelation than most assume, because "what we mean by 'Divine revelation' may be less external or mechanical than many Jews now think."[52]

In his follow-up letter, Greenberg clarified that he absolutely does not identify with the "liberal" Jewish acceptance of modern scholarship's conclusion, "that Torah is merely the product of humans."[53] He explained, furthermore, that his comment regarding revelation simply meant that the Torah was received by Moses, "in a particular time and setting and its images and conceptual material may be expressed in that language and cultural context."[54] That said, he reiterated his prior assertion that despite its secular humanistic bias, "contemporary Biblical scholarship has enriched our understanding of the meaning of the *Tanach* [sic],"[55] and that he "anticipates an even greater enrichment when we develop our own Biblical scholarship by men who believe that God communicates with man but who will not work from an apologetic or stereotyped image."[56] Greenberg expressed confidence that these efforts would not facilitate the infiltration of heresy into Orthodoxy: "I believe that we can be disciplined enough to reject conclusions that do not meet our test of validity, when and if, this becomes necessary."[57] Relatedly, he noted that higher criticism is not the exclusive modern method. For example, in a public lecture delivered a few years before, "*Rav* Aharon Lichtenstein pointed to the possible uses of the techniques of literary criticism ... for deepening our insight into Torah."[58]

The reference was to a presentation that Lichtenstein offered at Stern College in 1962, in which he made abundantly clear that higher biblical criticism had no place in the intellectual oeuvre of those allegiant to traditional

---

52 "Greenberg Interview," 215–6. The article by Miri Freud-Kandel in this volume addresses the Greenberg-Lichtenstein conflict regarding Bible study as well.
53 "Greenberg Clarifies," 222.
54 Ibid., 223.
55 Ibid.
56 Ibid.
57 Ibid.
58 Ibid., 222.

understandings of revelation and Divine authorship. This opinion was echoed in the only comment relating directly to the theological implications of Bible study in Lichtenstein's 1966 retort to Greenberg, "I take exception not only to the apparent substance of the original section on revelation, but to the suggestion implied in the juxtaposition of the two adjectives in the statement that 'what we mean by Divine revelation' may be less external or mechanical than Jews now think."[59] On the other hand, a trained scholar of English literature in his own right, in his 1962 address Lichtenstein advocated strongly for the adoption of literary tools developed within the academy as a key to gaining more profound understandings of the characters and religious meanings of the biblical text: "I propose that we rediscover *kitvei kodesh* (sacred writings) as literature … and that in order to deepen our appreciation of them as such, we seek to approach them critically."[60]

The text itself was only published fifty years later in 2012, and in the interim he barely addressed methodological issues revolving around Bible study in print. Furthermore, by his own later accounting, Lichtenstein never devoted himself personally to teaching or writing this type of Torah analysis—though his oral presentations on the weekly portion often demonstrated a keen literary sensitivity.[61] All the same, in retrospect, the 1962 discourse intimated a new approach to Orthodox Bible study, that was subsequently developed from the 1970s by the faculty and graduates of the Israeli institution headed by Lichtenstein, Yeshivat Har Etzion, and its affiliated Herzog Academic College.[62]

Since its 1968 establishment, one of the distinguishing elements of this yeshiva was its emphasis on Bible study alongside the traditional focus on the Talmud and its commentaries. The initial driving forces in this endeavor were the founding yeshiva head, Rabbi Yehudah Amital, and two early Bible instructors, Rabbis Mordechai Breuer and Yoel Bin-Nun. With the start of the educational college in 1973, Lichtenstein was appointed rector (chief academic officer).

---

59 "Lichtenstein to Greenberg," 230.
60 Aharon Lichtenstein, "Criticism and *Kitvei Kodesh*," in *Rav Shalom Banaiyikh: Essays Presented to Rabbi Shalom Carmy by Friends and Students in Celebration of Forty Years of Teaching*, ed. Hayyim Angel and Yitzchak Blau (Jersey City, NJ: Ktav, 2012), 15–32.
61 For a published example that is based on a summary of his oral remarks, see Aharon Lichtenstein, "Joseph's Tears," *Torah miEtzion—New Readings in Tanach: Bereshit*, ed. Ezra Bick (Jerusalem: Maggid, 2011), 533–8.
62 For a discussion of Bible study at Herzog College that focuses on its role in raising the interest of Modern Orthodox Jews in this discipline, see Chaim I. Waxman, *Social Change and Halakhic Evolution in American Orthodoxy* (Liverpool: Littman Library, 2017), 156–8.

Some of the early instructors, such as Breuer and Bin-Nun, stemmed from the yeshiva milieu, but integrated approaches that arose from academic writing.[63] Over time, faculty members were recruited who had earned doctoral degrees from Israeli universities and were integrated with members of the yeshiva's staff. Today, Herzog graduates serve as Bible teachers and lecturers throughout Israel, many have gone on to earn doctoral degrees, and some are renowned lecturers at Israeli university Bible departments. In addition to its BA and MA degree programs in Bible, Herzog publishes the Bible studies journal *Megadim*, runs the Bible study website hatanakh.com, and sponsors an annual five-day summer Bible seminar/jamboree that attracts thousands of people from Israel and abroad to its rich program of classes, workshops, and Bible-based outings.[64]

The core approach to biblical interpretation that has become associated with Herzog dovetails, to a great degree, the concept promoted by Lichtenstein in 1962. It emphasizes making use of a broad gamut of literary tools to address the text independently or as a complement to the exegetical traditions of rabbinic midrash and medieval exegesis. Yet, as evidenced by the numerous publications emanating from this circle, a variety of stances exist in parallel within the institution regarding the degree to which academic methods can be drafted. While some have maintained a strict boundary between literary analysis and instruments associated with higher criticism or that take historical context into account, other Herzog scholars have not stuck to such clear distinctions. Breuer actually accepted the Documentary Hypothesis' four-part division of the Pentateuch, but asserted that this was divinely orchestrated, and Bin-Nun has predicated much of his work on reading the Bible in light on modern archeological discoveries. As Rabbi Ezra Bick writes in the preface to the first in a series of English-language collections of articles authored by Herzog scholars: "Because the understanding of a literary work necessarily requires understanding of external factors in its writing, the studies will incorporate findings from history, archeology, Semitics, and not only literature per se."[65]

---

63 On Breuer's approach, see Meir Eckstein, "Rabbi Mordechai Breuer and Modern Orthodox Biblical Commentary, *Tradition* 33, no. 3 (1999): 6–23. On Bin-Nun, see Hayyim Angel, "Torat Hashem Temima: The Contributions of Rav Yoel Bin-Nun to Religious Tanakh Study, *Tradition* 40, no. 3 (2007): 5–17. See the illuminating discussion of Bin-Nun's early Bible teaching at Yeshivat Har Etzion in Yossi Klein-Halevi, *Like Dreamers: The Story of the Israeli Paratroopers who Reunited Jerusalem and Divided a Nation* (New York: HarperCollins, 2013), 153–4, 203–4.
64 For the full range of Herzog's academic and public programs, see: Herzog.ac.il.
65 Ezra Bick, "Preface," *Torah miEtzion*, xviii.

Bible scholarship at Herzog College, then, has brought to fruition ideas articulated by Greenberg in his 1966 *Commentator* interview on three levels: critical Bible study has entered the mainstream of advanced Orthodox learning; a cadre of high-level practitioners of Bible study have emerged that are conscious of the spectrum of critical methods, but advance one that does not necessarily contradict Orthodox theological principles; and in certain cases, its adherents have demonstrated openness to comprehending the Bible within the historical context in which it originally appeared. Lichtenstein himself expressed very clear reservations regarding the potential damage to foundational beliefs that some of these developments portended, but he did not categorically reject them. As he indicated in a preface to a book on biblical interpretation authored by a close student that engages aspects of modern scholarship: "… this book is, admittedly, not every *ben Torah*'s cup of tea … A measure of knowledge, sensitivity and sophistication—and, above all, discretion and discrimination rooted in commitment—is requisite in order to extract from these studies that which they have to offer. Those who approach them with the appropriate spiritual mindset and proper intellectual array can find themselves amply rewarded."[66] Indeed, some of the harshest criticism of Yeshivat Har Etzion from within more intellectually conservative sectors of Israeli Orthodoxy have focused their attacks on its innovative methodology for studying and teaching the Bible.[67]

In recent years, prominent Israeli Religious-Zionist rabbis, among them prized students of Lichtenstein, have actually expressed more radical attitudes regarding Bible scholarship than those held by Lichtenstein himself as well as the approaches most-closely associated with Herzog College. Some of these statements might have even challenged Greenberg's 1960s Orthodox articulations. A prime example is Rabbi Yuval Cherlow, a prized student and alumnus of Yeshivat Har Etzion and founder of the Tzohar rabbinic organization, who

---

66 Aharon Lichtenstein, "Preface," to Nathaniel Helfgot, *Mikra and Meaning: Studies in Bible and Its Interpretation* (Jerusalem: Maggid, 2012). For broader evaluations of his approach to Bible study, see Yaakov Beasely, "A Question of Character: R. Aharon Lichtenstein and the Interpretation of Biblical Texts," *Tradition* 47, no. 4 (2014): 126–36; Regarding Lichtenstein's complex attitude toward academic endeavors, see, for example: Ariel Horovitz, "Yahasim Murkavim," *Makor Rishon—Shabbat Supplement*, May 7, 2016, https://musaf-shabbat.com/2016/05/; Schwartz, "Haguto she ha-Rav Aharon Lichtenstein," 32–3.

67 See Adam S. Ferziger, "The Role of Reform in Israeli Orthodoxy," in *Between Jewish Tradition and Modernity: Rethinking an Old Opposition*, ed. Michael A. Meyer and David Myers (Detroit: Wayne University Press, 2014), 60–2.

heads the Yeshivat Amit Orot Shaul in Ra'anana.[68] In an eye-opening article on contemporary Orthodox approaches to biblical criticism, Marc Shapiro highlights Cherlow's argument that it is acceptable to believe that multiple verses in the Torah, beyond the final passages, were not authored by Moses. This, as long as one accepts that the Torah itself is of divine origin. Cherlow's understanding, notes Marc Shapiro, is in direct contradiction to the Eighth Principle of belief of Maimonides.[69] Furthermore, Cherlow does not feel bound to the Bible's actual historical account, "The Torah does not intend to tell us what happened, but what we are to build within ourselves as a result of these events."[70]

Rabbi Chaim Navon, another well-regarded Yeshivat Har Etzion alumnus, is a prolific author of works on Jewish thought and law who teaches at Herzog College and Midreshet Lindenbaum in Jerusalem.[71] With the exception of the Sinaitic revelation, which had to have occurred as presented in the text, Navon too does not assume that the Hebrew Bible necessarily offers a fully accurate historical account. As such, he has no difficulty accepting archeological findings that contradict the book of Joshua's description of the fall of Jericho's walls, and if historical evidence indicates that camels were not domesticated animals during the period when the stories of the book of Genesis took place: "Perhaps in truth the Patriarchs did not ride on camels, but on donkeys, or on bulls, or on winged horses … Does this matter to anyone? God, for his own considerations which relate to how the Torah will influence its own and later generations, preferred to write that the Patriarchs rode on camels."[72] Navon's article appeared in in *Alon Shevut*, the official Torah journal of Yeshivat Har Etzion, and received a strong rebuttal from Rabbi Yaakov Meidan, himself a highly respected practitioner of the "Herzog" literary approach who subsequently was appointed one of the heads of the yeshiva.[73] Notwithstanding, this did not interfere with

---

68 "Rabbi Yuval Cherlow," Koren Publishers Jerusalem, https://www.korenpub.com/koren_en_usd/rabbi-yuval-cherlow/.
69 Marc Shapiro, "Is Modern Orthodoxy Moving toward an Acceptance of Biblical Criticism?," *Modern Judaism* 37, no. 2 (May 2017), 170–1 (165–93).
70 Yuval Cherlow, "Bikoret ha-Mikra ve-Yir'at ha-Shamayim Sheli: She'elah le-Rav," in *Be-Einei E-lohim ve-Adam: Ha-Adam ha-Ma'amin u-Mehkar ha-Mikra*, ed. Yehudah Brandes, Tova Ganzel, and Hayota Deutsch (Jerusalem: Beit Morasha, 2015), 295 (cited and translated in Shapiro, "Is Modern Orthodoxy," 171).
71 "Chaim Navon," TivahFund.org., https://tikvahfund.org/faculty/chaim-navon/.
72 Chaim Navon, "Iyov lo Haya ve-lo Nivra: Al Mikra ve-Historia," *Alon Shevut* 159 (2001), www.asif.co.il/?wpfb_dl=1316 (cited and translated in Shapiro, "Is Modern Orthodoxy," 184).
73 Yaakov Meidan, "Ahat hi ha-Emet," *Alon Shevut* 161 (2002), www.asif.co.il/?wpfb_dl=1268.

Navon being invited to teach in Herzog College, and to posthumously edit, together with Lichtenstein's son Shai, a book on the Jewish concept of *kedushah* (the sacred) that Rabbi Aharon Lichtenstein had been completing at the time of his passing.[74]

A few months after penning these words, an essay entitled "Rabbi Aharon Lichtenstein and Academic Talmud Study" appeared in the *Lehrhaus* online scholarly forum that aims to enrich the diversity of discourse within Orthodox Judaism.[75] Written by Rami Reiner, a Yeshivat Har Etzion graduate and professor of rabbinic thought at Ben-Gurion University in the Negev, it explores a parallel but unidentical issue regarding Lichtenstein to that discussed above. Reiner focuses on Lichtenstein's antagonism toward critical scientific inquiry of the Talmud, highlighting the complexity of a yeshiva head who celebrated the wisdom that could be gained from those outside the Jewish orbit, yet in certain areas erected formidable boundaries to its application. Reiner's perspective shares much in common with a major point made here, that despite Lichtenstein's own strong reservations, through Herzog College he actually played a key role in facilitating the introduction of academic Talmud into mainstream Religious-Zionist Orthodoxy. Due to the commonalities of the arguments, I am including an extended direct citation from Reiner's work:

> The broad, rich, unique world that Rabbi Lichtenstein brought to Yeshivat Har Etzion coexisted, in those days, with his strong opposition to any whiff of academic Talmud study. Thus, some of Rabbi Lichtenstein's students ultimately continued their search for the truth, but they found it elsewhere, and in different kinds of truth. The driving force was Rabbi Lichtenstein's strength and spirit, but the end result was something far from his spirit, and far from the destinations toward which he strove … What happened subsequently? It seems that the history of Herzog College, which is adjacent to, affiliated with, and influenced by Yeshivat Har Etzion, and for which Rabbi Lichtenstein served as rector, shows that sometimes lines that may never intersect can nevertheless grow closer. …

---

74 Aharon Lichtenstein, *Kedushat Aviv: Iyunim be-Kedushat ha-Zeman ve-ha-Makom* (Jerusalem: Maggid/Yeshivat Har Etzion, 2017). For an expanded focus on geographical distinctions, see: Adam S. Ferziger, "Fluidity and Bifurcation: Critical Biblical Scholarship and Orthodox Judaism in Israel and North America," *Modern Judaism* (forthcoming).

75 Rami Reiner, "Rabbi Aharon Lichtenstein and Academic Talmud Study," trans. Elli Fisher, *Lehrhaus*, February 1, 2018, https://www.thelehrhaus.com/scholarship/rabbi-aharon-lichtenstein-and-academic-talmud-study/.

In the early 1990s, as the college steadily grew and developed, prospective teachers of Talmud and halakhah were disqualified one after another as it became clear to Rabbi Lichtenstein, in his capacity as rector, that these teachers had been trained in academic Talmud departments. From that point forward, however, and in contrast to everything we have thus far described, the Faculty of Oral Law at Herzog College developed in a different direction, to the point that eventually, every one of its members was the product of research institutions where they had studied Talmud and related disciplines. These facts speak for themselves …

In contrast with Reiner, I do not suggest that Lichtenstein had a more fundamental change of heart at the end of his career and became less equivocal regarding certain aspects of the academic enterprise that had previously troubled him.[76] As late as 2011, Lichtenstein opined regarding the orientation the Bible instructors in Herzog College that, "We need a method of Bible study that is both humanistic and religious … If you ask me, does this balance exist in the [Har Etzion] yeshiva and [Herzog] College on the level that I would like? There are people here who exemplify this characteristic … [And] there are people of whom I disapprove …"[77] Notwithstanding this clear censure, the comment itself concedes that the latter figures were full-fledged members of the Herzog College faculty.

Unlike the case regarding relations with the non-Orthodox and nonobservant, then, the gap between Greenberg's 1966 proposals and Lichtenstein's subsequent attitudes toward Bible study remained more easily delineable. All the same, if Greenberg's primary goal was, in his words, to "develop our own Biblical scholarship by men who believe that God communicates with man," then Lichtenstein can be credited with having a hand in advancing this project.

---

76 For a critique of this aspect of Reiner's essay, see Lawrence Kaplan, "An Alternate View on Rav Aharon Lichtenstein and Academic Talmud Study," *Lehrhaus*, March 19, 2018, https://www.thelehrhaus.com/scholarship/alternate-view-on-rav-aharon-lichtenstein-talmud-study/. For additional perspective on Lichtenstein and academic study, see the recent translation from Yiddish of a 1968 talk that he presented on the topic at the YIVO Institute in New York, Shaul Seidler-Feller, "Rabbi Aharon Lichtenstein on the Divide Between Traditional and Academic Jewish Studies," *The Seforim Blog*, March 27, 2018, http://seforim.blogspot.co.il/2018/03/rabbi-aharon-lichtenstein-on-divide.html, and the erudite discussion based on this newly available source, in Shlomo Zuckier, "Rav Lichtenstein on Wissenschaft in his Own (Yiddish) Words," *Lehrhaus*, March 26, 2018, https://www.thelehrhaus.com/scholarship/rav-lichtenstein-on-wissenschaft-in-his-own-yiddish-words/.

77 Hayyim Sabbato, *Mevakshei Panekha: Sihot im Ha-Rav Aharon Lichtenstein* (Tel Aviv: Yedioth Ahronoth, 2011), 201. I thank Shlomo Zuckier for pointing me to these comments.

He articulated a vision for critical Orthodox Bible scholarship as early as 1962, modeled personally a form of textual analysis that integrated deep awareness of literary factors and that was rooted at least in part in his own academic training, and he gave his imprimatur to the development of the only research and training center in the world that is dedicated exclusively to cultivating and popularizing Orthodox Bible scholarship. Not only those who formally set out upon academic careers in Bible research, but also some of his most visible rabbinic protégés, have demonstrated their willingness to engage aspects of Bible study that Greenberg encouraged and Lichtenstein rejected. In their underlying aim of synthesizing a "critical" orientation with unequivocal allegiance to the divine origins of the Torah, even when they deviated in significant details from Lichtenstein in crucial matters, it was his fundamental direction toward the road "less traveled" that "made all the difference."

ORTHODOX ATTITUDES TOWARD SEXUAL BEHAVIOR

The topic for which Greenberg's 1966 *Commentator* interview received the sharpest criticism was his statement in the original article that "sex" was the most pressing area in which Orthodoxy needed to reevaluate accepted approaches.[78] Broadly, he asserted that there was a prevailing negative attitude within Orthodoxy toward sex that turns what should be seen as holy conduct into a secular activity. "Today the poskim (adjudicators) should recognize that there is nothing wrong with sex per se, and should promulgate a new value system and corresponding new *halachot* [sic] about sex. The basis should be the concept that experiencing a woman as a *zelem Elokim* [an image of God] is a *mitzvah* just as much as praying in shul [synagogue] …"[79]

As an example of the problem, Greenberg noted that "[t]he fact that unmarried girls are not permitted to go to the *mikvah* reflects the reaction of *Poskim* in the middle ages to looseness in morals …"[80] This sentence was understood by readers to mean that he advocated permitting premarital sex as long as the woman immersed in a ritualarium in advance. Such a position was in

---

78 For an examination of the Sixties "sexual revolution," see David Allyn, *Make Love, Not War: The Sexual Revolution* (New York: Routledge, 2016).
79 "Greenberg Interview," 219. A broader and more detailed account and analysis of Greenberg approach to sexuality and its position in the development of Modern Orthodoxy's positions on this issue, appears in Sylvia Barack Fishman's contribution to this volume.
80 Ibid.

clear opposition to accepted Orthodox norms and practice, and caused a considerable uproar.

In his subsequent letter to the editor, Greenberg claimed that he was misunderstood and never intended to change Jewish law regarding unmarried individuals, but he now recognized the ambiguity of his words and therefore, "I must take the blame for not having clarified the language."[81] That said, he reaffirmed his focus on "the positive strand in halachah ... that use[s] sexual imagery as the highest relationship of G-d and Israel—and [the need to] shift the emphasis to the positive value of sex as a mode of encounter rather than as exploitation."[82] Such a redirection would welcome the fresh accent within some corners of contemporary civilization on "sex as an expression of the communication of love in a husband-wife relationship with particular emphasis on a new mutuality and significance for the woman."[83] Although this might be seen by some as leading to "legitimate sinning," he felt that it was more likely to raise the overall level of religious sensitivity, for "even those who sin might well have criteria for restraint and reduction in sinning."[84]

In his June 1966 rejoinder, Lichtenstein pointed to the "vague" quality of his colleague's formulations, which opened the door to interpretations that deviated from Orthodox norms and challenged Greenberg's credibility. Even before Greenberg's clarification, however, "I did not think, as did many, that you were referring to premarital sexual relations. I know you too well and regard you too highly to have considered this."[85] Yet once Greenberg attested that his words were addressed to a reevaluation of the Orthodox sexual ethos within the context of marriage, Lichtenstein was confused. For he did not see the novelty of the critique, since there were plenty of rabbinic sources that spoke positively about sexual relations. That is, unless Greenberg was suggesting a complete overhaul of the laws of Jewish family purity, "Within the existing Halachic framework, concerning marital life, there is little in the way of absolute norms which could be changed so as to produce the axiological shift you advocate."[86]

---

81 "Greenberg Clarifies," 223.
82 Ibid., 224.
83 Ibid.
84 Ibid.
85 "Lichtenstein to Greenberg," 232.
86 Ibid., 233.

Lichtenstein's remarks were consistent with his fundamental assessment that Greenberg's open-ended statements meant to encourage novel thinking and renewal, were irresponsible and could instigate questioning that undermined entrenched religious norms. Yet referring to Greenberg's revised presentation regarding sex in the *Commentator*, he adjured, "The thesis against which you argue in your clarification is rather different; those remarks I understand perfectly, and I might add, I've thought about them myself."[87]

Lichtenstein does not detail which aspects of the thesis he "understood perfectly." Yet based on a programmatic essay on marriage that appeared in 2005, he shared the sentiment that from a religious perspective, sexual relations should be viewed extraordinarily positively, as a covenantal act that unites husband, wife, and the sphere of the Divine. In his typically rigorous dialectic fashion, Lichtenstein's essay explores the gamut of rabbinic statements regarding sexual behavior, especially those that are not focused on its necessity for procreation. Indeed, he portrays a sharp conflict between the classical Tannaitic and Amoraic sources that for the most part, celebrate sexual union as a key element in a healthy marital union (the kabbalistic literature going even further by emphasizing its mystical significance within the esoteric realm), and the tendency of many medieval "*rishonim*" who expressed disgust with an act whose foundation was in the *yezer ha-ra* (evil will). Unwilling to explain away this dissonance through "historicizing" analysis that connects the medieval turn with the influence of Christianity or Sufi asceticism, Lichtenstein simply acknowledges that these two trends existed in conflict within legitimate Jewish tradition. All the same, he argues that in modern times, both the most influential figures in the Modern Orthodox and Religious Zionist camps—Soloveitchik and Kook—and literature regarding marriage that received the imprimatur of prominent Haredi authorities, promoted a highly positive view of sexual relations within the marital context.[88]

Yet the inability to resolve the contradiction between the two premodern rabbinic approaches to sex troubled Lichtenstein's Talmudist religious sensibility as well as his overall propensity—unlike Greenberg—to hedge the innovative character of his own pronouncements: "I am left, nonetheless, with a lacuna. Even while adhering to the Rav's (Soloveitchik's) position, one may

---

87 Ibid.
88 Aharon Lichtenstein, "On Marriage: Relationship and Relations," *Tradition* 39, no. 2 (2005): 7–35.

freely concede wishing that he had done for us what we have been challenged and constrained to do here: examine the various tiers of tradition and elucidate the basis for his own judgment and commitment."[89] Lacking such a precedential explication, in the end Lichtenstein did not settle for neutrality. Rather he concluded his article with a vociferous endorsement of the positive approach to sexual intimacy that is reminiscent of the aspects of Greenberg's 1966 declarations with which he apparently identified:

> ... impelled by our spiritual instincts and animated by the faith instilled in us by our Torah mentors, we opt for consecration rather than abstinence. In this most sensitive area, we strive for a life which is energized rather than neutralized—not merely sterilized and sanitized, but ennobled and ennobling. We are challenged to sanctify—by integrating sexuality within total sacral existence, characterized by the systole and diastole of divinely ordained denial and realization, and by infusing the relationship itself with human and spiritual content.[90]

While defining appropriate heterosexual behavior was clearly a central challenge for the generation of the 1966 Greenberg–Lichtenstein exchange, the existence of openly homosexual and lesbian Orthodox Jews and the question of how to relate to them only began to draw considerable attention in the twenty-first century.[91] Both Greenberg and Lichtenstein addressed this issue in ways

---

89 Ibid., 30.
90 Ibid., 31.
91 As early as 1974, Yeshiva University President and Orthodox thinker Norman Lamm authored, "Judaism and the Modern Attitude to Homosexuality," *Encyclopaedia Judaica Yearbook* (Jerusalem: Keter, 1974), 194–205, available at http://www.ezrabessaroth.net/leadership/rabbi-s-blog/entry/rabbi-lamm-s-1974-article-on-judaism-and-homosexuality. Other Orthodox-oriented discussions appeared from time to time, but the turning point can be attributed to the 2001 appearance of Sandi Simha DuBowski's documentary film *Trembling Before God* (available at https://www.youtube.com/watch?v=Ts7bhOau0Wc), which portrays the lives of gay and lesbian Orthodox Jews, and the 2004 publication of Steven Greenberg, *Wrestling with God and Men: Homosexuality in the Jewish Tradition Updated* (Madison: University of Wisconsin Press, 2004), in which the openly gay author and Orthodox rabbi explores the sources and attitudes of Orthodoxy toward homosexuality. By late 2009, a panel discussion of gay students and alumni was held in a large auditorium at YU and drew both a standing-room-only crowd of over 600 and strong censure from leading RIETS rabbis. See Steve Lipman, "Gay YU Panel Broadens Discussion, Debate," *The New York Jewish Week*, December 30, 2009, http://jewishweek.timesofisrael.com/gay-yu-panel-broadens-discussion-debate/; E. B. Solomont, "Fallout from Gay Debate Rocks YU," *Jerusalem Post*, January 1, 2010, http://www.jpost.com/Jewish-World/Fallout-from-gay-debate-rocks-YU. For an

that demonstrate consistency with their respective foundational 1966 attitudes toward both nonobservance and sexuality. These iterations offer further evidence of their differences both in temperament and priorities. All the same, they also testify to an ongoing proximate conversation.

In a 2011 *Moment Magazine* symposium, rabbis from across the American denominational spectrum were asked to pen a hypothetical letter to their child on learning from them that they were gay. Representing the Modern Orthodox, Greenberg wrote as follows:

> My heart goes out to you. As you were raised as an Orthodox Jew, you already know that since the time of the Torah, homosexuality has been condemned in our community, especially in more traditional circles. While treatment is improving, I fear that you will face much rejection and hostility, and I wish that I could prevent it or protect you.
>
> Nevertheless, if you live your life this way, I would hope that you would apply the Torah's other guidelines for sexuality to your own practice. Sex should not be casual or promiscuous. It should never be exploitative or abusive. Sexuality should express relationship and love; the deeper the sexuality, the deeper the relationship that it should express. You should try for the Jewish ideal, which remains family and creating/nurturing life via children (by conception or adoption). This is a great joy and a fulfillment in life.
>
> Your mother and I love you very much as a total person. This feeling has not changed with your announcement.[92]

Greenberg noted the traditional "condemnation" and the personal price to be paid for deviating, but he did not express a clear stand on the ongoing prohibition. Rather he highlighted the core relationship values that he considered to be of prime importance, and expressed his unequivocal acceptance of his child regardless of their untraditional choice.

In 2013, Lichtenstein shared his views on homosexuality, which both echo his overall "fragmentary" approach to halakhic nonobservance, and add an

---

overview, see Sylvia Barack Fishman, "Introduction: Paradoxes of a Social Revolution," in *Love, Marriage, and Jewish Families* (Waltham, MA: UPNE/Brandeis, 2015), 18–20.

92 Yitz Greenberg in Amy E. Schwartz, "Ask the Rabbis: What Advice Would You Give if Your Child Told you He or She was Gay," *Moment Magazine*, November 16, 2011, http://www.momentmag.com/ask-the-rabbis-11/.

additional layer to the "less traveled" character of his Orthodox worldview. Consistent with his positions of categorically forbidding premarital sex and reaffirming the fixedness of Jewish family purity laws, Lichtenstein fully supported traditional understandings of the biblical prohibition against homosexual behavior. At the same time, he argued that this topic underscores an unhealthy double standard that commonly pervades Orthodox Jews. Whereas other sins referred to in the Bible as an abomination (*to'evah*), such as "cheating on weights and measures" are often overlooked or at least easily forgiven, vilification of homosexuals is incessantly supported by the fact that the same term (*to'evah*) is applied in its regard. Similarly, he found it difficult to countenance the fact that few contemporary Orthodox Jews are sensitive to the seriousness of public Sabbath desecration among their brethren and take pains not to pass judgment on them, while at the same time they forcefully and consistently campaign against homosexuals. It is not that he encouraged intolerance toward nonobservant Jews. He simply felt that the pervasive antagonistic attitudes toward homosexuals were rooted in personal "revulsion" instead of a sincere desire to uphold Jewish law standards. With this in mind, he recalled with considerable consternation the "threat" a few years back by a group of Orthodox high schools not to march in New York's Israel Day Parade that ultimately prevented a Jewish gay contingent from participating:

> Is it proper, is it fair, and I say this without relenting in our opposition to homosexuality—to decide that all the sins which the whole entire Jewish community has—all of that we can swallow and march with them, with pride and with their flags and everything that they want, but this is the [scapegoat]— dispatched to *erets gezerah* [a barren wasteland] ... (Leviticus 16:22). I discussed this point with people for whom I have the highest regard and I asked them this question.[93]

From Lichtenstein's perspective, homosexuality was historically always treated as a private transgression rather than a communal one. In an age in which the prevalence of traditional public sins such as Sabbath desecration or failing to give charity had transformed them into bearable private ones, ironically the opposite makeover has taken place regarding homosexuality. Not only did he protest that this was inconsistent and unfair, but—in a similar fashion to the understanding position adopted by many halakhic authorities of the last two centuries

---

93   *Pages of Faith*, April 4, 2013, http://pagesoffaith.wordpress.com/2013/04/.

regarding those who grew up in an environment in which nonobservance is the norm—he reflected that in regard to homosexuality: "as the phenomenon becomes more prevalent, which is unfortunate in itself, but at the personal plane it has become a more common *aveirah* [transgression], it is less of an *aveirah* on the part of the individual." Indeed, such a position might not qualify a homosexual individual as upholding the most pristine personal standards of observance, but for the most part it would neutralize day-to-day sanctions and pave the way for acceptance as a full-fledged member of the Orthodox community.

The distinctiveness of this assessment of homosexuals is set in bold through comparison to the tone and content of prominent YU rabbinical figures. In December 2009, a public forum was held at YU in which gay students and alumni discussed their personal identity struggles, particularly with being part of the Orthodox community.[94] In response, four RIETS rabbis publicized a joint statement entitled "Torah View of Homosexuality," that included the following:

> … today's *galus* [exile] seeks to legitimize and mainstream the abominable practice (*toeiva* [sic]) of homosexuality … Homosexual behavior is absolutely prohibited and constitutes an abomination. Discreet, unconditionally *halachically* committed Jews who do not practice homosexuality but feel same sex attraction should be sympathetically and wholeheartedly supported. They can be wonderful Jews, fully deserving of our love, respect, and support. They should be encouraged to seek professional guidance … How painful, sad and sobering is the sharp contrast between the clear attitude that should prevail in a pure Torah community and the confusion that exists among well-intentioned individuals within our communities … Due to the influence of today's *Mitzrayim*, appropriate sympathy in discreet settings has become conflated with public, celebratory identification of people with an urge for forbidden behavior. In today's *galus* same-sex-attraction is not viewed as a challenge of *kevishas hayetzer* (overcoming and taming impulses for forbidden behavior), but rather as a troubling *halacha* lacking in compassion, *rachmanah litzlan* [Heaven forbid].[95]

---

94 Steve Lipman, "YU Gay Panel Broadens the Discussion, Debate," *The Jewish Week*, December 30, 2009, http://www.thejewishweek.com/news/new_york/gay_yu_panel_broadens_discussion_debate_0 (accessed April 1, 2014).

95 Herschel Schachter, Mordechai Willig, Michael Rosenzweig, and Mayer Twersky, "Torah View of Homosexuality," *TorahWeb.org*, 2010, http://www.torahweb.org/torah/special/2010/homosexuality.html (accessed April 1, 2014).

Rather than perceiving homosexual behavior as a particularly "abominable" act, Lichtenstein isolated the Orthodox and gay person's transgressive behavior from the overall religious character of the individual. This facilitated a less judgmental and more inclusionary communal approach; it does not preclude the type of parental empathy expressed in Greenberg's letter. Nonetheless, Lichtenstein remained more formally concerned with the halakhic implications, and as such unwilling to address homosexuality through his foundational outlook on intimate relationships. Some of his students, however, have been more forthcoming.

In 2010, Rabbi Nathaniel Helfgot, an American Orthodox pulpit rabbi, educator, and scholar, who is an alumnus of Yeshivat Har Etzion and a close disciple of Lichtenstein, authored a petition entitled "Statement of Principles on the Place of Jews with a Homosexual Orientation in Our Community."[96] The final document, which to date has been signed by over 200 Orthodox rabbis and educators, is a consensus-oriented document that is clearly more guarded than the original draft. It resonates to some of the points made by Lichtenstein three years later, both the unequivocal nature of the prohibition on homosexual behavior and the isolation of private sexual behavior from other aspects of their religious identity, but it also goes further in embracing Orthodox homosexuals. Acknowledging their emotional needs, it states that "it is critical to emphasize that halakha (sic) only prohibits homosexual acts; it does not prohibit orientation or feelings of same-sex attraction, and nothing in the Torah devalues the human beings who struggle with them."[97] Moreover, the statement encourages synagogues to welcome "Jews with homosexual orientations or same sex-attractions ... as full members of the synagogue and school community ... they should participate and count ritually, be eligible for ritual synagogue honors, and generally be treated in the same fashion and under the same halakhic and hashkafic (worldview) framework as any other member of the synagogue they join."[98] As to those who choose to formalize their homosexual and lesbian relationships,

> Halakhic Judaism cannot give its blessing and imprimatur to Jewish religious same-sex commitment ceremonies and weddings, and halakhic values proscribe individuals and communities from encouraging practices

---

96 Nathaniel Helfgot, "Statement of Principles on the Place of Jews with a Homosexual Orientation in Our Community," July 28, 2010, http://statementofprinciplesnya.blogspot.co.il/.
97 Ibid.
98 Ibid.

that grant religious legitimacy to gay marriage and couplehood. But communities should display sensitivity, acceptance and full embrace of the adopted or biological children of homosexually active Jews in the synagogue and school setting, and we encourage parents and family of homosexually partnered Jews to make every effort to maintain harmonious family relations and connections.[99]

On the other side of the ocean, Beit Hillel is an organization of Religious Zionist rabbis and female religious leaders founded in 2012, that is dedicated to presenting Israeli society with an "authentic, enlightened, inclusive Judaism—whose ways are pleasant and peaceful." Among its members and leadership are to be found many Yeshivat Har Etzion alumni, including its chairman Rabbi Meir Nehorai, a core teacher in Migdal Oz, the women's division of Yeshivat Har Etzion headed by Lichtenstein's daughter Esti Rosenberg. One vehicle by which Beit Hillel aims to achieve its goals is by issuing Jewish legal decisions that reflect sensitivity to contemporary realities.[100]

A 2016 responsum entitled "The Congregation and People with Homosexual Tendencies," piggybacks on much of the 2010 American statements authored by Helfgot, with some notable novelties. Most pronounced is its tacit recognition of the viability of same-sex couples, even as it supports the technical prohibition on homosexual sex: "An individual whose sexual orientation precludes him or her from entering into a union sanctioned by the laws of Moses and Israel, and seeks a way to avoid solitude, may forge ties of friendship and partnership with a person of the same sex. Despite the apprehensions and suspicions that may arise from such a relationship, the congregation should assess the possibility of embracing them."[101] Such a position is a radical departure from the YU rabbis, who insisted on applying the "*toevah*" label to contemporary homosexuality. But it also goes beyond Lichtenstein's isolation of the specific transgressive act and gravitates toward Greenberg's more empathic encouragement of healthy same-sex relationships that remain grounded in the Torah's foundational relationship ethic.

---

99 Ibid.
100 On Beit Hillel, see https://eng.beithillel.org.il/.
101 The responsum was authored by a team of twenty-one rabbis and female religious leaders led by the head of the "Beit Hillel Beit Midrash," Rabbi Amit Kula. The abridged English version appears as "The Congregation and People with Homosexual Tendencies," April 2016, https://eng.beithillel.org.il/responsa/the-congregation-and-people-with-homosexual-tendencies/. For the full Hebrew decision, see "Ha-Kehillah ve-Anashim Ba'alei Netiyah Had-Minit," *Halakhah ve-Hakhalah—Hoveret* 11 (April 2016): 3–8, http://upload.kipa.co.il/media-upload/beitHilel/18926293-4112016.PDF.

Rabbi Dr. Binyamin "Benny" Lau is an alumnus of Yeshivat Har Etzion who leads the Ramban synagogue in Jerusalem and is an influential public figure in the liberal camp of Religious Zionism.[102] He has spoken out against religious homophobia, and in 2014 presented a ruling to his congregation entitled, "And You Should Choose Life: On Partnership for People with Homosexual Tendencies." Lau also did not give his approbation to actual homosexual intercourse and made clear this must be avoided, but he puts forward a distinction articulated by Soloveitchik between two aspects of Jewish marriage: collective (outward) oriented procreation and togetherness (inward) commitment. For the latter, in the words of Soloveitchik, "The main value of marriage is to be found … in its creating a personal experience that enriches and enhances the lives of two individuals who were drawn to each other … A childless marriage is just as sacred as a one blessed with offspring, since the meaningfulness of the matrimonial union is to be found in self-fulfillment of the wedded partners themselves rather than in the benefits which accrue to society."[103] Based on this second aspect, Lau permitted homosexuals to establish an exclusive partnership agreement and create a monogamous shared life. Lau argued that this was a matter of preserving life, since "loneliness is the narcotic of death."[104]

Unlike Greenberg's hypothetical 2012 letter, Lau did not offer guidance that introduced fundamental elements of holiness into a forbidden sexual relationship. Yet he sanctioned a permanent connection between two homosexuals based on the conviction that companionship, in this case between two people of the same sex, is axiologically meaningful and even critical to maintaining a healthy reality, and must therefore be supported.[105]

CONCLUSION

The analysis in this article was not intended to diminish from the substantial ideological divides that arose from the late 1960s between Greenberg and Lichtenstein. What it does illustrate, however, is that the initial 1966 debate may be understood not as a polar struggle between an emergent archetypical deviant and a staunch centrist "mainstream" representative. Rather, it highlights two

---

102 On Lau, see http://ramban.org.il/english/rabbi-benjamin-lau/.
103 Joseph B. Soloveitchik, "Marriage," in his *Family Redeemed: Essays on Family Relationships* (New York: Toras HoRav, 2000), 32 (31–72).
104 Binyamin Lau, "U-Baharta ba-Hayyim: Al Zugiyut le-Anashim in Netiyot Had Miniyot," April 26, 2014, http://ramban.org.il/.
105 Lau, "U-Baharta ba-Hayyim." Most recently, see *Homosexuality, Transsexuality, Psychoanalysis, and Traditional Judaism*, ed. Alan Slomowitz (New York: Routledge, 2019).

novel and related roads that were percolating within 1960s American Modern Orthodoxy, neither of which became the dominant path. Initially, one was "not taken" while the other was merely "less traveled." More contemporaneously though, new intersections have come to a fore.

The juxtaposition of Greenberg with Lichtenstein, then, offers evidence of "Insider-Outsiders" who reexamined accepted group paradigms in ways that those who grew up exclusively within a certain milieu may have been less inclined. Moreover, it illustrates both the fickleness and rapidity of historical change, especially in contemporary times. Innovative ideas expressed by radical individuals that quite recently were viewed as beyond the pale, can after a short interval gain traction within normative settings. Meanwhile, the same figures who were perceived as the conservative guardians of tradition at a previous juncture may turn out in retrospect to have been the catalysts of a fundamental transformation.

Editors and Contributors

Steven Bayme is national director of the Contemporary Jewish Life Department and the Koppelman Institute on American Jewish-Israeli Relations, American Jewish Committee.

Sylvia Barack Fishman is an emerita professor of contemporary Jewish life in the Near Eastern and Judaic Studies Department at Brandeis University. She edits the Brandeis Series on Gender and Jewish Women, and was the founding codirector of the Hadassah Brandeis Institute (HBI). She is the author of eight books, including *Double or Nothing? Jewish Families and Mixed Marriage* (Brandeis University Press, 2004) and *Love, Marriage, and Jewish Families: Paradoxes of a Social Revolution* (Brandeis University Press, 2015). In 2014, she received The Marshall Sklare Award from the Association for the Social Scientific Study of Jewry.

Alan Brill is the Cooperman/Ross Endowed Chair for Jewish–Christian Studies at Seton Hall University, where he teaches Jewish studies in the department of religion and the Jewish–Christian studies graduate program. He is the author of *Thinking God: The Mysticism of Rabbi Zadok of Lublin* (Yeshiva University Press, 2002), *Judaism and Other Religions: Models of Understanding* (Palgrave Macmillan, 2010), *Judaism and World Religions: Christianity, Islam, and Eastern Religions* (Palgrave Macmillan, 2012), and *Rabbi on The Ganges: A Jewish-Hindu Encounter* (Lexington Books, 2019).

Adam S. Ferziger holds the S. R. Hirsch Chair in the Department of Jewish History and Contemporary Jewry, Bar-Ilan University. He is co-convener of the annual Oxford Summer Institute on Modern and Contemporary Judaism and a senior associate of the Oxford Center for Hebrew and Jewish Studies, University of Oxford. His most recent book, *Beyond Sectarianism: The Realignment of American Orthodox Judaism* (Wayne State University Press, 2015), received the National Jewish Book Award in American Jewish Studies.

Miri Freud-Kandel is fellow and lecturer in modern Judaism in the Faculty of Theology and Religion at the University of Oxford, and co-convener of the annual Oxford Summer Institute on Modern and Contemporary Judaism. She researches the theological development of modern Jewish religious movements, focusing on Orthodoxy, British Judaism, and gender. She is the author of *Orthodox Judaism in Britain Since 1913: An Ideology Forsaken* (Vallentine Mitchell, 2006) and coeditor of *Modern Judaism: An Oxford Guide* (Oxford University Press, 2005). She is currently completing a full-length monograph examining the theology of Louis Jacobs in light of the contemporary Jewish quest.

Samuel C. Heilman holds the *Harold Proshansky Chair* in Jewish Studies at the Graduate Center and is *distinguished professor of sociology* at Queens College of the City University of New York. His most recent book is *Who Will Lead Us: The Story of Five Hasidic Dynasties in America* (University of California Press, 2017).

Alan Jotkowitz is professor of medicine, director of the Jakobovits Center for Jewish Medical Ethics, and director of the Medical School for International Health and Medicine, Ben-Gurion University of the Negev, and a senior physician at Soroka University Medical Center, in Beer-Sheva, Israel. His main academic interest is in the field of medical ethics and modern Jewish thought, and he has published more than one hundred peer-reviewed papers in leading academic journals.

Steven T. Katz holds the Slater Chair in Jewish and Holocaust Studies at Boston University, where he was the founding director of the Elie Wiesel Center for Jewish Studies. He serves on the Academic Committee of the United States Holocaust Memorial Museum, chairs the Holocaust Committee of the Conference for Material Claims Against Germany, and edits the journal *Modern Judaism*. His most recent work is the two-volume *The Holocaust and New World Slavery: A Comparative Study* (Cambridge University Press, 2018). Katz was awarded the University of Tübingen's Lucas Prize, and a Distinguished Achievement Award from the Holocaust Education Foundation at Northwestern University.

Irving (Yitz) Greenberg has served in the Orthodox rabbinate, in academia, and in Jewish communal life (founding president, CLAL: The National Jewish Center for Learning and Leadership; founding president, Jewish Life Network/Steinhardt Foundation). He is a pioneer in Holocaust education and commemoration as well as in the Jewish–Christian dialogue. He has written extensively on Jewish theology after the Holocaust, the ethics of Jewish power, Jewish–Christian relations, and religious and cultural pluralism. His books include *The Jewish Way: Living the Holidays* (Touchstone, 1988), *Living in the Image of God* (Jason Aronson, 1988), *For the Sake of Heaven and Earth: The New Encounter of Judaism and Christianity* (Jewish Publication Society, 2004), and *Sage Advice: A New Edition of Pirkei Avot: Ethics of the Fathers* with commentary and translation (Koren Publishers, 2016).

Darren Kleinberg is head of school at Kehillah Jewish High School in Palo Alto, California. He is the author of *Hybrid Judaism: Irving Greenberg, Encounter, and the Changing Nature of American Jewish Identity* (Academic Studies Press, 2016).

James Kugel served as Starr Professor of Hebrew Literature at Harvard University from 1982 to 2003 and subsequently professor of Bible and chairman of the Bible Department at Bar-Ilan University. He is editor in chief of *Jewish Studies: An Internet Journal*. A specialist in the Hebrew Bible and the Dead Sea Scrolls, and the author of more than eighty research articles and seventeen books. His more recent books include *How to Read the Bible* (Free Press, 2007), awarded the National Jewish Book Award for the best book of 2007, and *The Great Shift: Encountering God in Biblical Times* (Houghton Mifflin Harcourt, 2017). In 2016, he was awarded Israel's Rothschild Prize in Jewish studies and in 2017, he was elected a member of the Israel Academy of Sciences and Humanities.

Tamar Ross is professor emerita of the Department of Jewish Philosophy at Bar-Ilan University and continues to teach at Midreshet Lindenbaum in Jerusalem, with which she has been associated since its inception in 1976. She has published widely on various topics relating to Jewish thought and theology, including feminism, historicism, biblical criticism, postmodernity, concepts of God, divine revelation, religious epistemology and hermeneutics, philosophy of halakhah, the Musar movement, and the writings of Rabbi A. I. Kook.

Marc B. Shapiro holds the Weinberg Chair in Judaic Studies at the University of Scranton. His most recent book is *Changing the Immutable: How Orthodox Judaism Rewrites Its History* (Littman Library, 2015).

Jack Wertheimer is professor of American Jewish History at the Jewish Theological Seminary. He writes on American Jewish religious, communal and educational life since World War II. His most recent book is *The New American Judaism: How Jews Practice Their Religion Today* (Princeton University Press, 2018), which received the National Jewish Book Award.

Index

Abraham, 110, 130, 166
Abraham Ibn Ezra, 158
Academic Jewish Studies, 21, 29, 31, 277
Agudath Israel of America, 34, 50, 162, 197, 212
Agunot (chained women), 203–204
Algeria, 181, 188
Akedah, 4, 110
American Jewish Committee, 6, 30, 289
American Jews, 197–198, 258, 266
Amital, Yehudah, 272
Angel, Marc, 46, 245
Archeology, 273
Arnovitz, Andi, 249
Association of Jewish Studies (AJS), 61
Auschwitz, 61
Autonomy (Human and God), 117–118, 122, 125–126, 155
Aviv, Caryn, 247

Barack Fishman, Sylvia, 184, 224–253, 278, 282, 289
Bar-Ilan University, 74, 289, 291
Barzun, Jacques, 188
Bayme, Steven, 1–2, 4, 6–7, 30, 233–234, 289
Beit Yosef Novaredok (Yeshiva), 9
Beker, Harvey, 6
Belkin, Samuel, 16, 31, 176, 183
Bendheim, Giti, 6
Bendheim, Jack, 6

Berkovits, Eliezer, 176
Berman, Saul, 46, 169, 177, 193, 206, 235
Bernays, Isaac, 174
Beth Medrash Govoha (Lakewood Yeshiva), 258
Bible, 12, 29, 58, 67, 71, 98–101, 150, 159–160, 213, 271–275, 277–278, 291
Biblical Criticism, 107, 110, 112–113, 116, 124, 146–148, 153, 158–161, 205, 207, 227, 270–271, 275, 291
Biblical Interpretation, 98, 100, 103–104, 273–274
Bigman, David, 159
Bioethics, vii, 67, 69–70, 77–78
Bin-Nun, Yoel, 272–273
Birnbaum, Jacob, 18, 20
Birthright trip, 38, 46
Blau, Yosef, 234, 243, 245
Bleich, J. D., 75, 109, 169–170, 218
Borough Park (Boro Park), 2, 8, 9, 196, 257
Borowitz, Eugene, 17
Boston, 11, 207
Boston Chevra Shas, 11
Breuer, Mordechai, 184, 272–273
Brill, Alan, 138, 172–192, 200, 255–256, 286, 289
Brisk, 109
Britain, 4, 40, 153–154, 156–157, 188, 290
British Jewry, 39, 147–148, 151, 153–157, 174

Brodie, Israel, 153–155
Brooklyn College, 10, 150, 222, 259
Brisker (Soloveitchik), Hayim, 8
Buber, Martin, 81
Bulka, Reuven, 265

Canadian Center for Advanced Jewish Studies, 17
Centrist Orthodoxy, 54, 80, 260
Chabad-Lubavitch Hasidism, 187, 213
Cherlow, Yuval, 159, 170, 274–275
Christianity, 4, 17, 28, 34, 52, 93, 131, 136, 143, 188, 280
    Interfaith dialogue, 4, 28, 39, 48, 97, 135, 141, 144
    and Judaism, 41, 130–134, 140–144
    and other monotheistic religions, 136, 138
Churgin, Pinchas, 183
City College of New York (CCNY), 31–32, 290
Church of England, 83, 153
CLAL, 17–18, 39, 44, 117, 262, 290
Cloning, 75, 77
Cohen, Steven M., 168, 177, 194, 247
Cohen, Jeffrey, 40
Commentator (YC Student Newspaper), 24, 27, 169, 228–231, 235, 237–238, 254–256, 261–262, 270, 274, 278, 280
Conservative Judaism, 151, 162–163, 174, 193, 209
Cosgrove, Elliot, 155
Covenant, 3, 7, 13, 16, 23, 45, 47, 52–53, 55–58, 60–61, 71–73, 77, 89–90, 92–94, 105, 116–119, 121–122, 126, 130–133, 135–136, 140–141, 144–145, 215, 239, 261–262
Cover, Robert, 68
Cross Currents, 163, 164–166

Da'at (Da'as) Torah, 219, 260
Daf Yomi, 212–214
Dating (Courtship), 233–235
Debow, Yocheved, 239
Dewey, John, 86, 95

Ecumenism, 90, 134, 136
EDAH, 46, 138, 142, 206, 239, 242, 255
Edrei, Arye, 5
Egypt, 56–57, 181
Eisen, Arnold M., 149, 183
End of Life Protocols (Bioethics), vii, 67, 69, 77, 78
Engaged Yeshivish, 178, 186–187
England, 39, 64, 178, 181, 183
Church of England, 83, 153
Europe, 85, 180–182, 222
    Eastern Europe, 6, 188, 197, 213
    Western Europe, 182
Euthanasia, 69, 72, 76
Ettlinger, Jacob, 174, 263

Fackenheim, Emil, 17, 18
Farber, Zev, 5, 80, 161–164, 166–168, 170, 193, 265
Feinstein, Moshe, 73–74
Feminism
    Orthodox and, 3, 29, 45, 111, 114, 171, 204, 214
    RYG and, 185, 291
Ferziger, Adam S., 2, 4, 6, 148, 160, 166, 187, 191, 193, 216, 221, 254–288, 289
Feuerstein Family (Boston), 11
Fishbane, Michael, 5, 98
Fletcher, Joseph, 69
Foxman, Abraham (Abe), 30
France, 178, 181, 188
Frances, Koby, 239
Freud-Kandel, Miri, 1–2, 4, 6, 146–171, 193, 271, 290

Friedlander, Michael, 174
Friedman, Menachem, 213, 265

Gandhi, Mahatma, 140
Gender, 2, 25, 28, 51, 62, 74, 163, 185, 191, 206, 215, 224–227, 232–233, 236–238, 242–243, 246, 248–249, 251, 253, 289–290
Germany, 71, 83, 178, 181–182, 184, 290
Giddens, Anthony, 4, 178–179, 182, 184
Glazer, Nathan, 4, 86, 94
Goldberg, Hillel, 94, 228, 255
Goldman, Ari, 176
Goodman, Martin, 5
Gordon, Milton, 87, 94
Goshen-Gottstein, Alon, 138, 141, 143
Greenberg, Blu, 204, 235
Greenberg, Irving "Yitz" (RYG), 3, 54–67, 70, 77, 81, 83, 89, 91–94, 107, 117, 120, 122–124, 130, 132–134, 140–142, 144, 150, 169, 193, 202, 222–231, 234–235, 237–238, 242, 244–245, 250–263, 270–272, 274, 278–282, 287–288, 290–291
    tikkun olam, 53, 58, 116, 119, 121, 131
Grinspoon, Harold, 6, 46
Groningen Protocol (Euthanasia), 69
Gruber, Dean, 62
Gurock, Jeffrey S., 139, 152, 156, 163, 197, 201, 206, 256

Hain, Kenneth, 193, 198, 205, 209, 235
Halakhah (Jewish Law), vii, 55, 57, 59–65, 73–74, 76–77, 80, 82, 97, 108–110, 121–122, 150, 160, 176, 182, 189, 206, 208, 220, 253, 262, 277, 286, 291
Hardal – Haredi Leumi, 49
[Haredi Orthodoxy], Haredim, 4, 8, 13–14, 20, 23–24, 27–28, 35–36, 39–41, 44, 47–52, 55, 62, 147, 160, 191, 196–202, 204, 206, 210, 213–215, 219–221, 226–227, 236, 240–241, 248–250, 258–259, 263, 280
Hartman, David, 17, 27–28, 41, 116, 139, 232, 236, 244, 25
Hartman, Tova, 244, 259
Hartman, Moshe, 232
Harvard University, 2, 69, 94, 100–101, 222, 237, 221, 291
HaShomer Hadati (Bnei Akiva), 9
Ha-Tzaad ha-Rishon (the First Step, Ethiopian Jewry), 21
Hazon Ish (Avraham Yeshayahu Karelitz), 263, 268
Hebrew, 1, 5, 9, 12, 14, 17, 19, 21, 29–30, 39, 67, 99, 102–103, 112, 115, 149, 155, 159, 160, 162–163, 184, 191, 197, 239, 248, 258, 260
Heilman, Samuel C., 4, 177, 189, 197, 199, 207, 211–223, 240, 248, 256, 290
Helfgot, Nathaniel, 135, 166–167, 245, 274, 285–286
Hertz, Joseph Herman, 152
Hebrew Institute of Boro Park (Etz Chaim Yeshiva), 9
Heresy, 22, 29, 34, 140, 142, 146–148, 151–153, 155, 157, 159, 161, 163–167, 169, 171, 271
Hester Panim (Divine Hiddeness), 117, 125
Hier, Marvin, 30
Hirsch, Samson Raphael, 289
    Hirschian Orthodoxy, 173
Hoenlein, Malcolm, 30
Hollinger, David, 82–84, 87, 92, 94
Holocaust, 2–3, 7, 13–18, 20, 23–24, 30–33, 36–37, 43–45, 52–53, 56–57, 59, 62–63, 65, 71–72, 77, 81, 89–90, 93–94, 107, 116–120, 125, 130, 197–198, 211, 213, 222–223, 227–228, 231, 258, 266, 290

Holocaust studies and memory, 7, 16–20, 23–24, 31, 33, 36–37, 44, 52, 56–57, 59, 62, 77, 81, 94, 107, 290
Hollinger, David, 82, 84, 88, 92, 94
Homosexuality, 242–245, 247, 281–286, 203
Hutner, Yitzchak, 258
Hybrid Judaism, 81, 82, 89, 92–93, 291

Incarnation, 130–132
International Rabbinical Fellowship (IRF), 46, 163, 167, 206
Irshai, Ronit, 74
Islam, 40, 97, 133, 135–136, 138
Israel, State of, 9, 13, 16–17, 20, 23–24, 31–33, 36, 38, 41, 48–49, 52, 54, 56–58, 61, 63, 238–239, 241, 244–246, 248–249, 256, 259, 263, 273, 279, 283
Isserles, Moses (Rema), 213, 251
Italy, 181–183, 188

Jacobs, Louis, 4, 146–161, 163, 165, 167–171, 290
"Jacobs Affair," 146–148, 153–157, 161, 170
Jakobovits, Immanuel, 39, 67, 76, 135, 153–154
Jesselson, Michael G., 6
Jesus, 130–132, 143, 168
Jewish Life Network/Steinhardt Foundation, 38, 46, 290
Jewish Observer, 34, 169
Jewish Orthodox Feminist Alliance (JOFA), 46, 203, 206–207, 241, 245
Jewish Theological Seminary (JTS), 291
Jews' College, 40, 153–155, 174
Joshua ben Sira, 101
Jospe, Raphael, 134

Jotkowitz, Alan, vii, 3, 67–80, 138, 260, 290
Judah ha-Hasid, 158

Kabbalah, 114, 179–180
Kallen, Horace Meyer, 83–88, 90, 94–95
Kansas City, 207
Kaplan, Lawrence, 23, 160, 166, 175, 193, 258, 277
Kaplan, Mordecai, 62
Karo, Yosef, 251
Katz, Steven T., vii, 3, 7, 55–66, 81, 94, 109, 116–117, 153, 219, 222, 290
Katz, Ysoscher, 166–167
Kelman, Ari, 247
Kibbutz Hadati, 190
Klapper, Aryeh, 62, 247
Kleinberg, Darren, 3, 81–95, 291
Knohl, Elyashiv, 239
Kook, Abraham Isaac, 3–4, 111–115, 118, 121, 126–127, 139–140, 263, 268, 280, 291
Koren, Irit, 137, 244, 275, 291
Korn, Eugene, 4, 134, 140–144
Kotel/Western Wall, 48, 267
Koussevitsky, David (Cantor), 8
Koussevitsky, Moshe (Cantor), 8
Krasner, Jonathan, 247
Kugel, James, vii, 3, 96–106, 158–159, 170, 291

Lamm, Maurice, 22, 33–36, 46, 112, 139, 235–236, 242, 281
Lamm, Norman, 176, 235
Susan and Jack Lapin Fund, 6
Lau, Binyamin (Benny), 245, 287
Law, 3, 17, 22, 25, 28, 34, 55–56, 64–65, 67–68, 74–75, 77, 79, 82, 99, 101–102, 109–110, 119, 121, 135, 139, 150, 160, 186, 191, 193, 202–204, 206, 209–210, 218–219,

225, 228, 230, 234–235, 240, 242, 247, 258–259, 265–267, 269, 275, 277, 279, 283
Lefkowitz, Jay, P., 169, 193, 210, 225
Lichtenstein, Aharon, 4, 15, 22, 24–25, 41–42, 95, 168, 169, 229–230, 234, 254–260, 262–274, 276–283, 285, 287–288
Lichtenstein-Greenberg Exchange, 24
Liebman, Charles S., 15, 156, 175–177, 184, 259, 270
Linzer, Dov, 193, 241
Lopatin, Asher, 166–167, 242
Los Angeles, 168, 196, 207
Luzzatto, Shmuel David (Shadal), 180

Maimonides, v, 6, 11, 56, 127, 131, 158, 192, 213, 219–220, 275
   Mishneh Torah, 131, 220
Maimonides Fund, 6
Maimonides School, 11
Mannheim, Karl, 179
Marriage, 58, 72, 101, 203, 224–226, 231–240, 243, 247, 249–250, 252–253, 279–280, 282, 286–287, 289
Maryles, Gladys, 6
Maryles, Matthew, 6
Masorti Judaism (United Kingdom), 157
Meiri, Menachem, 143
Melting Pot, 84–86, 94–95
Messiah, 124, 130–132,
Modern Orthodoxy, 3–5, 7–10, 11, 13–19, 131, 133, 135, 172–190, 192–194, 197–201, 203–210, 216, 218, 223, 225–227, 229, 249, 253, 255–259, 270, 275, 278
   move to the right of, 22–24, 27–31, 33–36, 38–42, 44–48, 50–51, 53–54, 111, 116, 129
Montagu, Ewen, 152

Montefiore, Claude G., 174, 182
Mount Sinai, 68, 102–103, 105–106, 116, 136, 149
Mussar, 9, 259
Mussar Movement, 9

Nehorai, Meir, 286
Neustadter, Naomi, 6
Neustadter, Peter, 6
Newman, Louis, 73, 95, 153, 174
New London Synagogue, 149, 154
New York, 2, 3, 6, 12, 31, 39, 81, 83, 135, 195–196, 207, 210, 241, 259, 290
Nishma Survey, 5
Nonobservant Jews, 33, 257, 261, 268–270, 283
Novaredok, 9–10, 259

Open Orthodoxy, 80, 162–170, 206–209
Orthodox Judaism, 3, 19, 44, 55, 59, 93, 96, 108, 146, 147, 148, 153, 156–157, 160, 162–163, 166, 169–170, 174, 177, 184, 186–187, 191, 200, 228, 248–249, 254–256, 260, 263, 273, 289–291
Orthodox Forum, 198, 205, 209, 233–234, 238–239
Oxford, University of, 1, 3, 5–7, 67, 96, 98, 146, 160, 168–169, 289–290
Oxford Summer Institute on Modern and Contemporary Judaism, 1–3, 5, 96, 156, 188, 193, 289–290

Partnership Minyanim, 29
Petuchowski, Jakob J., 17–18
Pew Survey of American Jewry, 5, 32, 51
Philo of Alexandria, 101
Pluralism, 3, 14, 17–18, 21, 31, 33–34, 36, 41, 43, 45–46, 52, 61, 64, 70,

82–95, 123, 131, 133–134, 138, 140, 143, 223, 226, 270, 291
Podhoretz, Norman, 22, 290
Poland, 8, 10, 212
Post-Ethnicity, 82–83, 87–90, 92
Postmodernity, 42–44, 47, 51, 54, 168, 185, 291
Post-Orthodoxy, 168, 200
Prayer, 20, 63, 65, 140, 158, 180, 194, 200, 203–204, 206–207, 209, 246, 264, 267
Pre-Nuptial Agreement, 203
Prins, Michal, 239

Qumran, 98–99

Rabbinic Authority, 166, 186, 204, 218–220, 234
Rabbinical Council of America (RCA), 28, 34–35, 46–47, 163, 197
Rackman, Emmanuel, 76, 176, 183
Ramsey, Paul, 72
Raphael, Melissa, 5
Ravitzky, Aviezer, 191
Reconstructionist Judaism, 34, 61, 247
Reform Judaism, 55, 262
Reform Jews, 18, 63, 236, 269
Reiner, Rami, 276–277
Revel, Bernard, 183
Religious Zionism, 49, 168, 173, 182, 184, 260, 287
Reshit zemihat geulateynu (the beginning of the dawn of our redemption), 63
Revelation, 3–4, 12–13, 45, 53, 56–57, 64–66, 96–98, 100–117, 124–127, 130, 132, 141, 146–153, 155–163, 165–171, 189, 271–272, 291
Ribner, David, S., 240
RIETS – Rabbi Isaac Elchanan Theological Seminary, 109, 201, 206–207, 209, 222, 229, 257, 281, 284

Riskin, Shlomo (Steven), 4, 41, 143–144
Risman, Barbara, 237
Riverdale Jewish Center, 2, 16, 20
Roman Catholic Church, 63
Romania, 181
Rosenberg, Shimon Gershon (SHAGA"R), 45, 159, 286
Rosenfeld, Jennie, 239–240
Rosman, Doreen, 179–180
Ross, Edward Alsworth, 85
Ross, Tamar, 4, 107–128, 134, 139–140, 151, 158–160, 170, 289–291
Roth, Sol, 176
Rothschild Foundation (Hanadiv), The, 6
Rubenstein, Richard, 62
Rubin, Aryeh, 6
Rubin, Raquel, 6
Russia, 181–182

Sabato, Haim, 260, 267–268, 277
Sacks, Jonathan, 4, 40, 76, 134–139, 141–143, 155, 243
  Koren Sacks Siddur, 134, 137–138
Salanter Akiba Riverdale Academy (SAR), 3
Sarah, 166
Sarna, Yehudah, 209
Schick, Marvin, 199
Schneerson, Menachem Mendel (Lubavitcher Rebbe), 62
Sexuality, 4, 25, 43, 224–225, 228, 230–231, 233, 235, 237–245, 248–253, 278, 281–282
Shapiro, Marc B., 4, 129–145, 132, 134, 136, 138, 140, 142, 144, 146, 158, 160, 170, 275, 291
Shapiro, David, S., 176
Shapiro, Meir of Sanok, 212
Shaw, Steven
Shechem, 101
Shrage, Barry, 30

Shtibbelization, 216, 223
Simon Wiesenthal Center, 30
Singer, David, 169, 229–230, 255–257
Singles/singlehood, 225, 231, 233–234, 239, 250, 252
Smith, Ramie, 186, 241
Solomon, Norman, 51, 101, 152, 157–158
Soloveitchik, Aaron, 258
Soloveitchik, Joseph, B., 4, 11–12, 14, 22, 23, 25, 27–29, 62, 70, 80, 109–110, 116, 135, 144, 197, 201, 203, 215, 220, 222, 227, 241, 257–259, 263–265, 280, 287
Halakhic Man, 100
Soloveitchik, Haym, 110, 220
Soviet Jewry, 20, 21
Spektor, Isaac (Yitzchak) /Elchanan (Elkhanan), 109, 201, 222
Spero, Shubert, 176, 264
Steinsaltz, Adi, 41, 213
Stern College for Women (YU), 257
Stollman, Aviad, 217, 220
Straus, Moshael, 6
Straus, Zahava, 6
Student Struggle for Soviet Jewry (SSSJ), 20

Taragin, Lea, 248–249
Targum Shlishi Foundation, 6
Tel-Aviv University
Temple Emmanuel (Borough Park), 8
Temple Bethel (Borough Park), 8
Theology, 2–3, 116, 118, 89–90, 93, 116–120, 123–125, 213, 222, 228, 231
Theology, 3, 28, 30, 45, 53, 55, 67–70, 77, 80–83, 89–90, 92–93, 107, 111–112, 114, 116, 120–121, 123–124, 127, 129, 131, 134, 136, 138, 140, 143, 144, 148–152, 155, 158, 160, 162, 164–165, 167, 170, 176, 205, 209, 224, 262, 290–291

Tikkun Olam, 17, 43, 52–53, 58, 116, 119, 121, 131
Tinok she-nishbah (an infant taken captive), 268
Torah.Com, 161
Torah min hashamayim, 4, 13, 45, 146, 151, 163, 166–167
Torah U'Madda, 29, 114, 197, 201, 206
Torah U'Mesorah, 11, 28
Tolstoy, Margie, 5
Transcendental Withdrawal of God, 58
Twersky, Isadore, 176
Tzelem Elo-him (in God's image), 229

Union of Orthodox Jewish Congregations of America (OU), 49
United States Holocaust Commission, 2
United States Holocaust Memorial Museum, 2, 290
United Synagogue (United Kingdom), 39–40, 152–156, 173–174, 182
Unterman, Isaac, 29

Vegetarianism, 77
Vietnam War, 21, 226
Voluntary Covenant, 7, 52, 55, 89–90, 92, 94, 117–118, 122, 261–262

Waldenberg, Eliezer, 72
Washington D.C., 21, 77, 94, 207, 244, 257, 259
Waxman, Chaim I., 152, 155–156, 170, 201–202, 212, 221–222, 272
Weber, Max, 179
Weinberg, Yaakov, 197, 291
Weiss, Avraham (Avi), 46, 99, 162, 206
Wertheimer, Jack, 4, 109, 163, 193–210, 291
Wexner Heritage Program, 44
Wiesel, Elie, 21, 30, 32, 37, 290
Wolosky-Wruble, Anna, 239

World Health Organization (WHO), 71
Wurzbuger, Walter, 176–177, 183
Wyschogrod, Michael, 28

Yad Vashem Holocaust Memorial Authority, 15
Yarnton Manor, 1
Yavneh (Orthodox Student Organization), 3, 19, 22, 26
Yeshiva Chaim Berlin, 258
Yeshiva College (Yeshiva University), 2, 3, 9, 10, 15–16, 18, 20–22, 26–29, 31, 33, 35–36, 45, 47, 50–51, 111–112, 159, 169, 175, 183, 197, 201, 208, 217–218, 228–230, 234, 243, 255–257, 259, 265, 281, 289
  teaching there, 15–16, 18, 26–29, 31, 33, 35–36, 41, 47, 289
  and the 1960s, 2–3, 9–10, 22, 228–230, 234, 255, 272,
  role in American Orthodoxy, 50, 51, 111–112, 159, 169,175, 183, 197, 201, 208, 217–218, 243, 256–257, 259, 265, 281
  and Soviet Jewry, 20–21
Yeshivat Chovevei Torah (YCT), 16, 46, 162–164, 166–168, 206–208, 241
Yeshivat Har Etzion (Gush), 111, 259, 272–277, 285–287
Yeshivat Maharat, 46, 162, 193, 206–207
Yeshiva University High School (Brooklyn Talmudic Academy–BTA), 257–259
Yom Ha-Shoah (Holocaust Memorial Day), 37
Young Israel of Brookline, 11
Yichud (laws regarding a male and female meeting in private), 25, 235

ZACHOR Holocaust Resource Center, 37
Zikui Harabim, 10–11, 19, 37
Zimmerman, Deena, 215
Zimzum, 57, 61, 63, 114–115, 121–122, 124
Zionism, 7, 14, 23, 24, 27, 29, 49, 84, 95, 116, 168, 173, 182, 184, 191, 198, 209, 260, 287

www.ingramcontent.com/pod-product-compliance
Lightning Source LLC
Chambersburg PA
CBHW051111230426
43667CB00014B/2527